CONTENTS

SELECTED
READINGS
ON
AMERICAN
INDUSTRY

Edited by

T. J. Morrisey

State University College
at Buffalo

MSS Information Corporation
655 Madison Avenue, New York, N.Y. 10021

This is a custom-made book of readings prepared for the courses taught by the editor, as well as for related courses and for college and university libraries.   For information about our program, please write to:

MSS INFORMATION CORPORATION
655 Madison Avenue
New York, New York 10021

MSS wishes to express its appreciation to the authors of the articles in the collection for their cooperation in making their work available in this format.

Library of Congress Cataloging in Publication Data

Morrisey, Thomas J   comp.
    Selected readings on American industry.

    1. United States — Industries — Addresses, essays,
lectures. 2. Industry — Social aspects — United States —
Addresses, essays, lectures. 3. Technological innovations
— United States — Addresses, essays, lectures.
4. Business enterprises — United States — Addresses,
essays, lectures. I. Title.
 HC106.6M648   338'.0973   74-12244
ISBN 0-8422-5199-5
ISBN 0-8422-0440-7 (pbk.)

INTRODUCTION

The Nation is in an era of rapid change — knowledge has been increasing exponentially; new discoveries and inventions have mushroomed; efficiency in many sectors of industry has risen beyond the wildest dreams of many; and communications have become almost instantaneous. Proper application of new knowledge and technological advances could enable us to become more efficient architects of our destiny.

American industry is rapidly changing. It is facing new challenges on every front. Increasingly, American industry is being called upon to solve complex national social and economic problems.

Recently, American industry has encountered pressures from a number of sources. However, the basic structure of our industrial system is sound, flexible, and viable. The system has been very responsive to change. It has been a very powerful instrument in obtaining social and economic progress in the United States.

This collection of selected readings presents an overview of the development of American industry to the latter part of this century. The various readings are authored by key decision makers who consider the issues, challenges, and opportunities confronting American industry during the next two decades.

For ease in reading, this text is divided into the following sections: An Overview of American Industry, Tomorrow's Jobs, The Private Enterprise System, The Social Responsibility of Business, Technology and Resources for Business, and the Human Side of Enterprise.

T.J. Morrisey

SECTION I

AN OVERVIEW OF AMERICAN INDUSTRY

Section I presents an overview of American industry for the next two decades through the following articles.

A VIEW OF THE ECONOMIC WORLD OF 1990

KEY CHOICES OF THE NEXT TWO DECADES

TRENDS IN PUBLIC ATTITUDES TOWARD BUSINESS
AND THE FREE ENTERPRISE SYSTEM

THE U. S. ECONOMY IN 1990

A View of the Economic World of 1990

Herman Kahn

T HE UNITED STATES in 1990 will still be the world's greatest economy. But, instead of being the overwhelmingly dominant economy it was in the immediate post-World War II years, it will simply be the largest among many large economies. It will have only about one-quarter of the Gross World Product (GWP), or but one-half of that in the immediate post-war years. The comparative GNPs of principal areas of the world will, in 1980, be about as shown in Table 1. We are a big economy and will remain a big economy, although we are smaller relative to the remainder of the world than we used to be.

By 1980 the Japanese economy should be about one-third the size of the U.S. economy (up from one-fifth today). By 1990 the Japanese economy should be about one-half our size. It is likely to be more highly internationalized than the U.S. economy. Thus, even by 1980 it begins to have an effect on the remainder of the world about equal to that of the United States. From the viewpoint of Asia and most of the remainder of the world, Japan's economy might seem equal to or larger than that of the United States over the whole decade of 1980-1990.

In other words, an economy about the size of

Address by Herman Kahn, Director, Hudson Institute, Croton-on-Hudson, New York.

the present European Economic Community (EEC) will suddenly have been created off the coast of Asia by 1980. Further, this economy will tend to grow during the ensuing ten years at almost twice the rate of EEC. This will have all kinds of consequences for the world in general and for American business in particular.

I believe that the rapid growth of Japan will contribute enormously to the creation of dynamic and prosperous economies everywhere, particularly in Asia and in North and South America. Despite the recent criticism of Japan, I believe that, in fact, even in the past, its huge growth rate has contributed helpfully to the U.S. growth rate and is likely to do so even more in the future.

Incidentally, although Mainland China and India have about one-half of the world's population, neither is likely to play a major role in the world economy in the 1990 period, but it will be greater than at present.

Character of the Work Force Changes

The character of the U.S. work force has changed enormously over the last 20 years, and will continue to change. In 1950 the United States had almost 60 million workers, about equally divided between goods-producing industries and service industries. About another 20 million has been

A LOOK AT BUSINESS IN 1990: A Summary of the White House Conference on the Industrial World Ahead, Washington, D.C., February 7-9, 1972 (U.S. Government Printing Office: 1972 0—467-348) pp. 13-27.

Area	GNP
United States	1. 5
U.S.S.R.	0. 9
Japan	0. 5
France and West Germany	0. 25
China, United Kingdom, Italy, Canada, India	0. 1–0. 2
Brazil, Australia, East Germany, Mexico, Sweden, Poland, Argentina, Indonesia	0. 05–0. 1

added since—almost all in the service sector. Between 1947 and 1980 the workers in service-producing industries (transportation, public utilities, finance, insurance, real estate, government, services, and trade) will have risen from about 24 million to some 60 million, while those in goods-producing industries will be showing a rise from about 27 million to only a little over 30 million. In some ways these numbers underestimate the rate of change, because even in the goods-producing industries, people, increasingly, are white-collar workers. While the service industries have large numbers of blue-collar workers, their percentage is decreasing. And, the white-collar workers are less likely to be relatively unskilled women workers than highly trained professional and technical workers. This, in the most literal terms, is what we mean by the postindustrial culture: the relative number of blue-collar workers declines; the construction and manufacturing industries become a smaller and smaller part of the nation's activity, and, relative to the total national effort, become easier and easier to do; and the technical and professional labor force increases enormously (an increase by a factor of 1.5 in the decade of the '60s).

The situation in agriculture is similar. In 1850, half of all Americans worked in agriculture. Today, less than three percent of the American work force produces more than 95 percent of the foods and fibers we need. It could probably increase production by half or more without particularly increasing the number of people engaged in agriculture. Thus, we in the United States live in a "post-agricultural culture." It is not that the product is unimportant; it is that the national effort in producing the product is small relative to other efforts in the economy. Most of the growth of the U.S. economy today is in the service sector—at least in terms of additions to the work force.

One of the present problems of the United States is that we may not be making these additions to the work force wisely. In New York City in the last five years 100,000 city government employees have been added while the population of the city was declining by about the same number. The cost of city services has increased by about 50 percent, yet it is difficult to find service much improved as a result of these additional city employees and city costs.

In general, service industries have the unfortunate characteristic that output is difficult to measure quantitatively—and quality even more so. As a result of this, both governments and companies have a tendency to add service personnel who do not increase productivity significantly. They may produce something measured by the institution itself, but this may be a part of the process of "institutionalizing"—when the institution starts to serve its own interests instead of those of the general community. In any case, one of the standard characteristics of an institution in the process of institutionalizing is a large increase in service personnel and a relative decrease in the number of people who directly turn out useful products.

The World of 1990

Some revival, some evolutionary development. A general but irregular movement toward a multipolar but economically unified half of world that participates intensely in the world economy* but with countervailing tendencies toward anarchy as well as order. The nation-state system is largely maintained with about 15 large nations and more than 100 small nations.

This politically increasingly multipolar world should see in the '70's the end of the post-World War II era (including an effective political settlement of that war)and the following consequences:

• Rise of Japan as an economic, financial, and technological superstate (and possibly political and/or military superpower).

• Rise of France to the largest national economy (at least nominally in terms of GNP) in Western Europe.

• Almost full reemergence of both Germanies (but some political disabilities are likely to remain).

• An emergence of new regional and/or large powers.

• United States-Soviet strategic equality—or possibly even Soviet superiority—accompanied by a relative decline of both super-powers in power, prestige, and influence.

- An enlarged EEC with perhaps a new role for France as the leading nation of the community—also possibility of a breakup of the current enlarged EEC.
- Possible creation of an Eastern European EEC.
- At least ad hoc creation and perhaps self-conscious advancement of a dynamic (economically) Pacific Hemisphere trading/investment area (PAHTIA).
- Many other new possibilities: e.g., new alliances, new arms races, politically unified Europe, intensely isolationist United States, etc.

Some acceleration, some continuation but also some selective topping off of multifold trend (and perhaps some temporary reversals):

- Further intensification of many issues associated with a 1985 technological crisis; growing need for worldwide (but probably ad hoc) zoning ordinances and other forms of self-restraint involving environmental, social, and perhaps knowledge controls.
- Other problems in coping with sheer numbers, size, and bigness of almost everything.
- With important exceptions, erosion of 12 traditional societal levers; a search for meaning and purpose, some cultural confusion, ideological polarization, social conflict, growth of discretionary behavior, etc.
- Increasingly revisionist communism, capitalism, and Christianity in Europe and the Western hemisphere; perhaps a crisis of liberalism—some persistence and even eruption of the counterculture.
- Populist, conservative backlash, and/or counter-reformation movements.
- Increasing problem (worldwide) of educated incapacity and/or illusioned, irrelevant, or ideological argumentation—greater explicit emphasis on feeling and emotion.

Emergence of various styles of postindustrial culture for nations with about 20 percent of world's population and in enclaves elsewhere and possibly also by:

- New political milieus; rise of "humanist left"-"responsible center" confrontation in at least high culture of developed nations (but in particular in the United States and northwest tier of Europe).
- Emergence of mosaic cultures (at least in the United States) incorporating esoteric, deviant, communal and/or experimental life styles. Some increase in anarchistic behavior movements—ideological and political development of the counterculture.
- Possible successful synthesis between old and new in France, Japan, Scandinavia, northwest tier, or elsewhere.

Above sets context for further development of a unified but multipolar and (partially) competitive (half) global economy.

- A general understanding of the process and techniques for sustained economic development.
- A worldwide green revolution; also a worldwide capability for modern industry and technology.
- Growing importance of TNC's as innovators of economic activity and engines of rapid growth.
- High (3-15 percent) GNP growth almost everywhere—five especially dynamic areas.
- Sustained growth in trade, communications, travel.
- Increasing unity from technology, private industry, commercial and financial institutions, but relatively little by international legal and political institutions.
- Some development of year 2000 (and/or compound interest) ideologies.
- Little or no long-term overall catastrophic difficulties with environment, pollution, or scarcity of resources though there will be many temporary crises and doubtless some limited catastrophies.

Thus, a relatively anarchic but also relatively orderly and unified world, but with new issues of international control:

- Continuing growth in discretionary behavior, corresponding worldwide (foreign and domestic) law-and-order issues. Some growth in violent, deviant, or criminal behavior—possible irreverent use of terror, violence, subversion, unilateral changes of international rules, etc.
- Some bizarre issues may arise.
- Some ad hoc countermeasures may be taken.
- Some important but nonsignificant surprises and perhaps some significant ones as well.

---

* About half of the world's population lives in two relatively isolated cultures—a fourth in Communist Asia (a relatively isolated Sinic culture) and a fourth in a relatively isolated Indian culture (India, Bangladesh, Ceylon, Burma, and perhaps West Pakistan).

Service industries are, of course, important and valuable. One characteristic of a successful large company or a successfully developed nation is an emphasis on the service sector—on managers, engineers, designers, marketers, financial experts, the people who deal with other kinds of knowledge, administration, etc. The wave of the future is service, not production. It is easier to be incompetent in service industries than in any other; sometimes the very concept of competence does not have any clear-cut application.

Two Major Changes in History—A Third Is Imminent

What I am suggesting is that whereas today we no longer have an agricultural state, but a postagricultural state, we will, in the future, have a postindustrial state—not a new industrial state. All manner of changes and innovations will ensue from this. I shall first emphasize the changes; later, the continuities.

In a review of the history of man, two incidents of first-order magnitude stand out.

The first incident was the agricultural revolution about 10,000 years ago, which laid the foundation of civilization. Civilization means civic culture or living in cities. But not many lived in cities. Roughly only about one in twenty did so. Rather surprisingly the average per capita income did not change much during this prolonged agricultural era. This era survived until about 200 years ago, as basically characterized by an income in the range of $50-$250 per capita, or roughly $100 per capita average. China, India, and Indonesia are still in this category.

The next big change was initiated about 200 years ago in England. It was the so-called Industrial Revolution. For the first time man achieved sustained growth rates. Medium-term British growth rates have been remarkably constant—averaging between 2-2½ percent per year for the last 200 years or so. This is impressive. An average of 2.3 percent per year means that every 100 years change is by a factor of 10, or an increase of 900 percent. From a historical point of view, that is a big change. In fact, a change of this magnitude, particularly if it is in GNP per capita rather than total GNP, changes the character of a culture enormously. Just as the preindustrial culture is roughly $50-$250 per capita, industrial culture is a factor of 10 higher, or $500-$2500 per capita.

Many people, including myself, believe that in the next 10, 20, or 30 years we will see another

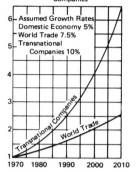

A Surprise free Projection: Relative Importance of World Trade and Transnational Companies

Figure 1

factor-of-10 change: the attainment in many countries of GNP per capita will be in the range $5000 to $20,000 (in 1970 dollars). This will induce as great a transition in society—or at least initiate the early phase of such a transition—as these first two great historical transitions did some 200 and some 10,000 years ago.

The Skyrocket Rise of Transnational Companies

Another phenomenon on the industrial scene is the recent rapid rise and even greater future growth of multinational companies, or transnational companies as I prefer to call them. By this I mean any corporation doing significant business, other than simple import/export operations, in many sovereignties. This is shown in Figure 1. Already, for the United States, such corporations sell about $5 for every dollar we export. The dynamism of the transnational companies (TNC) is suggested by the following. Basically, Gross World Product—or the total amount of goods and services produced around the world—grows by about 5 percent per year. Today, talk about gross product brings ideas of pollution, or overcrowding, or traffic. However, we are simply trying to measure the amount of goods and services produced, whether or not these are useful, healthful, or wholesome.

The United States grows at a slightly lower rate than the world as a whole and hence we have a declining portion of GWP. World trade, including that of the United States, grows about 50 percent faster than GWP, as Fig. 1 makes clear. Business has developed an increasingly internationalized world economy. Rather interestingly—and mostly overlooked by economists heretofore—the true internationalization of the world economy is now beginning to derive less from the movement of the products of industry from one country to another than from the movement of actual resources and national ownership and management. The transnational corporation now grows at a rate almost double that of GWP.

Despite many difficulties it is likely to continue—for a while—to grow at that rate. Thus the world is being increasingly internationalized, but less by world trade than by the operations of transnational corporations. These themselves are increasingly becoming multinational in the simple sense of multinational operation, multinational decision making, and multinational ownership. The transnational company is becoming the major engine of rapid economic development in both the Third World and in the rapidly developing world.

Shifting National Positions in GNP Growth

The economic performance of the seven largest countries is set forth in Fig. 2. Two of these are superpowers—the United States and the U.S.S.R.—which we expect to grow in GNP by about 4 to 6 percent a year—or about the same as the world average. Gross World Product has grown by about 5 percent a year for about 15 years and seems likely to continue doing so—at least on the average. Many believe that in something between 20 and a 100 years we will run out of one or another kind of resource, causing these curves to turn down. The resource may be pollution-type resources—that is, reservoirs or space in which to dump things—or it may be actual raw materials. My own strong belief is that this view is not correct. That is, I believe that the next 100 years or so should not see any particular slowdown in overall growth rates because of resource constraints. Eventually all curves rising exponentially have to top out—even including economic growth rates—but actually, as we go into a postindustrial culture, even this statement may turn out to be wrong.

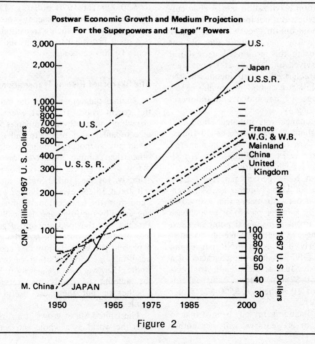

**Postwar Economic Growth and Medium Projection
For the Superpowers and "Large" Powers**

Figure 2

14

An interesting point is illustrated by the three basic kinds of economies. The British economy, the largest of the five "large" powers in 1950, is probably surpassed by China today—or is close to China. The British economy has grown by a steady 2.3 percent or so rate for about 100 years, which markedly affects the quality of an economic society. The differences between a traditional economy, an industrial economy, and a postindustrial economy are just this factor-of-10 change in per-capita income. Gross World Product grows by about 5 percent per year, and that is just about twice as fast as traditional British growth. That means a factor of 10 in 50 years. In one sense, from a historical point of view, what does it matter if you get a factor-of-10 change in 50 or 100 years? But these are competitive issues and it makes a big difference to the countries involved—at least during the transitional period. In other words, it is an important fact to Britain that most of the world's economies are growing almost twice as fast as Britain's.

Also, it is noted that the Japanese economy grows by about 10 percent per year. If sustained the economy would double in seven years. The Japanese culture, while quite different from that of the Chinese, is still Sinic. It seems that wherever members of the Chinese culture have gone they have reached the top—except in China. Today, if an economy is dominated by people raised in the Chinese culture, whether it is in the diluted Thailand form or in the more or less modernized feudal form as in Japan, or in a diluted British framework as in Hong Kong or Singapore, the result is economic growth rates of about 10 percent. This is likely to mean some big changes for the world.

As Fig. 2 indicates, from 1975 or so France rises above Germany. I would not take that 1975 figure too seriously, but I believe that some time in the late 70's the French economy is likely to pass the West German economy, and become the largest economy in Western Europe.

One of the most interesting happenings in Europe right now is the enlargement of the EEC, accompanied at the same time by an emerging eminence or preeminence of France in GNP. I wish to emphasize that this slight, new edge of France in GNP over West Germany is in itself insignificant.

But it is not the actual economic "heft" of France that counts here. It is the fact that if France has the largest economy in Europe it is impossible to take France lightly. It also means that the traditional problem of Europe since 1870—of an automatic domination by Germany because of the German economy and military power—is no longer a problem. When one discusses this issue with Frenchmen, they always raise the real possibility that the French will experience political problems that will prevent their economy from growing in this way. This is certainly a reasonable fear. I believe that the actual success of France itself increases the possibility of French stability.

All this can easily mean a fairly large change in Europe—these two events together, the enlargement of the EEC and the emergence of France as leader of the EEC. One of the main reasons why such countries as The Netherlands want England in the EEC is to dilute both the German-French rivalry and to dilute the French leadership.

By 1980 even Communist Asia ought to reach a level of about 200 billion dollars, as Table 2 indicates. This assumes that—as now seems likely—Mainland China spends the next decade in what can be called reconstruction and consolidation. If they do this their growth rates should be at least 6 percent or so. Indeed, this estimate may be, if anything, low. If they indulge in more "great leaps forward," or cultural revolutions, the figure is probably high.

TABLE 2—THE ECONOMIC CONTEXT OF 1970 AND A SIMILAR PROJECTION FOR 1980 (an approximation)

	GNP (in Trillions of 1970 Dollars)		Population (in Billions)		GNP/CAP (Thousands of 1970 Dollars)	
	1970	1980	1970	1980	1970	1980
United States	1.0	1.5	0.2	0.22	5.0	6.7
Remainder of OECD	1.2	2.0	0.5	0.54	2.4	3.8
Communist Europe	0.7	1.2	0.35	0.38	2.0	3.2
Developed Countries Subtotal	2.9	4.7	1.05	1.14	2.8	4.1
Non-Communist Less Developed Countries	0.4	0.7	1.65	2.0	0.24	0.35
Communist Asia	0.1	0.2	0.8	1.0	0.12	0.20
Less Developed Countries Subtotal	0.5	0.9	2.45	3.0	0.22	0.30
Total or Average	3.4	5.6	3.5	4.2	0.97	1.36

Growing Internationalization

The 1980 global economy, Table 3, gives a feeling of the increasing internationalization of the world economy. As stated before, GWP grows by around 5 percent per year, world trade by 7½ or 8

TABLE 3—THE INCREASING INTERNATIONALIZATION
OF THE WORLD ECONOMY
1970 to 1980
(Using mostly rough estimates)

	In Billions of 1970 Dollars	Percent of Gross World Product
GWP	3400 to 5600	100
World Exports *	300 to 600	8. 7 to 10.7
Total Sales of MNC's *	500 to 1200	14. 5 to 21. 4
Total Foreign Sales of MNC's *	350 to 1900	10. 2 to 16. 1
Total Foreign Sales of U.S. MNC's *	200 to 450	5. 7 to 8. 0
Total U.S. Exports	40 to 75	1. 6 to 1. 3
World Tourism	15 to 50	0. 5 to 0. 9

* All these numbers include a good deal of double counting, e.g., when a country exports items that are in part made of imports or when the output of the one MNC is part of the input of another MNC.

percent per year, the multinational concerns by something like 10 percent per year. Then we have an approximation for tourism growth, some 12 to 12½ percent per year.

This figure takes into account the increase in South American, Japanese, and Asian tourism. Usually the figures concentrate on Europe and the United States. As a result of all this an increasing proportion of the world's transactions takes place internationally. There is a limit to internationalization of course, 100 percent, which means that at some point all of these curves that are rising faster than GWP have to turn downward. This is particularly true of growth of the transnational concern, and to many of us this implies a kind of collision between the transnational concern and something in the system. I emphasize the belief held, at least among some of us at Hudson, in contrast to the belief of many governments, that the transnational concern is a weak organization politically—as compared to national governments. While it has great strength in its ability to withhold or reallocate resources, this is its main strength, and it is not the strongest weapon in the world.

A second factor worth noticing about Table 3 is that we probably still have not reached past levels of internationalization as measured, say, by the ratio of world trade to GWP. Probably we have not reached levels of internationalization achieved before 1914 or before 1929. This observation may be important because it indicates—probably correctly—that this kind of internationalization is a delicate growth. If the process is interrupted it is difficult to restore rapidly. Indeed, it may literally take a generation or two to restore current trends of internationalization if there were to be catastrophic breakdown in the system. So a serious depression or a serious trade war could really make a difference to our future.

The central role of the transnational corporation as an instrument and engine of worldwide and rapid development is to again be noted. If the transnational concern becomes self-conscious about this role, it will perform even better and presumably will also make more profits. So it could be both self-serving and altruistic for them consciously to understand and improve their performance in this function.

Hostility to the transnational company has been common throughout the world, outside the United States. In our own country we are seeing increasing hostility toward the American TNC—on both the liberal and conservative sides of the house. In particular, American labor and many in the American Congress are now angry at a move by American automobile manufacturers to tie in with the Japanese. This tendency in the United States to criticize the transnational companies is mostly new. You will soon be able to say with reasonable accuracy that of the 120 sovereignties in the world, all 120 are hostile to the American multinational corporation. Indeed there may be few government officials anywhere in the world who are really friendly to the American—or even their own—transnational companies. Nevertheless the odds are still in favor of the transnational companies despite hostility. Factors that encourage TNC growth are given in the box on page 20.

Currency Status of the World

A rough assessment of the currency status of the world is given in Table 4. It essentially ignores short-term movements. Almost all countries want reserves equal to about three to six months' imports. This is considered important to national safety and flexibility. If foreign reserves drop to less than three months, generally something is done to increase them. If reserves increase to more than six months—unless it is West Germany or the United States—the country generally feels uncomfortable since it is wasting capital by keeping it in the bank. The country starts investing it. One of the reasons, I believe, for West Germany's relatively slow growth rate in recent years is that the Germans have held foreign reserves that are too large. They should have been investing.

All this means that to run world trade under present conditions, world foreign-currency reserves should about equal one-third the volume of world trade. World trade runs at 330 billion dollars a year of imports or exports, and, in fact, world foreign reserves are about 120 billion. World foreign reserves are at about the right point to finance world trade.

Arguments can be made that as world trade increases a smaller percentage of reserves is acceptable. Whether these arguments are right or wrong, governments still do not believe them; they act as if the arguments are wrong. The one-third rule is a kind of sacred rule because it is the way many countries actually behave. That means four months of imports—scarcely too much. It means that if world reserves do not grow at about 10 percent per year, world trade will suffer. The 10 percent per year consists of some 7½ percent to take account of real growth, and 2½ percent, or so for inflation. Obviously, if inflation is more than that, world reserves have to grow even faster.

How can world reserves grow? One can add more gold to the system, but that is a slow process and there is no sense relying on it. The only convenient way for world reserves to grow today is for dollars to go into the system. There is literally no other way.

Gold reserves are about 40 billion dollars, or about 40 percent of the total. Many people talk about a smaller role for gold. I am convinced that the role of gold does not go down much—and may go up. Or at least world reserves of monetary gold will hold their own or increase over time rather than decrease despite the fact that today the free market price of gold is one-third or so higher than the official price paid by central banks.

The best means to finance world trade would be, in my opinion, to accept the suggestion put forth by the French some years ago (which they no longer advocate) and increase the price of gold some two and one-half times. That would raise the 40 billion dollars to 100 billion, which is about right to finance world trade. The increase in the

Ten Aspects of the World Context That Encourage MNC Growth

- Continuation of world peace, relative political stability, and worldwide economic growth.
- Dispersion of resources and markets—disparities in labor costs.
- New or emerging technologies, sources of resources, markets, and methods of rationalizing the economies of various industries.
- Increasing "similarity" or standardization of markets.
- In some cases continued protectionist policies, but in others decreasing protectionism.
- Increasing importance of economics of scale—requirements for large amounts of capital, competent management, and advanced or new technology to accomplish desired or required tasks.
- Proportionate decrease in transportation and communication costs.
- Pressures to maintain a competitive market share.
- "Momentum" from current investment and experience.
- No pervasive and/or effective interference from political authorities.

price of gold would draw gold back into the international system at, I would guess, about the right rate for financing the increase in world trade. Just the same, the possibility of going back to gold as the main international reserve is, I think, under existing conditions, zero. Even the French gave up this position. So I am not arguing for gold. But a substitute must be found. This raises intrinsically difficult problems.

If gold is not a base, what can be used as a base? One of the main purposes of currency is to act as what economists call a store of value. If it is kept in gold, it does not deteriorate and is always marketable. It has the beautiful characteristic that during hard and difficult times—civil war, world war, insurrection—the price tends to go up not down. Every other commodity is less reliable—many have a tendency to go down during troubled times. But gold has a tendency to go up. In fact, in much of the world, the actual local "free market" price for gold tends to be well over $50. For this reason Frenchmen have three and a half billion dollars in gold in hiding (that is the more-or-less official estimate—but it may be five or six billion). Many people simply do not trust scraps of paper as a store of value.

Many, however, are willing to trust the U.S. dollar as a store of value. They have the feeling that, whatever else happens in the world, the United States is not likely to repudiate its currency completely—and in the meantime their savings earn interest, which normally cannot be done with gold holdings. That belief, however, is not universal. When I was in Germany in September of last year I found some bankers were worried that the United States would, in effect, repudiate its overseas funds—at least for the time being. But many Germans tend to have a slightly hysterical attitude towards inflation because of the historical experience of that country.

Some major parts of the world would be willing to accept special drawing rights issued by the IMF. Most likely the Scandinavian countries, Atlantic Germany, The Netherlands, the Flemish part of Belgium, Switzerland, the United States, Canada, Australia, and New Zealand would. Japan probably would. But, most likely France, Italy, and the remainder of Germany would not.

Major Role for the Dollar

I believe that SDR's will not be the answer to the international monetary reserve problem within the the next decade or two—and perhaps even longer. What then is the answer? I believe the long-term answer is probably a combination of currencies— that is, the yen, the dollar, the ECOR (which is the European currency unit to be launched), SDR's, and gold. Gold will not pay interest. Money in one of these other four will earn, say, five-percent interest. People who have held gold have not made money on it because over time the five-percent interest lost was not made up by the gain in the value of gold. Nevertheless there will be enough lack of faith in these pieces of paper that there will be no lack of people willing to hold gold.

Surprisingly, most countries still prefer to hold large amounts of gold, despite the fact that they lose five-percent or more interest by doing so. It shows a basic distrust of these pieces of paper. It is also difficult to imagine the West Germans or the Japanese running the large balance-of-payments deficits necessary if the mark or yen were to play appreciable roles as world-reserve currencies.

World trade in 1980 can be assumed to be at least 600 billion dollars in real terms. Assume a 20- or 25-percent inflation, so it would be around 750 billion in 1970 dollars. That means the world will need 250 billion dollars or so of reserves, which is about 150 billion more than is currently available. This has to be supplied under existing operating conditions. I think the only big supply can be the U.S. dollar. The others, the SDR, the possible ECOR, the yen, the mark, will provide relatively small contributions. If this is so, then the current idea that the U.S. dollar will play a much smaller role in world reserves is, I think, incorrect. It also means that the dollar deficit must continue, because this is how you get the currency in wide supply.

This is understood in the United States, and it is probably why Secretary Connally, when he talked about reversing the deficit, said that we want to reverse it only for a few years so as to restore confidence in the dollar. He did not talk about a permanent reversal. I think it is a bad thing for the United States to have this dollar deficit because it leads to bad habits. In effect, we send pieces of paper overseas and exchange them for hard goods and property. The second problem is that the world banker must accept a certain responsibility for its internal conduct—which the United States may or may not wish to do.

The U.S. balance-of-payments situation is, I believe, about right. It supplies about five to ten billion dollars or so a year to the system. (See the lower portion of Table 4). When the Europeans and the IMF people meet with the Americans, the first thing they look at is U.S. direct investment abroad ($6 billion). They say, "Why don't you cut out that direct investment? This would almost immediately eliminate the dollar deficit." The answer is that such direct investment is the wave of the future. It happens to be perhaps the most valuable money we spend. It also happens to be one of the hardest things in the world to cut because it involves extremely large firms that can raise money anyway. Therefore, the chance is small, if any, that interference with this investment will do much more than is already being done. We already have some interference with this direct investment, and I doubt we can expect much more effective interference.

How Overcome the Deficit?

If you are opposed to American military policies, you observe the military contributions to the

World Monetary Reserves		
Gold (Countries' Holdings)	36	
International Agency Gold	5	
Total Gold		41
Foreign Exchange		
Dollars	46	
Sterling	7	
Difference (Other)	16	
Total		69
SDR's	6	
IMF Position	6	
Total		122
Total World Imports		330

U.S. Currency Flow		
Imports (Goods and Services)	−68. 4	
Exports (Goods and Services)	+68. 9	
Net		+0. 5
Selected Components		
U.S. Tourism In	+ 3	
U.S. Tourism Out	5. 4	
Net Tourism		−2. 4
U.S. Military Aid		−5. 0
(Direct Defense Expenditures)		
Other Government Expenditures		−2. 2
U.S. Direct Investment Abroad		−6. 0
Reinvested Earnings		−3. 0
U.S. Investment in Foreign		
Securities		−1. 2
Direct Foreign Investment in U.S.		−0. 4
Foreign Investment in U.S.		
Securities		+1. 7
Repatriated from Overseas		
Investments		+8. 4
Net Balance (approx.)		−10

but some disagree, that it is relatively easy to increase the plus 68 to a plus 75 or so, or to decrease the 68 of imports to 60 or so, or even easier to work on both sides of the ledger simultaneously. How do we decrease imports? One way is by such measures as a 10-percent surtax. Or you could do it with something like a serious export substitute program—or even a serious "Buy American" campaign.

Or one could work on the other side of the equation. The United States has never gone on an all-out export drive. If we did, I suspect we could—at present prices—easily increase exports by 10 to 20 billion—at least if the potential markets did not take counteractions. Thus, despite much concern, normally the balance-of-payments problem is not really as serious as usually pictured. Now this was not true in 1971. So it may be well to ask what happened in 1971.

If a trade balance is to be maintained year after year, a basic equation must be satisfied, i.e., the productivity increase (approximately averaged) minus inflation (wholesale inflation, not consumer inflation) must equal the productivity increase of the other country minus its inflation. United States consumer inflation is quite low—lower than the Japanese, lower than the German. But in the last two years our wholesale inflation got out of control—it went to about 10 percent. It happens that the Japanese have kept this equation balanced since 1949 by tinkering with their inflation. That is one of the reasons why the yen ratio, which was set at 360 to the dollar in 1949, was satisfactory for the next 21 years. It got out of balance in 1969 and 1970.

Normally international trade is not sensitive to this equation. That is, when a nation changes its currency value, it normally takes two or three years for international trade to react. But in addition to letting the equation get out of line we had a shipping strike and a steel strike in America. As a result, every businessman had to reconsider who his suppliers were. The normal inertia of the established pattern did not exist. For this and other reasons we had a large imbalance that soon resulted in betting against the dollar. This quickly provided a 20-billion dollar deficit, resulting in the President's August 15th speech. If this equation is not maintained, something must be adjusted. The currency rate can be adjusted, or the country that is more competitive can start exporting currency—through tourism, in loans, in direct portfolio, or investments in foreign aid, and so on. But some action is necessary.

deficit (five billion) are almost equal to the deficit (in 1970 almost exactly equal). Why not cut that out? And again the answer is that if these military expenditures are desirable, they are probably among the highest priority items on the list. If they are undesirable we should cut them out whether or not we want to reduce the balance-of-payments deficit. In other words, military policy should be treated outside of financial considerations. To achieve a payments balance, obviously you look at the imports and exports of goods and services, which is roughly 68 billion both ways. I believe,

Governments today will not stand for one nation taking five billion dollars a year in reserves out of the system. The Japanese have done almost exactly this in the last three years. Whether this is done because of accident, or productivity increase, or inflation, it must be put back via currency adjustment, direct investment, portfolio buying, loans, credits, or anything else, so that the multinational trading system creates as much purchasing power as it destroys. This seems to me to be an absolute obligation for a nation such as Japan—which, after all, benefits enormously from this system. As far as business in 1990 is concerned, all of these issues will probably have been worked out and today's ills will have been largely replaced by ills associated with the cures to the existing problems. But this cannot be discussed here.

Protectionism or Free Trade?

The United States will not, in my view, go protectionist despite recent changes. While the attitude in the United States will change—it will probably not change as much as many now believe. From 1934 to 1967 every major initiative for free trade

RAW STEEL PRODUCTION
U.S., U.S.S.R., JAPAN and EEC (including U.K.)
(millions of net tons)

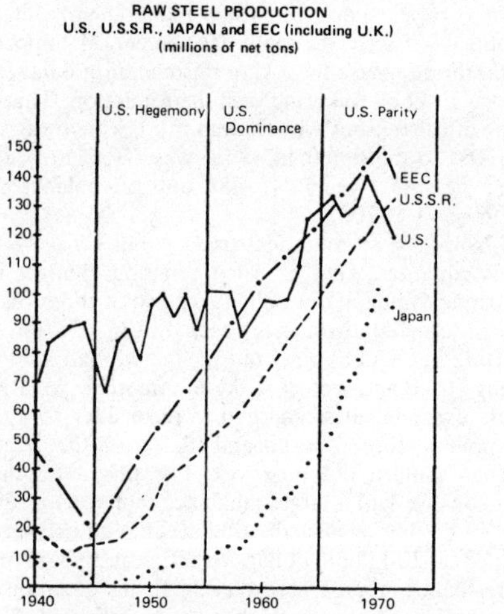

Source: American Iron and Steel Institute, European Economic Community Information Service, British Information Service

Figure 3

came from the United States. This will not happen in the future—that is my guess. To have free trade, somebody else will be needed to fight for it. Who will take the initiative in the future? Rather interestingly, the Council of Ministers of the European Economic Commission issued a statement in late 1971 that went completely unnoticed in the world press. It said that it was willing to discuss, with the United States and others, all issues of free trade, including things like agriculture policy. Previously the Commission had absolutely refused to consider this kind of issue. If this is a straw in the wind, it indicates that the Commission may be willing to take the initiative in free trade. My own reading of the European mind is that this is unlikely. It is hard for me to believe that even an expanded EEC will take any serious new initiatives on lowering external tariff barriers. Let us hope I am wrong.

Flight-and-Return of Products

Let us examine what has been happening to steel production, for example. Raw-steel production appears in the curves of Fig. 3. For the first decade after the war, the United States produced 60 to 80 percent of the steel in the world. Nothing that happened in steel could bother the United States. This can be called the U.S. hegemonial period. Right after the war we had more than half of the world's gross product. The United States was the main world actor.

During the period 1955 to 1965—the period of U.S. economic dominance—we still were the main steel producer in the world, but others had begun catching up. Particularly the EEC. Today, in what I term the period of U.S. parity, at least three international actors produce about as much steel as we do.

Several things are happening. Compare the curves for the steel industry with those for the automobile industry, Fig. 4. In the early '50s the United States produced 75 percent of the world's automobiles and trucks. Once again our industry was largely immune from what was happening in the remainder of the world. Today we produce about 30 percent. This represents a big proportional decrease. But another 20 to 30 percent (depending on how the counting is done) is produced by American firms outside the United States. In other words, U.S. business has suffered a relatively small loss in its market share while the United States as a country has suffered a large loss in market shares.

20

This is quite different from the steel industry. Part of the difference reflects the nature of the industries. Everybody knows how to make steel, and much national emotion is attached to the existence and ownership of so basic an industry in a nation. It is difficult for a transnational company to get into the steel business abroad. I also think there were big differences in management. In this context (but not in all others) people in American steel management were relatively unentrepreneurial—at least compared to other parts of the American system. The automobile industry was more entrepreneurial—much more global, more cosmopolitan, more willing to take chances in international investment.

Many industrial production shifts take place among nations. They cannot always be well predicted. For example, consider steel reinforcing bars. In 1960 it seemed that this product would no longer be made in the United States. Production was moving overseas. That seemed irreversible. But continuous-casting steel mills came into existence, representing both high technology and high capital investment. Reinforcing-bar manufacture came back to the United States. Technology is unpredictable.

The movement of a product out of the United States can occur suddenly. In 1960 the largest home-entertainment tape-recorder industry in the world was in the United States. In 1970, except for some expensive high-fidelity tapes, not a single magnetic tape was manufactured in the United States for home entertainment. Almost the entire industry had been lost.

Also, the United States once had a large radio industry. By 1970, four-fifths of our radios were manufactured abroad. Of the one-fifth remaining still made in the United States, 90 percent had foreign parts.

During these departures almost no effective complaint from American industry was heard. Many protested, but in the existing milieu their complaints and recommendations went unheeded. This probably would not happen today—or at least not go as smoothly—and there might even be limits set to the operation of the market forces. Other manufacturers—some after finding that their products were ineffective—were willing to accept the movement as part of an inevitable comparative advantage process, in part because they themselves did the importing.

We can all cite examples of products whose manufacture has taken flight abroad, usually because of lower labor rates. Conceivably the United

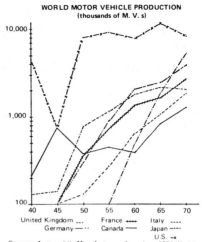

WORLD MOTOR VEHICLE PRODUCTION
(thousands of M. V. s)

United Kingdom ...   France ++++   Italy ----
Germany —··   Canada —   Japan --··
U.S. -x
Source: Automobile Manufacturers Assn. Inc., 1971 World Motor Vehicle Data

Figure 4

States could change its technologies or reorganize the manufacturing system to become more productive, or somehow just encourage the workers and managers to be more productive. It is also clear that if our currency is out of line, then it will not be economically efficient to do a number of things in the United States, not because of real comparative advantage problems but simply because of misaligned currency. But the currency is not likely to be off by more than 20 or 30 percent. Anything that is noncompetitive by much more than that will, in the long run, present issues of protection or subsidy on the one hand, or on the other, of allowing untrammeled—and sometimes undesirable—market forces to work freely.

Many American manufacturers fear that this kind of thing can happen for all of American industry, so that in effect the Far East could, in principle, underprice us almost across the board. Actually, if we have a reasonably priced currency, this is impossible no matter how efficient or inefficient the two trading partners are. That is, one can always set the currency ratio so that it pays each country to buy as much as it sells from each other. If one does set the currency ratio this way, both sides will gain from trading. In fact, this is exactly what is meant by the concept of comparative advantage. No country can be at comparative advantage (or disadvantage) in everything.

An important set of issues relates to our willingness to have the shape of our economy determined by purely market forces of this sort. No U.S. government would be willing to see 100 percent of any really important or basic manufacturing enterprise leave this country. This is particularly true of manufacturing enterprises that involve a lot of encouragement of research and development, because here such cautions as hedging against future changes, security, flexibility, dependability, and so on become important.

By 1990 we may be, for example, importing about 100 million tons of steel a year and manufacturing about 50 million tons—but I cannot imagine dropping much below 50 million tons a year. I could also imagine that if the technology of steel production changed, the United States could become a major exporter again. In fact, in some ways, the worst case would involve both major exportation and major importation. This last is even more possible in the automobile industry. However, one could also easily imagine, as one extreme, importing about 10 million cars a year and producing about 5 million; and at the other, that the manufacture of automobiles might become so automated and take so much capital investment that the United States could achieve a commanding position once more. Or, the in-between situation where the United States concentrates on things like large, expensive cars, mass produced, while overseas industries concentrated on smaller, less expensive cars or specially made cars.

To give a feel for some of the issues that arise I will discuss briefly factors affecting the rate of change. It should be first of all understood that in some places—Japan might be a typical example—the other side can decide where to put its resources and in effect determine where its comparative advantage will exist. I cannot imagine, for example, allowing Japanese industry, which is more or less coordinated, to make a conscious decision to be competitive in certain kinds of computers and not in other kinds, thus causing the U.S. computer industry to adjust rapidly to the Japanese decision. In some sense, we have a right to vote on that decision, particularly if the United States is being asked to make a rapid transition. This kind of issue is likely to come up in the near future.

In any case, the United States has some obligation to its manufacturers—they should not have to ammortize expensive plants overnight—and has an equal obligation to its workers that they should not, on a large scale, be asked to pick up new skills and become apprentices again. I repeat, there will be forced ammortization of American capital, and there will be forced retraining or retirement of American workers. The question is the scale and rapidity with which these processes occur, and how far they are allowed to go before the entire industry vanishes—or whether cutback will simply be large and orderly.

A Trade/Development/Investment Policy Is Essential

One thing, however, is certain. Before much can be done about any of these policies, an overall trade/development/investment policy is required. This policy must take into account the fact that, for the advanced countries of the world, much of the wave of the future lies in the more technologically advanced products. If such countries try to maintain too large or strong a position with the somewhat simpler, conventional lines—unless of course the fundamental issues are also changed—they will run into serious trouble. On the other hand, it is not likely that many of these emerging postindustrial economies will be willing to allow untrammeled market forces to work out their destiny, certainly not in the short or medium run, and possibly not even in the long run.

Most of the income of advanced economies today still comes from the more traditional product lines, but if they stay in that category too long they will be in serious trouble. The United States, so I believe, is more likely to pursue reasonable policies here than Canada is. Further, the United States and Canada are more likely to be reasonable than the Europeans in the sense that European countries are likely to try to maintain the status quo too long and too vigorously. On the other hand, only the United States is likely to make the mistake of going too far. Ours is practically the only country that has the ability to control events to some degree, but large biases of an ideological sort favor letting our market forces work out the solution almost independent of government interference.

One of the real points of superiority of the Japanese has been an extreme willingness to move from relatively low-technology industries to higher technology industries. Despite all the current intense complaints about the textile industry, the Japanese are trying to get out of the manufacture of simple textiles as fast as possible. The government has already bought up about one-third of the textile looms in the country and put them out of business, and plans to continue. To some degree Japan is rapidly getting out of some of the simpler forms of the consumer-electronics business. At least one company is moving its entire business to South Korea, Taiwan, and elsewhere. Even a country such as Singapore today has a tendency to discourage simpler kinds of consumer-electronics plants. It tends to think of simple transistor radios as being too primitive for Singapore, and might better belong in Hong Kong. This could be an intelligent policy. Almost any city in the United States with an unemployment problem would be pleased if someone opened exactly this kind of electronics plant, even though in the long run it will not compete with overseas manufacture.

It is just such a sense of having a specific, clear public policy, designed towards the medium-or long-term future that is very keen and strong in Japan and Singapore, but largely absent in Europe and America. In fact, in some sense we have never really had a trade policy of this sort in the United States. Many people believe that the political system of the United States is such that a trade policy is not possible in the same way, for example, that we have a national security policy.

Before World War II we usually did not have a national security policy either. We just drifted from event to event. We have in the United States a group called the Peterson Committee, whose objective is to try to set up a trade policy for the United States. This is not likely to be completely successful because no federal official is likely to be willing to say that any particular product should be abandoned to a foreign competitor. Nor can I imagine many European government officials saying that—although the Swedes, I am told, have done so.

In some European countries this is being done in agriculture. I do not believe we have a plan for this in America. We now have four million agricultural workers, which is a million or so too many, but no President will admit that we would like to move these surplus workers off the land. The system eventually does do this, but no admitted government policy exists for facilitating it.

Much of the shift we are postulating from the industrial to the postindustrial-type activities is something that is likely to be inevitable, but the rate at which the shift occurs could still be under national control. If a nation stretches out the shift too long it is likely to sharply decrease its growth rates; if too fast, it may also decrease growth rates. Whether or not it decreases growth rates, it will at least increase human suffering.

I emphasize that foreigners should not be allowed to disrupt capriciously, or excessively rapidly, orderly transitions in the United States or to determine, by themselves, which U.S. industries shall survive and which shall not.

Rise of Pacific Basin Trade

Another important trend in world trade is the movement of trade from the Atlantic to the Pacific in much the same way that it once moved from the Mediterranean to the Atlantic. We are accustomed to the idea that the great volume of world trade is conducted among the nations bordering the North Atlantic. Several developments of the last few years suggest that the next decade will see the development of a new trading and investment area, the business and economic reality of which may in turn underlie important political and eventually perhaps military possibilities.

Consider some likely magnitudes. By 1980 each of the major nations of the Pacific hemisphere will probably be conducting more than half of their trade and making (or receiving) more than half of their investments with other countries in the Pacific hemisphere. The principal components of this Pacific hemisphere trading and investment community (PAHTIA) are Japan, the Sinic culture areas on the border of Asia (South Korea, Taiwan, Hong Kong, Singapore, Thailand, South Vietnam), Indonesia, Philippines, Australia, New Zealand, Brazil, Colombia, Venezuela, Mexico, the United States, Canada, and perhaps Argentina and Chile.

The principal economic forces operating today, which we expect will continue to operate strongly through the '70s that will create this PAHTIA are these:

- The continued economic growth of Japan at a much greater than world rates and the growth of Japanese international trade at at least the rate of world trade in general.
- The continued rapid growth of the Sinic culture areas and their increased share of world trade.
- The expanding need of the developed countries, particularly the United States and Japan, to export manufacturing operations to areas of low labor cost, such as the Sinic culture areas of Asia, and increasingly by the end of the decade to such areas as Malaysia, the Philippines, and Indonesia as well.
- A shifting orientation of Australia and New Zealand away from Europe and toward Japan, the Pacific, and the United States.

23

This will come in part from England's move into the Common Market and in part from the increased availability of Japanese capital and Japanese markets, and other factors as well.

- Increased Japanese investment and marketing interest in South America, and especially in Brazil, the only other major country in addition to the United States where Japanese have gone in large numbers to settle as immigrants. (There are now about 750,000 Brazilians of Japanese descent, and, on the whole, they have tended—unlike the United States—to back up ties with Japan.)

Inasmuch as the Americas face both across the Atlantic and across the Pacific, it is possible for an Atlantic hemisphere trading and investment area and a Pacific trading and investment area to exist simultaneously, and for the members of both to trade at least 50 percent with each other. The Pacific hemisphere trading area deserves special attention of the two because it is the newer development in economic and business life and during the '70s (and quite possibly the '80s) the more dynamic. Important business events are often generated by changes in the underlying economic factors, so it is important to focus on that which is most rapidly changing—particularly as those new constellations of trade and investment may require changing business orientations elsewhere as well.

PAHTIA can be thought of as the merger of the area that has been dominated by the United States with the area that Japan seems to be in a position potentially to dominate in a similar way. (Japanese dominance is not likely to be like that of the United States for several reasons; it comes a century later; Japan has a smaller percent of the total population of the area; distances are larger; and other countries in the area were developed before Japan.) The merger of these two areas means that in the natural struggle between small countries and large ones, small countries will have two large countries to play off against each other. Both the struggle and the playing off of one country against the other can be, and well may be, a relatively benign process.

It is better for a small country to be in an area containing two large countries than one. To some extent the United States (and Japan) also benefits from being part of an area of two large powers. The other large power, in effect, will rake off some of the heat. Today, in much of the world, modernization tends to be synonymous in people's minds with Americanization. While almost everybody in the world wants to be modern, this is a painful process with many ugly and evil by-products. If Japan catches up with the United States as the most advanced nation, and the one most present in a particular country, then it may become true that modernization is as much identified with Japanization as it is with Americanizaton. To the extent that this becomes true—and it isn't clear whether this is a possibility for the '80s, for the '90s, or for the next century—many of the political, psychological overtones of international affairs can be expected to change, partly to our detriment, but perhaps even more to the benefit of the United States.

One of the real advantages of having a double leadership of some group over a single leadership is not just that it dilutes the hostility toward the single leader, but that it really changes the relationship almost completely. The smaller members of the group can find a considerable self-assertion and self-actualization and independence in the fact that the leadership is divided, and that the whole relationship then changes extensively. Power that is divided is simply much smaller than power that is unified. This can make for a much more wholesome relationship for all concerned. ∎

Key Choices of the Next Two Decades

Willis W. Harman

A KEY QUESTION facing men of business is: Will the private enterprise corporate business system have proven, by 1990, to have been inadequate to the challenges presented to it?

New evidence and accusations are presented daily that what is seemingly good business policy frequently turns out to be poor social policy. Rational business decisions too often turn out to have resulted in irrational squandering of natural resources, fouling of the environment, technological disemployment, debasing of persons, and—in some dimensions at least—lowered quality of life. National policies attuned to requirements of the domestic economy and of international trade have led to an interminable and morally questionable war. Present trends and present business strategies extrapolated to 1990 lead to projected states of society that are undesirable if not intolerable.

Many in the business community have become convinced, by the abundance of sober forecasts and doomsday descriptions, that some fairly fundamental change is required. Others are not so convinced. But the nagging question remains, Why should not really good business policy also be good social policy?

Those who see an inherent and insuperable

Address by Dr. Willis W. Harman, Director, Educational Policy Research Center, Stanford Research Institute, Menlo Park, California.

discrepancy between good business policy and good social policy often assume the need for more and bigger governmental structures. Government is called on to provide jobs for all who can work; doles for those who cannot; policing of the environment; regulation of the impact of new technology; salvation for failing cities; financial aid for failing railroads and aerospace corporations; water and air cleanup; public housing for the poor; higher education for all—the list grows interminably. Wherever private enterprise, working through the market mechanism, fails to satisfy social needs, or where the associated profit margins would be low compared with alternative investment opportunities—hand the problem to the government.

Is there another way? Are there new, vital roles the private and voluntary sectors can play? Can the system be adjusted so that good business policy is congruent with good social policy? These are among the questions to be viewed against a background of alternative futures.

Alternative Paths to 1990

Few informed persons now doubt that technically advanced societies like the United States are undergoing a major historical transformation to some sort of postindustrial age. This is characterized by diminishing dominance of industrial production as a social function, by increasing

A LOOK AT BUSINESS IN 1990: A Summary of the White House Conference on the Industrial World Ahead, Washington, D.C., February 7-9, 1972 (U.S. Government Printing Office: 1972 0—467-348) pp. 28-36.

prominence of service activities, and by increasing concern with value questions related to quality of life. The differences among opinions lie on how rapid and extreme this change will be in values, perceptions, and institutions. I forecast that the shift is likely to be rapid, extreme, and hazardous.[1]

This forecast is in distinct contrast to the view that the available alternative futures comprise modest deviations from a "long-term multifold trend,"[2] with slow changes in social institutions and cultural values. It is not possible now to demonstrate which view is the more correct. Five years hence the situation may be clearer. Today both views are held by groups of reasonable men.

Rapid, Drastic Changes Ahead

I propose to examine the arguments suggesting that forces toward an abrupt and drastic modification of the long-term multifold trend may lead to a revolutionary social change within the next two decades. Further, this revolutionary change may free up the system so that satisfactory answers to the questions raised above can be found.

I say this soberly. History gives us little reason to take comfort in the prospect of fundamental and rapid social change—little reason to think we can escape without the accompanying threat of economic decline and disruption of social processes considerably greater than anything we have experienced or care to imagine. If indeed a fundamental and rapid change in basic perceptions and values occurs, such a chaotic period seems inevitable as the powerful momentum of the industrial era is turned in a new direction, and as the different members and institutions of the society respond with different speeds.

Present trends and present business strategies extrapolated to 1990 lead to projected states of society that are undesirable if not unacceptable.

Accurate interpretation of this disorder is crucial. The form—and the success—of the nation's policies will depend a great deal on whether the disruption is seen as accompaniment to a change toward a more workable system, or is perceived as essentially destructive. Or, alternatively, whether it is seen as a rather bothersome episode as a result of which things will be neither particularly better nor worse, just different.

Indicators of Revolutionary Change

Several clues indicate that the industrialized world may be experiencing the beginning phase of a sociocultural revolution as profound and pervasive in its effects on all segments of the society as the Industrial Revolution, the Reformation, or the Fall of Rome. I am not speaking of *The Greening of America*,[3] or of the achieving of any of the popularly promoted Utopias. The shape of the future will no more be patterned after the hippie movement and the youth revolution than the industrial age could have been inferred from the "new-age" values of the Anabaptists.

The transformation that we call the Protestant Reformation affected all aspects of the society, from the nascent science to the new capitalist commercial structure. Similarly, in the present case, we should expect impacts on the economic system, on science, on government, and on community and work life. As we look back at the Reformation, the most fundamental change appears to be in those tacitly agreed on, largely unquestioned basic premises on which every culture is based. Only a half dozen or so times in the history of Western civilization did this basic paradigm[4] undergo revolutionary change.[5] The Reformation was the most recent of these. It was characterized by a shift from the otherworldly, inner-directed, teleological paradigm of the Middle Ages to this-worldly, outer-directed, relatively nontelelogical paradigm of the industrial age. These characteristics are summarized as follows:

- Development and application of scientific method; wedding of scientific and technological advance
- Industrialization through organization and division of labor; machine replacement of human labor
- Acquisitive materialism; work ethic; economic-man image; belief in unlimited material progress and in technological and economic growth
- Man seeking control over nature; positivistic theory of knowledge; manipulative rationality as a dominant theme
- Individual responsibility for own destiny; freedom and equality as fundamental rights; nihilistic value perspective, individual determination of the "good"; society as an aggregate of individuals pursuing their own interests

26

Thus we are talking about an event that is historically improbable because of its rarity. It is a transformation that has not yet occurred; therefore, we can make only an informed guess at the main characteristics of the substitute paradigm. If this interpretation begins to appear more or less correct, the consequences for economic and political decision making are profound. Hence we can ill afford not to take the possibility seriously.

The Reformation period lasted about a century. Earlier major transformations, such as the agricultural revolution, were far more dispersed in both space and time. How can such a profound shift as we are contemplating take place in the space of a decade or two? One reason is the general speedup of change. Another, of course, is the impact of modern communication media. Still another reason may lie, as we shall see, in the acceptability of the paradigm that may be replacing the beliefs and values of the industrial age.

This impending revolutionary-change view is plausible for three major reasons. 1—The complex of social problems confronting the developed world appears to require changes in cultural values for their satisfactory resolution; 2—a competitor to the industrial-state paradigm, embodying the requisite kinds of value shifts, may be arising spontaneously; and 3—various "lead indicators" that have preceded historic cultural-change periods have been prominent during the past decade.

New values required. It is almost a truism that most of our severe social problems are essentially the consequence of our technological and industrial successes. For example, success in reducing infant mortality has contributed to excessive population growth. Technology-created affluence poses resource-depletion problems. New materials (e.g., plastics, detergents, aluminum) have interfered with natural recycling processes. Machine replacement of manual and routine labor has exacerbated unemployment and poverty problems. Development of nuclear, biological, and chemical weapons has led to the potential worldwide decimation. And so on.

The nature of these problems is such that many analysts have seriously questioned whether those basic values and premises that have served to build up our present technological and industrial capabilities are now suitable for the humane application or even rational control of those Faustian powers.[6] As long as this remains a question, values that appear more suitable will be able to mobilize social power. We will return to this point later.

Emerging paradigm. Several signs visible here and in other industrialized nations point to the possible emergence of a new dominant paradigm:

- Surveys and polls indicate significant value shifts among certain elite groups, such as students and corporate executives. Increased emphasis is placed on humanistic and spiritual values, quality of life, community person-centered society, and so forth. Emphasis on materialistic values, status goals, and unqualified economic growth [7] is diminished.

- Numerous cultural indicators (e.g., books read, voluntary associations, rock lyrics, themes of plays and motion pictures, content of magazine articles, "New Age" subculture) show greatly increased interest in and tolerance for the transcendental, religious, esoteric, occult, suprarational, mystical, and spiritual.

- New scientific interest in exploring subjective states, altered consciousness, partly as a consequence of new tools relating inner experience to physical and physiological correlates, (e.g., galvanic skin response, body electric fields, EEG components, biofeedback signals),[8] is resulting in a new legitimation of studies of religious beliefs, psychic phenomena, mystical experiences, and meditative states.

From these indicators, particularly the last, we can infer something about the direction in which values, and the dominant vision of man-in-the-universe, are likely to shift. Wherever the nature of man has been probed deeply, the paramount fact emerging is the duality of his experience. He is found to be both physical and spiritual, both sides being real, and neither describable in terms of the other. At various times and places the spiritual or the material has been temporarily dominant. A fundamental characteristic of the candidate paradigm is the relationship of complementarity in which it places such troublesome opposites as spirit/body, science/religion or determinism/free will, in much the same way as modern physics reconciles the previously opposing wave and particle theories of light. Suggested characteristics of the emergent paradigm are:

It is almost a truism that most of our severe social problems are essentially the consequence of our technological and industrial successes.

- Complementarity of physical and spiritual experience; recognition of all "explanation" as only metaphor; use of different non-contradicting "levels of explanation" for physical, biological, mental, and spiritual reality.
- Teleological sense of life and evolution having direction/purpose; ultimate reality perceived as unitary, with transcendent order.
- Basis for value postulates discoverable in own inner experience of a hierarchy of "levels of consciousness"; potentiality of supraconscious as well as subconscious influence.
- Goals of life—aware participation in individual growth and the evolutionary process, individual fulfillment through community; integration of work, play, and growth.
- Goals of society—to foster development of individuals' transcendent and emergent potentialities. Economic growth, technological development, design of work roles and environments, authority structures, and social institutions all are to be used in the service of this primary goal.
- "New naturalism, holism, immanentism" (V. Ferkiss); "re-discovery of the supernatural" (P. L. Berger); "The counterculture is essentially an exploration of the politics of consciousness" (T. Roszak).

Thus the challenging paradigm assumes some sort of transcendent spiritual order, discoverable in human experience, and against which human value choices are assessed. Ultimately reality is unitary. There is a teleological sense of life and evolution having direction or purpose. Other levels of consciousness than the usual are explorable, with different appropriate levels of explanation. Hence the scientific explanation of the level of sensory experience is in no way contradictory to religious, philosophical, or poetic interpretations of suprasensory experience. Rather, it is complementary to them.

The candidate paradigm extends, rather than contradicts, the modern scientific world view, much as relativity theory extended Newtonian mechanics. Moreover, it is in its essence not new at all, having formed a central stream of thought in the humanities, in Western political tradition, in "transcendentalist" movements in our own history.[9] (However, never has anything like it been the guiding paradigm of an entire society. Popular religions, East and West, have been at best some watered-down version.) Part of the growing acceptability of the New Age world view undoubt-edly has been due to this drawing on what is already well established in the culture, together with the bridging of the "two cultures" of science and the humanities.

Lead indicators of revolutionary change—From studies of historical occurrences of revolutionary cultural and political change come the following list of typical occurrences in the period leading up to that change:[10]

- Decreased sense of community
- Increased sense of alienation and purposelessness
- Increased occurrence of violent crime
- Increased frequency of personal disorders and mental illness
- Increased frequency and severity of social disruptions
- Increased use of police to control behavior
- Increased public acceptance of hedonistic behavior
- Increase in amount of noninstitutionalized religious activities

To anyone who has read the newspapers over the last decade, the list alone makes the point, without the necessity of further comment.

A Fundamental Problem

All the above is not to say that such a revolutionary change and paradigm shift will inevitably occur. Rather, the three assertions listed argue that among the alternative "future histories" to be considered, needs to be included this possibility. Whether or not the social forces for such a transition are gathering sufficient strength to bring it about remains to be seen. The probability is not negligible at any rate.

Consider the first of these three propositions—namely, that the nature of society's problems necessitates significant value change for satisfactory resolution. At the risk of seeming to oversimplify, I will make this assertion much more explicit:

Industrial societies in general, and this nation in particular, are faced with one fundamental problem that is so pervasive and so pernicious that the related societal problems (e.g., poverty, unemployment, inflation, environmental deterioration, crime alienation) will defeat all attempts at solution until that fundamental problem is satisfactorily resolved. Such resolution hinges on value change.

The problem to which I refer has puzzled Adam Smith and most economists since his time. It is this: individuals, corporations, government agencies in the course of their activities make microdecisions (e.g., to buy a certain product, to employ a man for a particular task, to enact a minimum-wage law) that interact to constitute a set of macrodecisions of the overall society (e.g., a five-percent growth rate, failing cities, polluted air and water). The problem is that perfectly reasonable microdecisions currently are adding up to largely unsatisfactory macrodecisions.

Some specifics will illustrate:

- *The tragedy of the commons* [11]—Microdecisions regarding utilization of resources (e.g., land, air, water, fuels, minerals), which are reasonable from the viewpoints of corporate management and stockholders, developers, and local governments, but result in macrodecisions of resource depletion, environmental degradation, urban crowding, which are unsatisfactory to society at large.

- *Insufficient work opportunity*—People need opportunities to contribute meaningfully to the society and be affirmed in return (commonly with wages). Individual decisions to create and accept jobs fail to result in a satisfactory full-employment policy, and thus lead to the incongruity that work opportunity becomes considered as a scarce commodity that needs to be rationed.

- *Unintended technological impact*—Even with technology assessment we do not know how to preserve market microdecision making regarding technological innovation and yet achieve satisfactory macrochoices with regard to technological disemployment, quality of the environment, infringements of human rights, interference with natural recycling processes, and resource depletion.

- *Inflation*—Decisions to pass productivity increases from technological innovation on to workers in the form of increased wages, rather than apply them to reducing prices to consumers (plus demands for similar increases for service-sector workers whose productivity is not appreciably increasing), have contributed to persistent inflation.

- *State of the economy*—Decisions of hundreds of U.S.-based corporations to transfer manufacturing operations to low-labor-cost countries, while economically sound as individual decisions, collectively constitute a serious temporary threat to U.S. economy and industrial capability.

- *Alienation*—Individual, corporate, and government decisions are widely believed to have been guided by such principles as economic growth as a self-justifying end, "the business of business is business," the affluent society, the underdeveloped world as supplier of raw materials for that affluent society, and the "technological imperative" that any technology that can be developed and applied should be—and that this fact is leading the world toward an intolerable future. Further, individuals feel themselves forced by pressures of "the system" to act in ways that they perceive as neither what they want to do, nor what would be in general social good. The result is a serious alienation from the society and its institutions.

This fundamental problem is not simply a matter of trade-offs—as a recent cartoon quip had it, "There's a price tag on everything. You want a high standard of living, you settle for a low quality of life." Rather, it is a flaw in the decision-making system such that individuals are encouraged to choose on the basis of their own short-term, imprudent self-interest, instead of their long-term, enlightened self-interest. [12]

Classical economic theory attempted to explain how the market mechanism could operate to constitute, from individual self-interest microdecisions, macrodecisions that would operate for the general good. As time went on, the invisible hand clearly needed a little help in the form of government rule-making and umpiring, from antitrust laws to Keynesian manipulations of the money supply and interest rate. Yet the basic dilemma of unsatisfactory macrodecisions worsens, as illustrated above.

Why is the system in such trouble now when it worked satisfactorily before? Some of the contributing factors are:

- Interconnectedness, so that laissez-faire approaches are less workable
- Reduction of geographical and entrepreneurial frontier opportunities
- Approaching limits of natural recycling capabilities
- Sharpened dichotomy between "employed" and "unemployed" (e.g., virtual elimination of the small farmer, partially or sporadically employed)
- More adequate supplying of deficiency needs (improved diet, material advance) plus more education, resulting in higher expectations and keener perception of the gap between actualities and potentialities
- Transition from a basic condition of labor scarcity to one of job scarcity

- Approaching limits of some resources (e.g., natural gas, domestic petroleum, fresh water)
- Faustian powers of technology and industrialization that have reached the point where they can have a major impact on the physical, technological, sociopolitical, and psychological environment
- Expanded political power of labor that, forcing industrial wages to follow increasing productivity, constitutes an inflationary force
- Weakening of the force of "American civil religion," partly through the eroding effect of positivistic science, and hence a weakening of the will to self-regulation in the interest of the whole.

A Crucial Choice

If this is the diagnosis, what then is the prescription?

A key characteristic of the future of this society lies in the way in which the nation handles this fundamental dilemma. By and large, two significantly different approaches can be considered.

One of these is a continuation of the collectivist trend that has characterized the past four decades. If this path is taken, as the kinds of problems mentioned earlier grow more severe, they will be turned over to an expanding public sector to handle. Individual decisions will increasingly be regulated by government, through coercive controls and manipulative incentives. That this outcome is intrinsic is emphasized in John Galbraith's 1967 analysis of *The New Industrial State,* in which he predicted that " . . . a system of wage and price restraints is inevitable in the industrial system . . . neither inflation nor unemployment are acceptable alternatives." [13] On this path of deprivatization it will be difficult to avoid the well-known disadvantages of centralized control and bureaucratic giantism. Nevertheless, many today seem inclined to accept the inevitability of this drift.

The other direction is toward a reversal of the collectivist trend and a revitalized role for the private sector. However, it will not return to some previous state—it will move forward to something we have never known.

The "entrepreneurial capitalism" of the 19th century involved a view of economic man in a freemarket society, a state of scarcity, and minimal governmental intervention. Over the past few decades, it has been replaced by "managerial capitalism," picturing man as consumer in an affluent industrial state, with government regulating growth, employment, and wage-price stability. The alternative to which I am alluding might be termed "humanistic capitalism."

Again it is necessary to oversimplify to make the point easily. If the basic problem concerns unsatisfactory macrodecisions arising from self-interest-directed microdecisions, then the almost obvious thing to do is to turn the situation upside down. That is, select appropriate macrodecisions—which is to say, national and planetary goals—that are in accord with the best available knowledge regarding human fulfillment. Then see what patterns of microdecisions would be necessary to achieve those goals.

But there is a catch. The means used to obtain those necessary individual actions have to be compatible with the ends. This nation affirms the goal to " . . . guard the rights of the individual . . . enhance the dignity of the citizen, promote the maximum development of his capabilities, stimulate their responsible exercise, and widen the range and effectiveness of opportunities for individual choice . . . to build a nation and help build a world in which every human being shall be free to dedicate and develop his capacities to the fullest." [14] However, if we take this seriously, then the necessary patterns of microdecisions cannot be obtained through coercion, as in a totalitarian

---

Several clues indicate that the industrialized world may be experiencing the beginning phase of a sociocultural revolution as profound and pervasive in its effects on all segments of society as the Industrial Revolution, the Reformation, or the Fall of Rome.

---

state, nor through manipulative behavior-sharing as in B. F. Skinner's version of a technocratic state. The only means compatible with goals such as those declared above is through reeducation toward appreciation of wholesome goals and understanding of the microdecisions necessary for reaching them.[15]

In sum, the more unsatisfactory the macrodecisions, the stronger the government required. Thus we have two routes—stronger government or changed culture.

Some Characteristics of "Humanistic Capitalism"

The basic characteristic of the political economics I am referring to with the term humanistic capitalism is that society would be what Robert Hutchins describes as *The Learning Society*,[16] one that will have transformed "its values in such a way that learning, fulfillment, becoming human, had become its aims and all its institutions were directed to this end." Postindustrial society, whatever its other characteristics, must answer the question of how men shall occupy the portion of their time that is not required to provide goods and services and keep the essential processes of the society functioning. Learning is the major such activity that is nonpolluting, nonstultifying, humane, and socially beneficial.

Large privately owned and managed corporations, we 'may assume, will continue to be the dominant economic institutions in American society. If their modes of operation move toward humanistic capitalism, corporate goals would broaden to include, besides the present economic and institutional goals, authentic social responsibility and the personal fulfillment of those who participate in the corporate activity. This would not be as a gesture to improve corporate image or as a moralistically undertaken responsibility, but as operative goals on a par with profit making and institutional security. With humanistic capitalism not production, but productiveness in human life would be the goal.

The manpower concept of contemporary business management has resulted in job structuring for efficient production and incentive structuring to shape the men to fit the jobs. Among the consequences of this policy have been "unemployable" welfare recipients, overtrained aerospace engineers, under-utilized employees, and alienated production and office workers. The policy is basically analogous to approaching the problem of air pollution by breeding smog-resistant humans. Under humanistic capitalism jobs would be structured to fit people. Production processes would be designed to reinstill pride of craftsmanship. Goods and services would be tailored to fit consumers' needs and desires, not consumer wants shaped by manipulative advertising to meet the needs of business. Employees would work for pay, of course, but also because they believed in and identified with the operative goals of their employing corporation.

Government would probably remain the organizer and regulator of large, complex systems (e.g., for transportation, communication, health care, energy supply, financial operations, food production, education) composed of relatively autonomous self-organizing and self-monitoring subsystems, coordinated mainly by shared values and goals. Adequate governmental regulation would be required to ensure that future social costs and

---

Perfectly reasonable microdecisions currently are adding up to largely unsatisfactory macrodecisions.

---

benefits are adequately represented in private decision-making procedures. However, government would tend to reduce its role in the direct provision of goods and services (e.g., education, health insurance, property protection, welfare services) and instead adjust incentives to encourage supply of these from the private sector.

In short, private-sector institutions would assume a significantly expanded range of responsibilities in the implementation of new postindustrial values. Large institutions that retained narrow self-serving goals, be they corporations or labor unions, would find their legitimacy questioned.

Does this sound like idealism? I mean it to be intensely practical. Let me mention three reasons why I think a humanistic capitalism is completely feasible, assuming that recent trends in shifting cultural values continue:

- The public can exert tremendous power through engaging in political buying, stock purchase, and job seeking, favoring those corporations of whose operative values they approve. Thus the balance could easily shift to where it is the corporations that display serious social responsibility, which have the competitive advantage, not the reverse. (Recent truth-in-lending and truth-in-advertising pressures exemplify the principle.) Changes in tax laws, antitrust provisions, corporate charters, and so forth, might be introduced to encourage broader corporate responsibilities.

- Requirements for effective functioning of large, complex systems naturally support such values as personal honesty, openness, (to ensure accurate information flow); responsibility (hence self-actualization); and cooperative trust. The values required in the team that puts a man on the moon and gets him back are a far cry from those that suffice for operation of a used-car lot. Thus as the production and service tasks of the society become more complex, humane values become not only moral but also functional imperatives.

- As such institutions as industrial conglomerates, multinational corporations, and international labor unions, not directly accountable to the public, become larger and more powerful relative to representative governments, their operative goals have to become more congruent with those of the overall society—else the goals of the society will become distorted toward those of the dominant institutions. Thus, political pressure will urge corporate goals toward personal fulfillment of participants, public good, and social responsibility. If multinational corporations are to be dominant social institutions in the future, the fate of the world will hinge on the operative goals and values of those corporations.

The Role of Value Change

Thus we have postulated a direction toward resolution of the fundamental dilemma that the resultant of the microdecisions is so typically an unsatisfactory macrodecision. It does not depend on Adam Smith's "invisible hand," or on the manipulation of motivations and behavior by a technocratic elite, or on the socialist solution of the private sector abdicating to the public. Rather, it depends on reeducation to perceive suitable macrodecisions and appropriate microdecisions to lead toward them, and on a shift in cultural values to support the process.

This last point is key. A modern banking, checking, and credit-card system requires for its operation that the trust level in society be above a threshold value. The quality of good family life

---

If multinational corporations are to be dominant social institutions in the future, the fate of the world will hinge on the operative goals and values of those corporations.

---

rests on shared values that would not be present if a number of people with diverse self-interests were living together. Institutional change requires value change for its support—just as new institutions may be required to implement new values.

Earlier arguments about the nature of social problems strongly indicate that the decision-making system will break down without an increase in the amount of caring for fellowman, for future generations, for nature, and for planet earth. No doubt it would have been nice all along if we had more of the traditional values of integrity, humility, and caring—now it may be a necessity if the system is to work at all.

But to have power over men's actions, values cannot stand in isolation or be arbitrarily chosen. They must be rooted in some sort of "vision of reality," some guiding philosophy. A recent book by Victor Ferkiss [17] argues, from an analysis of the present predicament of the technological-industrial state, that an adequate new guiding philosophy would have to incorporate three basic elements. First is what he terms a "new naturalism," which affirms that man is absolutely a part of a nature, a universe, that is always in process of becoming. The second element, a "new holism," recognizes that "no part can be defined or understood save in relation to the whole." The third, a "new immanentism," sees that the whole is "determined not from outside but from within." Men's actions and the forces they set in motion are all part of the developing whole; "every part of the whole has power and influence; every living particle is a source of direction and life." If man is to acquire the necessary sense of responsibility for the impact of his own actions on the shaping of the whole, he "must so internalize these ideas and make them so much a part of his instinctive world view that they inform his personal, political, and cultural life."

But these characteristics are precisely those found in what we described earlier as an emerging "new paradigm." They are the characteristics that would make the candidate paradigm socially useful, and give it staying power. And this is why the historically improbable paradigm shift and cultural revolution is even plausible as a future alternative worthy of consideration.

Conclusion

Among the future alternatives to be considered is one that comprises a rapid and drastic break with trends of the recent past, characterized essentially by a change in that basic vision of man-in-the-universe in which the operative values of the society have their origins. The main reason it is of interest, and that it seems plausible at all, is that the change would be in such a direction as to assist in the resolution of the society's most serious problems—particularly the central problem that reasonable actions according to the rules seem to be leading us toward such an unacceptable future.

In this view, *contemporary political, military, economic, ecological, and social crises are reflections of an underlying moral and spiritual crisis of civilization, and their resolution depends on the resolution of that deeper crisis.* The underlying dilemma is that somehow humanistic and transcendental values have come to be a luxury superimposed on economic values, rather than being the measure of the appropriateness of economic values. The result is that, rather than reinforcing the best we know, the economic institutions of the society seem to be at odds with the society's highest values. Further alienation, economic decline, and social disruption are likely to occur before this situation is corrected.

The extent to which our deliberate actions can affect the future is undoubtedly limited. Continuity of cultural change, institutional inertia, unexpected events, and subliminal social forces conspire to shape the course of history and to thwart attempts to design the future. Quite apart from our desires, the transformation postulated in these remarks is either upon us or it is not—it is not our choice to make. However, we can choose either to understand and move with the tides of history, whatever they may be—or to attempt to resist them. Upon that choice may rest in great measure the state of business in 1990—and beyond. ∎

Notes and References

1—This opinion is based on work reported in the following publications of the Educational Policy Research Center, Stanford Research Institute, Menlo Park, Ca., 94025: *Contingent U.S. Patterns, 1970 to 2000,* RM 69-3, December, 1969 (JRA Assocs.); *Projecting Whole-Body Future Patterns—The Field Anomaly Relaxation (FAR Method,* RM-10, February, 1971 (R. F. Rhyne); *Forces for Societal Transformation in the United States, 1950-2000,* RM-13, (N. B. McEachron); *Contemporary Societal Problems,* RR-2, June, 1971 (O. W. Markley, D. A. Curry, and Dan L. Rink).

2—The "long-term multifold trend" was originally described by Herman Kahn and Anthony Wiener in *The Year 2000,* MacMillan Co., New York, 1967.

3—The smooth transition to a "Consciousness III" society, portrayed by Charles Reich in his *The Greening of America,* seems to ignore the data of history regarding the chaos and conflict typical of profound social change. Random House, New York, 1970.

4—The term "paradigm" is used by Thomas Kuhn in his *The Structure of Scientific Revolutions* to signify the basic pattern of perceiving, thinking, and doing, associated with a particular vision of reality. University of Chicago Press, 1962.

5—Lewis Mumford discusses these historic transitions in *The Transformations of Man.* Harper and Brothers, New York, 1956.

6—The applicability of the term "Faustian powers" is discussed by Kahn and Wiener in *The Year 2000,* MacMillan Co., New York, 1967. A discussion of the unsuitability of the present paradigm can be found in Richard Means, *The Ethical Imperative,* Doubleday, Garden City, N.Y., 1969.

7—Numerous studies by D. Yankelovitch, J. Katz, P. Heist, R. Flacks, and others.

8—A summary of this area will be found in Charles Tart, *Altered States of Consciousness.* John Wiley & Sons, New York, 1969.

9—One of the best descriptions of the candidate paradigm will be found in Aldous Huxley's *The Perennial Philosophy.* Harper and Brothers, New York, 1945.

10—Based on McEachron, N. B., *Forces for Societal Transformation in the United States, 1950-2000.*

11—The term "Tragedy of the Commons" was introduced in Garrett Hardin's article of that title in *Science* 162, December 13, 1968, pp 1243-48. Hardin argues the unlikelihood of technical solutions to problems of this sort, the inefficacy of appeals to conscience, and the need for new social arrangements—"mutual coercion, mutually agreed upon."

12—Schelling, T. C., "On the Ecology of Micromotives," *The Public Interest,* No. 25, Fall, 1971, pp 61-98.

13—Galbraith, John, *The New Industrial State,* p 259. Houghton Mifflin, Boston, 1967.

14—*Goals for Americans,* report of the President's Commission on National Goals. Prentice Hall, Englewood Cliffs, N.J., 1960.

15—An excellent discussion of this important point is given by Adolph Lowe, *On Economic Knowledge,* Harper and Row, New York, 1965. Robert Theobald comes to a similar conclusion in *The Economics of Abundance,* Pitman, New York, 1970.

16—Hutchins, Robert, *The Learning Society.* Praeger, New York, 1968.

17—Ferkiss, Victor C., *Technological Man: The Myth and the Reality.* George Braziller, New York, 1969.

Trends in Public Attitudes Toward Business and the Free Enterprise System

Thomas W. Benham

AMERICAN business can achieve its goals only with the full support and backing and understanding of the American public. Yet today business has been declining sharply in favor with the public. The mass media have turned the spotlight on many of the defects and problem areas in our society. Concern over ecology, consumerism, and the social responsibilities of corporate management has created a skeptical—if not hostile—atmosphere in which industry must do its work.

In examining the opinions of the public, we should ask, who are these people who are speaking to us through these data? They are not the same fellows we talk to at lunch, or play golf with, or engage in business discussions with. Eighty-four percent of them have not traveled by air during the last year. Eight in ten do not own stock. Three-quarters of them have never been outside of the country. Half of them have not been 200 miles from home in the last year, and half of them do not use credit cards.

Thus, if their attitudes do not seem to match the attitudes that we run into every day, you can understand why. They are a different kind of people. But they are typical of the public generally.

Address by Thomas W. Benham, President, Opinion Research Corporation, Princeton, New Jersey.

A LOOK AT BUSINESS IN 1990: A Summary of the White House Conference on the Industrial World Ahead, Washington, D.C., February 7-9, 1972 (U.S. Government Printing Office: 1972 0—467-348) pp. 37-44.

General Attitudes toward Business

Consider some basic trends showing how these people are feeling and thinking today about business. First, look at their financial sense of well-being, as portrayed by the data in Table 1. Since 1965 to the present, we see a steady climb in the percentage who say they are worse off. These people believe they are treading water economically, slipping back in the picture.

When we measure public sentiment in terms of agreement or disagreement with a series of general statements about business, we see a steady decline in favorability. For example, "large companies are essential for the nation's growth." This concept draws little argument, as Table 2 indicates. Between eight and nine in ten people agree. But a slight downtrend is evident, even though agreement is still at a high level.

Similarly with some other propositions: "The profits of large companies help make things better for everyone." The trend line since 1965 shows about half of the public still agree, but the trend is sharply downward.

Taking the other side of the question, the disagree side: "as they grow bigger, companies usually become cold and impersonal." The number who disagree has been declining.

Look at the response to: "Too much power is

TABLE 1—SENSE OF FINANCIAL WELL-BEING

	1959	1961	1963	1965	1967	1969	1971
Worse off, %	18	20	14	14	17	20	22
Better off than a year ago, %	31	29	35	38	39	34	36
Same, or no opinion, %	51	51	51	48	44	46	42

concentrated in the hands of a few companies." The number who were willing to disagree with this are on the decline, down from 31 to 21 percent of those responding.

"For the good of the country, many of our largest companies ought to be broken up." Again the number of people who agree with this proposition is increasing sharply.

Now, if we sum up the opinions on these and other propositions in an overall measurement, we can classify people into three logical groups: those who express a high degree of approval of business,

those who give moderate approval, and those who give little approval to business. These categories and relative shifts among them are set forth in Table 3. The proportion who give little approval outweighs the other two by a sizable margin. And this group has been growing in proportion to the remainder. Examination of the high-approval group shows that their numbers have been cut in half since 1965, from about one in five to about one in ten.

Now, within the population, which are the groups who have been changing their opinion? The results are presented in Table 4. Notice that among younger people the decline here has been sharper than in the other age categories. Similarly, observe the views of the professional and managerial group, normally thought to be favorable toward business. They registered a quite sharp decline in approval of business.

College graduates, more sophisticated, more knowledgeable, have been more favorable toward business traditionally; but they have slipped badly since 1965. So it is with the more affluent, shrinking in terms of approval. In the initiator measure-

TABLE 2—RESPONSES TO SPECIFIC QUESTIONS ABOUT BUSINESS, PERCENT

	1959	1961	1963	1965	1967	1969	1971	Difference 1965-1971
Agree:								
Large companies are essential for the nation's growth	82	83	85	88	87	85	83	−5
Profits of large companies help make things better for everyone	60	59	64	67	63	55	51	−16
Disagree:								
As they grow bigger, companies usually become cold and impersonal	27	24	28	30	30	24	19	−11
Too much power is concentrated in the hands of a few large companies	24	24	28	31	30	23	21	−10
For good of the country, many of largest companies ought to be broken up	37	37	40	45	46	37	35	−10

TABLE 3—OVERALL ATTITUDE TOWARD BUSINESS

	1959	1961	1963	1965	1967	1969	1971
Little approval, %	52	55	52	47	46	56	60
Moderate approval, %	28	27	27	31	32	26	27
High approval, %	16	15	18	20	20	15	11
Unclassifiable, %	4	3	3	2	2	3	2

ment we have scored people on three factors: their degree of input of information; the level of interest they show in public affairs and business, and their degree of output, that is, their opportunity to pass on and express their opinions and ideas to others. We arrayed people on a scale from zero to one hundred, cutting off the top 12 percent and rating them high as initiators. It now becomes evident that the decline in favor toward business has been greatest among this group. Today they show no higher approval than people in the lower categories of initiative.

TABLE 4—HIGH APPROVAL OF BUSINESS, percent

	1965	Latest	Change
Total public	20	11	− 9
Men	25	12	−13
Women	16	10	− 6
15–20 years	24	12	−12
21–29 years	23	12	−11
30–49 years	21	13	− 8
50 or over	16	9	− 7
Whites	21	12	− 9
Nonwhites	14	7	− 7
Professional, managerial	28	16	−12
White-collar	25	12	−13
Manual	18	11	− 9
Grade school or less	9	7	− 2
High-school graduates	22	12	−10
College graduates	36	17	−19
Under $5000	14	6	− 8
$5000–$9999	21	9	−11
$10,000 or over	30	17	−13
Initiators	33	11	−22
Average initiative	20	11	− 8
Lowest initiative	13	10	− 3

Thus, it is not only the enemies of business who have been intensifying their attacks; the friends of business also have been weakening in their support at the same time.

Attitudes toward Specific Industries and Companies

Now these are generalizations. When we look at attitudes toward specific industries we unfortunately see confirming trends. The data below and following are from a series of Opinion Research Corporation surveys, either our biennial corporate-image studies or our twice-each-month Public Opinion Index reports.

Data are not available in every year for all industries. Nevertheless we see a uniform picture in the measurements we have—every industry is down in favorability. This is brought out in Table 5. These are the two favorable categories in a five-way rating scale. Opinions are asked of those who express some degree of familiarity with each industry.

TABLE 5—FAVORABILITY TRENDS BY INDUSTRY
(Very or Mostly Favorable)
percent

	1965	1967	1969	1971	Change
Telephone, communications	—	—	77	64	−13
Banking	—	—	65	58	− 7
Electric light and power	—	—	77	58	−19
Electrical equipment, appliances	73	68	69	57	−12
Food	—	72	64	54	−10
Aluminum	69	60	60	47	−13
Building materials	—	—	—	47	—
Electronics	—	—	58	46	−12
Tire and rubber	70	62	63	45	−18
Oil and gasoline	73	65	65	45	−20
Computer	—	—	47	43	− 4
Steel	64	56	47	43	− 4
Automobile	75	67	63	43	−20
Packaging, containers	—	—	—	43	—
Travel, tourist services	—	—	49	40	− 9
Prescription drugs	—	—	51	37	−14
Book and magazine publishing	—	—	38	36	− 2
Insurance	—	—	57	34	−23
Chemical	55	49	43	32	−11
Tobacco	—	—	24	22	− 2

Consider individual companies whose reputations we have measured over the same period of time (without mentioning names). Results are shown in Table 6.

From 1963 to 1965, of 39 companies measured, 26 stayed the same in favorability, 13 improved. From 1965 to 1967, only one improved its rating, 27 stayed the same, 11 declined. From 1967 to 1969, five went up, ten went down. In the latest measurement, of 39 companies, only six stayed the same and 33 showed a decline in the public's favorable rating.

TABLE 6—TRENDS IN FAVORABILITY FOR INDIVIDUAL COMPANIES

Time Period	Number of Companies Measured	Improved in Favorability	Stayed the Same	Declined in Favorability
1963–1965	39	13	26	0
1965–1967	44	1	27	11
1967–1969	58	5	43	10
1969–1971	39	0	6	33

Another piece of research suggests that it is not business alone that is dropping in favor with the public. Lou Harris, in one of his newspaper columns, showed some data that measured what we can call confidence in institutions. In 1966, and again in 1971, Harris asked people about the degree of their confidence in the leaders of various major institutions in our society. The results are shown in Table 7, which shows sharp declines in the percentages of those who give a high-confidence rating to the leaders of these institutions. This confirms more or less what we have observed in our corporate-image study, relating to business.

Not only has business fallen in favor. Public opinion of the scientific community, education, religion, organized labor, and various aspects of government has similarly diminished. Finally, at the bottom of the list we get to the media—the press, advertising, and television—never high on the scale but now at new low levels of confidence.

These last data must have a message for communicators in terms of credibility. When you talk to the public, you are handicapped by a large measure of skepticism, if not outright hostility among many.

TABLE 7—CONFIDENCE IN INSTITUTIONS, percent

	1966	1971	Change
Banks, financial institutions	67	36	−31
Big companies	55	27	−28
Local retail stores	48	24	−24
Scientific community	56	32	−24
Mental health, psychiatry	51	35	−16
Medicine	72	61	−11
Education	61	37	−24
Organized religion	41	27	−14
Organized labor	22	14	− 8
Congress	42	19	−23
Executive branch of government	41	23	−18
Supreme Court	31	23	− 8
The press	29	18	−11
Advertising	21	13	− 8
Television	25	22	− 3

The Factor of Inflation

Let us try to identify a few of the complex causes behind these major negative changes in the public's attitudes toward business. We observe three interdependent factors. Inflation is one. When people talk about the major causes of inflation, they talk about the Vietnam War, but they also talk about companies raising prices, wages outpacing productivity, interest rates going up, other nonwar government spending, and so on. This is set out in Table 8.

TABLE 8—MAJOR CAUSES OF INFLATION MOST COMMONLY MENTIONED, percent

Vietnam war spending	53
Companies raising prices	41
Wages outpacing productivity	34
Banks raising interest rates	24
Government spending at home	21
Consumers buying too much	20

Since 1946 a massive shift has occurred in the public's confidence in competition as a mechanism to keep prices fair. Table 9 shows this.

When people are asked which products or services give the most value for the money, or the least

TABLE 9—RESTRAINTS ON PRICES *

	Can Depend on Competition %	Government Control Needed %
Total public	27	62
By race:		
White	29	60
Black	15	73
By education:		
Some college	39	53
High-school graduates	33	59
High-school incomplete	16	69
By type of household:		
Managerial	40	55
Stockholder	30	61
Union	22	71
By party preference:		
Independent	36	52
Republican	28	63
Democrat	23	69

* "No opinion" omitted

value for the money, only the regulated industries score well, Table 10. Most of the other product categories—autos, grocery products, appliances, etc.—rate quite low in terms of value. At the bottom in value are cosmetics and toiletries, auto insurance, and prescription drugs.

Thus, in the face of this widespread general feeling, a businessman may well ask himself how convincing a claim will be that "we're really giving you value for your money." Incidentally, we believe

TABLE 10—VALUE FOR YOUR MONEY

	Most Percent	Least Percent
Electricity	62	5
Telephone service	50	7
Life insurance	23	12
Major appliances	21	7
Grocery products	16	30
Autos	13	19
Gasoline	11	15
Home furnishings	9	10
Prescription drugs	8	29
Automobile insurance	8	27
Cosmetics, toiletries	2	31

part of the problem is a result of the fact that businessmen are at the tail end of the pricing process. Regardless of the cause of inflationary prices—falling worker productivity, high wage settlements, government spending, or whatever—it is the businessman who ultimately jacks up the price.

Consumerism

Consumerism has also added its bit to negative attitudes toward business. And it is not all smoke—there is some fire. In a recent study, when we asked about recent purchasing experience, we found, in a nationwide probability sample, some 21 percent said they had been cheated or deceived in their dealings as consumers. The items most often mentioned were groceries, meats, automobiles, and appliances. Some of our clients have asked why we have not emphasized the 79 percent who do not report having been cheated. The fact is that 21 percent adds up to many, many millions of people. They are grist for the Nader mill or any other group that wants to assert leadership.

How were people cheated? The most common replies: the product was faulty; the packaging was deceptive; I was overcharged; the ads did not tell me the truth; or, the service was "lousy." Undoubtedly enough real examples of unfair treatment exist that a certain skepticism now applies to almost anything that is put on the market. Will it work? Will the service be good? Is the price fair?

Personally, I think for many years the public had a rather low level of expectation. If you had some problem with a new car, you worked with it; you did not get too excited. In other words, our consumer tolerance for defects and poor service has been wearing thin. And the politicians and the consumerists have been helping the erosion process.

Consequently, on a general proposition, we have seen a sharp uptrend in those who favor federal laws to help consumers get value for their money. It has risen from 55 percent in 1967 to 68 percent in 1969, and most recently 66 percent.

We asked the business editors of the one hundred largest newspapers, the major news weeklies, and the wire services this question: "Do you favor new laws to help consumers get full value for their money?" Of these, 54 percent said yes, 41 percent no, and 5 percent had no opinion. Even this group, who understands business problems well, and who is generally sympathetic, nonetheless believes that some type of legislation in the consumer field is needed if we are to see action.

The Factor of Concern about the Environment

Another whole facet of the cause behind these great attitude changes is found in the area of attitudes on environmental problems. We have compared people's awareness of different threats to the environment to everyday newspaper items: namely, drugs, crime, and auto accidents. Note in Table 11 that air pollution and smog are as much in the news these days as unsafe drugs. Public awareness of water pollution is on a par with awareness of violent crimes. Littering and garbage are as familiar to John Q. Public as are automobile accidents. Mercury in fish, and DDT in animals and humans,

outrank coal-mine explosions as subjects for popular discussion. Note the trends. Air pollution and smog, 79 percent, up 12 points. Pollution of lakes, rivers, and seas up 16 points since 1969. Earthquakes up, obviously a reflection of the California mishap. Notice the change in awareness of mercury, from three percent to thirty-seven percent. People are getting the message. Oil spills almost double in awareness. Cyclamates, petering out somewhat, but still well in the forefront of people's awareness. Notice lead poisoning of children. Press coverage of this has increased and awareness has grown.

Throughout these environmental problems, industry is always in evidence. It is the one that pollutes; it is the one that litters; it is the one that creates the problems. Obviously, companies do not throw beer cans on the side of the road; but it is the company that makes the can, and it becomes the target for legislation. Thus, the public's growing sensitivity to many aspects of environment brings industry into focus over and over again.

Many realize that companies want to do the right thing. When people are asked if large companies want to correct pollution, a large majority say yes, as Table 12 shows. But notice youth's response. Many are skeptical. It is also interesting that even among executives as many as one in five question company sincerity in wanting to do something to reduce pollution.

TABLE 11—SUBJECTS HEARD A LOT ABOUT, percent

	1969	Latest	Change
Air pollution, smog	67	79	+12
Unsafe drugs	74	78	
Pollution of lakes, rivers, seas	57	73	+16
Violent crimes	67	71	
Earthquakes	33	63	+30
Littering and garbage	—	61	
Automobile accidents	65	60	
Mercury residues in fish, other foods	3	57	+54
Oil spills	30	56	+26
Overpopulation	—	56	
Fish kills	26	48	+22
Cyclamates	62	45	−17
DDT in animals and humans	45	41	
Phosphates	—	37	
Lead poisoning of children	16	36	+20
Noise pollution	—	36	
Changes in weather or climate	29	35	
Coal-mine explosions	22	35	+13
Accidents involving dangerous substances	26	27	
Sonic booms due to aircraft	25	27	
Thermal pollution of waterways	13	25	+12
Radioactive wastes	16	23	
Underground nuclear explosions	26	22	
Mid-air collisions of aircraft	32	17	−15
Military accidents, poison gas	16	—	
Nuclear fallout	17	14	
Silt buildup a problem	13	—	

TABLE 12—MOST LARGE COMPANIES WANT TO CORRECT POLLUTION THEY MAY BE CAUSING *

	General Public	Youth	Executives
Agree, %	61	47	78
Disagree, %	29	45	19

* "No opinion" omitted

It is also interesting here—in a period perhaps when companies are doing more about pollution than ever in history—that the realization that something is going on has been diminishing, Table 13. The percent who say companies are doing little about pollution has been rising. In other words, tolerance is diminishing at a faster rate than awareness of company actions to correct the problems.

Consequently, do we need new federal laws to protect the public's health and safety? Yes, say a large majority: 70 percent in 1967; recently, 76 percent.

TABLE 13—OPINION AMONG BIG CITY RESIDENTS
OF HOW MUCH COMPANIES ARE DOING TO
CONTROL POLLUTION

	1967	1968	Latest
Great deal, %	10	9	10
Fair amount, %	33	35	35
Very little, %	41	44	53
No opinion, %	16	12	2

TABLE 14—COMPARISON OF PUBLIC ESTIMATE OF
PERCENT PROFIT TO BUSINESS AFTER TAXES
TO ACTUAL

	1945	1951	1962	1965	1967	1969	1970
Median adult public estimate	18	21	20	21	23	27	28
Actual	5.2	5.1	4.5	5.6	5.0	4.8	4.0

Should we close plants that violate the laws? The opinion is up sharply from an already high level: 70 percent in 1967 to 81 percent in the latest survey.

Now, how much would you personally be willing to pay to help correct pollution? Of the total public, 22 percent would pay something; 40 percent would pay nothing; and 38 percent do not know. People do not think they created the problem. They do not think they should pay for it. Obviously, however, the bill is paid, whether in higher prices or taxes. Regardless of on whom taxes are imposed, it ultimately will be the man in the street who will foot the bill.

What is Ralph Nader's role in all of this? He certainly did not invent consumerism or concern about the environment. But he did come along at a time in which he has helped to crystallize the thinking and concern of many. And business editors, as friendly as they may be to business, nevertheless feel that Nader's influence, in the long run, will be a plus: 75 percent agree; 10 percent believe his influence is harmful. In other words, things will happen faster, companies will do more as a result of his influence than they would without it.

Basic Attitudes toward Our Business System

The latest public estimate is that the average manufacturer makes 28 cents out of every dollar of sales after taxes. The actual figure is around four cents. In the '50s, people estimated about 20 cents on a dollar, Table 14. That has now gone up to almost 30 cents. Thus, when a businessman is trying to tell a value story, this misconception stands in the minds of his listeners. They believe he is making a fat profit. A so-called "bargain" may not be credible to me, if I have this notion fixed in my head. Also, the public tends to think companies

can raise wages without raising prices. This is shown by Table 15.

If we ask people to classify themselves ideologically as liberal or conservative, they tend to say, "Well, I'm in the middle-of-the-road, or I'm fairly conservative." Only about one in five admits to being liberal or fairly liberal: very conservative, 11 percent; fairly conservative, 28 percent; middle-of-the-road, 29 percent; fairly liberal, 19 percent; very liberal, 7 percent; and no opinion, 6 percent. Many of the ideas that people hold, however, cannot be considered too conservative.

TABLE 15—COMPANIES COULD RAISE WAGES 10 cents
PER HOUR WITHOUT RAISING PRICES

	1953	1955	Latest
Agree, %	55	57	66
Disagree, %	29	27	25
No opinion, %	16	16	9

The idea that the federal government is responsible for seeing that everyone who is willing and able has a job is broadly accepted, as Table 16 makes clear.

TABLE 16—SHOULD GOVERNMENT ASSURE A JOB
FOR EVERYONE WILLING TO WORK? *

	1946	1948	1953	1955	1962	Latest
Yes, %	68	51	44	45	55	59
No, %	30	44	50	48	36	35

* "Don't know" omitted

What is the most practical way for workers to improve their standard of living: produce more, or get more of what companies make? Table 17 gives the results. Since 1948 "produce more" has been getting a substantially larger vote. Today the balance is shifting in the other direction.

Similarly, what is the best way to provide jobs for our population, private business or government projects? In 1955 some 69 percent of the people said business should provide the jobs. Today, as many (47 percent) say it should be a government or joint responsibility.

The impressions of high-school seniors about business 20 years ago and today are shown in Table 18. In 1951, when these teenagers evaluated our business system, one in twenty-five felt that the bad in the system outweighed the good. Today that same proportion has gone up five times. Today, one in five thinks our system is so bad that it needs to be completely overhauled. These are the future adults.

The Task of Industry

Business must stem a flood tide of adverse public opinion if it is to continue to prosper. The business

TABLE 18—TEENAGER IMPRESSIONS OF U.S. BUSINESS SYSTEM

	1951	Today
Very good, %	8	5
Good outweighs bad, %	45	31
Good equal to bad, %	29	40
Bad outweighs good, %	2	7
Very bad, %	2	13
No opinion, %	14	4

community must educate in those areas where half truths dwell and must hold itself accountable in those areas where it has fallen down in its responsibilities. The public will no longer accept lip service on pressing issues. Large numbers see their air becoming poisoned, their water undrinkable, their quality of life deteriorating. Large numbers see—and badly exaggerate—unequal distribution of wealth, hunger and poverty in the richest nation in the world, and housing unfit for human habitation. Large numbers feel cheated on what they purchase, see products judged unsafe, experience poor quality, and the like.

Business must, by its deeds and words, correct these basic feelings of suspicion and resentment about its contributions to American life. If businessmen fail in this, the areas of decision within which business will be able to operate will be shrunk smaller and smaller. Already the government is partner in many of your business decisions. The government's voice will grow louder and more insistent, and that of business will be reduced. Perhaps nothing is more urgent than this tremendous problem of public dissatisfaction when we lay plans to grow and expand to meet the needs of American society in the future. ■

TABLE 17—THE MOST PRACTICAL WAY FOR WORKERS TO INCREASE THEIR STANDARD OF LIVING *

	1948	1953	1955	Latest
Produce more, %	43	44	42	37
Get more of what companies make, %	27	23	27	34

* "Both" and "No opinion" omitted

The U.S. Economy in 1990

The Conference Board

ANY SET of projections depends heavily upon the assumptions on which they are based. The projections of the gross national product presented in this study were prepared from the "input side" and depend therefore on assumptions about the utilization of labor and the rate of productivity change.

The principal assumption underlying the projections in this study is that of full employment. That is, the projections are the most likely outcome, in our opinion, that will result if the economy is operating at full capacity. The projections are not based on an assumption that cyclical fluctuations will not take place in the next 20 years; that would be highly unrealistic. Rather, the growth rates are the paths about which business fluctuations will take place. In line with this assumption, the base year for most of the projections is 1969, a year of full employment.

The unemployment rate at "full employment" in the coming decade is assumed to be 4.5%. This relatively high rate reflects the large proportion of younger workers in the labor force, who are subject to unemployment rates well above the average. In the Eighties, this proportion will decline, and

our assumed "full-employment unemployment rate" is reduced to 4.0% by 1990 to reflect that fact.

Our projections incorporate annual rates of growth of labor productivity in the private sector of 3.0% from 1969 to 1980, and of 3.4% from 1980 to 1990. The rate for the earlier period is lower than the average since World War II, and reflects the slowdown of U.S. productivity in the last five years to an annual rate of 1.8%, compared with an average annual increase of 3.4% from 1948 to 1966. The slowdown was partly related to the recent recession, but other factors of longer term duration contributed, including a decline in the growth rate of expenditures on research and development, a reduction in efficiency from the price inflation that has bedeviled the economy since the mid-Sixties, and the increase in the proportion of young inexperienced workers in the labor force.

We assume that these negative factors will be reduced by 1980, and that the rate of productivity growth will, therefore, be higher in the Eighties. The composition of the labor force is almost certain to change in the direction of greater productive potential; the problem of inflation is expected to ease; and a pickup in research and development expenditures is anticipated.

A report prepared for the White House Conference on the Industrial World Ahead by The Conference Board, New York, New York.

A LOOK AT BUSINESS IN 1990: A Summary of the White House Conference on the Industrial World Ahead, Washington, D.C., February 7-9, 1972 (U.S. Government Printing Office: 1972 0—467-348) pp. 45-73.

Growth Potential of the U.S. Economy

The total output of the U.S. economy in dollars of constant purchasing power has more than doubled in the last 20 years. Goods and services are now being produced at an annual rate of more than $1 trillion. Under conditions of full employment of capital and labor, the gross national product of the nation in 1971 prices is projected to reach a total of more than $2.4 trillion by 1990.

Owing to variations in the level of activity as a result of the business cycle, war, and inflation, the growth rate of GNP has fluctuated widely from year to year. The pace of economic growth has also varied considerably over periods of similar cyclical activity. Measured from peak to peak of the business cycle, the growth rate was more than twice as great from 1948 to 1953 as it was from 1957 to 1960, for example.

In preparing our projections, we assume that the economy will experience cyclical variation during the next 20 years; however, the growth paths shown are those that represent the long-term trend, rather than forecasts of individual years. For the entire period from 1948 to 1969, the rate of growth of real output averaged 3.9%. This rate is expected to accelerate to 4.2% for the period from 1969 to 1990 largely as a result of a more rapid rate of growth of employment anticipated in the next two decades than in the previous two.

The main source of growth in the next 20 years will be the rise in GNP per worker, which is expected to go from $12,500 in 1970 to $22,500 in 1990, in 1971 prices. This was also the principal source of the doubling of gross national product in the preceding two decades. One of the conven-

tions in measuring the gross national product is that the general government sector, unlike government enterprises, has no change in productivity. Both the historical and the projected gains in GNP per worker, therefore, stem entirely from the private sector.

The composition of expenditures for the gross national product is not anticipated to show substantial changes on a long-term basis over the next 20 years. Cyclical variation produces wide short-term swings in composition, affecting primarily investment expenditures and consumption of durable goods. Considerable variation also results from activities of government, particularly in periods of war.

Over the long term, we project that consumption expenditures will account for about 60% of the gross national product in 1990, approximately the same proportion as held in the last two decades, aside from the irregular fluctuations just discussed. By 1990, therefore, consumption expenditures should exceed $1.5 trillion in terms of 1971 price levels, a rise of 135% in consumer purchases of goods and services from the present. The importance of government expenditures is expected to remain stable, at about 24% of GNP, yielding a dollar total of $570 billion in 1990.

Investment expenditures, at 15% of GNP through the 1960's, are expected to decline slightly in relative importance in the two following decades. The dollar amount is projected at $330 billion in 1990. Net exports of goods and services, a relatively minor component of GNP, are expected to rise in the first decade, and then to level off, in absolute terms, after 1980.

43

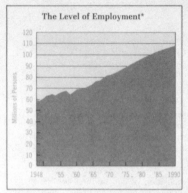

The Level of Employment*

*Includes Military

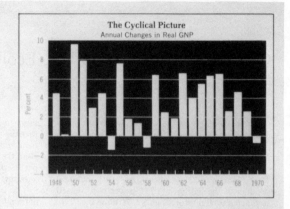

The Cyclical Picture
Annual Changes in Real GNP

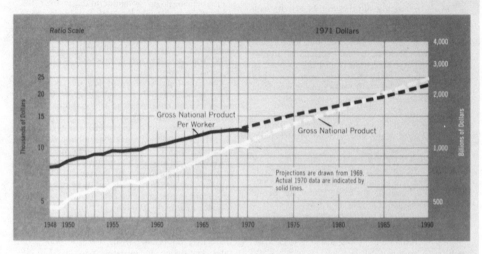

Ratio Scale   1971 Dollars

Gross National Product
Per Worker

Gross National Product

Projections are drawn from 1969.
Actual 1970 data are indicated by
solid lines.

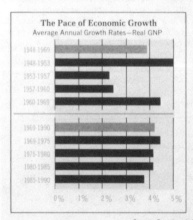

The Pace of Economic Growth
Average Annual Growth Rates—Real GNP

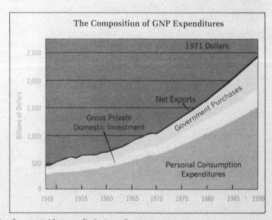

The Composition of GNP Expenditures

1971 Dollars

Net Exports

Government Purchases

Gross Private
Domestic Investment

Personal Consumption
Expenditures

Sources: Department of Labor; Department of Commerce; The Conference Board

44

Inputs in the Private Sector

Nearly 90% of today's GNP is produced by the private sector, and that percentage is projected to rise during the next two decades, with private sector GNP reaching a total of $2,257 billion of goods and services by 1990. General government purchases about one fourth of final output, but actually produces only one tenth. In addition to its predominant size, the private sector is also the source of all the productivity gains of the economy, according to the conventions of national income accounting.

Gains in labor productivity stem largely from two sources: improvements in the skill of the labor force and increases in the quantity and quality of capital. Expenditures on education and job training are major determinants of the skills of the labor force, while expenditures on plant and equipment and on research and development are major factors affecting the quantity and quality of capital.

The measurable inputs in the private sector are manhours worked and the net stock of capital. The number of manhours worked in a period is determined by three factors: the size of the labor force, the unemployment rate, and average weekly hours.

The projections start from a full employment year, 1969, and the figures for the succeeding years represent the quantities of output that would be produced under conditions of full employment. For 1975 and 1980, we have defined full employment as obtaining when all but 4.5% of the labor force are employed; for 1985 the rate is defined as 4.2%, and for 1990, 4.0%. The higher levels in 1975, 1980, and 1985 reflect the large proportion of younger workers in the labor force who are subject to unemployment rates well above the average; by 1990, this proportion will fall to a level similar to that of 1960.

Average weekly hours worked in the private sector are expected to decline from the 1969 level of 38.3 to 36.0 by 1990, resulting mainly from a shorter workweek. This represents a 6% overall decline, substantially less than than the 9% decline registered in the previous 21 years from 42.2 hours per week in 1948.

The manhour input is projected to grow at 1.1% per year from 1969 to 1990, nearly 50% faster than from 1948 to 1969. This acceleration stems largely from the expected rapid growth in the labor force, examined in detail in a later section of this study.

Increases in the capital input, measured as the net physical stock in the private sector, are expected to average 4.8% per year from 1969 to 1990, somewhat higher than the rate of the previous 21 years (4.3%). With private sector real output projected to rise at an average annual rate of 4.4% between 1969 and 1990, up from the 4.0% rate that occurred from 1948 to 1969, the ratio of output to net capital is expected to continue the downward drift that has characterized the postwar period. There is evidence (not charted) that the past decline in the output/capital ratio is traceable in large degree to the increasing importance of those subsectors of the private economy that have low ratios of output to capital, such as public utilities. These trends are projected to continue during the next two decades.

Growth in labor productivity is expected to average 3.0% per year in the Seventies. This level reflects the slowdown that has taken place in the last six years; however, a return to the 1948-1966 rate of 3.4% is projected for the Eighties, as the impact of the negative factors discussed in the introductory paragraphs is moderated.

Utilization of Labor

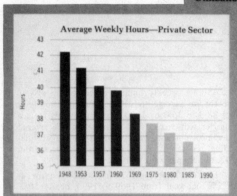

Average Weekly Hours—Private Sector

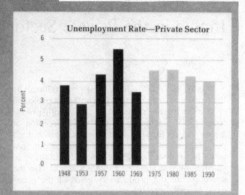

Unemployment Rate—Private Sector

GNP and Factor Inputs

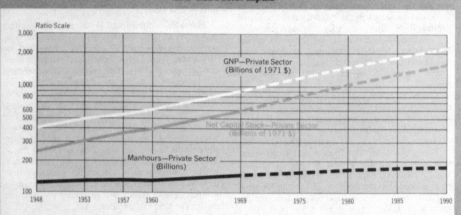

Ratio Scale

GNP—Private Sector
(Billions of 1971 $)

Net Capital Stock—Private Sector
(Billions of 1971 $)

Manhours—Private Sector
(Billions)

Productivity of Labor and Capital

Output per Manhour—Private Sector

Index: 1971 = 100

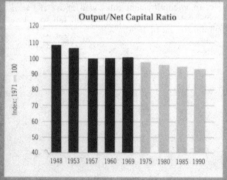

Output/Net Capital Ratio

Index: 1971 = 100

Sources: Departments of Commerce and Labor

Population and the Labor Force

Both the size and the composition of the nation's labor force will change appreciably over the next two decades, an echo of the sharp fluctuations in the birth rate experienced since World War II. In the next few years, the number of persons working or looking for work will continue to expand rapidly, as the youngsters born in the baby boom of the late Forties and the Fifties come of employment age. In the Seventies, however, the growth rate will begin to fall as a consequence of the leveling in births that began in the late Fifties and the decline that took place during most of the Sixties.

Over the past five years, for example, the labor force expanded at an average annual rate of about 2.0%, appreciably faster than in the late Fifties and early Sixties. But the pace has already begun to slacken, and it is expected to decelerate to about 1.0% in the second half of the Eighties. All told, the U.S. labor force will increase by about 30% or by some 27 million persons over the next two decades. Almost three fifths of this increment will be experienced during the Seventies, two fifths during the Eighties.

The age composition of the labor force is changing, again in response to the sharp fluctuations in past fertility rates. For example, persons under 25 now make up 23% of the labor force, but the fraction will decline to only 18% by 1990. In the same period, the age group 25-34 will expand from 21% currently to 27% of the labor force. This relative increase also reflects the higher level of births in the years following World War II.

Persons in the middle years of the life cycle— from 35 to 54—now represent almost 40% of the labor force, but this ratio will contract to about 35% during the next ten years. This demographic development suggests that there will be a shortage of executive- and management-level personnel. The size of this age group will, however, begin to expand rapidly in the Eighties, and by 1990 will account for over 40% of the labor force.

The gender mix of the labor force is also changing. Over the past 20 years, an increasingly large proportion of women have been going to work. For instance, between 1950 and 1970, when the number of employed males grew by 20%, the number of employed females expanded by 70%. Three fifths of the entire growth in the size of the nation's work force in the past 20 years was accounted for by women. The incidence of working women will continue to increase in the coming years, but more slowly in the future than in the past. Today over half of all women 35-54 are employed, up from 38% twenty years ago.

The disposition of a growing number of women to go to work reflects in part our changing social values, but also a sharp expansion in the availability of relatively pleasant white-collar jobs. Since the end of World War II, there has been a significant alteration in the occupational mix of the nation's labor force. Over the past two decades, total employment increased by a third, but white-collar jobs grew about 70% more numerous. Blue-collar employment, meanwhile, increased by only a fifth. The number of persons working in service occupations rose roughly 50% in the same time interval. It is anticipated that in the years ahead white-collar jobs will again increase at a substantially faster than average pace.

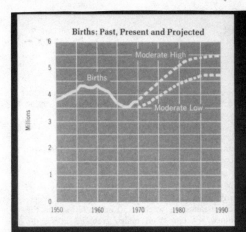

Births: Past, Present and Projected

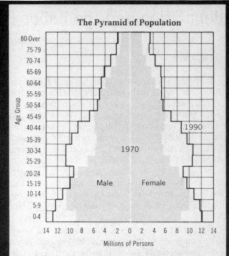

The Pyramid of Population

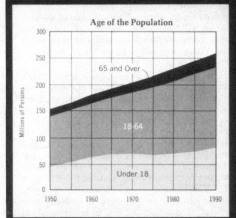

Age of the Population

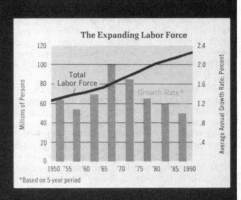

The Expanding Labor Force

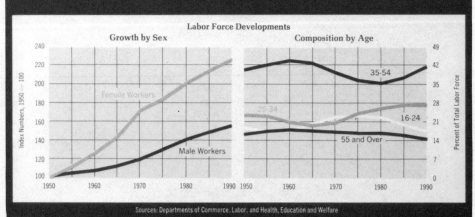

Labor Force Developments

Sources: Departments of Commerce, Labor, and Health, Education and Welfare

R&D and Economic Growth

Investment in machines and structures is necessary to bring technological improvements into the production stream. Investment is also required for the research and development that is the ultimate source of most technological innovation. In the postwar period, investment in R&D expanded at relatively high rates of annual increase until the mid-Sixties. As a proportion of GNP, expenditures reached a peak of about 3% in 1964. In more recent years, however, annual increases in R&D spending have been tapering off, and the total has been declining in relation to GNP.

Much of the past expansion is attributable to Federal mission-oriented research: crash programs for new weapons systems, space exploration, and atomic energy. About two thirds of all R&D expenditures in the mid-Sixties were directed toward this type of research. With the fulfillment of the more pressing missions by the mid-Sixties, the proportion of R&D for Federal objectives fell to slightly more than one half, comparable to that in the early Fifties.

The decline in the importance of Federal mission-oriented research is the cause of the deceleration of R&D expenditures in constant dollars. Congress has not provided the sums for non-Federal objectives in the amounts necessary to offset the slowdown in spending for Federal objectives. This slowdown has meant that R&D expenditures adjusted for price changes have actually declined since 1968. This is true not only for total R&D expenditures but also for outlays for basic research. Unless corrected, possibly by greater privately funded R&D, the latter situation could have serious consequences for the growth of the U.S. economy in the Eighties. In the twentieth century, at least, the ultimate source of technological innovations is the expansion of the frontiers of knowledge. This expansion in turn results primarily from scientific or basic research, defined as pure fundamental work, aimed at increasing the pool of scientific knowledge.

In the second half of the Sixties, the main performers of basic research were the universities and colleges, and industry. The remainder of approximately 30% was the province of the Federal Government itself and nonprofit organizations other than educational institutions. In terms of sources of funds, however, the Federal Government was predominant, providing 64% of all funds expended on basic research in the five-year period, 1965-69. Even this understates the role of the Federal Government for it fails to include the substantial sums provided in the form of scholarships and fellowships for the development and training of new scientists. The continued reduction, beginning in 1968, in Federal funds in constant dollars both for the maintenance of an adequate supply of trained scientists in the future and for the expansion of scientific research itself may have serious consequences. It may well, if it has not done so already, disrupt the sustained advance of scientific knowledge and, in due course, the substantial pace of technological innovations. Unless real efforts are made to restore funding to former levels, by either increased Federal support or its replacement by industry funds, the probabilities of achieving the rates of growth projected in this report are significantly lowered.

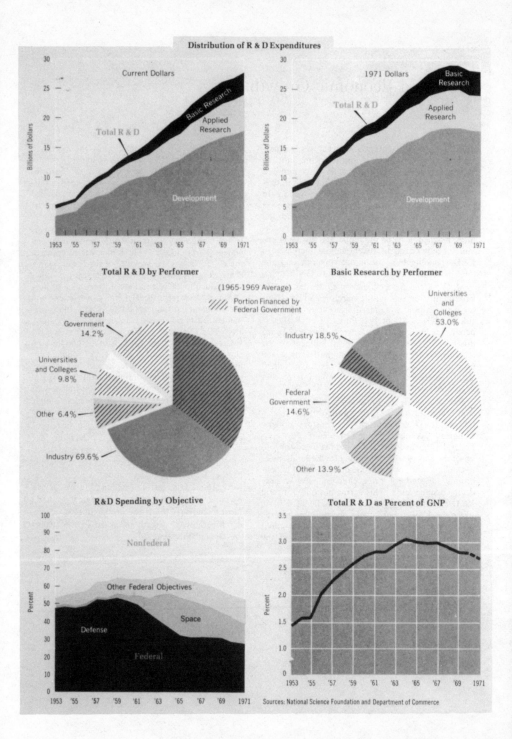

Distribution of R & D Expenditures

Current Dollars

Basic Research

Total R & D

Applied Research

Development

Billions of Dollars

1953 '55 '57 '59 '61 '63 '65 '67 '69 1971

1971 Dollars

Basic Research

Total R & D

Applied Research

Development

Billions of Dollars

1953 '55 '57 '59 '61 '63 '65 '67 '69 1971

Total R & D by Performer

(1965-1969 Average)

Portion Financed by Federal Government

Federal Government 14.2%

Universities and Colleges 9.8%

Other 6.4%

Industry 69.6%

Basic Research by Performer

Universities and Colleges 53.0%

Industry 18.5%

Federal Government 14.6%

Other 13.9%

R&D Spending by Objective

Nonfederal

Other Federal Objectives

Defense

Space

Federal

Percent

1953 '55 '57 '59 '61 '63 '65 '67 '69 1971

Total R & D as Percent of GNP

Percent

1953 '55 '57 '59 '61 '63 '65 '67 '69 1971

Sources: National Science Foundation and Department of Commerce

50

Consumer Income and Spending

Rising population in conjunction with rising incomes will add up to a sizable growth in consumer demand over the next two decades. In that interval, real personal consumption expenditures will, like GNP, substantially more than double. Since the economy will be growing at a considerably faster pace than the population, there will also be a steady escalation in real per capita consumption. Currently, each American spends, on average, about $3,300 annually, but by 1990 this figure will be close to $6,000, in terms of today's dollars. This anticipated improvement in living standards will be faster than experienced in the prior two decades, principally because, in the coming period, a larger proportion of the population will be of working age.

We are, in fact, experiencing a significant reshuffle in the distribution of income in real terms; each year, many millions of families move upward in the earning scale. In the past, this process consisted mainly of a shift from adequate to comfortable levels of income. In the coming decades, however, a large proportion of American families will have the means to purchase the products and services generally associated with an abundant life. Currently, about 12 million, or less than one fourth, of all families have annual earnings exceeding $15,000, but 20 years from now such families will be a substantial majority. By 1990, families with incomes exceeding $15,000 (in 1971 dollars) will number well over 40 million and account for close to 60% of all families. About one out of every four families in 1990 will have an income of over $25,000 a year, compared with one out of twenty today.

This upward progression will not, however, entirely eliminate poverty. Although poverty will be less widespread, its persistence will represent an even greater social issue, precisely because of the economy's increased capacity to alleviate it. For example, 4½ million families today have annual incomes less than $3,000; there will still be about 2½ million families with incomes below $3,000 (in 1971 dollars) in 1990. This, however, is entirely a statistical projection, which does not take into account social programs which might be initiated in the coming years.

As a family moves up in the earning scale, each dollar of additional income is spent differently—relatively less goes for necessities, more becomes available for other things. For example, consumer outlays for food and for footwear increased by about 2½% a year, on average, between 1955 and 1970, whereas consumer spending for foreign travel and for higher education grew more than 6%, on average. In the future as in the past, some sectors of the consumer market will grow much more rapidly than others. The response of consumers to rising spending power in the recent past provides at least a rough indication of what might be anticipated for the era ahead.

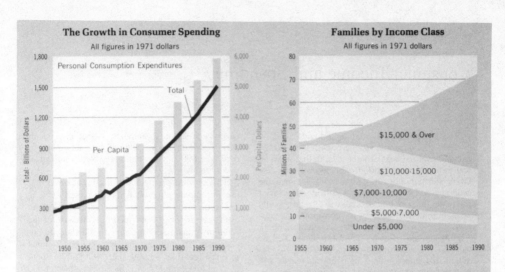

The Growth in Consumer Spending

All figures in 1971 dollars

Personal Consumption Expenditures

Total

Per Capita

Families by Income Class

All figures in 1971 dollars

$15,000 & Over

$10,000-15,000

$7,000-10,000

$5,000-7,000

Under $5,000

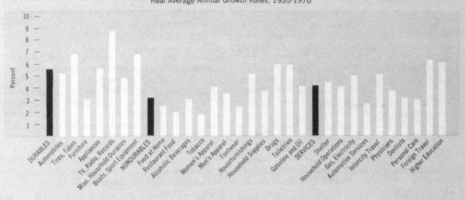

The Discretionary Effects of Rising Income

Real Average Annual Growth Rates, 1955-1970

DURABLES, Automobiles, Tires, Tubes, Furniture, Appliances, TV, Radio, Records, Misc. Household Durables, Boats, Sport Equipment, NONDURABLES, Food at Home, Restaurant Food, Alcoholic Beverages, Tobacco, Women's Apparel, Men's Apparel, Footwear, Housefurnishings, Household Supplies, Drugs, Toiletries, Gasoline and Oil, SERVICES, Shelter, Household Operations, Gas, Electricity, Automotive Services, Intercity Travel, Physicians, Dentists, Personal Care, Foreign Travel, Higher Education

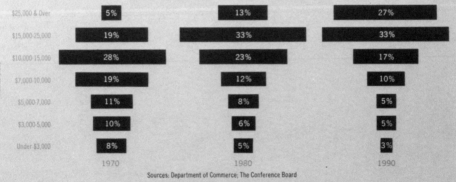

The Changing Pyramid of Income Distribution

Total Families Each Year = 100%; Based on 1971 Dollars

Income Class	1970	1980	1990
$25,000 & Over	5%	13%	27%
$15,000-25,000	19%	33%	33%
$10,000-15,000	28%	23%	17%
$7,000-10,000	19%	12%	10%
$5,000-7,000	11%	8%	5%
$3,000-5,000	10%	6%	5%
Under $3,000	8%	5%	3%

Sources: Department of Commerce; The Conference Board

52

Investment

Real gross private domestic investment is expected to more than double by 1990—reaching a level of about $330 billion (in 1971 prices), compared with the 1969 total of $154 billion. This would represent an average growth of 3.7%, as against 2.8% a year between 1948 and 1969. Private investment is projected to constitute about 14% of GNP (in 1971 prices) in 1990, a slightly lower proportion than the average levels of the Fifties and Sixties.

This broad picture of investment growth is subject to many uncertainties. For example, if the United States chooses to pursue the goal of material economic growth less vigorously in the future than it has in the past, through a change in national priorities or in individual life style, investment will clearly grow more slowly than projected. On the other hand, if the nation seriously undertakes to preserve and restore its environment, investment will have to grow more rapidly than would otherwise be needed to achieve a given level of GNP. This is because a given level of final output will require additional spending—for pollution abatement, for example—that is nonproductive in the traditional sense.

Another uncertainty in the investment picture is governmental policy, as reflected, for example, in tax and depreciation laws. Investment spending in the Sixties thrived in part because of a cut in the corporate income tax rate and the institution of a 7% investment tax credit.

The overall growth in investment, discussed above, masks some important changes taking place among the different types of investment spending. For example, real nonresidential fixed investment grew at a 3.6% average annual rate between 1948 and 1969, while real residential fixed investment grew only 1.2% annually. Thus, while nonresidential fixed investment (mainly outlays for plant and equipment) accounted for 61% of total investment in 1948 (in 1971 prices) and residential structures for 32% of the total, by 1969 the respective figures were 72% and 23%. This trend is expected to continue—although moderated—through 1990, with nonresidential fixed investment reaching three fourths of total investment and residential housing dropping to slightly under one fifth.

The mix of nonresidential fixed investment is changing also. Since the late Fifties, the proportion accounted for by equipment has been steadily increasing, and that accounted for by structures, decreasing. This trend probably reflects in part the much more rapid rise in construction costs than of equipment prices—two to three times as fast—during the interval, and the consequent tendency of businessmen to utilize existing structures more intensively where possible, rather than expand old structures or build new ones. In addition, equipment technology has been advancing more rapidly inducing greater investment in equipment to take advantage of increased capabilities. Rapidly increasing labor costs, also, may have spurred expenditures in labor-saving equipment.

Spending for plant and equipment has not grown at the same rate in the different geographical areas; nor is it likely to during the projection period. Rather, its increase in each region will reflect the rate of overall economic growth in that region. Hence, since U.S. population and industry have, on balance, shifted to the South and West, investment in plant and equipment has increased faster in those areas than in others.

The Composition of Investment

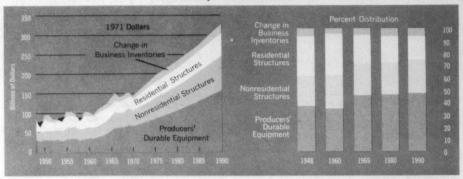

Regional Growth in Real Plant & Equipment Expenditures
Annual Growth Rates 1947-1968

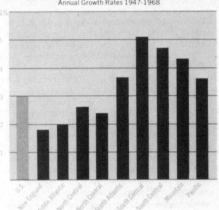

The Nonresidential Fixed Investment Mix
1971 Dollars

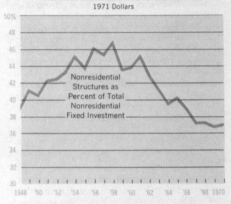

The Changing Pattern of Structures in the U.S.
1971 Dollars

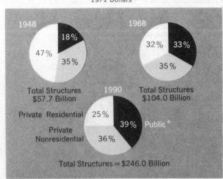

Growth in Producers' Durable Equipment Purchases by Type
Annual Growth Rates, 1948-1970
1971 Dollars

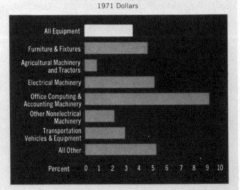

Housing

Until the housing boom that began in mid-1970, progress in satisfying housing needs had, for about two decades, generally been intermittent and unsatisfactory. Unlike most other markets, housing has operated within a tangled skein of restrictions, bottlenecks, and inefficiencies. Our projections are made under the assumption that some progress will be made toward resolution of those problems, as follows: (1) Mortgage market vulnerability to swings in monetary policy will be reduced; (2) building codes will begin to be modified to permit new materials and methods; (3) new materials and methods will permit increasing substitution of capital for labor; (4) all of the foregoing will lead to growth in the size of construction firms, and to decline in the power of building trades unions; (5) property tax structures will increasingly be shifted away from the use of the building as a tax base toward a land-based tax, providing incentives for investment in real property.

In long-period projections such as these, estimates of demand for housing must be based primarily upon real factors. Monetary conditions, as they affect mortgage flows, play a minor role. Basic demand for housing arises from net increases in the number of households, demolition of existing units, changes in vacancy rates, and demand for second homes.

The total units data in these projections can be viewed with somewhat more confidence than the components—conventional housing starts, and mobile homes. It should be noted that the definition of conventional units includes prefabrications, such as modular units, as well as traditionally built structures. Our analysis suggests that growth will occur mainly in conventional structures; it thus means that the phenomenal rate of growth of mobile homes experienced recently will decrease. Two main factors account for this expectation. First, we assume that preferences are for traditional dwellings—that an average home buyer confronted with a choice of mobile versus conventional dwellings is more likely to choose the latter. The second factor is the tendency toward urbanization, which is expected to continue. This implies that space will command an increasing premium. Moreover, some indications of a preference for apartments have been observed among younger households. Consequently, mobile homes, which do not utilize space as efficiently as multi-unit structures, are less likely to find markets in rapidly growing metropolitan areas. In addition, the zoning laws in many suburban regions exclude mobile homes.

On the other hand, modular units and similar prefabricated structures are well suited to multi-unit construction. Thus, manufacturers presently producing mobile homes may find an increasing demand for related outputs—modules and other kinds of prefabrication.

These tendencies imply a continuation of the decline in single family dwellings as a percentage of total residential structures. Of course, the projections are the result of one particular scenario. Several others are possible. As a brief example, if an intensive program were undertaken to develop high-speed mass transportation, many areas presently out of easy reach of job centers would become suitable for residential development. Consequently, the pressure on space would decrease, and one might well find single-family dwelling units predominating.

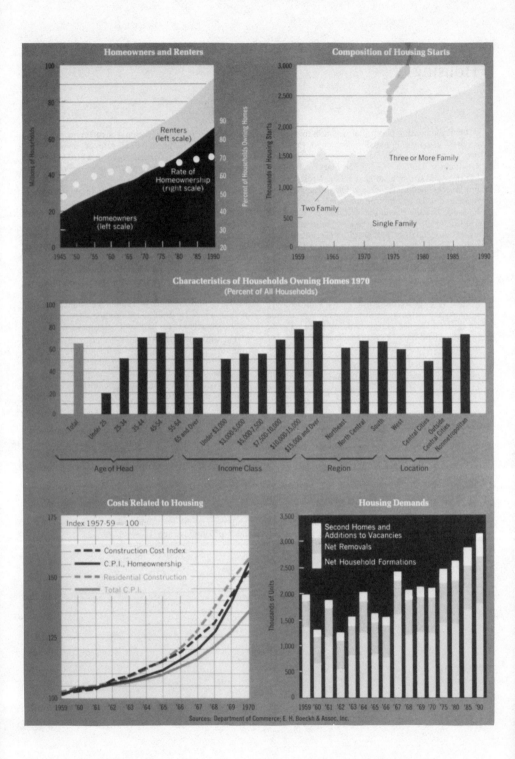

Homeowners and Renters

Renters
(left scale)

Rate of
Homeownership
(right scale)

Homeowners
(left scale)

Millions of Households

Percent of Households Owning Homes

1945 '50 '55 '60 '65 '70 '75 '80 '85 1990

Composition of Housing Starts

Thousands of Housing Starts

Three or More Family

Two Family

Single Family

1959   1965   1970   1975   1980   1985   1990

Characteristics of Households Owning Homes 1970
(Percent of All Households)

Total | Under 25 | 25-34 | 35-44 | 45-54 | 55-64 | 65 and Over | Under $3,000 | $3,000-5,000 | $5,000-7,500 | $7,500-10,000 | $10,000-15,000 | $15,000 and Over | Northeast | North Central | South | West | Central Cities | Outside Central Cities | Nonmetropolitan

Age of Head   Income Class   Region   Location

Costs Related to Housing

Index 1957-59 = 100

- - - Construction Cost Index
—— C.P.I., Homeownership
- - - Residential Construction
—— Total C.P.I.

175

150

125

100

1959 '60 '61 '62 '63 '64 '65 '66 '67 '68 '69 1970

Housing Demands

Thousands of Units

3,500
3,000
2,500
2,000
1,500
1,000
500
0

Second Homes and
Additions to Vacancies
Net Removals
Net Household Formations

1959 '60 '61 '62 '63 '64 '65 '66 '67 '68 '69 '70 '75 '80 '85 '90

Sources: Department of Commerce; E. H. Boeckh & Assoc. Inc.

Government Employment

Between 1970 and 1990, total Federal, state, and local government employment—including employment in government enterprises—is expected to grow at an average annual rate substantially below that of 1950-1970, i.e., at 1.6% versus 3.3%. However, the growth in government employment will exceed the rate of increase in the private sector; thus the portion of the total labor force accounted for by government workers will still rise, although only from 17% in 1970 to 18% in 1990.

During 1950-1970, all components of government employment grew more rapidly than the total labor force. The number of employees in public education increased most rapidly (5.2%), and Federal civilian employment, the slowest (1.7%). During 1970-1990, in contrast, state and local employment other than education is the only component of the public sector expected to grow substantially faster than the total labor force (3.1% vs. 1.4%). The average annual rate of growth of state and local employment in education will be only slightly above that of the total labor force (1.6% vs. 1.4%); Federal civilian employment will grow much slower (0.7%), and Federal military employment is projected to remain virtually constant. The size of the armed forces is expected to decline from the 1968 peak of 3.5 million men and women to a low of 2.7 million in 1973. Assuming there will be a volunteer force with higher pay scales, the military will have to economize on manpower. Consequently, rapid growth after 1973 is unlikely in the absence of international crises. Peacetime increase in the armed forces will, in fact, be very slow.

Since 1950, there has been a little-noticed trend toward administrative decentralization of government in the United States. Congress now legislates and raises funds for many purposes (such as education and combating pollution) which received little or no Federal support twenty years ago. Yet, Federal civilian employment fell from 26.7% of all public sector employment in 1950 to 19.6% in 1970. Increasingly, state and local governments administer expenditures, under congressional guidelines, from funds raised by Federal taxes. State and local governments, though less efficient as tax collectors, are considered more responsive to the needs of individual citizens—the consumers of governmental services—than is the Federal system.

Present proposals for increased revenue sharing continue this movement towards decentralizing administrative decisions. Moreover, the trend is unlikely to be reversed, for it is inherent in the large population of the United States—208 million today and projected to be 260 million in 1990. In servicing such a large constituency, Federal officials cannot be as flexible as state and local officials who administer programs for much smaller numbers and, thus, are able to tailor each legislative program to the particular needs of localities. But at the same time that administration is being decentralized, it is expected that legislation will continue to be more centralized in Congress. These two trends are likely to produce a more appropriate mix of diversity and uniformity in American government.

Because of this continuing trend toward decentralization of expenditures, state and local employment other than in public education will account for 40% of total government employment in 1990, compared with 30% in 1970. The share of Federal civilian employment will decline to 16% in 1990 from 20% in 1970.

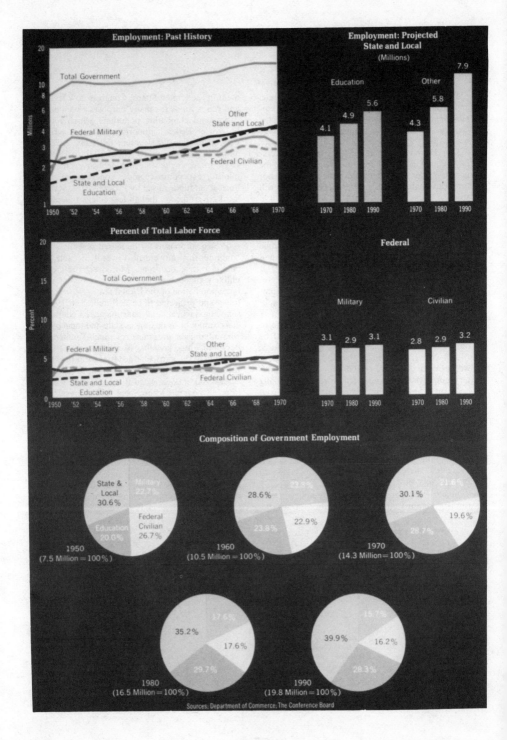

Employment: Past History

Total Government

Federal Military

Other
State and Local

Federal Civilian

State and Local
Education

Millions

1950 '52 '54 '56 '58 '60 '62 '64 '66 '68 1970

Percent of Total Labor Force

Total Government

Federal Military

Other
State and Local

Federal Civilian

State and Local
Education

Percent

1950 '52 '54 '56 '58 '60 '62 '64 '66 '68 1970

**Employment: Projected
State and Local**
(Millions)

Education

| 4.1 | 4.9 | 5.6 |
| 1970 | 1980 | 1990 |

Other

| 4.3 | 5.8 | 7.9 |
| 1970 | 1980 | 1990 |

Federal

Military

| 3.1 | 2.9 | 3.1 |
| 1970 | 1980 | 1990 |

Civilian

| 2.8 | 2.9 | 3.2 |
| 1970 | 1980 | 1990 |

Composition of Government Employment

State &
Local
30.6%

Military
22.7%

Education
20.0%

Federal
Civilian
26.7%

1950
(7.5 Million = 100%)

28.6%

23.5%

23.8%

22.9%

1960
(10.5 Million = 100%)

30.1%

21.6%

28.7%

19.6%

1970
(14.3 Million = 100%)

35.2%

17.6%

29.7%

17.6%

1980
(16.5 Million = 100%)

39.9%

15.7%

28.3%

16.2%

1990
(19.8 Million = 100%)

Sources: Department of Commerce; The Conference Board

58

Public Education

Public education accounts for 87% of total school enrollment in the United States—88% in elementary, 92% in secondary, and 77% in higher education. Employment in public education—including classroom teachers, other teaching personnel, and supporting personnel—rose at an average annual rate of 5.2% between 1950 and 1970. During the next 20 years, the average growth rate will be down to 1.6% per annum.

The two principal sources of growth in the past were a rapid expansion of the school-age population and increase in school enrollment rates among the age groups that account for most secondary and higher education. A less important but still significant source of growth was the decline in the ratio of students to teachers in elementary and in secondary education, although it was small in the former. In higher education, the student/teacher ratio has fluctuated around an average of fifteen students per classroom teacher since 1950.

During the next twenty years, the school-age population will decline, reflecting the fall in births during the Sixties. The elementary school-age population (5-13) peaked in 1970, and will decrease about 5% over a 5-year period until it hits 35.3 million in 1975. It will rise at an average annual rate of 1.4%, through 1990. The secondary school-age population will continue to increase until it reaches a peak of 16.9 million in 1975. It will then decline—by about 7% between 1975 and 1985—and return to just below its 1975 peak in 1990. The higher education age group will continue to grow—although at a decelerating rate—through 1980, to a high of 29.6 million; it will subsequently decrease so that by 1990 it will be 6% below its 1980 peak.

Increases in school enrollment in the next twenty years will be limited by the fact that many enrollment rates—the proportions of children attending school in the various age groups—are close to their upper limit. Virtually all children of elementary school age go to school; and in secondary education, the margin for improvement in enrollment has narrowed sharply in the last two decades. In higher education, there is considerable margin for increase, but the rate of growth in enrollment from 1950 to 1965 was so high that it is unlikely to be matched.

With fewer children per family as a consequence of the drop in births, parents will be able to afford a better education for each child. Increasing family income will also help. This will mean higher qualified teachers and fewer students per teacher, unless new teaching methods, more efficient educational plant and equipment, and the use of the mass communications—television in particular—allow for increased educational output with the same labor input as before. In elementary education, which accounts for about 50% of teacher employment, such productivity increases are unlikely to reduce the number of classroom teachers.

In secondary and higher education, large gains in labor productivity could enable one teacher to handle more students than before without any decline in educational output. In higher education, however, projected increases in enrollment will very likely lead to greater teacher employment despite innovations. On balance, it seems likely that teacher employment will continue to rise more rapidly than total employment but at a much reduced pace. As a result, education will probably claim more of GNP rather than less in the next twenty years, even though it may not duplicate its sharp rise of the last twenty years from 2.5% of GNP in 1950 to 5.2% in 1970.

School Age Population

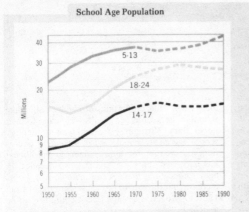

Enrollment

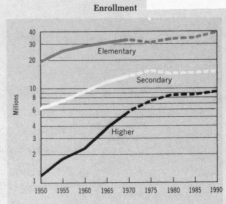

Student/Teacher Ratios

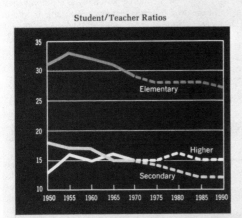

Classroom Teachers

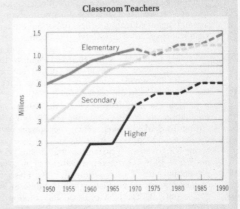

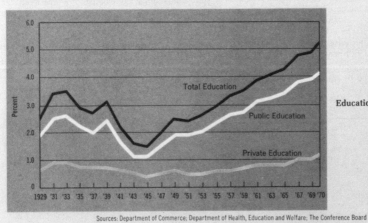

Education as Percent of GNP
1929-1970

Sources: Department of Commerce; Department of Health, Education and Welfare; The Conference Board

International Sector

Net exports of goods and services—the excess of exports produced in the United States over imports purchased by the various market groups distinguished in the national accounts—traditionally have contributed a considerably smaller share to overall gross national product than in most other countries. While both exports and imports of goods and services will continue to grow more or less steadily between now and 1990, their growth rates are projected to be only slightly above the growth rate of gross national product as a whole. In other words, even by 1990, both exports and imports will not account for a much larger share of total GNP than they do now and the contribution of the net exports to aggregate output will still be well below 1%.

However, within the total flow of goods and services from and to the United States (the so-called current account in the balance of the payments), some significant shifts will have occurred. Merchandise exports—which in 1970 accounted for two thirds of exports of goods and services—are projected to fall to little over one half by 1990. A similar drop, from two thirds to about three fifths of total imports, is projected for merchandise imports. This increasing share of nonmerchandise transactions reflects, on the export or receipts side, a continuing growth of income (in the form of dividends, fees, and royalties) from U.S. direct investments overseas as well as rising foreign travel to the United States. On the import or expenditures side, it similarly stems from continuing growth of U.S. tourist outlays abroad and, to a much smaller degree, from some increases in the rate of earnings on foreign direct investments in this country.

As a result of these diverse and only partially offsetting developments, the traditional U.S. merchandise trade surplus—already in jeopardy in 1971—is projected to disappear permanently by the mid-1980's. An eventual excess of merchandise imports over merchandise exports looms increasingly likely since, according to some recent studies, identical percentage rises in the gross national products of the United States and of other countries do not lead to equal relative increases in U.S. imports from those countries and in their imports from the United States. Rather, a similar percentage increase in GNP in both the United States and the rest of the world would tend to raise U.S. imports proportionately more than it would boost total world imports from the United States. The disparity is even greater between the United States and the major foreign industrial countries. It has been estimated that, if the U.S. trade balance with these countries as a group were not to deteriorate further, the rate of growth in their combined GNP would have to exceed the U.S. growth rate by almost 30%.

The merchandise trade deficits projected for 1985 and 1990, however, will be more than offset by surpluses on nonmerchandise transactions. These reflect largely the anticipated sharp growth in the return on U.S. overseas investments as the United States increasingly comes to assume the characteristics of a "mature creditor" country—a country whose gap between exports and imports is financed by income from investments abroad built up through past excesses of exports over imports.

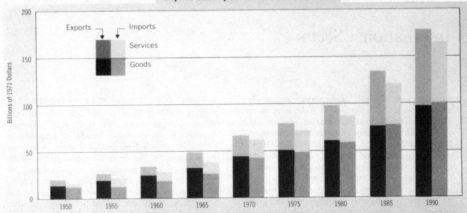

Exports and Imports of Goods and Services

Exports   Imports

Services

Goods

Billions of 1971 Dollars

1950 1955 1960 1965 1970 1975 1980 1985 1990

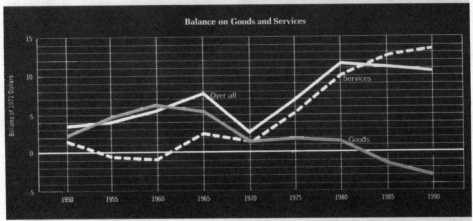

Balance on Goods and Services

Billions of 1971 Dollars

Over-all

Services

Goods

1950 1955 1960 1965 1970 1975 1980 1985 1990

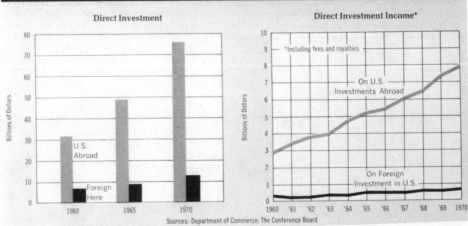

Direct Investment

Billions of Dollars

U.S. Abroad

Foreign Here

1960 1965 1970

Direct Investment Income*

Billions of Dollars

*Including fees and royalties

On U.S. Investments Abroad

On Foreign Investment in U.S.

'60 '61 '62 '63 '64 '65 '66 '67 '68 '69 1970

Sources: Department of Commerce; The Conference Board

62

The Changing Spectrum of Production

In the next two decades, the mix of national output by industry and by type of product is expected to continue to shift slowly, from goods and structures, toward services associated with goods production and distribution, and toward services for final sale to consumers.

The rate of growth of an industry today tends to be positively related to its state of technology and to the extent to which the industry is involved in service activities. Advances in technology usually result in the development of new products (including services) and processes, which permit greater real output to be produced from the same volume of purchased material inputs. For example, output originating in communications and in electric, gas, and sanitary services—where improved technology has led to production efficiencies internally as well as in the industries they service—has been growing much faster than GNP as a whole and is projected to continue to do so.

While the trend is not strong and clear, demand for services (private and governmental) in the post-war period has been increasing faster than that for goods and structures, and The Conference Board expects this to continue during the projection period. On a type-of-product basis, services represented 38.0% of real GNP in 1970, compared with 34.4% in 1947; the ratio is projected to rise to 42.8% by 1990. On an industry basis, real product originating in trade, finance, insurance, real estate, private services, and general government—generally considered to make up the service sector—has been increasing at virtually the same rate as the rest of the economy; for the next two decades, output of service industries is expected to grow slightly less rapidly than the output of other industries. However, the output of many service industries is extremely difficult to measure; and it is widely believed that in some cases the present level of output and the rate of growth of output have been significantly underestimated in the official accounts.

Inasmuch as the rate of improvement in productivity varies by industry and will continue to do so, changes in employment by industry in the next two decades will not correspond to output changes by industry. Between 1947 and 1965, the average annual increase in output per man in private industry ranged from less than 2% in finance, insurance, and services to nearly 6% in communications and public utilities, according to estimates by the National Bureau of Economic Research. Since the service industries are mostly near the lower end of the range, employment is increasing much faster in the service sector than in other sectors.

Because advances in productivity are responsible for a large part of economic progress (in terms of GNP per capita), and because growth in productivity has been shown to be slower in the service industries than in those producing goods, some have feared that continued increase in the share of employment accounted for by services will lead to a long-term slowdown in the rate of economic progress. Service employment has, however, been increasing relative to total employment for many decades, and despite this, the rate of productivity increase for the economy as a whole has actually risen in the long run. This is because productivity growth in nonservice industries has accelerated.

Gross Product by Major Industry, 1970

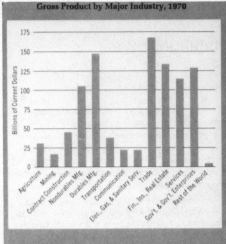

Growth in Real Output

Average Annual Percent Increase

BY MAJOR INDUSTRY
- Electric, Gas & Sanitary Services
- Communication
- Transportation
- Durables Mfg.
- Finance, Insurance, Real Estate
- Services
- Contract Construction
- TOTAL GNP
- Nondurables Mfg.
- Wholesale & Retail Trade
- Mining
- Gov't. & Gov't. Enterprises
- Agriculture

1947-1970
1970-1990

BY SECTOR
- Rest of the World ▲
- Nonfarm Business △
- Farms, Households, Institutions
- General Government

BY TYPE OF PRODUCT
- Services
- Durable Goods
- Structures
- Nondurable Goods

Distribution of GNP, 1970

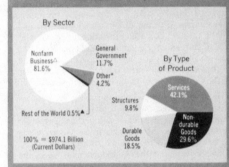

By Sector

Nonfarm Business△ 81.6%
General Government 11.7%
Other* 4.2%
Rest of the World 0.5%▲

100% = $974.1 Billion (Current Dollars)

By Type of Product

Services 42.1%
Nondurable Goods 29.6%
Durable Goods 18.5%
Structures 9.8%

Productivity Change by Major Industry

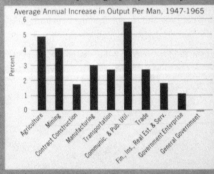

Average Annual Increase in Output Per Man, 1947-1965

Employment Change by Major Industry

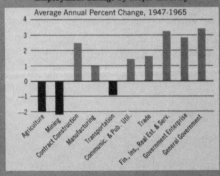

Average Annual Percent Change, 1947-1965

△ Includes government enterprises.
* Farms, households, & institutions.
▲ Gross product originating in the "rest of the world" is the net international inflow of incomes, or the excess of output not produced in the U.S. but accruing to factors of production supplied by U.S. residents over that output produced in the U.S. but accruing to foreigners.
NOTE: Projections are derived on the basis of values in 1958 dollars. Because this entails use of 1958 expenditure weights in the process of deflation, the data differ from those that would be obtained by using, for example, 1971 dollars and, therefore, 1971 expenditure weights.
Sources: Department of Commerce; Department of Labor; National Bureau of Economic Research; The Conference Board.

Inflation and the Money Supply

Gross national product (GNP) in current dollars and the money supply are projected here on the assumption that the economy is moving along a full-employment path (as defined earlier in the study) which generates real GNP—in 1971 dollars—of $1.6 trillion in 1980 and $2.4 trillion in 1990.

Separate projections are provided on the basis of three different rates of inflation: a "moderate" rate of 3.0%, somewhat above the 2.6% average of the preceding two decades; a "high" rate of 4.5%, roughly in line with the most recent experience; and a "medium" rate of 3.75%, which is roughly consistent with the latest estimates of the long run "Phillips Curve" for the U.S. economy. The lower average of 2.6% of the last 20 years included an extended period of relative price stability with high unemployment rates. During 1958-64, the annual rate of inflation of the implicit GNP deflator averaged 1.5%, while unemployment rates ranged roughly between 5% and 7% and fell below 5% only during three isolated months. Moreover, recent research has indicated structural changes in the composition of the labor force which imply that the rate of inflation associated with any given unemployment rate is higher now than it was during the 1950's and early 1960's.

For 1980, current-dollar GNP is projected at $2.1 trillion under conditions of "moderate" inflation, $2.3 trillion with 3.75% inflation, and $2.4 trillion under the most inflationary assumption. This spread increases sharply by 1990 to $4.3 trillion, $4.9 trillion, and $5.6 trillion, respectively.

Three levels of money supply are projected, consistent with the moderate, medium, and high rates of inflation. For 1980, they are $362 billion, $387 billion, and $417 billion, respectively; for 1990, they are $613 billion, $706 billion, and $813 billion. The lowest money supply, associated with 3% inflation, reflects an average annual growth rate of 5½% over two decades; the higher money supply reflects a 6% growth rate; and the highest figures reflect a rate of monetary expansion of 7%. In each case, the average annual rate of increase of the money supply projected for the first decade is slightly higher than that for the second (because real economic growth is expected to be slightly faster during the first decade). All projected rates of monetary increase are well above the average annual rate of about 3% during the past two decades, reflecting faster real growth, as well as more inflation, during the next twenty years.

All projections of the money supply imply that the income velocity (GNP divided by the money supply) will continue to rise roughly in line with its postwar trend. In 1980, the implied income velocity of money would be roughly 5.8—compared with roughly 4.6 in 1970; by 1990, it would have risen to 6.9. Underlying this rise in velocity would be a combination of past trends toward improved techniques of cash management and the movement toward a "checkless society."

As in the postwar period, the future rise in velocity will be gradual. A slower growth in velocity than projected here would require higher rates of growth of the money supply for any given full-employment GNP.

Gross National Product, Money Supply, and Inflation

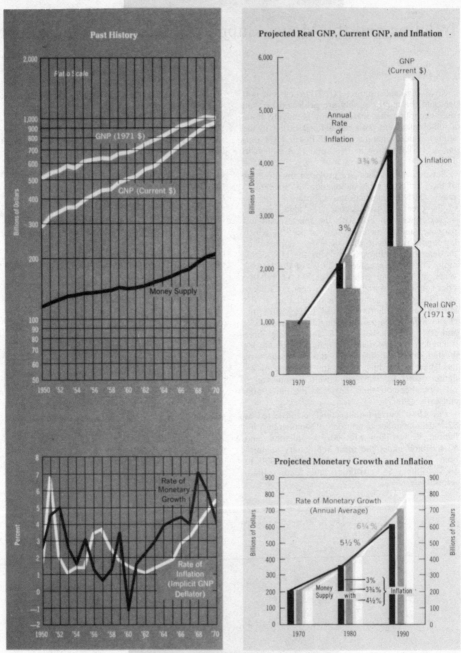

Sources: Department of Commerce, Federal Reserve, The Conference Board

66

Calls on Our Resources

Past and future growth in population and in output place increasing demand on the non-human resources available. For example, the manner in which water, land, and forests are being used is attracting considerable attention. But it is anticipated that, *for the span covered by these projections,* market forces and appropriate public actions will ensure a sufficient supply of resources.

While there are limits to particular natural resources in particular places, resources in general do not necessarily grow increasingly scarce in economic terms. The *cost* of producing needed materials is the key question. Thus far in the nation's history, advances in technology—that have facilitated new discoveries and improved methods of recovery and use—and the importation of products have enabled the total supply to meet domestic demand with little or no rise in resource prices relative to prices in general. The mix of materials has changed, because the relative costs of *individual* resources vary with changes in the relative difficulty of their recovery and use. Many experts expect these market-induced changes to continue to be effective in providing extractable resources with a negligible change in overall relative cost. In cases such as land and water, efficiencies will probably be effected through dual or multiple use, and through renewal after alteration.

Total energy consumption probably will grow less rapidly than GNP, as it has done historically. A U.S. Bureau of Mines "medium-range" projection shows a 95% rise in energy consumption between 1968 and 1990 resulting from a 145% increase in real GNP. This projection rests on the assumption that the present conventional energy system will continue with "normal" improvements in efficiency and with interfuel competition and substitution within evolving energy markets; and it

is assumed that technological gains in the use of fossil fuels will offset the effects of any restrictive regulations aimed at controlling environmental pollution.

Continued increase in water use by industry, particularly for cooling in electricity generation, and growing recreation and conservation demands are expected to account for most of the rise in U.S. requirements over the next 20 years. Less than 5% of withdrawals by industry are consumed (disappear from runoff), but much of the discharge needs treatment to prevent spoilage of the receiving body of water for downstream uses. Recreational and conservational uses entail very large volumes and require relatively clean flows; but virtually no withdrawals or disappearance (other than natural) are involved.

Recreation and conservation are also expected to increase demand for land greatly, as population, leisure time, and recognition of ecological principles grow. Resources for the Future projects that acreage devoted to nonurban parks, reservoirs, wildlife refuges, etc., will nearly double between 1960 and 1990. Large portions of grazing land and commercial forest may have to be also used for recreation.

Metals present the greatest problem of future adequacy even though nonmetals—plastics, for example—continue to win away markets. Domestic ore deposits of the major metals are much smaller in relation to current and anticipated domestic demand than is the case for fuels. From one third to three fourths of apparent domestic consumption of iron, aluminum, copper, lead, and zinc ores is now supplied by imports; it is likely that the United States will become even more dependent on foreign resources.

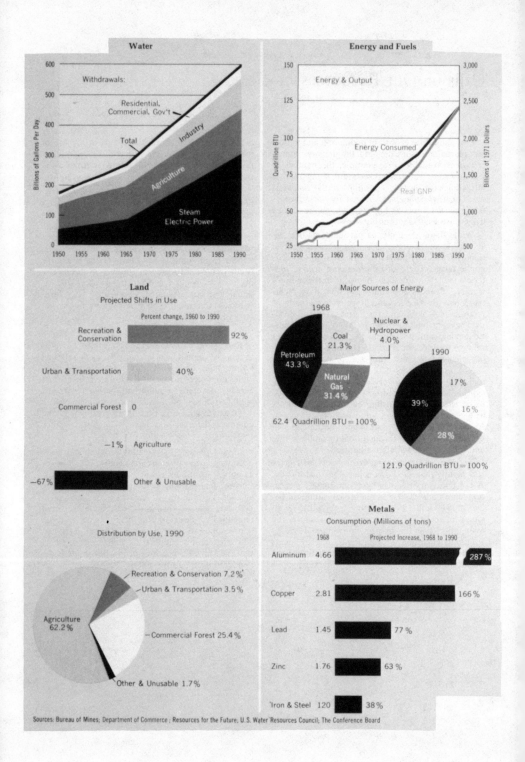

Water

Withdrawals:

Residential, Commercial, Gov't

Total

Industry

Agriculture

Steam Electric Power

Billions of Gallons Per Day

1950 1955 1960 1965 1970 1975 1980 1985 1990

Energy and Fuels

Energy & Output

Energy Consumed

Real GNP

Quadrillion BTU

Billions of 1971 Dollars

1950 1955 1960 1965 1970 1975 1980 1985 1990

Land

Projected Shifts in Use

Percent change, 1960 to 1990

Recreation & Conservation — 92%

Urban & Transportation — 40%

Commercial Forest — 0

−1% Agriculture

−67% Other & Unusable

Distribution by Use, 1990

Recreation & Conservation 7.2%

Urban & Transportation 3.5%

Agriculture 62.2%

Commercial Forest 25.4%

Other & Unusable 1.7%

Major Sources of Energy

1968

Coal 21.3%

Nuclear & Hydropower 4.0%

Petroleum 43.3%

Natural Gas 31.4%

62.4 Quadrillion BTU = 100%

1990

39%

17%

16%

28%

121.9 Quadrillion BTU = 100%

Metals

Consumption (Millions of tons)

	1968	Projected Increase, 1968 to 1990
Aluminum	4.66	287%
Copper	2.81	166%
Lead	1.45	77%
Zinc	1.76	63%
Iron & Steel	120	38%

Sources: Bureau of Mines; Department of Commerce; Resources for the Future; U.S. Water Resources Council; The Conference Board

Social Indicators

The changing quality of American life has become a major theme in the national debate. As a people, we are disposed to take accomplishment for granted but are restless with our imperfections. With each new achievement, we define more ambitious goals. This—the rising tide of aspirations—is the wellspring of our growth.

By many standards, certainly, the quality of our daily life has improved since the end of World War II. For one thing, medical breakthroughs and an increased ability and willingness to spend for medical care has made us a healthier and longer living people. Back in the Thirties, spending for health came to about 3.5% of our gross national product; currently, the figure is over 7%, and, conservatively estimated, it will be 10% by 1990. Our improving health standards are dramatically documented by longevity statistics. Americans born in 1920 had a life expectation of less than 55 years; children born today can expect to live to the year 2040.

Longevity increased sharply immediately following the war, principally because of new drugs which appreciably reduced deaths from infectious diseases. With a growing prevalence of older persons, however, there has been a rise in the incidence of cancer, cardiovascular disorders, and other diseases generally associated with aging.

A telling indicator of a people's material well-being is the proportion of resources required for essentials. By this measure, the quality of American life has improved imposingly in the past two and a half decades. In 1947 an estimated 27% of consumer outlay went for food; in 1971 the figure was 18%. It is expected that the ratio will probably not be higher than 14% by 1990. While the proportion of family income that goes for food has declined, real per capita consumption of food has increased by 10% over the past two decades.

As the relative claim of necessities on the family's budget declines, the resources available for other things increases. In the postwar period, we have experienced boom demand for a wide range of goods and services that are generally associated with the affluent life. For example, the number of Americans with the inclination and the means to travel abroad has increased more than eightfold in the past two decades. Real consumer spending for recreational goods has more than quadrupled in the same period.

A further measure of progress is the rising level of educational attainment. Each upcoming generation remains in school longer. For example, in 1950 about 18% of men 30 to 34 years old had some college experience; by 1970 the ratio had increased to 33%; and by 1990 it is expected to exceed 38%. At present, about 23% of women aged 30–34 have been to college; by 1990, the proportion will exceed 37%. Not only are we becoming better schooled, but the education-gender gap is narrowing.

Unmistakably there has been appreciable progress in the quality of American life, but no less unmistakable is the fact that there are important areas of deterioration. The crisis of the city, crime and drugs, the wide and persisting inequity in living standards, and the distressing pace at which we are polluting our environment have created a sense of urgency. The problems ahead are perhaps more awesome than those of the past. ∎

Resources for Health

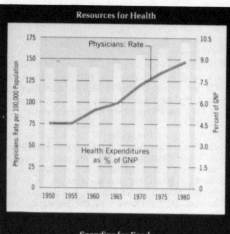

Longevity

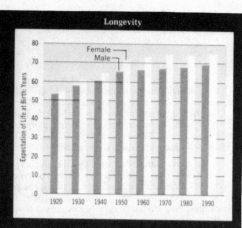

Spending for Food
All Figures in 1971 Dollars

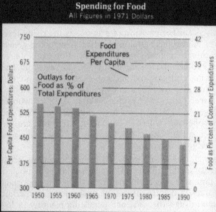

Spending for Travel

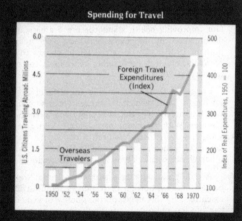

Educational Attainment
Level of School Completed, Persons 25 Years and Over

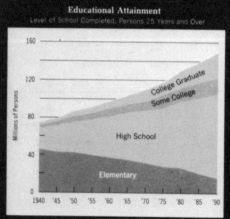

Education by Generation
Percent College Educated in Age Group 30-34

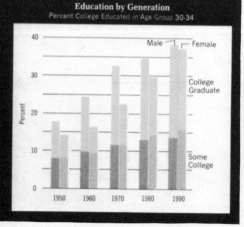

SECTION II

TOMORROW'S JOBS

Section II presents an overview of the employment opportunities available in American Industry. This section is from the Occupational Outlook Handbook. The handbook is updated every other year. It is published by the Bureau of Labor Statistics, U.S. Department of Labor.

"Tomorrow's Jobs" presents, through the use of some excellent charts, trends in employment opportunities during this decade. American industries are classified according to the following categories:

1. Manufacturing
    a. Durable
    b. Non-durable
2. Trade
    a. Wholesale
    b. Retail
3. Services
4. Government
    a. Local
    b. State
    c. Federal
5. Agriculture
6. Transportation and Public Utilities
7. Contract Construction
8. Finance, Insurance, and Real Estate
9. Mining

The occupational classifications within the various American industries are grouped according to the following categories:

1. Professional, Technical, Kindred
2. Managers, Officials
3. Sales
4. Service
5. Clerical, Kindred
6. Skilled
7. Semi-skilled
8. Laborers, except farming
9. Farmers, Farm Managers, Laborers

TOMORROW'S JOBS

Bureau of Labor Statistics

Young people in an ever growing and changing society are faced with the difficult task of making sound career plans from among thousands of alternatives. As the economy continues to expand, this planning process becomes more difficult. Making career plans calls for an evaluation of an individual's interests and abilities, as well as specific information on occupations. This *Handbook* provides counselors, teachers, parents, and students with occupational information on training and education requirements, employment opportunities, and the nature of the work.

Several questions are of major importance to young persons as they view the variety of occupational choices open to them. Among these questions are: What fields look especially promising for employment opportunities? What competition will other workers furnish? What type and how much training and education are required to enter particular jobs? How do earnings in certain occupations compare with earnings in other occupations requiring similar training? What types of employers provide which kinds of jobs? What are the typical environment and working conditions associated with particular occupations?

Of importance in evaluating information that answers these and related questions is knowledge of the dynamic changes that are continually occurring in our economy —the trends in the Nation's work force and its business, industrial, and occupational development. New ways of making goods, new products, and changes in living standards are constantly changing the types of jobs that become available. To throw light on the changing characteristics of occupations and to provide background for understanding the outlook in specific occupations, this chapter focuses on overall patterns of change in the country's industrial and occupational composition. It also discusses the implications of these changes on education and training in relation to occupational choice.

No one can accurately forecast the future. Nevertheless, by using the wealth of information available, extensive economic and statistical analyses, and the best judgment of informed experts, the work future can be described in broad terms. Of course, some aspects of the future can be predicted more accurately than others. For example, the number of 18-year-olds in 1980 can be

OCCUPATIONAL OUTLOOK HANDBOOK, 1972-73 Edition (U.S. Government Printing Office: Bulletin 1700) pp. 13-21.

estimated with a very high degree of accuracy because individuals 8 years old in 1970 are accounted for in our vital statistics, and the death rate of children between 8 and 18 is extremely low and stays about the same from year to year. On the other hand, forecasting employment requirements for automobile assemblers in 1980 is extremely difficult. Employment of these workers can be affected by the changing demand for American-made automobiles, shifts in buyer's preference (toward the compact car, for example), changes in the ways cars are made (more automation or the use of turbine engines), and unpredictable economic developments outside of the automobile industry.

To project the demand for all workers in the economy, specific assumptions have to be made about general economic movements and broad national policy. The picture of the future employment outlook reflected in the *Handbook* is based on the following fundamental assumptions:

1. Maintenance of high levels of employment and of utilization of available manpower in 1980;

2. that no major event will alter substantially the rate and nature of economic growth;

3. that economic and social patterns and relationships will continue to change at about the same rate as in the recent past;

4. that scientific technological advancement will continue at about the same rate as in recent years; and

5. that the United States will no longer be fighting a war. On the other hand, a still guarded relationship between the major powers will permit no major reduction in armaments but defense expenditures can be reduced from the peak levels of the Vietnam conflict.

The *Handbook's* assessment of 1980 industrial and occupational outlook assumes a projected total labor force of 100.7 million in 1980, an Armed Forces of 2.7 million, and a resulting civilian labor force of 98 million.

Knowledge of specific industries is necessary because employers seek a wide variety of skills, for example, many different industries employ engineers, salesmen, and secretaries. Employment patterns have shifted considerably over the years and are expected to continue to do so. These changes greatly affect employment opportunities and occupational choices.

Industry employment and occupational requirements change as a result of many factors. A new machine or a newly automated process may require different occupational skills or may even create an entirely new occupation; a change in product demand may affect the number of workers needed; an invention may all but eliminate an industry or create a new one.

Industrial Profile

To help understand the Nation's industrial composition, industries may be viewed as either goods producing or service producing.

They may further be grouped into nine major divisions according to this product or service. (See chart 1.)

Most of the Nation's workers are in industries producing services, in activities such as education, health care, trade, repair and maintenance, and in government, transportation, and banking and insurance service. The production of goods—raising food crops, building, extracting minerals, and manufacturing of goods —has required less than half of the country's work force since the late 1940's. (See chart 2.) In general, job growth through the 1970's is expected to continue to be faster in the service-producing industries than in the goods-producing industries. However, among industry divisions within both the goods-producing and service-producing sectors, the growth pattern will continue to vary. (See chart 3.)

Service-producing industries. In 1970, about 47.3 million workers were on the payrolls of service-producing industries—trade; Government; services and miscellaneous; transportation and other utilities; and finance, insurance, and real estate—about 13.5 million greater than the number employed in 1960. The major factors underlying this rapid post World War II growth have been (1) population growth; (2) increasing urbanization, with its accompanying need for more city service; and (3) rising income and living standards accompanying demand for improved services, such as health, education, and security. These factors are expected to continue to result in rapid growth of service industries as a group, and to employ 59.5 million by 1980, an increase of about 26 percent above the 1970 level.

Trade, the largest division within

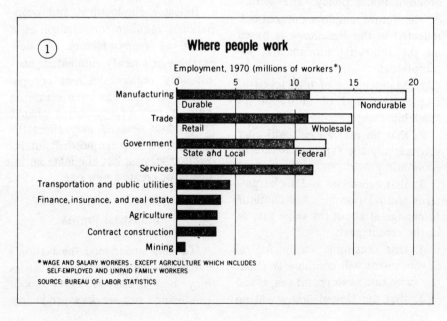

① **Where people work**

Employment, 1970 (millions of workers*)

Manufacturing — Durable / Nondurable
Trade — Retail / Wholesale
Government — State and Local / Federal
Services
Transportation and public utilities
Finance, insurance, and real estate
Agriculture
Contract construction
Mining

*WAGE AND SALARY WORKERS. EXCEPT AGRICULTURE WHICH INCLUDES SELF-EMPLOYED AND UNPAID FAMILY WORKERS
SOURCE: BUREAU OF LABOR STATISTICS

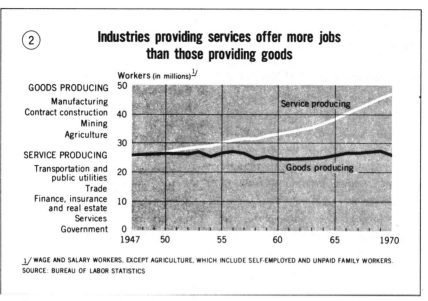

② **Industries providing services offer more jobs than those providing goods**

Workers (in millions)$^{1/}$

GOODS PRODUCING
Manufacturing
Contract construction
Mining
Agriculture

SERVICE PRODUCING
Transportation and public utilities
Trade
Finance, insurance and real estate
Services
Government

Service producing

Goods producing

1947   50   55   60   65   1970

$\underline{1/}$ WAGE AND SALARY WORKERS, EXCEPT AGRICULTURE, WHICH INCLUDE SELF-EMPLOYED AND UNPAID FAMILY WORKERS.
SOURCE: BUREAU OF LABOR STATISTICS

the service-producing industries, has expanded sharply since 1960. Wholesale and retail outlets have multiplied in large and small cities to satisfy the need of an increasingly urban society. Employment in trade was about 14.9 million in 1970, about 31 percent above the 1960 level.

Employment in trade is expected to grow by about 18 percent between 1970 and 1980. Although an ever-increasing volume of merchandise will be distributed as a

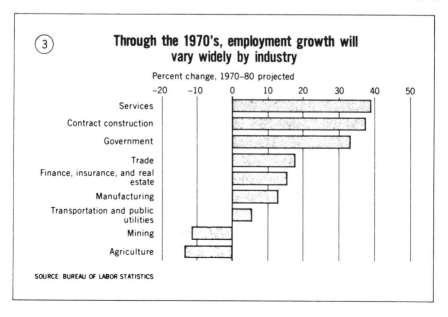

③ **Through the 1970's, employment growth will vary widely by industry**

Percent change, 1970-80 projected

−20   −10   0   10   20   30   40   50

Services
Contract construction
Government
Trade
Finance, insurance, and real estate
Manufacturing
Transportation and public utilities
Mining
Agriculture

SOURCE: BUREAU OF LABOR STATISTICS

result of increases in population and consumer expenditures, the rate of increase in manpower needs will be slowed by laborsaving technology such as the greater use of electronic data processing equipment and automated warehousing equipment, growth in the number of self-service stores, and the growing use of vending machines.

Government employment has grown faster than any other industry division, and has increased by more than one-half from 8.4 million to 12.6 million between 1960 and 1970. Growth has been mostly at the State and local levels, which combined increased by almost two-thirds. Employment growth has been greatest in agencies providing education, health, sanitation, welfare, and protective services. Federal Government employment increased about 19 percent between 1960 and 1970.

Government will continue to be a major source of new jobs through the 1970's. By 1980, employment in Government may be as much as 33 percent higher than in 1970. Most of the growth will be in State and local governments in which employment needs may rise by 1980, to 13.8 million about 40 percent higher than the 9.9 million employed in 1970. Federal Government employment is expected to rise slowly to about 3 million to 1980, 300,000 or about 11 percent above the 1970 level of 2.7 million.

Services and miscellaneous industries employment has increased rapidly since World War II as a result of the growing need for mainte-nance and repair, advertising, domestic, and health care services. From 1960 to 1970, total employment in this industry division rose by about two-fifths from slightly more than 8.0 million to about 11.6 million.

Service and miscellaneous industries will continue to be among the fastest growing industries through the 1970's. About two-fifths again as many workers are expected to be employed in this industry division in 1980 as in 1970. Manpower requirements in health services are expected to grow rapidly due to population growth and the increasing ability of persons to pay for health care. Business services including accounting, data processing, and maintenance also are expected to grow very rapidly.

Transportation and public utility employment in 1970 at 4.5 million was only slightly more than one-tenth higher than in 1960. Different parts of this industry, however, have experienced different growth trends. For example, air travel employment increased rapidly but the railroad industry declined.

The number of jobs in transportation and public utilities as a whole is expected to continue to increase slowly through the 1970's and widely differing employment trends will continue to be experienced among individual industries within the division. Rapid increases in employment are expected in air transportation and a decline is expected to continue in railroad employment and little or no change is expected in water transportation, and electric, gas, and sanitary services. Overall employment in this industry division is expected to increase to more than 4.7 million in 1980, 5 percent above the 1970 level.

Finance, insurance, and real estate, the smallest of the service-producing industry divisions, has grown about 38 percent since 1960, from nearly 2.7 million in 1960 to nearly 3.7 million in 1970. Employment has grown especially rapidly in banks; credit agencies; and security and commodity brokers, dealers, exchanges, and services.

Job growth in finance, insurance, and real estate will keep in step with the overall employment increases of nonfarm employment through the 1970's. Finance, insurance, and real estate employment is expected to expand to nearly 4.3 million by 1980, about 16 percent above 1970 levels. The most rapid advances will be in banking and credit agencies, which combined account for nearly two-fifths of total employment in this industry division.

Goods-Producing Industries. Employment in the goods-producing industries—agriculture, manufacturing, construction, and mining—more than 26.9 million in 1970—has increased slowly in recent years. Significant gains in productivity resulting from automation and other technological developments as well as the growing skills of the work force have permitted large increases in output without corresponding increases in employment. Employment in goods-producing industries is expected to increase to about 30 million in 1980, 12 percent above the 1970 level. However, widely different patterns of employment changes have occurred and will continue among the industry divisions in the goods-producing sector.

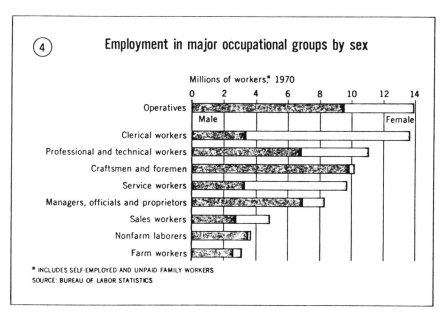

④ Employment in major occupational groups by sex

Millions of workers,* 1970

* INCLUDES SELF-EMPLOYED AND UNPAID FAMILY WORKERS
SOURCE: BUREAU OF LABOR STATISTICS

Agriculture, which until the late 1800's employed more than half of all workers in the economy, employed only 5 percent, or 3.4 million workers, in 1970. Employment in agriculture has dropped by about two-fifths since 1960. Increases in the average size of farms, rapid mechanization, and improved fertilizers, feeds and pesticides have created large increases in output at the same time that employment has fallen sharply.

Agriculture is facing a continuing decline in manpower needs. Factors resulting in past declines will continue and the outlook is for a 1980 farm work force 15 percent lower than in 1970.

Mining employment, at about 620,000 workers in 1970, has declined by nearly 13 percent since 1960, primarily because of labor-saving technological changes and a shift to sources of power other than coal.

This trend is likely to continue and mining is the only nonagricultural industry division that is not expected to increase between 1970 and 1980. Although minor employment increases are expected in quarrying and other nonmetallic mining, they will be more than offset by continuing declines in the coal mining, and in crude petroleum and natural gas extraction industries. The job level of the entire mining group is expected to decline about 12 percent to about 550,000 between 1970 and 1980.

Contract construction employment, at more than 3.3 million in 1970, has increased more than one-sixth since 1960. The Nation's growing need for homes, offices, stores, highways, bridges, dams, and other physical facilities resulted in this increase in employment.

Between 1970 and 1980, contract construction is expected to grow by about two-fifths to about 4.6 million. Construction activity will be spurred by several factors. An expanding economy will result in more industrial plants and commercial establishments such as office buildings, stores, and banks. The volume of construction maintenance and repair, which is now about one-third of new construction activity, also is expected to grow significantly through the 1970's. Home and apartment building will be stimulated by the increase in population, new family formations, and higher income levels. Also, large government expenditures for urban renewal, school construction, and roads are likely.

Manufacturing, the largest division within the goods-producing sector that had about 19.4 million workers in 1970, increased about 16 percent in employment between 1960 and 1970. New products for industrial and consumer markets and the rapid growth of the defense-space market has spearheaded the post World War II growth.

Manufacturing employment is expected to increase about 13 percent through the 1970's and reach about 21.9 million in 1980. Durable goods manufacturing is projected to increase slightly faster (16 percent) and nondurable goods somewhat slower (9 percent) than the total.

However, the rate of growth will vary among the individual manufacturing industries. The machinery industry is expected to have the largest need for additional people, as employment grows from nearly 2.0 million to more than 2.4 million. Producers of rubber and plastic products; furniture and fixtures; stone, clay, and glass products; and instruments, will be among other rapid growing manufacturing industries. In contrast, employment in some manufacturing industries may decline, for example, food, textile mill products, tobacco, and petroleum refining.

Occupational Profile

As American industries continue to grow large, more complex, and more mechanized, fundamental changes will take place in the Nation's occupational structure. Furthermore, occupations will become more complex and more specialized. Thus, an imposing and confusing number of occupational choices is provided to individuals who are planning their careers. An individual, in examining the vast number of choices should first look at broad groupings of jobs that have similar characteristics such as entrance requirements. (See chart 4.)

Among the most significant changes in the Nation's occupational structure has been the shift toward white-collar jobs. In 1956, for the first time in the Nation's history, white-collar workers—professional, managerial, clerical, and sales—outnumbered blue-collar workers—craftsmen, operatives, and laborers. (See chart 5.)

Through the 1970's, we can expect a continuation of the rapid growth of white-collar occupations,

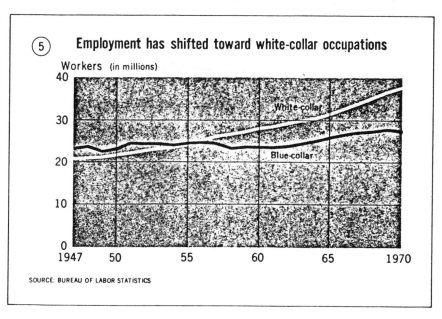

⑤ **Employment has shifted toward white-collar occupations**

Workers (in millions)

White-collar

Blue-collar

SOURCE: BUREAU OF LABOR STATISTICS

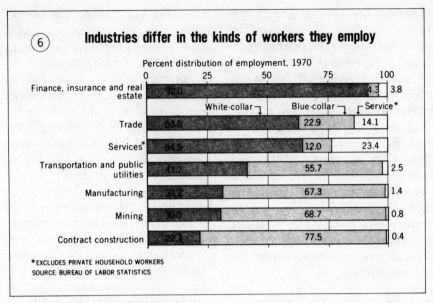

6 **Industries differ in the kinds of workers they employ**

Percent distribution of employment, 1970

Finance, insurance and real estate	92.0	4.3 3.8
	White-collar ⌐	Blue-collar ⌐ ⌐ Service*
Trade	63.0	22.9 14.1
Services*	64.5	12.0 23.4
Transportation and public utilities	41.7	55.7 2.5
Manufacturing	31.2	67.3 1.4
Mining	30.5	68.7 0.8
Contract construction	22.1	77.5 0.4

*EXCLUDES PRIVATE HOUSEHOLD WORKERS
SOURCE: BUREAU OF LABOR STATISTICS

a slower than average growth of blue-collar occupations, a faster than average growth among service workers, and a further decline of farm workers. Total employment is expected to increase about 21 percent between 1970 and 1980. In comparison, an increase of about 27 percent is expected for white-collar jobs, and only about 12 percent for blue-collar occupations. By 1980, white-collar jobs will account for more than one-half of all employed workers compared with about 48

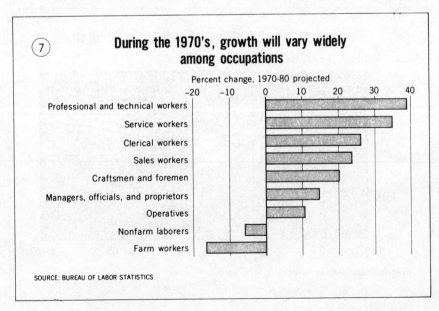

7 **During the 1970's, growth will vary widely among occupations**

Percent change, 1970-80 projected

- Professional and technical workers
- Service workers
- Clerical workers
- Sales workers
- Craftsmen and foremen
- Managers, officials, and proprietors
- Operatives
- Nonfarm laborers
- Farm workers

SOURCE: BUREAU OF LABOR STATISTICS

percent in 1970. The rapid growth expected for white-collar workers and service workers reflects continuous expansion of the service-producing industries which employ a relatively large proportion of these workers. (See chart 6.) The growing demand for workers to perform research and development, to provide education and health services, and to process the increasing amount of paperwork throughout all types of enterprises, also will be significant in the growth of white-collar jobs. The slower than average growth of blue-collar and farm workers reflects the expanding use of labor-saving equipment in our Nation's industries and the relatively slow growth of the goods-producing industries that employ large proportions of blue-collar workers.

The following section describes in greater detail the changes that are expected to occur among the broad occupational groups through the 1970's.

Professional and technical workers, the third largest occupational group in 1970, include among more than 11.1 million workers such highly trained personnel as teachers, engineers, dentists, accountants, and clergymen.

Professional occupations will be the fastest growing occupation from 1970–80. (See chart 7.) Personnel in this area will be in great demand as the Nation puts greater efforts toward the country's socio-economic progress, urban renewal, transportation, harnessing the ocean, and enhancing the beauty of the land. The quest for scientific and technical knowledge is bound to grow and raise the demand for workers in scientific and technical specialties. The 1970's will see a continuing emphasis in the social sciences and medical services. By 1980 the requirements for professional, technical, and kindred workers may be about two-fifths greater than 1970 employment.

Managers, officials and proprietors totaled about 8.3 million in 1970. As a group they will increase about 15 percent between 1970 and 1980, somewhat slower than the rate of growth for all occupations. As in the past, requirements for salaried managers are likely to continue to increase rapidly because of the increasing dependence of business organizations and government agencies on management specialists. On the other hand, the number of self-employed managers are expected to continue to decline through the 1970's as larger businesses continue to restrict growth of the total number of firms and as supermarkets continue to replace small groceries, general stores, and hand laundries.

Clerical workers numbering 13.7 million in 1970, include workers who operate computers and office machines, keep records, take dictation, and type. Many new clerical positions are expected to open up as industries employing large numbers of clerical workers continue to expand. The trend in retail stores toward transferring to clerical workers functions that were performed by salespersons also will tend to increase employment needs of clerical workers. The demand will be particularly strong for those qualified to handle jobs created by the change of clerical occupations to electronic data processing operations. However, the use of electronic computing bookkeeping machines and other mechanical devices to do processing and repetitive work are expected to reduce the number of clerks employed in jobs such as filing, making up payrolls, keeping tract of inventories, and billing customers. The need for clerical workers as a group is expected to increase more than one-fourth between 1970 and 1980.

Sales workers, accounting for about 4.9 million workers in 1970, are found primarily in retail stores, wholesale firms, insurance companies, real estate agencies, as well as offering goods door to door. Between 1970 and 1980 sales workers are expected to increase nearly 24 percent.

Increasing sales of many new products resulting from rapid population growth, new product development, business expansion, and rising business levels will be the major reason for increasing employment of sales workers. The expected increase in residential and commercial construction and urban renewal will increase the need for real estate agents. Continued extension of such laws as workers' compensation and automobile liability insurance should boost the need for insurance salesmen. The trend of stores to remain open longer hours should increase the need for retail sales persons. However, changes in distribution methods, such as self-service and automatic vending are likely to restrict the employment growth of sales workers.

Craftsmen, numbering about 10.2 million in 1970, include carpenters, tool and die makers, instrument makers, all round machinists, electricians, and type setters. Industrial growth and increasing business activity are the major factors expected to spur the growth of crafts occupations through the 1970's. However, technological developments will tend to limit the expansion of this group. Craftsmen are expected to increase nearly one-fifth, somewhat slower than the growth of all occupations.

Semiskilled workers (operatives) made up the largest major occupational group in 1970 with about 13.9 million workers engaged in assembling goods in factories; driving trucks, buses and taxis; and operating machinery.

Employment for semiskilled workers is expected to increase about 11 percent above the 1970 level, despite continued technological advances that will reduce employment for some types of semiskilled occupations. Increases in production generated by rising population and rapid economic growth, as well as the increasing trend to motor truck transportation of freight, are expected to be the major factors contributing to the increasing employment.

Laborers (excluding those in

farming and mining), who numbered nearly 3.7 million workers in 1970, for the most part move, lift, and carry materials and tools in the Nation's workplaces. Employment of laborers is expected to change little between 1970 and 1980 in spite of the rises in manufacturing and construction which employ most laborers. Increased demand is expected to be offset by rising productivity resulting from continuing substitution of mechanical equipment for manual labor.

Service workers, including men and women who maintain law and order, assist professional nurses in hospitals, give haircuts and beauty treatments, serve food, and clean and care for our homes, totaled about 9.7 million in 1970. This diverse group will increase about 35 percent between 1970 and 1980 and after professional workers will be the fastest growing group. Some of the main factors that are expected to increase requirements for these occupations are the rising demand for hospital and other medical care; the greater need for protective services as urbanization continues and cities become more crowded; and the more frequent use of restaurants, beauty parlors, and other services as income levels rise and as an increasing number of housewives take jobs outside the home.

Farm workers—including farmers, farm managers, laborers, and foremen—numbered nearly 3.1 million in 1970. Employment requirements for farm workers are expected to decline to about 2.6 million in 1980. This decrease is anticipated, in part, because of continued improvement in farm technology. For example, improved fertilizers, seeds, and feed, will permit a farmer to increase production without increasing employment.

Job Openings

In considering a career, young people should not eliminate occupations just because their preferences will not be among the most rapidly growing. Although growth is a key indicator of future job outlook, more jobs will be created between 1970–80 from deaths, retirements, and other labor force separations than from employment growth. (See chart 8.) Replacement needs will be particularly significant in occupations which have a large proportion of older workers and women. Furthermore, large occupations that have little growth may offer more openings than a fast growing small one. For example, among the major occupational groups, openings for operatives resulting from growth and replacement combined will be greater than for craftsmen, although the rate of growth of craftsmen will be more than twice as rapid as the rate of growth for operatives.

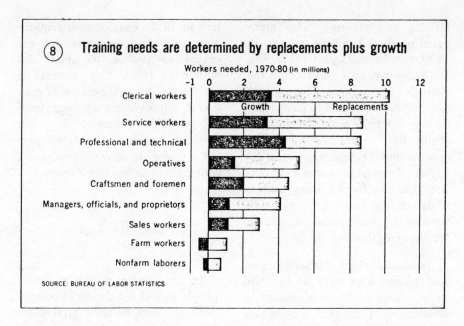

(8) Training needs are determined by replacements plus growth

Workers needed, 1970-80 (in millions)

Clerical workers	Growth / Replacements
Service workers	
Professional and technical	
Operatives	
Craftsmen and foremen	
Managers, officials, and proprietors	
Sales workers	
Farm workers	
Nonfarm laborers	

SOURCE: BUREAU OF LABOR STATISTICS

Outlook and Education

Numerous opportunities for employment will be available for job-seekers during the years ahead. Employers are seeking people who have higher levels of education because jobs are more complex and require greater skill. Furthermore, employment growth generally will be fastest in those occupations requiring the most education and training. For example, professional occupations requiring the most education will show the fastest growth through the 1970's. (See chart 7.)

A high school education has become a standard for American workers. Thus, because of personnel practices in American industries, a high school graduate is in a better competitive position in the job market than a nongraduate.

Although training beyond high school has been the standard for sometime for many professional occupations, many other areas of work require more than just a high school diploma. As new automated equipment is introduced on a wider scale in offices, banks, insurance companies, and government operations, skill requirements are rising for clerical and other office jobs. Employers increasingly are demanding better trained workers to operate complicated machinery.

In many areas of sales work, new developments in machine design, use of new materials, and the complexity of equipment are making greater technical knowledge a requirement for demonstrators; and repairmen must become familiar with even more complicated machines.

Along with the demand for greater education, the proportion of youth completing high school have increased and an even larger pro-

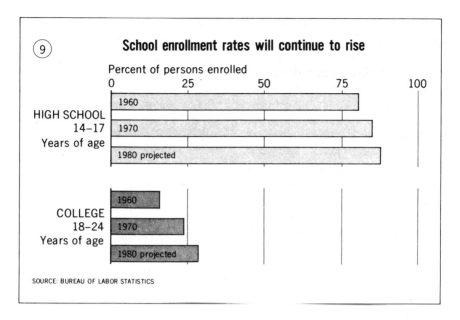

School enrollment rates will continue to rise

⑨

Percent of persons enrolled

HIGH SCHOOL
14–17
Years of age
- 1960
- 1970
- 1980 projected

COLLEGE
18–24
Years of age
- 1960
- 1970
- 1980 projected

SOURCE: BUREAU OF LABOR STATISTICS

portion of high school graduates pursue higher education. (See chart 9.) This trend is expected to continue through the 1970's. In 1980, high school enrollment is expected to be 21.4 million, 7 percent above the 1970 level and college degree credit enrollment is projected at 11.2 million, about 48 percent above the 1970 level of 7.6 million.

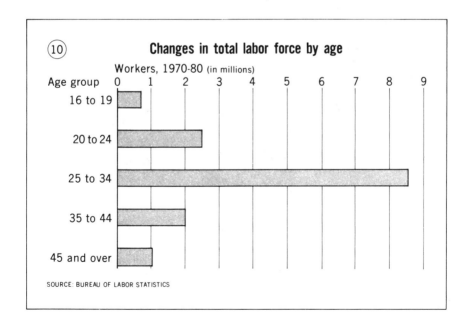

Changes in total labor force by age

⑩

Workers, 1970-80 (in millions)

Age group
- 16 to 19
- 20 to 24
- 25 to 34
- 35 to 44
- 45 and over

SOURCE: BUREAU OF LABOR STATISTICS

The number of persons in the labor force (including those in the Armed Forces) is a related aspect of job competition. Although the number of all workers and job-seekers will increase about 17 percent from 1970 and 1980, the growth in the labor force is really a story of young men and women between 16–34 who will account for about four-fifths of the net increase in workers between 1970 and 1980. (See chart 10.) Thus, in the 1970's the number of young workers will increase and these workers will have more education on the average than new entrants to the labor force in previous years.

With so much competition from young people who have higher levels of education, the boy or girl who does not get good preparation for work, will find the going more difficult in the years ahead. Employers will be more likely to hire workers who have at least a high school diploma. Furthermore, present experience shows that the less education and training a worker has the less chance he has for a steady job, because unemployment falls heaviest on the worker who has the least education. (See chart 11.)

In addition to importance in competing for a job, education is highly valued in the determination of income. In 1968, men who had college degrees could expect to earn more than $600,000 in their lifetime, or nearly 3 times the $214,000 likely to be earned by workers who had less than 8 years of schooling, nearly twice that earned by workers who had 1 to 3 years of high school, and nearly one and two-thirds as much as high school graduates. Clearly the completion of high school pays a dividend. A worker who had only 1 to

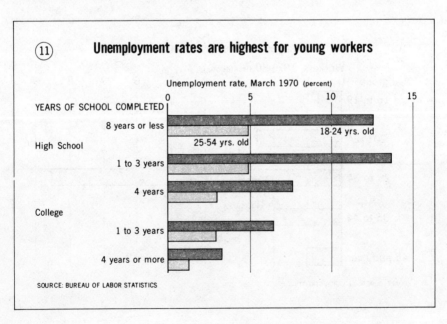

⑪ **Unemployment rates are highest for young workers**

Unemployment rate, March 1970 (percent)

YEARS OF SCHOOL COMPLETED

8 years or less

High School

1 to 3 years

4 years

College

1 to 3 years

4 years or more

18-24 yrs. old

25-54 yrs. old

SOURCE: BUREAU OF LABOR STATISTICS

86

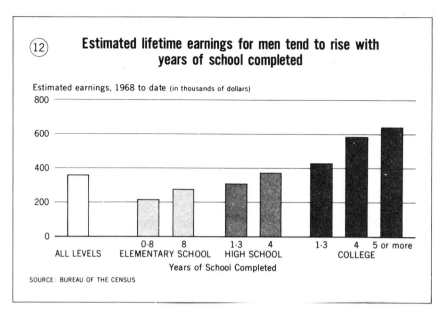

Estimated lifetime earnings for men tend to rise with years of school completed

Estimated earnings, 1968 to date (in thousands of dollars)

Years of School Completed

SOURCE: BUREAU OF THE CENSUS

3 years of high school could expect to earn only about $31,000 more than workers who had an elementary school education, but a high school graduate could look forward to a $94,000 lifetime income advantage over an individual completing elementary school. (See chart 12.)

In summary, young people who have acquired a skill or good basic education will have a better chance at interesting work, good wages, and steady employment. Getting as much education and training as one's abilities and circumstance permit therefore should be a top priority for today's youth.

SECTION III

THE PRIVATE ENTERPRISE SYSTEM

Section III presents an overview of the structure of the private enterprise system now and for the coming two decades through the following articles.

An Overview on the Structure of the Private Enterprise System

Weldon B. Gibson

T HE STRUCTURE of the American economic and business system will be determined during the next two decades by the progress made in resolving several key issues. In this paper, prime attention will be focused on eight basic questions or issues, of which several are understandably international in scope. These eight issues can be summarized as follows:

- *Competing Systems*—attracting greater support around the world for the private enterprise system in competition with the socialist systems.
- *The Corporation*—responding to new economic and social forces while maintaining capabilities for growth and profitability.
- *Multinationalism*—reconciling the needs for multinationalism in economic affairs with the inherent forces of nationalism in various countries.
- *Government-Business*—creating a more effective government-business relationship including a reappraisal of regulatory policies.
- *Balance*—maintaining a carefully adjusted balance of influence and an equitable distribution of income among major sectors of the economy.

An issues paper prepared by Dr. Weldon B. Gibson, Executive Vice President and President, SRI International, Stanford Research Institute, Menlo Park, California.

- *Trade*—reducing barriers to international trade and investment and increasing the competitiveness of American enterprise.
- *Capital*—generating greater amounts of capital to satisfy rising needs—both domestic and international—within business and government.
- *Monetary System*—devising a new international economic and monetary arrangement conducive to an expansion of both domestic production and world commerce.

This paper is being prepared at a turbulent time in the affairs of American business. The United States has taken strong measures to strengthen the domestic economy and is seeking a new international economic arrangement.

In spite of problems within the private enterprise system, the basic structure is sound and viable. It offers great promise to all mankind in the continuing search for greater economic and social progress. The system is responsive to change, and is itself a powerful agent of change in line with values and aspirations of the American public.

Competing Systems

In essence, the so-called western system of private enterprise is based on three main prin-

A LOOK AT BUSINESS IN 1990: A Summary of the White House Conference on the Industrial World Ahead, Washington, D.C., February 7-9, 1972 (U.S. Government Printing Office: 1972 0–467-348) pp. 247-263.

ciples—private ownership of property, decentralized planning and initiatives by business entities, and major emphasis on freedom of the individual in economic pursuits. On the other hand, the eastern or socialist system of enterprise springs from concepts of state ownership over the means of production, central planning and direction of national economies, and subordination of the individual to objectives of the body politic.

These two basic systems are by no means mutually exclusive beyond their conceptual characteristics. In many ways the socialist system has gradually absorbed some of the operating features of the private enterprise system while the latter has been modified in various ways around the world to encompass more and more relationships with government. Many of these permutations can be characterized as "mixed economies" involving a deep intermingling of business and government in economic affairs.

Partnerships

The days are long gone when the private enterprise system could be described in laissez faire terms or by such phrases as "the free working of supply and demand." In all the western nations dedicated to private enterprise principles, a so-called parternership arrangement has evolved in which the activities of corporations and entrepreneurs are intertwined with governmental policies, regulations, and operations.

Each partner in this relationship depends greatly on the other, and in many cases "joint venture" approaches have been created to pursue major national objectives in economic and social fields. Furthermore, state economic planning in various forms has been increasingly embraced in many private enterprise economics.

Proponents of the western principles of economic and business endeavors—especially in the United States—maintain, with high justification, that the private enterprise system is a far more efficient and effective engine for economic and social progress than are the many socialist or state-operated plans. Still further, the central feature of the private enterprise system, the corporation, has been called "the greatest economic and social invention since the Industrial Revolution."

A Global Issue

It is evident on the surface that both the private and state enterprise systems have been highly

In all the western nations dedicated to the private enterprise system, a so-called partnership arrangement has evolved in which the activities of corporations and entrepreneurs are intertwined with governmental policies, regulations, and operations.

successful in many respects—and that both have encountered fundamental problems on many occasions. The true meaning of success, however, depends largely on standards arising from precepts of the two systems and their variations.

The principles of the socialist or state-operated economies are being promoted in varying ways in all or almost all of the private enterprise nations. In scores of other countries around the world, proponents of the two basic systems—and their variations are engaged in a campaign to attract support to competing approaches in the organization of economic affairs. The tide ebbs and flows from time to time in many countries. It has been called a "struggle for men's minds."

The first basic issue greatly affecting the future of western enterprise might well be posed in question form.

Can the private enterprise system of the western world—and in particular the American version of that system—be further developed and presented in such a way as to attract greater support in the United States and elsewhere while at the same time preserving and enhancing its proven strengths?

Some success can—and undoubtedly will be—achieved in this direction during the next two decades, primarily because the private enterprise system is flexible and is itself a powerful instrument for progress in economic and social affairs. Eventual success depends on further adaptation, articulation, and promotion of the system—but more importantly on accomplishments measured in social as well as economic terms.

The future of the private enterprise system around the world depends first and foremost on the United States. Thus, it is vital that the sum total of American economic policies during the next two decades and beyond be aimed at strengthening the system on an international as well as a national basis.

Modern Capitalism

The socialist system of enterprise—with its many variations—attracts support in many nations because it appears to champion progress for the people at large. The mixed-economy concepts often gain support because they present apparent long-term solutions to troublesome economic problems. On the other hand, the private enterprise system often appears to be in a defensive position.

The inherent strengths and benefits of "modern capitalism" in the organization of human affairs are not fully understood by millions of people around the world. The system must be more vigorously promoted. The time has come for the western nations—and especially for private enterprise in the United States—to redefine modern capitalism in phrases that peoples everywhere can easily understand.

This portrayal of the new private enterprise system as one of the great developments of modern times is not an easy task. A "great essay" on emerging concepts of the system could have a far-reaching impact on the world of 1990 and beyond.

International Forces of Change

Any attempt to foresee the issues that by 1990 will call for vital decisions affecting the structure and conduct of business in the United States and other private enterprise nations must be an exercise in "political economy." Diplomacy, economic policy, and business planning can be fully effective only when operated with and through the forces of change. Alfred Marshall once observed that social reform depends on enlisting not only the

---

The inherent strengths and benefits of "modern capitalism" in the organization of human affairs are not fully understood by millions of people around the world.

---

highest but the strongest motives of human behavior.

Profound changes in the way in which nations organize their political and economic activities are evident after every great series of international conflicts. These conflicts reflect, and are largely caused by, underlying forces of social change that often shift the balances of power and economic activity. Like volcanic eruptions, diplomatic strife and war release and reveal the stresses that reshape the world.

The first attempts at economic reconstruction and reorganization after a great military conflict are inevitably influenced by the concepts and emotions generated by the conflict. The new arrangements eventually run their course and must be reshaped. Economic as well as political structures created soon after World War I collapsed in the early 1930s, when the Japanese invaded Manchuria, the Bank of England suspended gold transactions, and the Great Depression began. During this period, the organized labor movement brought a new dimension to the structure of western enterprise.

The basic economic arrangements among the nations following World War II came to an end in mid-1971 when the United States stopped exchanging dollars for gold and so abandoned one of the pivotal roles in monetary and economic affairs. The nation was forced to take strong measures because of a continuing decline in its balance of payments together with an economic recession and problems of unemployment.

Despite its productivity and its foreign assets (greater by far than any country has ever accumulated), rising doubt as to the nation's economic course precipitated a flight of capital and speculation against the dollar. In a mounting crisis, the United States did what every other country has done in similar circumstances; it took the measures necessary to safeguard the national economy.

It is obvious that a great new wave of economic as well as social change is now flowing around the world along with gradual creation of new economic and political relationships for the 1970s and 1980s. The new—and hopefully more flexible—order that emerges undoubtedly will have as significant an impact on the structure and operation of private business as did Bretton Woods arrangements following World War II.

It seems virtually certain that international forces of change will accelerate during the remainder of this century. New and wholly unforeseen trends will engulf the world of business. The life span of each new international order probably will be shorter than that of its predecessor. The leaders of world enterprise can and should help shape the course of events by being even more energetic in formulating and advancing feasible changes in multinational economic arrangements.

The Corporation

The instrument by which the United States has gained its dominant position in the world economy is the business corporation—a very different entity in terms of economic and social responsibility from that which evolved in the 19th century. The corporation has remained an entity whose many owners are limited in their liability. But the number of owners and the size of corporations have grown so much that the relations of the corporation and its management to workers, consumers, government, and the community have changed radically. Among other things, a new class of professional managers has evolved while powerful new interest groups are now exerting pressures on the system.

The mass-transport systems—road, rail, water, and air—that knit the United States into one vast market have facilitated mass production and distribution and enabled corporations to grow. During World War II these facilities were strengthened by a great influx of scientists and engineers as the United States became the Allied arsenal and later the main source of world economic recovery. The momentum thus gained through technology was accelerated during the decades of the 1950s and 1960s. One result is that the nation entered the 1970s with an annual GNP of about one trillion dollars. This enormous force generated by the corporate system is a wellspring for future economic progress throughout the world.

A New Division of Labor

American corporate management extended overseas during the last two decades and became a powerful "third force" in the Allied and ex-enemy countries alike. Its performance engendered both fear and envy but evoked emulation. Europeans, Japanese, Australians, and entrepreneurs in many Asian countries adopted not only the forms but the methods of American corporate enterprise.

During the post-World War II decades, the industrial countries rapidly developed concepts leading to world markets and multinational productive enterprises in which capital, management and technology tended to ignore national boundaries. International finance was not new but international management posed new problems for national governments as well as for business.

What provoked this transcending of national boundaries was the combination of new technology—including communications and transportation—with the needs of countries impoverished by war destruction, economic disorganization, and underdevelopment. The nerve centers of business—monetary and banking systems, transportation and distribution facilities, and power generation—had first to be restored in many countries. By and large they were rebuilt on a new international pattern with international private enterprise—including American companies—at the forefront.

One result of the recent spread of international business is that a great new world division of labor has been ushered onto the economic stage. The process continues slowly but inexorably despite many obstacles that appear from time to time. It will continue—perhaps at an accelerated rate—during the next two decades. The significance of this movement on the structure of American business and the world economy is comparable in many respects to the impact of the first Industrial Revolution.

Social Pressures

Powerful as it has become during the last two decades, the American corporation has never lacked critics both at home and abroad. Until recently, they attacked its values and objectives but did not dispute its efficiency. The burden of their attack was that "things are in saddle and ride mankind."

In recent years the attack has sharpened and

The guiding principles in evaluating the size and ownership question should be to maintain competition and to create an environment conducive to the formation and flourishing of small business as well as large corporations. Arbitrary limits on the size of business do not appear to be in the public interest.

intensified. Moreover, it has encompassed the citadel of corporate strength—efficiency and productivity. The attack has taken many forms—complaints about destruction of natural resources, pollution of the environment, the power exercised by huge enterprise, the weakness of several corporate structures during the late stages of a long inflation, the price and quality of products, and the alleged inability of "owners" to influence the development of their enterprises.

Particularly in the case of the largest corporations, almost all of which now operate in many countries, the disposition of funds among possible claimants has been brought into question. Critics complain that among these claimants—the business itself, government, management, labor, and owners—too much importance is attached to growth and not enough to the distribution of benefits.

That business attaches significance to these and other criticisms is indicated by widespread programs demonstrating real concern for the environment and public needs, and also by appointments to boards of directors intended to give representation to special interests.

The latter trend raises new questions. How many such groups can a business corporation recognize—students, the young labor consumers, minorities, religious sects, political parties? Do such appointments give effective influence to the interest groups or merely increase the power of the corporation itself—and do they make it more difficult or easier for business to operate?

Undoubtedly, these and other social pressures on the private enterprise system will continue unabated during the years to come. However, business will do more than merely respond. Gradually, American corporations are taking new initiatives to serve more fully a range of public interests. This adaptability, flexibility and capacity for leadership are perhaps the most powerful assets in the private enterprise system.

Size and Ownership

One of the most controversial features of the private enterprise system in the United States during the 20th century involves the size and ownership of business corporations. Concern about concentration of power led to "trust-busting" moves at the turn of the century. The issue over ownership and control flamed anew during the Great Depression and has continued in various ways since World War II.

During recent decades, equity ownership of American business has spread enormously among many sectors of the population. In addition, ownership has become increasingly international in character. However, some maintain that effective control in the ownership of American business is shifting in various ways toward financial institutions.

One school of thought in the United States argues that "big business" has become too big and that these concentrations, however measured, should be diminished. The counterview is that the

Costs associated with the endeavors [in the public interest] must be borne by consumers through higher prices, by the general public through higher taxes, by corporations and their owners through lower profits and dividends, or by some combination of these three avenues.

present system is based on competition and that economic realities call for even larger business units in many fields. The thesis is that this permits economies of scale—broadly defined—in the interests of the nation and all citizens.

The question as to the size and ownership has no simple answer. Given the rising scale of capital needs and technology in American business as manufacturing and other physical production become more and more capital intensive, it seems likely that the size of large corporations will continue to increase during the next two decades. It also seems probable that equity ownership will continue to spread through the population—and that financial institutions will remain as great collectors of capital.

The guiding principles in evaluating the size and ownership question should be to maintain competition and to create an environment conducive to the formation and flourishing of small business as well as large corporations. Arbitrary limits on the size of business units do not appear to be in the public interest.

National Priorities

The business corporation is at the heart of the private enterprise system. It can and will respond to national priorities as they become clear to the American people. One of the great new emerging features of the corporation is a special sensitivity to the national mood and changing goals. Organization and operations are being increasingly modified to assist in the pursuit of a wide range of activities in the public interest. Costs associated with these endeavors must be borne by consumers through higher prices, by the general public through higher taxes, by corporations and their owners through lower profits and dividends, or by some combination of these three avenues.

However the various national programs are financed, and if the American enterprise system is to flourish, the need for business profits will surely increase during the next two decades. The profit motive and the profitability of American corporations must be nurtured and strengthened. This in itself should be a matter of high national priority.

The Corporate Issue

In many respects, business corporations of the United States are at the center of a rising tide of currents in the American society. They are urged by some segments of the population to invest more heavily in public programs; they are confronted with rising costs; they face difficulties in raising prices; they encounter more and more competition especially from other nations; they must generate more capital; and they must increase corporate profits.

The forces of these crosscurrents on the corporation are intense, and they probably will increase during the next decade or two. The basic issue reflected by these forces can be summarized in the following question:

Can the corporation respond sufficiently to new economic and social forces while maintaining its capabilities for growth and profitability?

The American private enterprise system is in many respects a marvelous economic framework. The system can be made to be whatever the nation as a whole wants it to be. It can and will respond to national needs. It deserves great and continuous support by the American people.

Multinationalism versus Nationalism

The spread of international business and the application of new technology on a world scale will continue, but the resistance of nationalism will be strong. Whatever may be the outcome of the economic change launched in 1971, governments and business corporations are likely by 1990 to be confronting more than ever before a choice between multinational and national solutions in many aspects of policy.

A new monetary system is evolving. Will it, like other features of international cooperation, remain subject directly to the actions of large nations or groups of nations? Or will sufficient sovereignty be delegated to multinational economic institutions to enable them to function effectively as organs of world government? The issue is fundamental and far-reaching.

The Developing Nations

The industrial countries—especially the United States—use geometrically increasing quantities of raw materials, e.g., petroleum, natural gas, basic metals, and timber. Their own supplies of many natural resources are progressively being reduced. Hence, their great enterprises turn increasingly to untapped reserves in developing areas of the world. Most of the latter countries lack the technology to discover, extract, and market their resources, but they often mistrust and fear the business corporations that have the necessary capital, management, technology, and world markets.

Must corporations especially in the United States turn their research increasingly to the formulation of substitutes as they have developed synthetic fibers? Or is it possible to create multinational enterprises in which the developing countries can participate to a much greater extent on a sound economic basis for both parties—and in the process hasten their mutual development?

International Agreements

Even the basic need of man—food—may be in short supply in many parts of the world if only because of increasing populations and transport problems. In many respects, the most productive areas of the earth are gradually becoming chemical factories using synthetic materials to produce food for human and animal consumption. Even so, it becomes ever more necessary to exploit the oceans as well as the land for food. The problem of international fishing agreements becomes intense. The ocean bed is explored for oil and minerals. International conflicts arise on offshore limits. It is inevitable that these international problems involving both government and business will continue? Or can further bilateral and multilateral agreements be forged to conserve and even enhance the resources of the oceans?

One can easily outline many more issues that call for decisive actions to reconcile international cooperation with national sovereignty. The business corporation—and particularly large American enterprises—will inevitably play a major role in these decisions. They already are an intermediate form of organization in this respect. Multinational enterprise is indeed a potentially powerful force in economic and other forms of cooperation among nations.

Many corporations are larger than some governments—at least in terms of assets and economic volume. However, the laws under which business entities operate are national. When they cross national boundaries, conflicts arise increasingly between the regulatory policies of different governments.

The Reconciliation Issue

The issues and problems in the further internationalism of business—and in creating favorable business environments around the world—are many and varied. They have a major impact on the structure of the private enterprise system in the United States and elsewhere. The impact will surely become more complex and significant during the 1970s and 1980s. The basic question can be posed in these words:

Can the growing needs for multinationalism so necessary for future effectiveness of the private enterprise system on an international scale be reconciled with the forces of nationalism inherent in both industrialized and newly developing nations?

The necessity for multinational solutions in the world economy will grow rapidly through 1990 and beyond. Progress in finding these solutions depends largely on the power and influence of the United States in helping develop a new economic order based on the principles of freer trade, international agreements conducive to the growth of private enterprise, the needs and aspirations of other nations, and the spread of business across national boundaries.

Although success along these lines depends heavily on government-to-government actions, private enterprise in the United States and elsewhere can and should take the lead in many cases. The proposed Pacific Basin Charter on International Investments and other privately sponsored statements on investment principles illustrate the possibilities.

It also seems apparent that the major enterprises of the world, and especially American firms, will increasingly become more truly "world corporations" with a greater denationalization of capital, ownership, and management. This, too, places a heavy demand on multinational solution of business problems.

The move toward "world corporations" is prob-

Disputes between Governments and Business Corporations

International law lacks effective application in many respects; the Court of International Justice does not take jurisdiction over disputes between governments and business corporations. Must the operation of American and other multinational enterprises continue to be restricted by the conflicts of national laws and the absence of international law? Or, will it be possible by 1990 to establish effective forms of world or regional law, and institutions empowered to administer them? Can this be done by the introduction of parallel legislation into national laws of groups of countries supporting the creation of a common code and adequate machinery for its interpretation and administration?

ably the most significant trend that will shape the structure of western private enterprise during the 1970s and 1980s. It should be aided and abetted by American policies—and by business initiatives—to the fullest extent. A set of guiding principles for this movement should be formulated perhaps by the private sector with support from government.

Government-Business Relationships

One of the foremost questions on structure that arises within most of the private enterprise nations has to do with the relationships between government and business. The affiliation appears in various forms ranging from the nationally owned corporations of many European countries to an intertwined system in Japan sometimes referred to as "Japan, Inc."

Within this spectrum—and especially in the United States—is a rising wave of "quasi-public" corporations in which both business and government are often involved in ownership and/or operation of major enterprises. Transportation, communications, and housing are examples.

National Planning

Another feature of the government-business relationship involves national economic planning. Again, the practices of western countries take many forms ranging from formal national plans to more subtle systems such as in Japan.

Many of the industrialized nations in the nonsocialist world are adopting features of the French system of "indicative planning" in which target objectives for business pursuits are set periodically and then monitored through various mechanisms. In general, the United States has confined its national economic planning to periodic forecasts on the likely course of events and to reports on desirable trends in business and in the economy generally. The country may well move during the 1970s and 1980s toward greater national economic planning.

Incomes Policy

Still another significant aspect—and increasingly so—in the government-business relationship involves guidance over prices, wages, rents, profits, and the like. The necessity for such measures usually arises in attempts to control inflation and/or

It seems probable that long before 1990 it will become increasingly necessary to revise the whole body of legislation governing American business so as to enable the private enterprise system to operate more effectively while ensuring pursuit of the public interest.

balance-of-payment problems. In many countries this approach is known as "incomes policy" and to a considerable extent the system has long prevailed in most of the industralized nations.

One line of economic thought in the United States maintains that some form of wage-price control must be sustained for a long time—if not permanently—if inflation and balance-of-payment problems are to be kept within reasonable bounds. Thus, it may be that current "temporary" measures in this respect will continue indefinitely in some form. The basic question is how to achieve a given national objective while preserving maximum freedom of decision for companies, entrepreneurs, and indeed for all citizens.

Regulation

Yet another troublesome element in the government-business affiliation is the increasing amount and degree of public regulation (aside from wages, prices, etc.) over the affairs of corporations large and small alike. Countless agencies at national and state levels have been created to supervise business in such areas as size, competition, services, advertising, product quality, labor relations, employment practices, financing, marketing, and protection of the environment.

It seems probable that long before 1990 it will become increasingly necessary to revise the whole body of legislation governing American business so as to enable the private enterprise system to operate more effectively while ensuring pursuit of the public interest.

In any such review it is obvious that the regulatory organs of government and their extensive body of administrative regulations, most of which have the force of law, must be included. It may be that redrafting the basic legislation can dispense with much of the apparatus of regulation.

In the multinational business world, it is particularly obvious that American enterprise is at some disadvantage with many foreign corporations that do not labor under the same type of policies designed originally to encourage competition and curtail monopolistic practices. The antitrust legislation and judicial interpretations that by 1990 will have covered more than a century surely need to be reviewed. The first attempts to restrict monopoly came in the "horse and buggy" and early railroad age.

In many respects, the need is urgent to reduce the present body of regulation and to rewrite gov-

97

erning legislation to meet the needs of 1990 rather than 1890, 1940 or even 1960. At the same time, new questions arise with the emergence of conglomerates, some of which have proved inefficient and unstable.

Taxation

The whole merger movement and other business operations often arise—or so it is alleged—from tax considerations with perhaps too little regard for productive efficiency or shareholder returns. Together with many other aspects of business law, the taxation of business enterprise calls for reconsideration. The nation must make sure that the tax policies do not unduly hinder growth and service of enterprise, and that they are fair and equitable to all parties involved as well as in the national interest.

This is particularly true with respect to corporations that operate internationally. One view maintains that taxation policies place undue emphasis on the retention of business profits abroad with a consequent accumulation of capital claims that complicates the U.S. balance-of-payments problem and creates controversy in other countries. Another view is that taxation policies in a great creditor nation should encourage even more the investment of capital and retention of earnings in other nations.

Many questions on taxation policies arise, and they will multiply as new national priorities emerge during the 1970s and 1980s. The tax situation can be formulated in such a way as to create greater incentives for business to become even more involved in problems associated with the cities, the physical environment, education, housing, transportation, health, technology and the like. Similar incentives can be used to stimulate the development of economically depressed industries and areas.

How far does the present tax system contribute to or restrict the growth and service of U.S. enterprises at home and abroad? Is it desirable for the nation to build up even greater capital assets in other nations? Should more emphasis be given to repatriation of earnings and to domestic capital formation? Are tax incentives being applied to maximum or optimum advantage to business and the public? What are the trade-offs in benefits over time from alternative taxation policies? These are only a few of the basic questions on business taxation.

The Government-Business Issue

If actions on the government-business question looking toward 1990 are to be based on adequate knowledge and insight, the time is at hand to begin the necessary studies. Thus, another major issue in future structure of the private enterprise system can be outlined in these words:

Can operation of the private enterprise system be made more effective—while fully serving the public interest—by a wide-ranging review and gradual change in government-business relationships including public regulation and taxation of business endeavors?

Under present circumstances, it seems certain that the interfaces between government and business in the United States will increase steadily during the next two decades. At the same time, the evidence suggests that business is becoming ever more socially conscious and motivated to serve the public interest. The key problem is how best to harness the energies of the private corporation in

---

The Government-Business Relationship

One approach to the government-business relationship involves possible creation of a high-level, public-private commission to analyze the needs and opportunities—with recommendations in time concerning both policy directions and ways to create a more effective "partnership" between government and business. This is an enormous undertaking; it must be approached with great care; five or more years may be needed merely for the examination process. Such a bipartisan Presidential body can well be the most important government-sponsored initiative of its type during the next two decades.

---

a combined pursuit of social goals and the usual corporate objectives. It may be that greater reliance can be placed on self-regulation pursuant to public policies maintained under government purview.

Structure of the Economy

It is widely recognized that large corporations occupy a dominant role in the U.S. economy. However, they depend on a vast network of smaller enterprises. General Motors quite rightly advertises that it has 10,000 partners. The relatively small corporation will still have an important place during the next two decades, especially in manufacturing specialized items for the large corporation or for general consumption.

Services

Moreover, an affluent society demands an ever-mounting volume of personal services that give scope and opportunity to the small, even the very small, business entity. Some of the small manufacturers and small businesses achieve enough growth to join the ranks of the large corporations. In the 1960s the electronics industry produced a number of such successes. The 1970s and 1980s will undoubtedly bring other successes.

Demand changes as income grows. The capacity of the human stomach is limited and there are limits also to other human necessities, e.g., clothing and shelter. The limits for both are transcended by the opportunities for variety and display.

The avenues of increasing expenditure on personal services lie especially in the occupations that cater to leisure, education, health, and to other professional pursuits. Shorter working hours and longer holiday periods offer scope for recreation, travel, avocations, and amusements. There will be more sailing and skiing, driving and flying, spectator sports and cultural events, adult education and medical clinics. The demand for conveniences will accelerate.

The American economy is increasingly service-oriented—more so by far than in any other industrialized nation. It seems certain that this trend will continue during the next two decades.

Technological Unemployment

On the other hand, machines increasingly take over the heavy manual and even routine occupations that formerly provided employment for the unskilled. Not only miners, railroad construction workers and laborers, but also typists and bank clerks tend to decline in numbers, at least relatively. Mechanical appliances, including credit cards that can be checked in a computerized clearing system, take over more and more routine labor.

One of the continuing major problems of the 1970s and 1980s is likely to be finding suitable employment for the unskilled and unlearned. Education is already one of the fastest growing occupations, but it must grow faster. It is still underpaid in comparison with the skilled crafts. As hospital and other personal services have grown, and yet have not been able to meet the demand, so educational services will grow and differentiate. Demand will increase for specialized educational skills—testing, remedial reading, special training for young adults and older people, as well as for classroom teaching at all ages. Schools and colleges will be dispersed increasingly through the community to offer a variety of educational services to old and young alike.

Even with this variety of available training and retraining, an increasing number of people, from choice or lack of skills, will be unable to find suitable places amidst technological employment. The problems of finding sufficient work and in developing effective welfare plans are likely to be as troublesome in 1990 as they are today.

The technological unemployment problem is not a symptom of weakness in the American private enterprise system. Rather, it reflects the dynamic effects of a Second Industrial Revolution. If the system is to be preserved and strengthened, more and more ways must be found to provide jobs—and train people for new jobs—within a rising labor force. High unemployment rates over a long period of time are unacceptable.

Organized Labor

The organization of American labor in many respects has been outpaced by events. It remains much as it was several decades ago; but the strength of labor is concentrated in a few strategic industries. Only one quarter of the 80 million workers employed in the United States are trade unionists, primarily in the skilled trades. Over the years the trade unions have gained a great measure of influence not only over wages, hours, and working conditions, but also over recruitment and allocation of employment particularly in light of possible innovations that reduce—at least relatively—the number of jobs available.

One result of this trend, more important than the leverage afforded in wage matters, is to complicate and make more expensive the introduction of labor-saving technology and higher productivity. Notable examples are afforded by difficulties in re-allocating labor on the railroads and by the price involved in the introduction of containers on the docks.

The United States is a country of high labor cost compensated to some extent—but not sufficiently—by high productivity. By 1990, if present trends continue, segments of the labor force that attempt to increase costs more rapidly than productivity may find themselves and their industries in increasingly severe difficulties. There is a case, therefore for re-examining the balance between organized labor and the economy generally—and especially corporate enterprise.

Organized labor itself would be well served by a self-sponsored study of its own long-range policies and position in the balance-of-forces within the American economy, and on ways in which labor can best advance the common interest of the private enterprise system.

It seems clear that the United States is moving toward 1990 with a network of laws and regulations devised to meet the problems of earlier days. Technology is vastly different. The patterns of production have changed and will change more drastically still. But the rules governing the association of men in organizing and discharging services remain much the same in many cases. Nearly half a century ago, an American philosopher pointed out that heavy labor had been lifted from the shoulders of men and transferred to the waterfalls. What is being shifted now is the routine.

Labor developments during the next twenty years probably will raise questions that have not hitherto been faced in the relations of government workers with public officials. Teachers, technicians, clerks, sanitary workers, police—possibly even professional soldiers—will be more highly organized, though not necessarily in trade unions as now known. They will gain increasing influence over their wages and working conditions, recruitment, promotion, and pensions. The authority of management in government services probably will be diluted. There will be more experiments in public corporate structures such as that on which the Post Office is now embarked.

Income Distribution

One basic issue in the structure of the American economy involves the distribution of income and influence among segments of the population. Agriculture remains a strong force in the economy even though the number of people engaged in agricultural pursuits has been greatly reduced. Consumer groups are on the rise as are many other special interests. Their views—along with those of business, government, and labor—must be heard in the system. The values inherent in the labor movement and in collective bargaining must be preserved and strengthened. Wages must rise but productivity must rise as much or more.

It seems apparent that a major issue during the next two decades will involve the income distribution problem. It can be summarized as follows:

Can the free enterprise system as now constituted with its three main foci of power—business, labor and government—bring about a more balanced relationship between these forces so as to enhance productivity while stimulating economic and social progress for the American people as a whole?

The adjustment process among economic and social forces in a democracy is a never-ending task. The United States has been quite successful in balancing the requirements of business, the needs of labor, the interests of government, and the desires of other groupings. The strength and future of the private enterprise system to 1990 and beyond depend greatly on continuing refinements in the system. Quantum jumps in progress over short periods of time are unlikely. The process of change and adaptation must be continuous with leadership at national, state, and local levels.

Organized labor itself would be well served by a self-sponsored study of its own long-range policies and position in the balance-of-forces within the American economy, and on ways in which labor can best advance the common interests of the private enterprise system.

Trade Currents

Already the scientific and technological revolution has diverted the currents of world trade into new channels. Many commodities, such as nitrates, have virtually disappeared from international markets. Ocean carriers have been transformed. The export of bunker coal on which British tramps depended for their outward freight is gone; but bigger ships carry bulk cargoes of coal from the United States to Europe and from Australia to Japan. Petroleum in still larger ships is carried from "where you find it" to European and Japanese and American ports. Networks of pipelines are laid over mountains and under seas. Anything that can be pumped in liquid form or suspended in water goes increasingly through pipes. The "transportation revolution" is indeed a significant factor in both domestic and international commerce.

Industrial Location

New methods of transport are shifting the location of industry in the United States and elsewhere as the railroads and automobiles did in earlier days. Cheap bulk transport by pipeline and large ships has gone far to reduce not only the advantages of proximity to raw materials, and even to markets, but also for what Alfred Marshall called "the momentum of an early start." In many cases, it has virtually become advantageous to lack raw materials and thus be forced to use bulk imports in heavy manufacturing. On the export side, container ships increasingly carry finished manufactures in bulk.

By 1990, therefore, the problems that have led to a revival of protectionism may be even more acute. Many manufacturing plants in American

---

Unless the developing countries and the great industrial corporations can reconcile their problems, there is little hope that the poorer countries will share fully in an expansion of trade that hopefully will continue in the 1970s and 1980s.

---

industries are in the wrong locations to take advantage of the new maritime revolution. They may shift in time to where they can gain greater access to cheap materials and mass markets. The shift from small riverports and narrow waterways as well as inland locations may ultimately leave many "Jarrows" and "Clydes" with decaying industries

and unemployment. More and more regional—as well as city—redevelopment programs will be needed. The forces of economic geography upon location of enterprises are inexorable in the long run.

Trade Expansion

Unless the developing countries and the great industrial corporations can reconcile their problems, there is little hope that the poorer countries will share fully in an expansion of trade that hopefully will continue in the 1970s and 1980s. Petroleum is found in unlikely places and can be made from coal, which is found everywhere. The common mineral ores—iron, tin, copper, lead, zinc, bauxite—are widespread. No country has a monopoly and substitution possibilities are numerous.

Unless the developing countries are willing to enter into arrangements that will serve their needs and purposes and yet be competitive, their natural resources will not enter fully into international commerce and they will remain poor. On the other hand, unless the great corporations increasingly meet justifiable needs of the developing countries, they will not gain access to what may prove to be the best and cheapest sources of supply.

Trade in food and agricultural raw materials is already diminished by agricultural protectionism. Prices have diverged (and fluctuated) so greatly in potential import markets that removal of quotas and trade agreements that govern the remaining trade would wreck subsidized domestic production. Yet it seems probable that, in the United States as well as the European Common Market, urban consumers will apply increasing pressure against higher and higher food prices. This could lead in time to substantial modification of quotas, to the mutual benefit of consumers and overseas producers. The latter, however, do not include the less-developed countries whose inefficient methods cannot meet the standards or the price competition of such food exporting countries as Canada, Australia, New Zealand, the Argentine, and the United States.

The trade that is growing and—unless hindered by exchange restrictions and controls—will continue to grow is the exchange of machines and equipment, specialized manufactures and manufacturing materials, semi-finished and even raw materials, among the industrial countries.

Industrialization is often a misused word. It is just as applicable to agriculture, forestry, and mining as to manufacture. The United States, using heavy earth-moving, planting, cultivating, chemical treating, reaping, and threshing machines—and with economies of scale—is able to out-produce the countries of hand-labor and compete on the world market for such products as wheat, corn, cotton, rice, and soybeans. In the same way, by use of sophisticated equipment and external economies such as transport, it can often produce minerals more cheaply than countries that lack the means to extract their richer resources efficiently.

The trade between the developed countries, therefore, covers a wide range of products, finished and unfinished. By a series of tariff reductions, of which the latest was the so-called Kennedy Round, negotiated under the auspices of G.A.T.T., duties on manufactured goods have been reduced considerably. This was one of the most important trade developments during the 1960s.

The lodgment of U.S. factories and the introduction of new methods of corporate management in Europe, along with the rapid development of Japan, have created vast new markets. Stabilizing of exchange rates and progressive removal of the impediments to international capital movements under the Bretton Woods agreements facilitated a

---

The U.S. future in world trade in industry after industry is being written now in the time and money spent on scientific research.

---

major increase in trade among the industrial countries in the 1950s and 1960s.

Trade Issues

Stubborn obstacles remained, however, during the recent trade expansion, and they were often at the expense of U.S. exports. Principal among the impediments is the steady rise in nontariff barriers and ever-rising prices for American products and services. These handicaps, added to defense and other overseas commitments, eventually proved intolerable and led to the abrupt measures of mid-1971.

It is too soon to know whether the multilateral decisions of late 1971, including a devaluation of the dollar and removal of the temporary surcharge on dutiable imports to the United States, will lead

to a new and more effective international trading system. Hopefully, within a reasonably short period international agreements can be reached on the full framework and mechanisms of a new parity system. Restoration and further expansion of the great industrial markets depend on progress in solving currency and other major trade restriction issues of the early 1970s.

In any case, the trade issues will not be fully resolved by 1980 or 1990. The conflict between protective measures promoted by particular interests, but using the persuasive arguments of nationalism, and the advantages to be derived from freer trade, has been evident for centuries. It will not be solved in one generation.

Trade between East and West is growing rapidly; the United States is showing new interest in its potential. Questions will arise frequently about the course of events. The basic issue will not be resolved by 1990, if ever. However, American interests including the business system are well served by a "bridge-building" policy.

Scientific Research

The United States must face the challenge of new competition in one industry after another. There was a time when the nation was primarily an agricultural community with the tremendous export advantage of vast new areas of virgin land. The scale on which it could produce brought into use many new devices that led the way to modern agriculture. This, in turn, led the way in many areas of transport and manufacture—with large markets making possible efficient methods based often on inventions borrowed from other lands.

After World War II, the United States became the leading country in basic as well as applied research, while continuing to be adept in commercial development. The technological movement has since spread throughout the industrialized nations. Their efficiency in production and distribution has grown tremendously. More and more American industries have felt the impact.

The path to future prosperity is through research aimed at the development of new products and new industries. The industries that have shown the greatest trade growth in the recent past are technological in character, e.g., electronics. The industries of future growth such as nuclear energy will be even more dependent on scientific research.

The present scientific industries benefited enormously from the basic research that was an essential part of the war and postwar effort. There is a meaningful correlation between scientific research and industrial growth. The U.S. future in world trade in industry after industry is being written now in the time and money being spent on scientific research. Even greater investment in such pursuits must be stimulated in the national interest.

The Current Trade Issue

The principal issue facing the United States in world trade during the next two decades can be summarized in these words.

Within a new international economic order, can the major barriers to trade and investment by American corporations be reduced to a basis of equality with other nations, and can U.S. industries with export potential be made sufficiently competitive in cost and prices?

The United States is launched on a course aimed at resolving this basic problem at least to some extent. It is highly important that a new international system be developed within a relatively short period of time. If this does not occur, impacts on the structure of American business may be far-reaching.

It seems likely that a new and more effective—and flexible—system will emerge in due course and usher in another sustained period of international trade expansion beneficial to the United States. No economic issue is of greater importance to the American economy and enterprise.

The Need for Capital

Karl Marx was right in describing the western economic system that developed in the 19th century as "capitalism." The difference between rich and poor countries is most evident in the surplus of production over current needs that can be devoted to future production. This surplus takes many forms. It provides consumption and social as well as industrial capital. Housing and public buildings, freeways, automobiles and trucks, television sets, and hospitals are evidence of productive capacity created by setting aside past production for future use.

The business corporation has proven to be an efficient instrument for the formation of capital. It

Non-Tariff Trade Barriers

A great need exists around the world for an organized multinational assault on nontariff trade barriers. The timing for such an exercise must await a more favorable international environment. Positive results are needed during the 1970s. The United States should bring its full influence to bear on this problem. The situation calls for a new "Round" of nontariff negotiations matching the tariff "Round" of the 1960s. An early announcement of American intentions in this respect could be helpful.

gathers large and small savings and puts them to productive use. As profits are made, a substantial proportion is retained for maintenance and expansion of the operation. A corporation unable to maintain and add to its capital soon disappears from the industrial scene.

As a country grows in wealth, it must set aside more capital to meet the demands of a population increasing in numbers and desiring higher living levels. This is particularly the case in a period of rapidly advancing technology. By 1990, the capital needs of the United States will be many times what they are in the early 1970s.

The changing industrial technology calls for new management methods and higher levels of skills in the labor force; but it also demands more complex and expensive machines, and machines to make machines. Each new generation of airplanes, locomotives, trucks, and buses is more expensive than the last.

The demand for higher living levels is not simply a demand for more goods and luxuries. It is also a demand for higher quality not just of goods for personal consumption but for the social capital that creates the environment in which we live.

Many large corporations already devote large amounts of capital to control pollution and to preserve the countryside. Pipelines are buried, grounds are landscaped, effluents are treated, smoke and gases are captured and treated or re-used, noise is reduced. But an alerted and alarmed public is now organized to demand a much greater effort to clean the water and air, prevent disfigurement of the landscape, and preserve the forests and mountains.

To achieve these and other desirable ends will require large capital expenditures by corporations and public agencies. The costs must be met largely by consumers and taxpayers. Even the industrially advanced nations are becoming increasingly short of capital in relation to mounting needs—consuming or investing almost immediately what they produce.

The need for greater capital generation in the United States is obvious. The requirements undoubtedly will rise steadily throughout the next two decades. Thus, a growing issue can be summarized as follows:

Can new economic policies and incentives be created that will generate greater amounts of capital for both private and public investments without unduly restricting a continuing rise in the living levels of the American people?

The shortage of capital in relation to rising needs is a relatively new experience for the American people. Thus the pressure rises for reductions in government spending abroad particularly for military and foreign-aid purposes. It seems likely that during the next two decades a greater proportion of current production will have to be shifted from consumption to capital formation.

If this be true, ways must be found to encourage and enable both business and individuals to increase their rates of capital accumulation. Indices of capital formation within companies—and for the nation as a whole—must increasingly be brought to public attention.

Money and the Balance of Payments

All the issues that confront business enterprise—national and international—come to a focus in the monetary system, which is now almost entirely a system of managed credit. Money is the common denominator, the unit of account, in which values are measured, compared, and exchanged. Taxes and all the relations between government and business, the distribution of goods and services, the rewards to those who contribute to their production—all take place through the medium of credit.

The long prosperity of the postwar period—a quarter of a century during which production and exchange expanded with only slight hesitations and no major setbacks—depended largely on the certainty with which credit was organized, nationally and internationally. The trend of prices was mildly upward but in most of the world the units of account—dollars, pounds, francs, pesos, and many other national currencies—were relatively stable in purchasing power and in relation to each other.

There were occasional breaks in this stability when countries allowed their credit creation to outrun productivity; it was not until the late 1960s that prices began to rise sharply in the United States. At the same time the external symptoms of inflation began to appear in a rapidly worsening balance of payments.

For twenty-five years the United States has underwritten to a major extent the world-wide credit expansion used in rebuilding economies and expanding international trade. It did so without impairing confidence in the dollar. The price of gold—$35 an ounce—was the fixed point on which the values of other currencies were based. Even though the purchasing power of the dollar fell steadily, the decline was in small increments and did not alarm traders and alert speculators—nor indeed business—until it accelerated in the late 1960s.

A New Monetary System

This period of relative stability came to an abrupt end in mid-1971. The United States no longer exchanges gold for dollars at a fixed price. The fixed rates at which currencies were exchanged gave way—at least temporarily—to floating rates with no fixed point of reference.

The theoretical assumption was that the price of one currency in terms of other currencies could float freely until it found its own level. But, in fact, all are interdependent and all are managed to some extent. An exchange rate is a ratio—it always involves at least two currencies and therefore two governments trying to manage it. There is really no such thing as a "clean float" over an extended period—governments do not stand idly by while the value of their currencies and thereby all the external economic transactions of their corporations and citizens are subjected severely to the

It seems likely that during the next two decades a greater proportion of current production will have to be shifted from consumption to capital formation.

stresses of an uncontrolled market.

So as to control the symptoms of inflation, the United States instituted a price freeze within its own borders and imposed drastic restrictions on external transactions. The surcharge on dutiable imports reversed the freer trading policies that were instituted in 1934 by the Reciprocal Trade Agreements Act. These external restrictions were temporary bargaining counters intended to persuade other countries to remove obstacles to U.S. exports and take a greater share in the common defense and aid programs of the free world.

It is hazardous to postulate what may be the final outcome of this bargaining and what sort of monetary and credit arrangements will emerge by 1980 or 1990. Many governments are allowing their currencies to appreciate in terms of the dollar by varying amounts. There has been limited response with respect to trade barriers and other governmental actions. Indeed there have been some threats of retaliation, but the latter seems unlikely so long as multinational negotiations offer promise for a long-term solution.

In these circumstances no one can foretell the immediate or long-term future on American enterprise. It is probable that the loosening of credit and reduction of taxes within the United States, at a time when inventories are low, defense economies have been achieved, and many long-term labor contracts have been concluded, will bring early economic recovery. But the impact of the American program on other countries has been severe, and also a "shock to confidence" in some cases. It could end in an international recession during the 1970s from which the United States would not be exempt. This is highly unlikely. Another possibility is neither sustained expansion nor recession, but some of both, followed by renewed inflation. National and international policy must—and undoubtedly will—be aimed at long-term healthy economic growth.

Although predictions for the short term are not feasible, it seems reasonable to expect that a rather more flexible system of exchange stability will accrue from the "IMF Agreements" of late 1971. In due course currencies probably will be allowed to fluctuate within a wider range than one percent of agreed parities, and depreciation (a euphemism for devaluation) will be made easier for countries that create credit beyond their productivity. Such assumptions carry with them the expectation of controlled inflation—a gently rising level of prices—which is in fact a practical method of re-

ducing the burdens of external debt carried by most countries.

The crucial issue is to determine who will do the controlling. Under the so-called gold standard of the late 19th century, which was really a sterling standard, exchange rates were kept stable by actions of the Bank of England in the London money market. Under the later gold-exchange standard, which was really a dollar standard, exchange rates were kept stable in a period of slow inflation largely by the United States permitting an outflow of dollars even after its gold supply had declined to a low level.

A new system for the 1970s and 1980s must necessarily be multinational. It probably will be operated by a modified International Monetary Fund or whatever institution takes its place. Such an institution may have larger powers but will inevitably be controlled by nations that have the largest trading and investment interests.

Gold may still have a role to play as a fixed point on which currencies can be pegged, even though the overwhelming bulk of transactions will involve credit and new instruments such as the Special Drawing Rights. The amount of gold now held privately—approximately equal to the total reserves of central banks—and its free price demonstrate that it has not lost its appeal. By 1990 gold will still be in demand for monetary as well as industrial purposes and its price probably will be higher.

Pressure for Imports

A question arises as to what will happen to the large foreign holdings of U.S. corporate enterprise. The value of production of American firms abroad is at least four times the value of exports from the United States. At the same time, the total value of corporate holdings abroad exceeds $70 billion. These holdings have been built up largely by ploughing back retained profits—but this cannot continue indefinitely. If increasing profits are to be brought back to shareholders in the United States —as eventually they should—imports must increase substantially.

To correct its recent adverse balance of trade, the United States has increased restrictions on capital exports. It has also imposed new restrictions on imports. The "turnaround" aimed at would restore a substantial surplus of exports over imports; but in the long run a creditor country has no way of collecting interest on its loans as well as dividends from its enterprises except by importing more goods and services. It can encourage foreigners to invest in the United States and Americans to travel abroad using foreign services. It can use foreign ships and planes, import foreign petroleum, steel, automobiles, cameras, textiles, meat, wool, butter, and other goods. But domestic industries affected by import competition understandably struggle to protect themselves.

An import surplus is more easily accepted when both imports and exports are increasing steadily. It is difficult to permit an excess of imports when men and women are out of work because of measures dictated by fear of high inflation. For international as well as domestic reasons, it is usually more expedient to tolerate controlled inflation than to accept the necessity for deflation. To achieve controlled inflation, however, government and business and labor must work closely together.

The ultimate question or issue on structure of the private enterprise system in the United States and elsewhere during the next two decades can be summarized as follows:

Can a new international credit system—with all of its requirements for sound economic policies especially by the major nations—be created and administered in such a way as to stimulate a new wave of national economic expansion and international trade and investment during the next two decades?

Several years may be needed to work out the details of a new international arrangement. The trend of events should emerge much sooner. This will reduce uncertainty in international business; the outlook is hopeful.

It is probable that by 1990 means will have been devised whereby the economy of the United States can operate more effectively based on interaction of organized labor and business management with government and other groups in what might be described—as Strindberg defined marriage—as a system of "antagonistic cooperation."

The task of government in this respect is to create the cradle and an environment for nourishment of the private enterprise system. The task of business is to seize opportunities, respond to needs and defend as well as promote the system. The task of labor is to assist in enhancing national productivity.

These pursuits should be the prime objectives of national economic and business policy during the 1970s and 1980s. ∎

The Structure of the Private Enterprise System

Walter E. Hoadley

"WHAT AMERICANS do not understand they seldom support" has always been a rather trustworthy principle. Applied to the American business system it follows that the future rests heavily on how well our system is understood and how relevant it is, especially for young men and women.

I am optimistic about what lies ahead. I am also certain we have a stiff fight on our hands to preserve our market-enterprise system and to keep it vital and alive for the American people.

I shall present my conclusions at the outset.

1. History and a careful analysis of current trends point to a potential weakening of our system by 1990, and a great loss of individual freedom unless undermining forces are checked.

2. The American system of enterprise is under major attack from within and without. It now requires reinforcement of public understanding of why and how it works in its interest.

3. Survival of our system will be largely determined by how well it can adjust to meet both the key qualitative and quantitative problems emerging in a rapidly changing national and world environment.

Address by Dr. Walter E. Hoadley, Executive Vice President and Chief Economist, Bank of America NT&SA.

4. Some changes in the characteristics of our private enterprise system will be required to meet the challenges ahead, including at least the following:
   a. The average American must be shown more convincingly that he or she has a personal stake in our system.
   b. Young people, better educated and more critical than ever, must become more directly involved in defining and solving our society's problems.
   c. A better way must be found to combine and strengthen the separate forces of business and government in the joint achievement of overall public goals and solution of attendant problems.
   d. More effective means must be developed to establish viable priorities in our country.
   e. To minimize destructive polarization, the will of the majority must make greater provision for the needs and aspirations of the minority.

5. Special government financial programs and unduly protective regulations or any other developments must not be permitted to weaken market competition as the principal economic force in our system.

6. Wherever we want to be in 1990, we will not get there without more profit-motivated business organizations, including large ones that can prove they have something valuable to contribute to the public at home and abroad.

A LOOK AT BUSINESS IN 1990: A Summary of the White House Conference on the Industrial World Ahead, Washington, D.C., February 7-9, 1972,(U.S. Government Printing Office: 1972 0—467-348) pp.264-271.

107

Which Way Are We Headed?

In looking to the probable structure of our American business system in 1990, even casual observation of present direct controls, and some sense of the trend toward greater government intervention in economic affairs can only alert us to danger of a progressive loss of individual and management decision-making freedom in coming years. This is also soberly supported by the historical perspective of a distinguished American business statesman of the recent past, the late H. W. Prentis, Jr., President of the Armstrong Cork Company during World War II and shortly thereafter. Mr. Prentis' scholarly research uncovered Ten Stages in the Cycle of Civilization: Bondage (i.e., loss of freedom), Spiritual Faith, Courage, Freedom, Abundance, Selfishness, Complacency, Apathy, Fear, Dependency (and back to Bondage).

Although this cycle analysis was rooted in past civilizations, Mr. Prentis was concerned that it could apply to the future of our country. On this scale, where do we stand? It may be significant that almost every person to whom I've directed this question has replied, "The United States does seem to be moving along this ten-stage cycle and probably is now somewhere between abundance and fear."

If so, our people and our system face an ever-mounting threat and challenge. To avoid dependency and bondage—perhaps by 1990—will require new spiritual faith and courage resting on a new base of widely accepted socioeconomic goals plus a strong determination to meet them. History says we will not escape bondage. Only by widespread public recognition of the imminent threat before us and by adding new dynamic dimensions to our system can we prevent a progressive loss of individual freedom.

Our American Business System is under Attack

Evidence continues to accumulate that American youth, including subteenagers, among others, is increasingly critical of our system. Many say, and seem to believe, that it is not working well. Individuals my age and older are tempted to respond with "so what's new if youths are critical?" But I am convinced that there is a difference now. Today we are dealing with a generation of educated young men and women who have been taught to be critical and who have grown up in an environment where they have come to take economic security pretty much for granted. Television has made them firsthand participants in society's problems—at least they feel so.

What are youth's criticisms? Many seem certain that our system causes—or in fact needs—war to perpetuate itself. Our system is held to be inflexible and controlled by so-called power structures, business in particular, which are unresponsive to the needs and wants of youth. All too often critics seem convinced that prompt solutions to society's ills are now impossible through the normal workings of the system.

Older people who have taken the time to discuss these and many related issues with young men and women are fully aware they are being challenged by exceedingly bright and idealistic youths who know our system's problems only too well. Perhaps a majority has been led erroneously to believe simplistic solutions are possible. Commonly, young people accept no responsibility to help find solutions. Moreover, they often look to business managements and other leaders as "the geniuses who got us into this mess" to provide the answers, contending that, "If *they* cared, *they* could quickly solve most of the difficulties."

Much could and should be said on several points: that our educational system and the media for a generation or more have pounded home chiefly our shortcomings and seldom our strengths; that relevant comparisons anywhere in the world demonstrate the overwhelming good in our system vs. others; and that youth is more free to speak and act here than elsewhere. For whatever reason, our American system is undeniably under greater attack from within and without than ever.

How can youths be expected to support a system they obviously do not understand? Should we really be surprised at their prevailing attitudes?

It has always been good sport to criticize Uncle Sam, but now it takes little courage for almost anyone to do so. We are held to be beyond the zenith of our power. Neither we nor any other single nation will dominate the world of 1990 as much as the United States has during recent decades. The U.S. public now fully realizes that we cannot—and never could—police, feed, and heal the world, and that the dollar is no longer the symbol of impregnable strength. Hence, there is a chorus of boos—frankly, because we are not perfect. But who is? Our system and our nation are being attacked by idealists and critics who knowingly or naively define our system's goals and standards so as virtually to ensure our failure to achieve them.

Frankly, the offensive against the American business system is so strong, and the efforts to defend it so weak, at times, that it is almost a mystery how the system manages to survive even now.

Business managements have a long and rather sad history of defaulting to their critics the responsibility for telling what our system is and what it accomplishes for the people. Executives in general have shunned direct involvement in "dirty" politics. Few have comprehensive plans to take their views directly to the voters. The paradox is that most business managements believe deeply in the merits of our system for all people, yet almost never feel they should try—or even have a chance—to "sell" their story in support of our system directly to the public. No wonder business has some credibility problems with the public.

Government spokesmen seldom are of help in this regard, probably because it has usually seemed politically attractive to strike out against business and the profit system (except when the nation faces a major crisis). Here again, criticism of our profit-and loss-system should not be surprising. Less than 30 percent of the elected officials in our nation have ever had any firsthand experience in private business, and considerably less in managing one. How can government leaders be expected to support what they do not understand?

What percentage of our teachers in primary and secondary schools or professors in our colleges and universities has had firsthand knowledge of how the American enterprise system and business really work? A small fraction, I am sure. How can we expect our educators to support a system that, in fact, they do not understand?

Perhaps here is a vital clue as to the durability of the American private enterprise system. It must rest on some deep, almost unconscious, spirit among our people, i.e., an understanding that comes through experience and a fleeting evaluation of the alternatives that all look suspect. Freedom, after all, is something an American only begins to appreciate in the prospect of its loss or in a visit to a place where the contrast can be seen, such as East Berlin or the DMZ in Korea. But, how much longer can we count on this underlying, intuitive spirit to defend our system from attack? Reinforcement of public understanding seems mandatory to demonstrate much more clearly how and why it works in the general interest, especially in relation to all other systems.

What Are the Key Problems Ahead for Our System to Solve?

How well our American enterprise system can survive and function in practice to 1990 will be determined largely by how well we meet some key problems ahead. What are they? My list now includes:

1—To improve the quality of life amidst probably slower economic growth.
2—To better balance population, jobs, and the labor force.
3—To control inflation.
4—To achieve less congested urban living (here is where our system will meet some of its most severe tests).
5—To increase creative productivity.

At first mention, most of these problems seem intangible and even nebulous. Indeed they are; that is the rub. Our American enterprise system over decades has been honed on meeting principally quantitative economic problems, particularly of the growth, employment, and GNP type. Putting men, materials, money, and minds to work in a market system for a tangible purpose has produced vastly superior living standards for our

---

Our system and our nation are being attacked by idealists and critics who knowingly or naively define our system's goals and standards so as virtually to ensure our failure to achieve them.

---

people and remarkable managerial skills, which have been carried across the world.

To be blunt, this is not good enough for the next two decades. Much more will be required. Our system will have to demonstrate its ability to achieve qualitative skills and output, now essentially taken for granted.

In short, we are on the threshhold of a new age where economic priorities and change, while still vital, will be subsumed in a system where social, psychological, and related noneconomic change and goals will become increasingly prominent. Longer range interests, especially of business, will become more critical in the entire decision-making process. The structure of our business system will

---

What percentage of our teachers in primary and secondary schools has had firsthand knowledge of how the American enterprise system and business work? A small fraction, I am sure. How can we expect our educators to support a system that, in fact, they do not understand?

---

not only have to be adapted positively to meet these developments, but there must also be vigorous leadership that understands the dynamics of American enterprise for the system to endure as we know it now.

Required Changes in the Structure of Our System

Frankly, all this will not be simple or easy for Americans. However, the blueprint for needed changes in certain characteristics of our system seems reasonably clear:

The average American must be shown more convincingly that he or she has a more personal stake in the health of our profit-and-loss system and, hence, more responsibility for it.

Many profit-sharing plans are already in operation or under discussion. No single or simple idea to broaden the base of income or ownership in enterprises can be expected soon, but more vigorous efforts will be essential to accomplish these ends. To increase direct public participation in our system, and to improve understanding about how it functions, several thought-provoking, albeit incomplete, suggestions have been advanced.

Lawyer Louis Kelso, for example, has proposed a Second Income Plan by which employees would be able to acquire a growing equity ownership

in their companies. Hopefully, in time, they would derive a sizeable dividend or second income to supplement their primary wages or salaries. Many unresolved issues involving inflationary financing and public attitudes toward equity holdings, however, remain.*

Publisher-inventor John Perry has offered a National Dividend Plan by which total corporate income-tax payments would be channeled into a public fund to be paid equitably to voters. The objective would be to demonstrate the role of profits and enterprise in the United States. Both conceptual and practical bottlenecks still must be faced.**

It is also clear that not all Americans will respond positively to financial incentives. Many derive their satisfactions on less economic grounds. Hence, broader participation in the benefits of our system must mean more nonfinancial as well as financial involvement and rewards, plus a greater sense of responsibility to help provide acceptable results from the system. The crucial question remains: How can we convincingly bring more Americans into the mainstream of understanding and participation in our system as it will operate in the future?

Young people, at an earlier age, must become more directly involved in the realities of defining and solving our society's problems.

On all sides we hear complaints from young people that they want "in" our system. I am convinced their request has merit. We must warn them, however, that "in" means to shoulder more real responsibility for problem solving. When they leave their spectator seats and come on the field to play, their Monday-morning quarterbacking days will be over.

Innumerable programs already are under way to give more young people some practical business experience. But few provide a solid opportunity to find out how our system—or any system—really functions in reaching decisions and affecting the lives of individuals.

A need clearly exists to devise a supplement to our educational process to give instructors and students alike opportunities to observe—and more importantly—to take a direct part in everyday business operations. This is no brain-washing sug-

Two-Factor Theory: The Economics of Realty, Louis O. Kelso and Patricia Hetter, Random House, New York, 1968.

**The National Dividend, John H. Perry, Jr., I. Obolinsky Publishing Co., 1964.*

gestion; it is an attempt to confront youth and educators with more reality. I have tested this practice so often myself that I can almost always anticipate the comment: "Oh, I never realized how complicated running a business really is. I thought it would be much easier to make a profit."

I am convinced much would be gained if each business field, including banking, offered to provide the essential elements for a classroom curriculum on "You Manage This Business." The objective would be to encourage teachers and students everywhere to try their hand at various decision-making levels of business of all sizes. Knowledgeable business people, of course, should serve as resource personnel to make the experience meaningful for every participant. The business representatives would, I am sure, also gain tremendously from the experience.

A better way must be found within our system to combine and strengthen the separate forces of business and government in the joint achievement of overall public goals and solution of attendant problems.

Many forces seem to be driving government and business closer together, but the gears are far from meshing. At present, government seems more and more nonprofit oriented, with little evident concern that profit margins in business are historically quite low. Accordingly, it is naive to believe that our private profit-making system is either working satisfactorily or its future can be safely assumed. Much more important, inasmuch as the key problems to be faced by our system to 1990 definitely involve both government and business interests and responsibilities, they can hardly be solved by strict adherence to our present government-business cooperation ground rules that deemphasize profits, sometimes to the point of their elimination.

A new system of government-business ground rules is simple to state in principle, but much more difficult to put into practice. In facing the complex qualitative and quantitative problems ahead,

---

It should be recognized that over a period of time what is now a social cost requiring full government (plus limited private special) funding may become a readily accepted economic cost for total private underwriting.

---

we must find professional and legal ways to separate economic from social costs on any given project. Private enterprise and private capital must be permitted to earn a normal competitive profit in return for assuming economic risks, while government carefully assumes the social costs or public risks without a profit return on the public capital invested—all in the same complex project.

This will require a whole new approach to accounting, cost analysis, and taxation. The need is urgent. If our nation is to combine the best elements of our system, working vigorously to solve the key problems ahead, we must recognize promptly that some basic changes must be made. With greater public understanding, government leaders must be made to feel more politically secure in espousing private profit; business managers must be encouraged to employ their highly successful profit-making techniques—all in the direct public interest.

At the outset it should be recognized that over a period of time, what is now a social cost requiring full government (plus limited private special) funding may become a readily accepted economic cost for total private underwriting. But no business alone can hope to cover a major social cost and survive.

Again, we can take encouragement from some limited beginnings. In at least a few companies, including Bank of America, social costing and social budgeting are being introduced by management. In general, the aim is to identify, separate, and measure expenditures for functions or activities that are not in the ordinary sense direct economic costs geared to immediate profit making. With experience, increased skills can be developed to judge the practical dimensions of ordinary economic and social costs as a guide to how much private and public funding and responsibility should be involved in any given endeavor to solve a major problem confronting the public.

Both government and business must direct major attention, including prompt practical experimentation, to this entire matter of economic vs. social costs with the goal of releasing the dynamic profit power of private enterprise and the social power of government in common projects for the betterment of the public. Until this is done, we must expect government and business all too often to continue to work at cross purposes.

More effective means must be found to establish viable priorities in our country.

In my view, growing polarization is blocking positive action in the United States, especially at the state and local levels. This is one of the greatest current threats to the future of our system of enterprise. We are being submerged in so much controversy these days that our system is not fulfilling its potential.

If business takes the lead in setting priorities, as it often has done, its motives are now suspect and the charge is commonly hurled: "Business power is cramming things down our throats." If business holds back until a community or national consensus forms, it never seems to come. Then, paradoxically, business is charged with callous indifference. Frankly, most business managements are now fed up with this "can't win no matter what" posture. They resent being caught up in the cross fire of individuals and groups who accept no responsibility for action except criticism of business and our system.

Accordingly, I strongly urge President Nixon and the Congress to redouble their efforts to clarify and establish our national priorities. We must realize as a people, we cannot do everything at once. That our wants will always vastly exceed our ability to meet them at any given time is a simple economic truth. Perhaps it may soon become necessary to strengthen our democratic process by placing the principal issues of interest and controversy on the ballot, debate them publicly and thoroughly for a limited time, and then literally take a priority vote to establish a practical guidance plan for greater action. But, even if this is accomplished, there is still more to be done.

To minimize destructive polarization, the will of the majority must make greater provision for the needs and aspirations of the minority.

We must now face squarely the issue in America of the will of the majority vs. the will of the minority. No longer will the minority on important issues accept the will of the majority calmly and with as much patience as in the past. The risk lies in a proliferation of interests, fractions, and parties, a condition incompatible with forceful progress under our system.

Under a system of using referendum or polls as a last resort measure, it should be more possible to gauge the strength of public feeling on the key controversial issues of the moment. Over time, it should help resolve lesser priority matters as it becomes known whether each is growing or slipping in public interest. Self-centered obstructionists who lay claim to media headlines for publicity purposes would be exposed as lacking a following. Where the evidence is impressive of growing interest or concern on some matter, not yet in a high-priority position, a program of research and experimentation could be launched to assure minority leaders that their interests are getting more effective attention.

Competition Must Not Be Weakened

Public officials and others are increasingly critical of our system as not bringing about the "proper" allocation of resources, especially credit. Accordingly, regular market forces are more and more being distorted. The traditional rights of the highest bidder are being questioned. Channelling of substantial amounts of funds into housing and other special areas by government certainly is not new, but recent developments seem to foreshadow far-reaching programs that will impede the force of market competition and replace it with government edict.

It is high time now, however, to review antitrust and related policies to determine whether they are as appropriate for the years ahead to 1990 as in past decades. I am convinced they are not.

Our system can withstand a considerable amount of nonmarket interference, but will face serious adjustments and loss of competitive vitality if present trends persist and increase. Basically, the problem is that some politically powerful groups, especially government bodies themselves at all levels, are facing enormous shortages of funds to offset inflation and continue increasing social expenditures above gains in tax revenue. Large, private savings flows and accumulations are easy targets for government direction. But, what the American people must understand is that undue public or private tampering with market flows and accumulations of funds will undermine the forces that generate them. Whenever a noncompetitive force, public or private, dominates a market, it is only a matter of time until all factors involved in the market become frustrated, to the detriment of the public.

The American enterprise system is rooted in the sound and long-tested principle that a properly functioning market may make small mistakes that are largely self-correcting at a minimum cost to society. The alternative of strong government intervention in markets inevitably destroys the creativity and vitality of the market participants and exposes society to the dangerous threat of major mistakes and major adjustments.

Our system depends upon savings and investment flows and confidence in its money and financial mechanisms for its every continuance. We risk great peril whenever impatience or partisanship is allowed to interfere seriously with these fundamentals. Government guidance and direction have a place in our system, but the market must be the stronger force through time or our system will falter.

The strength of our system through the years can be traced to the effectiveness of many policies, including antitrust measures, which have sought to ensure healthy competition. It is high time, however, to review antitrust and related policies to determine whether they are as appropriate for the years ahead to 1990 as in past decades. I am convinced they are not.

Antitrust policy probably as much as other factors, including management skill, has diverted resources and talent broadly across industry and service lines in contrast to greater developments within such fields. Similarly, narrow nationalistic restrictions have encouraged many ventures outside the United States. Labor-union exemption from the antitrust laws has contributed to major imbalance in sectors of our economy.

The point here is that powerful economic forces can never really be dammed up for long. No one should be surprised when they break out elsewhere. No patchwork of controls can contain them. If a serious problem for society exists, it should be corrected at the source, not where the symptoms appear.

Business Size and Scope

Let us examine the structure of American business organizations themselves. More than 10 million individual companies contribute to overall economic output. However, less than one percent produce half the total and employ less than 15 percent of the nation's active work force. Is this good or bad? Will the future for our system be brighter or dimmer if bigness persists?

Admittedly, these are emotional as well as economic questions. Many a political candidate is convinced he can be elected by attacking big business, conglomerates, and corporations in general. That the overwhelming evidence shows these institutions to be indispensable and making a strong positive contribution to society seems almost irrelevant to many people. Public attention is usually focused on the failures among the big,

---

My own research and experience point to the need for continuing strong big-business organizations amidst a host of smaller ones if our system of enterprise is to prosper.

---

almost never on their successes, which are either ignored or taken as just another indication of how "easy" it is to make a profit. Curiously, the critics of bigness or of business in general seldom, if ever, demonstrate how easy a profit is to make through personal experience.

It is almost impossible to keep any general public discussion of business, especially big business, on factual grounds. Many people, for example, know—others refuse to believe—that Bank of America has grown to its current position more by helping the "little guy" than the larger customer. We, and other business organizations, learned long ago to be continually sensitive and responsive to the wants of all types of people and all sizes of organizations.

My own research and experience point to the need for continuing strong big-business organizations amidst a host of smaller ones if our system of enterprise is to prosper.

Essential growth in our economy cannot and will not occur without the contribution of healthy, large organizations, including government. The world in which the United States must compete continues to reflect more and more public-policy decisions of foreign governments aimed at increasing, *not* decreasing, the size of their business establishments. The multinational corporation is the inevitable result of multinational economics as the world's people and markets more and more interact. The challenge to multinational-corporation managements must be to see that their enterprises are truly multinational operating in the interests of all nationals.

Low costs, low prices, and the most economic

use of resources require tremendous investments and broad management skills commonly available and possible on the scale required only through successful substantial organizations. Inflation cannot be checked by small business alone.

Far too many Americans ignore the fact that most private investments involve the government as a joint partner through the tax system sharing directly in about half of whatever profits are achieved. Our U.S. check-and-balance economic system requires large private institutions to cope with large government and other nonprofit organizations.

My conclusion is simply that the structure of our American system has long been one of various types and sizes of business organizations and must remain so. Criticisms against bigness will always be in order where inefficiency and poor leadership exist, but concerted attacks against bigness *per se* are against our system and ignore economic reality. Obviously, competition requires that markets be kept open for new firms, but our system properly gives no assurance of success, which comes only when management, economics, and social and political acceptance are correct through time.

Wherever we want to be by 1990, we won't get there without private, profit-motivated business organizations, including large ones, which are able to prove in the marketplace that they have something valuable to contribute to the public at home and abroad.

The United States in a World of Changing Systems

While my discussion thus far has seemed to center on the domestic U.S. scene, in reality I have had continually in mind that our American system is competing in a world of changing systems. Naturally our system must prove successful at home if it is to have any positive impact elsewhere. To date, at least, despite countless overseas critics, the American system has set the goal or example for more and more people across the world. The communist powers, for example, are seeing the practical value of tangible incentives and the positive power of profits in their economies.

All political and economic systems in one way or another will confront many or most of the difficult problems mentioned earlier as we look to 1990. Here is the main challenge to America and our system of enterprise—to solve these tough problems faster and better. The world will know by 1990 which system is winning.

Conclusion

We have the ingredients to achieve a vigorous and updated market system for 1990.

We will need a renewed spirit and greater understanding of our market system to stem the trend toward progressive loss of freedom through rising dependency on government.

History says we cannot or will not fight hard enough to adopt and preserve our system until 1990. I am predicting we will because we are too wise to give up our individual freedoms to allow a few people to make big mistakes at our expense.

Don't you agree?   ∎

114

Foundations of Private Enterprise

Weldon B. Gibson

T HE PRIVATE ENTERPRISE system is based on three main principles—private ownership of property, decentralized planning and initiatives by business entities, and major emphasis on freedom of the individual in economic pursuits. The system as it has emerged during recent decades involves three main foci of power: business, labor, and government. Other power centers are now arising in the economy but their membership cuts across the three principal groupings. Consumerism and environmental movements as well as minority programs illustrate new trends affecting structure of the American enterprise system.

The health, vigor, and potential of a private enterprise system—particularly one on the vast scale of the American pattern—depend greatly on maintaining a delicate balance of influence among the principal forces of power in the economy. The task of government in this respect is to create the cradle and an environment for nourishment of the private enterprise system. The task of business is to seize opportunities, respond to needs and defend as well as promote the system. The task of labor is to assist in enhancing national productivity.

The concept of checks and balances underlying our political and governmental system is equally applicable to the American private enterprise system. The balance of influence or power among major groupings in the economy changes slowly over time but it does change when public opinion embraces the idea that the pendulum has swung too far in one of the three directions. Thus it was that the balance between business and government shifted to some extent away from business during the early decades of this century. Then, during the middle of the century, the balance between business and labor moved in a series of steps toward organized labor.

In viewing our system of checks and balances and relative influences in the American economy during the next two decades, it seems apparent that the issues will become even more complex and intense than they have been during the recent past. Business as a whole advances the idea that the pendulum of strength has swung too far in the direction of labor and government. Labor holds the view that even greater strength in the balance-of-power equation is necessary in advancing the welfare of the working population.

Government is more and more concerned with directing the American economy toward national goals that seemingly override or alter the main pursuits of both business and labor. While responding increasingly to social forces emerging in this final third of the 20th century, business is concerned about its ability to generate profits at a rate consistent with growing demands placed upon the system.

Remarks by Dr. Weldon B. Gibson, Executive Vice President and President, SRI International, Stanford Research Institute, Menlo Park, California.

A LOOK AT BUSINESS IN 1990: A Summary of the White House Conference on the Industrial World Ahead, Washington, D.C., February 7-9, 1972 (U.S. Government Printing Office: 1972 0—467-348) pp. 272-273.

115

Six Imperatives

Although it is difficult within this complex balance of forces and needs to develop concrete lines of action appropriate to a rapidly changing society

---

The American private enterprise system is responsive to change, and is itself a powerful agent of change in line with values and aspirations of the American public.

---

in the 1970s and 1980s, a few imperatives in policy direction must be kept clearly in the foreground. They can be summarized briefly.

- *Profits.* The profitability of business enterprise must be increased. Profitability is without a substitute in meeting the growing risks and needs—public and private—of a free enterprise economy.
- *Jobs.* The number of jobs within private enterprise must be expanded more rapidly. High unemployment rates are unacceptable in the long run.
- *Income.* Salaries and wages must move upward but productivity must accelerate to make this possible. There is no sound long-term alternative to productivity advances in a private enterprise system.
- *Inflation.* National inflation must be kept within reasonable bounds. This is the only prudent course over time for a private enterprise economy.
- *Priorities.* The nation's goals and priorities —however formulated—must be vigorously pursued. Rising demands for such pursuits in the public interest will prevail.
- *International.* The American economy and its enterprises must become more and more international. Any other course is an upstream movement.

In spite of problems within the American private enterprise system, its basic structure is sound and viable. It offers great promise to all mankind in the continuing search for greater economic and social progress. The system is responsive to change, and is itself a powerful agent of change in line with values and aspirations of the American public.

Our business enterprise system is flexible; it can be what American people want it to be—in 1980, 1990, and beyond. The pursuit in which we now engage collectively, i.e., strengthening and improving our enterprise system, is most important. Moreover, it is potentially rewarding for all Americans and for the world at large.   ■

116

"Rebalancing" the Corporation

Carl A. Gerstacker

I PROPOSE to discuss some of the more important aspects and problems of the process of "rebalancing" the corporation

The Trend toward Bigness

Size of private enterprise has long been a bugbear of government, dating back to those days when the untrammeled growth of private enterprise allowed it to outstrip the growth of federal government, and to dominate some aspects of our national life for brief periods.

Size should no longer be a governing factor in government decisions concerning business. It has been abundantly proven that size is often a gigantic advantage, and often, for certain tasks, a necessity. The problems of our times will require for their solution bigger business organizations than we now have—not smaller ones. Historically, private enterprises of great size were feared because we thought that if they fell into the hands of tyrants we would be powerless to stop them. As a result, overly ample controls have been developed in the past two generations to control the nation's corporations. The recall of hundreds of thousands of the nation's most popular make of automobile by the nation's biggest corporation surely indicates the power of the controls.

Remarks by Carl A. Gerstacker, Chairman of the Board, Dow Chemical Company .

The advantages of size in corporations have been recognized in recent years by some of the more highly developed nations, some of which are now encouraging the merger of related firms within their economies. In some cases the marriage vows are being forced on reluctant corporate partners by the government. In such a climate, can the United States government continue to sponsor and enforce the same definitions of corporate legality as respects size that seemed appropriate and necessary a generation or two ago? Should we not liberalize our long-held notions of restraint-of-trade and monopoly and antitrust? Will they not surely be archaic by the standards of 1990? And can we not accomplish this without sacrificing the essential restraints on big business abuses that we have so laboriously built up over so long a period?

We must discard our outmoded notions of size and our fear of bigness. We must learn to take better advantage of bigness to solve problems that will otherwise remain insoluble.

One of the major reasons this is true is the rapid emergence of a world economy.

Emergence of a World Economy

We no longer have a sterling area and a franc area and a yen area and the like. We now have a genuine world economy. In many respects the corporation has been the leading edge of this development. The emergence of a world economy

A LOOK AT BUSINESS IN 1990: A Summary of the White House Conference on the Industrial World Ahead, Washington, D.C., February 7-9, 1972 (U.S. Government Printing Office: 1972 0—467-348) pp. 274-278.

and of the multinational corporation has been accomplished hand in hand. This will continue to be true, only more so.

The multinational corporation is in flux; it is still a developing form. The years to 1990 will see the adolescence of this form, I believe. This is bound to be so because the multinational corporation has now become the new melting pot. It provides a medium in which creed and color and caste can—indeed, must—mix, and work together, and produce together, solving problems together daily, working in harmony together for mutual benefits.

The futurists are fairly unanimous in their belief that the next 25 years will be characterized by vigorous, and sometimes virulent nationalism. This can be tempered to a large degree if we develop a countervailing force in the form of the world citizens now increasingly being nurtured in the multinational companies.

Some hold that the United Nations and kindred international organizations are the spawning ground of a new international breed—citizens of the world. On the contrary, international organizations tend to reinforce feelings of nationalism because the bulk of the representatives in such organizations represent the interests of one particular and specific nation and nationalism. I firmly believe the *real* world citizens are coming out of the companies that have branches in every nation and who are at home in every nation.

The "anational" company—We appear to be moving strongly in the direction of what will not be really multinational or international companies as we know them today, but what we might call "anational" companies—companies without any nationality, belonging to all nationalities. We generally conceive of the multinational company as one having a fixed nationality (that of the parent company) but operating in many nations. With the blossoming of a true world economy these multinational bees, whether they are American or British, German or French, Russian or Japanese, will be establishing more hives in the farther fields. We will see more foreign companies with large American holdings, and vice versa. They will tend for many reasons, political and economic, to become nationless companies.

The blurring of nationalism—One of the principal concomitants of this anationalism will be the blurring of a corporation's national origins. Parent boards of directors will gradually become genuinely anational vehicles, with personalities of varied origins and residences sitting about the table and

making decisions affecting worldwide operations. They will be in a sense junior counterparts of the United Nations Security Council. In this milieu nationalism will take a back seat to other matters of higher priority—such as the economic and social benefits provided by the organization.

As an example of the trend, two members of the board of directors of my own company, out of 17, are foreign nationals who have always worked outside the United States.

Corporate democracy—We will also see the flowering of new forms of democracy. At least three major factors are involved here. First, there

---

We must discard our outmoded notions of size and our fear of bigness. We must learn to take better advantage of bigness to solve problems that will otherwise remain insoluble.

---

is the impact of a continual and natural flow of personnel from nation to nation and from company to company, and such a flow is almost the lifeblood of the multinational, or anational company. These personnel carry with them not only technology directly related to their corporate tasks but also ideas about ways of living. Democracy, like water, seeks its own level. The impact on some nations will be greater than on others, but the effect of this seed-sowing process cannot be underestimated.

The Labor-Management Problem

The adversary system of labor vs. management has about run its course. It is often destructive rather than constructive, counterproductive rather than productive, tyrannical rather than democratic. Most of the time its failures—usually in the form of long, agonizing strikes—cause far more injury to third parties (the consumer, the supplier) than they ever do to the participants. Stick-in-the-mud unionism, with its featherbedding and make-work rules, will either be legislated out of existence or forced out of existence by those who suffer most from it, the innocent bystanders, once they become sufficiently outraged by its excesses.

We must move from an adversary system to some new system devised to accommodate to each other's needs without a constant power struggle. Organizations that work best, that are on the most solid footing, that are most prosperous, are those that have devised ways to eliminate unnecessary friction within the organization, whether the organization be corporate, governmental, academic, or ecclesiastic. We desperately need new patterns today for working together within our individual organizations. We need to explore new ways of accomplishing those goals closest to the hearts of union leaders—job security, good wages, good working conditions—without resorting to internecine warfare.

I suggest that, because of the scope, complexity, and potential benefit to be accrued, a special governmental commission might fruitfully explore the vast possibilities of this subject. Also, I suggest that far-sighted unionists themselves should take the lead in fomenting the new bloodless revolution that we need, and that, I believe, will take place.

John L. Lewis of the Mine Workers was the prototype of the advanced thinker that we now need. Lewis said to the mine owners, "Yes, we'll take the lead in installing machinery to automate coal mining, we'll raise the productivity of the mines—if you'll give us dignity and make it really worth our while." The mines did install power machinery; back-breaking toil was eliminated; miners' wages have now climbed to around $50 a day. And yet American coal is the cheapest in the world today, produced at the least physical effort by the miners. John L. Lewis understood that everyone gains if everyone works to make the pie bigger, and that fighting over the biggest slice of the pie is tough when the pie size is stable.

Democracy in Business

Another factor in these new democratic subcurrents is the campaign for equal rights and treatment by various minority groups—women and blacks notably, but also other groups, even including sexual deviates. It is rather startling to hear women, who compose 51 percent of the population, describe themselves as a minority, but as they also compose the majority of our stockholders, I am happy to believe them.

United States corporations are adjusting rather more rapidly than is generally recognized to the youth movement. In my own company, for example, eligibility for retirement begins at age 50, and members of the board of directors relinquish line responsibilities at age 60. Ten or 15 years ago we had directors who were 70 or 80 years old. Today the oldest member of our board is 63.

As more young people, more women, more blacks move into positions of top responsibility in our corporations, we will need better lubricating devices in a people sense. We will have more potential friction in the sense of man vs. woman, in the sense of youth vs. age, in the sense of black vs. white, and in the sense of (let us say) French vs. German, or Russian vs. Chinese. None of these frictions is new, but as we develop polyglot, ana-

---

We must move from an adversary system (of labor vs. management) to some new system devised to accommodate to each other's needs without a constant power struggle.

---

tional companies we will require more and better machinery for adjusting and adjudicating differences, rivalries, and personality clashes.

What new forms of democracy will develop within our corporations as a result I cannot say. But I am certain that we will be rebalancing our corporations to meet these problems. We must find ways to solve our "people problems"—to work together in harmony—while at the same time reinforcing the decision-making freedoms of both individuals and management within the corporation.

We have been underusing and continue to underuse the talents of women. Hiring more women purely for reasons of good citizenship is not attractive economically. But when we are fully awakened to the fact that women have talents that are equal to those of men and, in many cases superior, and that we can actually make more money employing these superior talents, then we will rush to hire women. The best way to motivate people to hire female talents is to show them that it is the way to make money. Women carrying picket signs and burning bras get attention, but not results. We'll get results and women's lib will get results when they tie their efforts to the profit motive.

In the same way, we have underused the talents of minority races in our nation. We have done a poor job of developing their talents and letting them use them. We will do a better job when we effectively tie this objective to the profit motive. The same is true for our young people, and for the underdeveloped nations and peoples.

119

The Business-Government Interface

The trends we now see present us with a striking opportunity to improve the interface of business both with government and with academia if we only have the grace and the good sense to exploit it. This opportunity is the growing frequency of two careers in one lifetime.

The average age of retirement is declining, but the average life span is lengthening. Consequently, the temptation of a second career will appeal to more and more people. Both government, which is keyed to election dates, Congressional appropriations, and other vagaries, and the educational world, which is still keyed, I believe, to the agricultural season and the marketing period, are better geared to short-term or part-time jobs than industry and commerce.

The opportunity for a greatly increased flow of personnel from business into a second career in either government or campus is one that we ought vigorously to encourage. One of the overriding problems of our time is a basic lack of understanding of the American business system, particularly by the young, an ignorance so pervasive that it may, in the view of some, be the undoing of the entire system. Studies show that less than a third of government employees in elective positions have had any experience in business. Probably no more than one in ten college-faculty members has had business experience. The generally antibusiness bias of the government employee and the professor is hardly astonishing.

It is distasteful to me to suggest any extension of bureaucracy, but perhaps we should provide a government clearing house or bureau to serve as a matchmaker between campus and government jobs and industry personnel who are seeking a second career.

We ought also to consider measures to ease any financial burden in such cases. A person's pension plan, for instance, should not be adversely affected.

American Business in the World Economy

We are likely to see a concerted effort to upgrade the living standards in many of the lesser developed countries, in keeping with the law of rising expectations. American know-how will most likely be called on to provide the basis of this development. Competition for the right to operate in various of these countries in the development of local resources will be intense, as it is now. This competition will continue largely to be between American corporations and those of other nations. In other words, if, for political or economic or moral reasons, we decline to provide know-how to country X in technology Y, some other nation will. This has often occurred.

When a lesser developed country is interested in developing its resources and seeks know-how from abroad, the United States should fight for the opportunity to provide such know-how. Furthermore, it should do so through the American business system, the American corporation, supported when and if necessary and appropriate by the U.S. government. If Bolivia, for example, needs plastic materials, the United States should not provide Bolivia a credit with which to buy such materials; it should negotiate the establishment of a Bolivian plastics plant using American industrial know-how and working with an American firm qualified to provide such know-how on a continuing, long-term basis.

Related to this, we must change our policies concerning direct foreign investment. Traditionally the United States has been cool to foreign investment. We see it, apparently, as an export of our capital that will never come back. This distaste seems to date from the time, many years ago, when capital was inadequate for the development of U.S. resources. Sending it abroad meant that some domestic project, providing jobs for Americans, might be crimped. Today we know this idea is not only antiquated but erroneous, but we still persist in frowning on foreign investments by Americans. They are controlled carefully through an Office of Foreign Direct Investments in the Commerce Department. We ought instead to encourage and facilitate useful, judicious, and appropriate investment abroad, particularly in the lesser developed countries, and particularly where we are in competition with other nations. I speak here of the manufacture of products to be sold

---

The opportunity for a greatly increased flow of personnel from business into a second career in either government or campuses is one we ought vigorously to encourage.

---

in such countries, and not for export back to this country.

The multinational, or anational corporation, is basically an American development although it

Recommendations to Improve Corporate Effectiveness

- My first and most urgent recommendation is that we establish a basis on which we can make truly neutral, truly anational corporations a reality.

- The anational company may be the major hope in the world today for economic co-operation among the peoples, for prosperity among the nations, for peace in our world.

- The truly anational company is possible only if it can be divorced from its mother country and thus no longer is a part of one culture or one nation. This cannot be possible if it is seen by any nation as a vehicle for forcing one nation's customs, mores, and politics on other countries. We must win better understanding of the profit system—which will, in 1990, still be the world's best economic engine. We must make certain that the system remains responsive to the needs of the society that nurtures it.

- I propose that the U.S. government should review, update, and liberalize its policies restricting the size of corporations, by legislation if necessary, maintaining, of course, essential safeguards against abuse of privilege.

- Means should be devised, possibly through a special study commission under governmental sponsorship, whereby new avenues to employee-employer harmony can be developed so that we can eliminate the labor-management adversary system and its attendant injury to innocent third parties, so that we can increase the productive capacity of the system.

- Consideration should be given to establishing a clearing house to match job opportunities on the campuses and in government with industry personnel seeking a second career.

- Methods should be developed whereby American companies may more effectively participate, with U.S. government support, in the development of third-country economic and technological development. The rules governing foreign direct investment should be revised to encourage American support and participation in appropriate foreign-development projects.

---

was not originated here, and is hardly an American monopoly. It is being emulated by most of the more developed industrial nations. Nonetheless, it is predominantly and clearly an American form of organization.

As we head into what is apparently to be a period of heightened nationalism, the official role of the United States government will become less effective in many countries, and in some it will be quite unwelcome. The quiet, unofficial operations of the anational corporation, I submit, are made to order for this kind of situation. They are, in fact, most effective when they are unofficial. The grass roots, people-to-people kinds of relationships that grow out of teaching situations, when know-how is passed on from person to person on the job, are a much better international cement than the best kind of diplomacy.

It was the Chinese philosopher Lao-tse who said that if you give a man a fish you give him food for a day, but if you teach him to fish, you give him food for a lifetime. Allow us in the anational corporations to teach those in the lesser developed countries our technologies, so that they can share our abundance, and not simply be envious of it.

Recommendations

One of the most disturbing aspects of the corporate structure today, here and abroad (perhaps *the* most disturbing aspect) is that by U.S. law an American corporation operating in another nation is obliged to conform to the dictates of the federal government, executive, legislative, and judicial. It is thus, through no choice of its own, to some extent an instrument of American policy. In many nations the American corporation is seen therefore as an arm of what is called American "imperialism." This leads me to several recommendations, which are listed above. If we do these things now, I am sure those in charge in 1990 will be grateful. ∎

The Financial Challenge of the 1970s and Beyond: Profits

Alan Greenspan

T HE MAJOR financial challenge to business during the next two decades is, in my view, the struggle to maintain profitability. With profit margins barely above their post-World War II lows, it is of major concern whether this year's projected increase in profits and profit margins signals a return to the higher margins of the middle or early 1960s. For that matter, is there any reasonable chance of a return to the relative corporate affluence of the 1950s? An analysis of profitability during the post-war period is not encouraging on this score for the years ahead.

The key questions that must be answered are: *Does the deteriorating profitability of American corporations result from unprofitable capital investments stemming from mismanagement and/or inadequate technological progress? Has the level of capital expenditures been inadequate to sustain profit margins?*

The answer to the second question must clearly be no. Capital outlays have held near historic highs in recent years, both relative to GNP and gross fixed assets. This is not to say that levels of investment could not be larger, or that they may not be deemed inadequate in comparison with other countries. I wish only to point out that the

declining level of profit margins in the United States cannot be explained in terms of a short fall of investment levels.

The question of the profitableness of the investments actually made is the more difficult to answer. The preliminary results of my analysis of the matter indicate that here, too, the answer is no.

Too often major physical improvements in a production process are not reflected in a company's (or industry's) earnings statement owing to price declines or cost increases engendered by forces essentially independent of the actions of the company. Or, as is too often the case, major capacity expansions leave the industry with a far superior plant but excessive capacity, and hence lower prices and subnormal profitability.

Even where profit gains from a particular process are clearly identified, bottlenecks in other segments of the production process may vitiate such gains in whole or in part. Conversely a single bottleneck-breaking outlay may free a whole synergistic process of profit creation.

Hence, to get at the underlying rate of return on capital investments, it is necessary to first strip away, where possible, the price, wage, and financial factors that frequently overwhelm the income statements and obscure true growth in technology and productive efficiency.

Remarks by Alan Greenspan, President, Townsend-Greenspan Company, Inc.

A LOOK AT BUSINESS IN 1990: A Summary of the White House Conference on the Industrial World Ahead, Washington, D.C., February 7-9, 1972 (U.S. Government Printing Office: 1972 0—467-348) pp. 279-282.

Return on Capital Investments in Manufacturing

For my analysis I chose to deal with manufacturing as a whole for the last two decades, although the techniques are equally applicable to non-manufacturing and to individual industries, or companies. I believe the results for the total corporate sector would match those for manufacturing.

Capital expenditures in manufacturing are made essentially for one of two purposes: either to increase capacity or to displace man-hours and/or materials. The extent to which such investments reduce labor and materials costs in physical terms is a proxy measure of the real rate of return associated with a particular capital expenditure. The rate of capacity expansion and labor-saving outlays doubtless does indirectly affect prices and wage rates. Nevertheless profit generated from new facilities must be first viewed in physical terms.

In principle, fully consolidated quarterly income statements for manufacturing should be capable of being factored into price and quantity elements, respectively. In such a case dollar sales would become the product of an index of physical volume and unit prices. Plant labor costs would be segregated into production worker and supervisory (nonproduction worker) man-hours, each with its associated average hourly labor cost, and materials purchases would be divided into physical quantities and unit prices.

Is there any reasonable chance of a return to the relative corporate affluence of the 1950s? An analysis of profitability during the post-war period is not encouraging on this score for the years ahead.

In my analysis, materials savings from capital expenditures, which over all tend to be small, have been disregarded. I was thereby able to go directly to an analysis of manufacturing value-added. Employment cost was segregated into its constituent elements; profit, taxes, interest payments, and depreciation were obtained as a single residual from value-added. Hereafter this residual will be referred to as property income. All prices and wages were then fixed at 1967 levels. Value-added in 1967 dollars, and employment costs as they would have appeared had wages and fringes been fixed at the rates prevailing in 1967 were generated. Constant-dollar property income was then calculated as the residual (value-added less employment costs). The resulting changes over time in constant-dollar property income can be ascribed generally to two elements: different rates of capacity utilization, and changes in physical costs and capacity owing to capital-investment programs.

To determine the improvement in property income attributable to capital-expenditure programs, it is necessary first to remove the fluctuations in the physical profit figure owing strictly to changes in the rate of operations. Obviously, if a company, in a short period of time, increases production from 60 percent to 90 percent of capacity, a sharp increase in physical-property income is to be expected that would not in any way reflect changes in the nature of the basic facilities of the company. The adjustment for this type of profit change required some notion of what man-hour requirements would have been during a specific year at a level of operations not actually experienced.

Also affected by the rate of operations is the proportion of nonproduction workers to total employment. This occurs because nonproduction workers and even some classes of production workers are a function of the size of the facilities rather than the short-term movements in production. The simulated trend of production worker man-hours to total man-hours at fixed operating rates was estimated. It is possible from these relationships to simulate value-added at capacity (in 1967 dollars), constant-dollar labor costs, and implicitly property income. As might be expected, such constant-dollar property income exhibits a relatively stable upward trend reflecting both increases in capacity and reductions in man-hours per unit of capacity. The latter, of course, represents output per man-hour simulated at fixed operating rates.

Although it is difficult to ascribe any specific increase in property income to a particular capital expenditure, it is possible to make some general comparisons. I have assumed that capital expenditures made in a given year would not immediately influence profitability owing to the lag between expenditures and facilities completions and the required "break-in" time. As a result, it was assumed, for example, that profit changes attributable to capital expenditures in 1970 would not be evident until 1972. To smooth out the relationship, I chose to attribute the increase in real

123

property income from the end of 1968 to the end of 1971 to plant and equipment expenditures (in 1967 dollars) made during the three years 1967–1969. The rates of return calculated on this basis suggest that returns on capital expenditures in recent years have been somewhat above the post-World War II average, as is indicated in Table 1.

This underscores the fact that the recent deterioration in profit margins results from financial factors, specifically wage-rate changes.

Wage-Rate Changes and Profit Margins

Through 1969 we were clearly caught up in a classical demand-pull inflation. The rapid rise in wages and prices was scarcely a puzzle to anyone. However, the failure of prices, and especially of wages, to respond to the growing unemployment of 1970 and 1971 led to the belief that a new cost-push inflation had taken hold, which required drastic action to abort. The most prevalent explanation for this phenomenon holds that large monopolistic unions and corporations are setting their wages and prices essentially independent of the general thrust of monetary and fiscal policy. This thesis argues that there is a self-perpetuating cycle in labor negotiations, each leap-frogging the

other in an accelerating wage pattern. Large businesses do not, according to this view, attempt to slow the wage increases but merely pass them on in the way of higher prices.

Evidence is slight that large manufacturing corporations' "monopolistic control" has increased during the past decade. Therefore, if this thesis is valid today, it must have been even more relevant in the early 1960s. Yet, price rises a decade ago, on average, were quite small. So far as industrial unions are concerned their power has, if anything, diminished during the past decade. Yet in the early 1960s union contracts in manufacturing were calling for average annual wage increases of only two to three percent.

To be sure unions have become stronger in two major areas. One is the construction trades. Owing to Supreme Court decisions of the late 1950s and the consequent onset of de facto exclusive hiring halls, wage gains in the construction trades have accelerated dramatically and far outstripped gains in the heavily unionized manufacturing area. Secondly, markedly higher unionization among federal, state, and local government employees has raised pay scales in the government area. Nonetheless, union membership still comprises little more than a fifth of the total labor force. Thus, prior to the institution of the Pay

TABLE 1–SIMULATION OF PROPERTY INCOME ($BIL. 1967) IN MANUFACTURING, OPERATING AT CAPACITY

Capital Expenditures			Increase in Property Income Owing to Expenditures			
Investment Period	Expend. ($Bil. '67)	Period During which Increase Computed	Lower Unit Cost ($Bil. '67)	Greater Capacity ($Bil. '67)	Total Increase ($Bil. '67)	Percent of Expend.
53–55	33. 43	4Q 54–4Q 57	1. 54	0. 55	2. 09	6. 27
54–56	36. 31	4Q 55–4Q 58	2. 70	0. 62	3. 32	9. 15
55–57	39. 28	4Q 56–4Q 59	3. 06	0. 66	3. 72	9. 49
56–58	39. 24	4Q 57–4Q 60	3. 21	0. 70	3. 92	9. 99
57–59	35. 26	4Q 58–4Q 61	2. 35	0. 79	3. 14	8. 93
58–60	32. 38	4Q 59–4Q 62	3. 86	1. 06	4. 92	15. 21
59–61	32. 37	4Q 60–4Q 63	4. 10	1. 19	5. 30	16. 38
60–62	33. 93	4Q 61–4Q 64	4. 16	1. 64	5. 81	17. 12
61–63	35. 10	4Q 62–4Q 65	3. 61	2. 06	5. 68	16. 19
62–64	38. 55	4Q 63–4Q 66	2. 64	2. 69	5. 34	13. 86
63–65	44. 68	4Q 64–4Q 67	1. 79	2. 90	4. 70	10. 52
64–66	53. 04	4Q 65–4Q 68	2. 74	3. 58	6. 32	11. 91
65–67	60. 04	4Q 66–4Q 69	3. 14	3. 72	6. 86	11. 43
66–68	62. 30	4Q 67–4Q 70	4. 82	4. 47	9. 30	14. 92
67–69	61. 92	4Q 68–4Q 71	4. 67	4. 26	8. 93	14. 43

Board, and perhaps even today, wage bargains are determined predominantly by broad free-market forces. (It is sometimes counter-argued that, even though unions comprise a small proportion of the work force, they are the price leaders and ultimately set the wage framework for the total labor force. The evidence for this, however, is questionable. No group has been able to match the construction-trades wage patterns. Desire is one thing, implementation is another.)

Yet, one cannot deny that wage increases had continued disturbingly high in the face of sizeable unemployment. However, an alternative and more credible explanation exists. A new force began to develop during the past five years whose effect on wages was initially obscured by the presence of a demand-pull inflation and is only now beginning to become clear. Past periods of high unemployment were associated with extraordinary hardship. Workers, with little savings or alternate sources of income, were forced to actively seek jobs at lower than their normal wage. It was not the level of unemployment that actually determined the balance of bargaining power between management and labor, but the level of hardship. Compared to five or ten years ago, at any given level of unemployment today, the level of hardship is clearly less, or obversely, a level of hardship comparable to a decade ago would now imply a much higher level of unemployment.

Expanded benefits coverage under unemployment insurance has been one factor in this change, especially among adult men. The proportion of unemployed men, for example, over 24 years of age, who received state unemployment insurance benefits rose from 60 percent in 1965 to 77 percent in 1970. The massive rise in average welfare benefits and extended welfare coverage has significantly decreased the supply of unskilled service workers, with a consequent large increase in wage rates for these job categories. Thus, both expanded unemployment insurance and greater welfare have had the effect, in recent years, of significantly reducing the hardship/unemployment ratios. The shift in the proportion of unemployed

who are teenagers has also contributed to this trend.

Less general hardship among the unemployed means less willingness to offer their services at any given wage. Consequently, other things equal, the wage-bargaining process must conclude with a higher average wage than it would have had with a higher hardship/unemployment ratio. This is equivalent to saying that a greater proportion of the national income is going to labor and less to capital. Thus, if the average level of labor-market hardship is permanently reduced, profit margins must be permanently lower. During the period of transition of recent years, while the hardship/unemployment ratio was declining, wage increases were abnormally large. However, the rate of increase can stay high only so long as profit margins continue to decline. But, there is a downside limit to the decline in margins and it has probably already been reached.

Business' ability to accept still lower profit margins has been significantly reduced. In a sense the countervailing force to the sharp drop in labor-market hardship has been the onset of long-term profit insufficiency.

It is thus likely that a new long-term equilibrium will be reached characterized by relatively lower profit margins than prevailed in past decades but margins still presumably adequate to maintain levels of capital investment and technological advance. Corporations doubtless will have to fund the rising costs of pollution control and presumably even higher taxes if the recent trend of government expenditures continues.

The challenge is clear. Corporate success in 1990 will not be as easy to achieve as in decades past. As a result the demands for skilled business management must clearly accelerate. The challenge is great. I am hopeful that we have the means to meet it. ∎

The Changing Pattern of Consumer Demand

Richard H. Holton

W E LIKE to think of the ideal economy as one marked by the economist's model of perfect competition. In that simplified model, the public's needs and wants are translated into votes in the marketplace. This demand for a complex of goods and services leads to the attraction of talent and resources into areas that meet the market demand. If we assume that each individual in society is interested in maximizing his income, then human talent and the associated resources are pulled into those uses that society values most. If the assumption and details of this model are fully specified, it can be shown that total welfare for society is maximized.

Desire for Nonfinancial Income

All this assumes that the society consists of "economic men," i.e., individuals who are interested in maximizing their real income. But what if the individual is not an "economic man" in the pure sense, i.e., what if he is interested not just in his money income but in a variety of other aspects of his life as well? We may be seeing an increase in the percentage of the population that is

Remarks by Dr. Richard H. Holton, Dean, School of Business Administration, University of California, Berkeley.

interested in total "life style," to use the popular term. Perhaps, in this style of life, income is distinctly secondary to a number of other objectives. A man may view the totality of his life to include not just income, but the objective of a minimum commuting time, minimum human congestion in his daily life, maximum vacation time, and flexibility in the scheduling of his vacation time. He may seek real satisfaction with the content of his work; he may want to be producing a physical product. He may, say, turn to woodworking. He may be willing to work longer hours and for less income if he is "doing his own thing." He may choose to live and work in up-country Vermont at considerably less income than he could obtain in New York City. He may want a great deal of variety in his life. And he may want to have an opportunity to pursue his education beyond his last formal degree, and perhaps even move into a second career.

Broadened Expectations Will Alter the Structure of Society

Many people, if not everyone, have long been interested in more than just money income, of course. The point here is that in the affluent society the nonmonetary components of the individual's

A LOOK AT BUSINESS IN 1990: A Summary of the White House Conference on the Industrial World Ahead, Washington, D.C., February 7-9, 1972 (U.S. Government Printing Office: 1972 O—467-348) pp. 286-287.

126

total rewards may be increasing significantly in importance.

The major problem we face, as Dr. Harman points out (page 28), is that somehow the summation of the countless microdecisions in ·our society has given us a macroeconomic picture that we do not find altogether pleasing. The totality of life for a high percentage of the population somehow is not as pleasant as we think it ought to be, given our incomes.

If we are no longer primarily interested in personal income but in the nonmonetary aspects of our enjoyment of life to an increasing extent, we may be in for restructuring of our society. This can be rather disappointing, perhaps. Here we thought we had an economy that was clearly the leader in the world, but now we are not so sure that we really have everything put together as we would like.

What are the consequences for the structure of the private enterprise economy? I suggest two possible consequences. I am sure there are others:

- The medium-sized or large corporation will not be able to accommodate the entrepreneurial personality, or the individual who wants to "drop out" of the large firm.
- As the citizenry at large comes to recognize that somehow our microdecisions lead to a totality that we think is significantly deficient in many respects, we may insist on certain public policies that are designed to constrain private decisions.

If we are correct in anticipating this change in the objectives of some significant proportion of the people we normally would expect to recruit into the ranks of management, then we should expect to find people dropping out to various degrees. At the extreme, some will want to escape to the rural commune. But other alternatives are available, and are being used today. The individual will want (does want, and is receiving) more leisure time on the job. He gets a longer coffee break, for example. Or he is willing to shift, or perhaps eager to shift, to a job that involves more elbow room, more space within which he can exercise his individual initiative. He may want to start his own enterprise, a common practice in the last decade or two.

Small business is by no means dead. The most recent Enterprise Statistics of the Bureau of the Census indicate that some 22 percent of the employment in the nonagricultural firms in the country is in companies with fewer than 20 employees. In manufacturing, the percentage of employment in such small firms is far less, about five percent. It is apparent that small firms are much more common in the service industries than in manufacturing, as one would expect. If proportionately more people are willing to sacrifice money income in order to pursue activities in which they find greater personal fulfillment, we may see a more rapidly growing small-business sector.

The effect of such a movement could well be to drain off from the large corporation some of its best talent. Recent news stories about second-echelon executives who quit the large firm to start their own suggest that this may already be happening. If this corporate "brain drain" reaches significant proportions, perhaps the "Fortune 500" community will have to make do increasingly with second-rate talent, on the one hand, and face more competition from new firms on the other.

The second consequence of this greater concern for the quality of life may be more far reaching. Recognition is growing that somehow the millions of microdecisions made at the level of the individual and the firm, each of which might well be a decision that leaves the individual or firm better off, add up to a macropicture less desirable or attractive than we think it should be. We are already witnessing the development of new government regulations designed to correct this situation. This will lead to further constraints on private activities at all levels.

One way to view this situation is to see that wants in our society are socially generated. Advertisers work to generate wants, but in the world of competition these advertisers are now competing, for example, with politicians who argue that we want a space program, a poverty program, or a clean-air bill. A Ralph Nader generates a public want for automobile safety. In the marketplace of ideas, more wants are likely to be generated in the nonbusiness sector. Business will thus increasingly have to adjust by one means or another to this set of forces. This development is not new; at least since the 1930s business has been faced with growing regulatory pressures. It is a compliment to the resilience of our system that business has on the whole, I think, responded well.

Business must participate in this process of assessing new public wants, and in particular in the process of designing legislation or other means of best meeting those public wants. If business does become a full and active partner in this process, rather than merely a reluctant and defensive culprit, I see no reason why we should not be able to have a fully satisfactory and viable private business sector operating in this country in 1990. ∎

Size and Growth of Enterprise

Joseph H. Allen

BUSINESS has grown to an enormous size in recent years, usually on the assumption that the bigger the business, the bigger the market it can serve efficiently. But that assumption is subject to question, and perhaps we should begin to test its validity. Certainly some segments of the U.S. government—notably the antitrusters—are raising some serious questions, as are some of the more vocal critics of today's society, such as Ralph Nader.

Last August, in a ruling on a long-standing ITT case, the Justice Department seemed to say to big business: "If you add a significant chunk to your business by merging with a company, you must divest yourself of a comparably sized chunk." The intent seems to be to let big businesses stay at their present size, and not to permit new entries to get to *comparable* size.

Big business can answer that business must be big to generate the kind of innovation and regeneration we need at home, and to compete with major competitors abroad. Certainly it is big business that has been given the role of problem-solver in many of today's social areas. When governments want training programs for minority employees, or contributions of executive time and money to make repairs in the social fabric, they turn to business.

Still, if we are to examine business 20 years hence, we must seriously consider the problems of

bigness in business, and the strong evidence that in that time business will grow even more.

Business Is Big, and Getting Bigger

A recent FTC survey showed that the one hundred largest manufacturing corporations in 1968 held a larger share of the manufacturing assets of the United States than had the two hundred largest manufacturing corporations only 18 years earlier, in 1950. In the 13-year period between 1954 and 1967, the following changes took place among some of the top-ranked companies of the United States: the company ranked No. 100 had expanded 188 percent; the 500th had expanded about 166 percent; and No. 1, General Motors, had expanded by 123 percent.

Other Segments of Society Are Getting Bigger, Too

The growth is by no means confined to U.S. companies and U.S. consumers. The experts all forecast the development of the huge multinational company in the coming decades, as well as the growth of the truly international labor organization. European and Japanese business is growing every bit as rapidly as U.S. multinational operations. Professor Howard Perlmutter of Wharton has estimated that, by 1985, three hundred of the world's largest corporations (with individual sales of $8 billion and up) will account for one-half of

Remarks by Joseph H. Allen, Vice President, McGraw Hill, Inc.

A LOOK AT BUSINESS IN 1990: A Summary of the White House Conference on the Industrial World Ahead, Washington, D.C., February 7-9, 1972 (U.S. Government Printing Office: 1972 0—467-348) pp. 288-290.

the world's industrial output.

At the same time, we can expect labor organizations, many of which have had the name "international" in their titles for years, to begin to take that name seriously. As multinational corporations develop, multinational unions are sure to follow.

All the present factors indicate greater bigness in government, too. We have seen the increase in size and scope of both regulatory and social-service agencies. As political awareness grows among the electorate, and such phenomena as consumerism and social-action groups continue to proliferate, the call will be for more and more of the same.

Problems, Also, Get Bigger

Consider two of the most important problems we face now: those of decision making, and its most necessary component, communications. As business has grown larger, a dangerous paradox has developed:

- Upper management, although removed by several steps from the marketplace, is making decisions affecting the marketplace in a direct and immediate fashion. It is also frequently making decisions that would be better made further down the line.
- At the other extreme, lower management, because it does not have simple and easy access to top management, is frequently required to make decisions that should be reserved for top management.

To keep private enterprise viable we must have reappraisal of its concepts and methods. Professor Peter F. Drucker puts it this way in his *Age of Discontinuity:* "Now we are entering again an era in which emphasis will be on entrepreneurship. However, it will not be the entrepreneurship of a century ago, that is, the ability of a single man to organize a business he himself could run, control, embrace. It will rather be the ability to create and direct an organization for the new. We need men who can build a structure of entrepreneurship on the managerial foundations laid these last fifty years."

The new, and complex, organization will of course be some variation of the group, or "executive office" concept. But the philosophy will be an older one. It is a case of the entrepreneur reborn—in a new managerial role, and within a new and more responsible managerial hierarchy—but still with a critical need for the enterpreneur's awareness, spirit, and—most important—grasp of the total business situation.

The most critical need of the effective executive,

if he is to cope with bigness in business and with the constantly accelerating change that will accompany the next two decades, is for reliable—and pertinent—intelligence. Communication in a steady flow, reliable, but most of all, relevant.

Today's executive, as did the old-time company president, must "go out to the shop and look around." The story is told of Josiah Wedgewood, who occasionaly walked through his pottery plant with a piece of chalk in his hand, marking for destruction those pieces that did not meet his standard. Another version is that of the commanding officer who checks the eating and sleeping arrangements for his troops before concerning himself with his own situation. He, too, must not rely only on a subordinate's reports; he must go into the mess hall, and out into the field, to see for himself.

And, like Mr. Wedgewood, today's entrepreneur/manager must have his chalk at the ready, not for individual products, but for systems, methods, and practices that require scrapping or reorganization. That willingness to "go out and look" is the best protection for the executive of the 1980s and 1990s. It becomes critically necessary because of the hazards of communication.

Professor John Dearden of Harvard sees a basic problem in the people and information systems now in use: "Staff personnel responsible for communicating change are not doing so. Management

---

If we are to examine business 20 years hence, we must seriously consider the problems of bigness in business, and the strong evidence that in that time business will grow even more.

---

must always operate with insufficient information, (but now) while the role of management becomes more complex, new information technology is not helping significantly."

I shall cite, from many possible, a single example of each. In 1971 *Business Week* reported on a Detroit auto company whose top management overruled a move by division managers to recall one model of a car because of a defect. The firm subsequently was *forced* to recall the model—with unfavorable publicity and at higher cost. Further, it lost the credit it could have gained by voluntarily making the move. Here, top management was too far from the dealer-customer relationship to make the best decision.

On the other hand, lower management in a major aircraft company went on a binge of accepting new orders when it really did not have the capacity to deliver all it promised. Before the firm resolved its problems, it went through a merger and underwent heavy transfusions of new management talent. Decisions of top-management magnitude were being made by individuals too far down the line.

The executive suite is not immune from growth mania either. Too often we hear of conglomerate fever leading to the acquisition of totally unrelated businesses, merely because they were attractive investments. The subsequent reaction is painful when it is found that some of those acquisitions are neither digestible nor manageable.

Some Answers to Some of the Problems

Today's effective executive has found a number of ways to cope with some of these problems. General Electric Company, of course, is a model of top management coping with a vastly diversified, yet compatible, group of companies and product lines. Like G.E., more than 50 of the top corporations function through some version of the "Executive Office" or a similar collective grouping that puts three or four top men in charge of groups of operating units within the company.

The structure is typical of the re-thinking aimed at the problems that come with concentration and the difficulties that arise when the groups find it difficult to communicate with the center.

Because the computer is a quantifying tool, the temptation for those who deal with it is to ignore considerations that cannot easily be quantified or put into a numerical statement.

Thus, the computer, which has encouraged bigness in business by the vast amount of information it can process and produce on command, also threatens the sound development of bigger business in the coming decades. It threatens in two fundamental ways: in the quantity of its material and in the quality of that data. Surely we have had enough warnings about the danger of drowning in a flood of seemingly relevant, but actually overpowering, data.

I emphasize another danger that can grow from too great emphasis on the computer, and too little exercise of the go out and look concept. Because the computer is a quantifying tool, the temptation for those who deal with it is to ignore considerations that cannot easily be quantified or put into a numerical statement.

Unless tomorrow's manager goes out and looks, and gets in touch with those analytically messy factors that do not fit neatly into the mechanized information system, he hasn't a prayer of coping with the bigness of business—and government, and labor, and the marketplace—that will inevitably continue. ∎

The Corporation in 1990

James P. McFarland

I AM PERSUADED that business can and will merit and maintain the support of the society it seeks to serve and on whose approval its survival depends. However, we must recognize and overcome some of the problems to be found along the way.

Modern capitalism, for all its strengths and proven record of achievements, is still a misunderstood concept and system—not just to millions of people around the world but to millions of people in our own country. It is ironic indeed that a system that has been so successful in selling goods and services has been so inept in selling itself, even to those who are a part of it. The kind of structure we will have in 1990 depends in good measure on our ability between now and then to redefine capitalism in a manner that is understood and believed.

Another problem facing us if we are to reach 1990 in a recognizable form lies in the rapidity with which both higher expectations and changed aspirations exert new pressures against the business system. While we have been remarkably imaginative and far sighted in anticipating the needs and wants of people for new or improved goods and services, we continue to underestimate the demand for social and economic change. We too often refuse to acknowledge that we are entering an era

where certain eternal verities like the Puritan work ethic may be giving way to a whole new set of human values. It is not a matter of agreeing with these new values; it is a matter of understanding them and adapting our structure to recognize their growing importance.

If we can assume that business will successfully cope with these problems, let us consider what in 1990 resembles 1972. To begin with, however much we alter the physical or organizational structure of our system, however much we move from national to multinational markets, however much we switch emphasis from manufactured goods to the providing of services, the private enterprise system in 1990 as in 1972 will rely on the competitive edge to survive and prosper. The competitive edge, tomorrow as today, will be largely the function of two components—productivity resulting in a lower cost, and technology resulting in a better product.

I believe also that in 1990 profits will be a basic source of motivation, the measure of performance and ability to serve, and the means to the maintenance and the strengthening of our economic system and, indeed, our entire society.

Employer-Employee Relationships

Any consideration of productivity of the private enterprise system must include a discussion of the corporate work force and especially that part represented by organized labor. We are a high-labor-cost nation. We must compete in world markets

Remarks by James P. McFarland, Chairman of the Board, General Mills, Inc.

A LOOK AT BUSINESS IN 1990: A Summary of the White House Conference on the Industrial World Ahead, Washington, D.C., February 7-9, 1972 (U.S. Government Printing Office: 1972 0—467-348) pp.291-293.

131

with an increasing number of countries whose labor costs are lower and whose goods are therefore lower priced. Our success as a world trader depends on our ability to reverse this trend. This in turn depends on a changed relationship between labor and the corporation. The private enterprise system of 1990 may well see dramatic changes in this relationship, with both parties abandoning

---

While we have been remarkably imaginative and farsighted in anticipating the needs and wants of people . . . we continue to underestimate the demand for social and economic change . . . It is not a matter of agreeing with these values; it is a matter of understanding them and adapting our structure to recognize their growing importance.

---

traditional positions at the bargaining table so as to achieve the greater productivity so urgently needed.

The business corporation of 1990 will, in all probability, have an employer relationship with its personnel that differs dramatically from that of today. The changes may occur in ways that are not only different but also to some extent contradictory. On the one hand the corporation of 1990 will be expanding services and benefits to its employees. This may be occasioned by government action, by competitive pressure, or simply because it seems "the right thing to do." However, its effect will be to increase in a real way the dependence of the employee on the corporation for which he works. Some of these developments may simply be extensions of benefits now being given in a more modest way, but others may be in areas where today the corporation assumes no responsibility, and where, indeed, no particular pressure is applied by the employee.

We may, for example, be providing "second career" opportunities through a substantive reduction in the retirement age but with full benefits. We may well see the rapid development of corporately sponsored day-care centers for employee children, and a great increase in programs that give employees lengthy leaves of absence to pursue interests in nonbusiness-related fields.

Government-Business Relationships

If we have difficulty believing these changes will occur, note the recent developments in other institutions, colleges and universities for example. One of our greatest mistakes would be to assume that we are somehow immune from the same winds of change that are blowing so violently through areas of our society.

Let us not make the mistake of believing that the corporate structure of 1990 will be one devised and implemented simply by those of us in big business. We are creatures of the society we try to serve, and our charter will be written therefore by the people acting through their elected and appointed representatives, chiefly in federal government.

It is customary today to cite the inevitability of changed government-business relationships as arising from social pressures. Few of us would be rash enough to predict anything but increased government regulation (or interference) in the future. We have seen this trend develop throughout the 1960s and gain momentum in the first years of this decade. Faced as we seem to be with an ever-mounting pressure in a great variety of business areas, it is easy to assume that the structure of the corporation in 1990 will stem from demands that are more often than not noneconomic in nature. This conclusion follows a reading of the results of polls and surveys purporting to tell us what people are thinking. In its most oversimplified form it goes like this: A) Many people think the country is in one whale of a mess. They cite such valid problems as war, racial tension and inequality, pollution, urban blight, etc. B) Most people think that the single most powerful force for change in the country is big business, i.e., the corporation. C) Therefore, so the reasoning goes, it is big business that must play the major role in cleaning up the mess.

These social-responsibility pressures must not be discounted. However, the changed government-business relationships of 1990 may emerge basically from the *economic* factors involved, i.e., the

---

One of our greatest mistakes would be to assume that we are somehow immune from the same winds of change that are blowing so violently through areas of our society.

132

realization that unless we do some things better and other things differently we may not be able to fulfill our essential role at home or to compete successfully with the state socialism of a USSR or the state capitalism of a Japan.

I believe strongly that our future prosperity as a nation will depend upon our ability to compete successfully in world markets—as an exporter, as

This is a time when government and business and labor should be sitting down to plan the future, to establish national priorities, and to agree on objectives and strategy.

an overseas partner or entrepreneur, and as a producer of goods and services here at home that meet the challenge of imports. World-wide markets and global companies appear to be feasible, desirable, and inevitable.

I am concerned that, as we pursue desirable social goals, we may neglect the economic reforms necessary to give us increased productivity and profit potential. While we are willing to see the factory smokestack disappear as a symbol of American industry, none of us can afford to see what the smokestack represents—know-how and output—disappear along with it. We must find the path to a genuine government-business partnership. We have talked about that for a long time, but, with the passage of years, it seems more remote than ever. This is a time when government and business and labor—and in fact all elements of our society—should be sitting down to plan the future, to establish national priorities, and to agree on objectives and strategy. Instead we find ourselves in far too many cases failing to look beyond what we deem to be the overriding rights of our individual constituencies.

At a time when we should all be working together to unleash the full economic potential of business we find ourselves divided. The various constituencies—capital, labor, and the marketplace, i.e., the consumer—that provide the basic resources for our economy are pursuing their own interests at the national political level. The result is that outmoded restrictions and obsolete laws remain on the books. More importantly and dan-

gerously, further legal detriments to successful competition are being constantly suggested. We must devise a new system of corporate enterprise that will involve more deeply than ever before the forces of labor and the marketplace, but, which, in the final analysis, gives the opportunity for management to manage.

Because I believe strongly in our adaptability, I foresee this kind of change coming to pass. It will mean that all of us will be asked to give up some of the prerogatives we have taken for granted. This will be a small price to pay if we can thereby resolve our conflicting interests. Given this analysis, one is led to believe that we can move reasonably quickly toward the kind of corporate structure and government relationship that allows for comprehensive and coordinated national planning, for agreement on national priorities and for a full partnership whose strength is derived from a unity of purpose. ∎

The Financial System in 1990

Henry C. Wallich

WHILE 1990 seems remote, some plausible predictions can be made in the financial field, because the technology, the financial trends, and the population pattern are already well defined.

Automated Payments

Something like 75 percent of all payments that today are made by check will, in 1990, likely be made by an automated mechanism. The movement of checks, some 22 billion per year recently, is likely to double each decade if allowed to do so. The associated paper shuffling would threaten to do to the banks what high-volume trading did to Wall Street. These checks will to a large extent have been replaced by home terminals and point-of-sales terminals feeding information into computers.

Automation of payments has been held back more by legal difficulties, human inertia, and lack of profit prospects than by technological obstacles. For instance, the danger of fraud must be met that will arise when signed documents are phased out and payors no longer have their cancelled checks as receipts. The hesitancy of individuals must be overcome when they confront computers that respond to human complaints with recorded announcements. The problems of the banks will have

Remarks by Dr. Henry C. Wallich, Seymour H. Knox Professor of Economics, Yale University.

to be met that foresee great initial costs with a payoff only after the facilities are in wide use. Some 18 years from now, these difficulties should be well on their way to a solution. But it is too early to start accumulating currency and check forms as potential collectors' items. Moreover, small purchases and payments will always be handled most efficiently by pocket change.

Shrinkage of Demand Deposits

Even without automation, the demand-deposit business of the banks, as a share of their total activities, is doomed to contraction. The upward trend in the turnover of checking deposits will continue even without automation, as firms and households learn to use their money more efficiently. Automation will greatly accelerate velocity. These developments will reduce the advantages that may accrue to thrift institutions from offering checking deposits, which likely they will be allowed to do long before 1990. Banks meanwhile will have to find new sources of funds if they are to maintain their share of financial business, and if they are to offer their customers the kind and volume of financing they will need. Financial services of all sorts will play an increasing role among bank earnings, partly displacing income from lending.

A Homogeneous Group of Deposit Institutions

In 1990 specialization among depositary institutions will no doubt exist, but much of it will not

A LOOK AT BUSINESS IN 1990: A Summary of the White House Conference on the Industrial World Ahead, Washington, D.C., February 7-9, 1972,(U.S. Government Printing Office: 1972 0—467-348) pp. 294-296.

be the kind of specialization that today exists among banks, mutual savings banks, and savings-and-loan associations. The report of the Hunt Commission, which proposes to broaden the lending and deposit powers of the thrift institutions, and to subject all these types of deposit institutions to the same taxes, reserve requirements, and regulation, indicates the trend. That trend is toward department stores of finance, even though different stores will still differ in the relative magnitude of particular departments.

Larger Institutions Competing Vigorously

The size of the average deposit institution will have increased significantly. This will be true not only in absolute terms—growth and inflation make that a certainty—but also relative to a much enlarged GNP. Many small institutions will have been merged, because the progress of automation and consequent legislative trends will favor this development. Branching areas will have been widened. Automation will have reduced the competitive capacity of small unit banks, while also cutting down the usefulness of branches. Large automated banks will be able to reach across larger distances, connected to their customers by wires instead of by mail. Automated equipment will demand large amounts of capital, and will probably raise the economies of scale. Even so, the American banking system will not resemble the Canadian or European banking systems. There will be no big five or big nine. Competition, moreover, will be intensified precisely because it will be possible to handle smaller transactions over longer distances so that the number of institutions competing regionally or nationally will be enhanced. The greater homogeneity of depositary institutions will further intensify competition.

Mutual Funds

Mutual funds for similar institutions will play a larger role for the average investor than they do today. The small investor probably will go on losing ground in the stock market owing to the high cost of servicing small transactions. Techniques meanwhile should have been developed to bring down the high cost of mutual-fund management. Mutual funds will be close to playing the role of banks for equity depositors who want to place funds for longer or shorter periods in the stock market, much as today they place them in thrift institutions. Meanwhile speculative activity of

funds will have diminished. The experience of the funds, increasingly publicized and scrutinized, will have made increasingly clear that the average fund cannot beat the averages. Stress will be placed on preserving principal by avoiding taxes, commissions, and other charges.

The Stock Market

In contrast to the 1950s and the 1960s, the stock market will probably be an important source of capital for American corporations. Mounting controls over capital use will compel corporations to finance more heavily through equities. Strong demand for equities will exist because, over many years, it should have been demonstrated that the stock market does broadly keep up with inflation and offers an acceptable hedge. While bonds with high coupons will be protecting the holder against moderate inflation, taxability of the inflation premium will work against high-income investors

---

The trend is to department stores of finance, even though different stores will differ in the relative magnitudes of particular departments.

---

in the bond market. Stock markets will have become unified, with widespread access for institutions, and transactions and the keeping of records, of course, wholly automated. Stock certificates will have vanished generically and not just individually as today. Increasingly sophisticated securities analysis, in a stabler economy, will make for increasingly correct pricing of stocks. Performance investment accordingly will have lost much of its appeal and turnover will be lower relative to the volume of securities outstanding than it is today. Social pressures, including heavier capital-gains taxation, will be working against speculative gains.

The Supply of Savings

The shortage of investable funds that many observers foresee for the decade of the 1970s will have faded somewhat by 1990. I feel less confident about this prediction, however, than about the others. Its realization will depend on the net outcome of conflicting trends that cannot be foreseen with certainty. Given present birth rates and population structure, the rate of population growth is due to slow sharply by 1990. The rate of labor-force growth may have slowed somewhat less depending as it does upon birth rates of the late '60s and early '70s, and on births during the 1920s and 1930s, the age bracket that will be retiring around 1990. Population and labor-force growth both suggest that the number of newcomers to be supplied with homes, schools, and jobs will be shrinking. So will the amount of capital required for those purposes. The reduction in population growth implies some decline in the fraction of GNP going into savings. Nevertheless, on balance more savings should be available each year per head of the then-existing population.

These conflicting trends, therefore, should work out to an easier supply situation for capital, although not to the extent of the 1930s when an exhaustion of the demand for capital was being forecast.

Growing Government Control over Allocation of Capital

No matter whether 1990 will see a capital shortage or a capital glut, the role of government in the allocation of capital is likely to be greater. If the supply situation of capital is eased, it may be necessary for government to absorb a larger proportion of the supply by public works, or at least make sure that it is invested privately. If, on the other hand, capital should still be in tight supply, for instance because of major environmental or scientific projects, one must assume that present trends toward the setting of social priorities for the allocation of capital will have led to a larger role for government. This means that business, which as a user of capital has been least affected by capital-market difficulties, will find access to the market limited in favor of housing, and of governmental units at all levels. This may mean somewhat higher borrowing costs, more frequent recourse to new equity issues, and lower dividends. The net effect would probably be a drag on the rate of growth of output. ■

SECTION IV

THE SOCIAL RESPONSIBILITY OF BUSINESS

Section IV presents an overview on the social responsibility of business now and for the coming two decades through the following articles.

AN OVERVIEW ON THE SOCIAL RESPONSIBILITY
OF BUSINESS

THE SOCIAL RESPONSIBILITY OF BUSINESS

THE PARADOX OF CORPORATE RESPONSIBILITY

ROLE OF THE CORPORATION IN THE ECONOMY

REDEPLOYING CORPORATE RESOURCES TOWARD
NEW PRIORITIES

THE NEW ENVIRONMENT FOR BUSINESS

CONSUMERISM, 1990 — ADAPTING TO
TODAY'S VALUES FOR TOMORROW'S IMPERATIVES

An Overview on the Social Responsibility of Business

Roy Amara

RAPID social change has increasingly become a way of life. Such change produces a variety of new social forces impacting on all our social institutions. As a result, new responses and new social mechanisms are required to adapt successfully to the future environment that is thereby created.

In the present context, "social responsibilities of business" are defined as expectations arising from the transactions between a corporation and the following principal societal claimants: shareholders and bond holders, employees, consumers, government, public, suppliers, and competitors.

The Changing Environment

I shall consider how the increasing velocity of social change might affect the size, form, structure, and internal and external relationships of the corporation. To answer such questions, the characteristics of the most relevant societal changes can be aggregated into four environmental trends.[1, 2, 3]

- Economic toward Social
- Industrial toward Postindustrial
- Technological toward Posttechnological
- National toward International

An issues paper prepared by Roy Amara, President, Institute for the Future, Menlo Park, California.

In some instances these trends are mutually reinforcing, in others they are conflicting. Technology has created an environment in which it is both necessary and possible for society to shift its concerns from predominantly economic ones toward social ones. However, the amount and kind of technological development required to satisfy social concerns may be at variance with that required to meet growing international challenges. As a whole, these four key trends may be seen as representing a transition from one type of society to another.

Economic toward Social—No simple phrase can capture adequately the changes in values and expectations that are taking place in society. They are characterized by such descriptions as youth culture, new "consciousness," equality of opportunity, and quality of life. The manifestations are also many: decreasing emphasis on materialistic, achievement-oriented pursuits; shifts from growth-motivated to person-centered orientations; concern with quality of physical environment; abandonment of the puritan ethic of hard work as an end in itself for stress on human self-fulfillment and the concept of leisure as a right; diversity of value systems; and so forth.

These changes are made possible in large part by present and expected future economic affluence

A LOOK AT BUSINESS IN 1990: A Summary of the White House Conference on the Industrial World Ahead, Washington, D.C., February 7-9, 1972 (U.S. Government Printing Office: 1972 0—467-348) pp. 77-84.

138

(about 40 percent per decade growth in per capita real income).[4] They are not restricted to the young nor is their effect likely to dissipate. Rather, they are expected to intensify because they represent, in many cases, basic shifts in value systems that underlie much of the attitudinal and belief structure of large segments of society. As a result, their societal effects can be expected to be fairly pervasive and fundamental. In particular, such shifts are at the root of the growing list of social and public concerns in contrast to prior emphasis on economic and private ones.[5]

Industrial toward Postindustrial—The economic history of the United States can be characterized by three distinct periods of economic activity. The agrarian period was featured by the dominance of agriculture as an economic pursuit with a correspondingly low per-capita income. The industrial age, beginning with the Civil War, and fueled by the development of the west, was characterized by the preponderance of workers employed in manufacturing and a moderate standard of living. The postindustrial age, which is now emerging, portends a much higher

---

Business will have to learn to become an even better listener to the variety of voices, a better integrator of conflicting demands bearing on it, and a better responder to the range of public it will need to serve.

---

standard of living, a decline in the importance of manufacturing, and the rise of service-oriented and knowledge-oriented activities. Among its more important features are: the expanding role and importance of education as a generator of wealth; greater individualization in access to and dissemination of information (now done through the mass media); the dominant role of computer and communication technologies in business and industry as well as in societal interactions; and the increased capability for citizen participation and feedback in political processes.

The growth of postindustrial applications of technology and the growth of channels of communication imply basic redistribution of influence and power—where more real power will now be exercised by better-informed citizen groups, consumer

---

The growing understanding that it is not technology per se that is at fault, but rather the way in which it has been applied or not applied will have widespread consequences.

---

groups, students, and the like. Ultimately, this will create basic changes in institutional forms. The full effects of such changes—particularly in politics, government, and education—are only now beginning to be felt through increased public awareness, growth of public participation in defining social issues, and in an increasing public insistence on reappraisal of national priorities. Virtually no sector of society will be left untouched by the effects. The end result may be a well-educated, leisure-oriented, informed society of highly interacting and participating citizenry.

Technological toward Posttechnological—It is being increasingly recognized that technology should be developed and applied with somewhat more deliberation than in the past, for the effects can be detrimental as well as beneficial. It has contributed to problems of population growth, threat of nuclear warfare, pollution, congestion, and so forth. Similarly, it has made possible an increasingly higher standard of living throughout society.

In the past, whenever technology has become available, it has been used without much forethought as to its long-run consequences—the urge to use it has normally been overriding. Private decisions to employ a new technology have generally been based on a short-run economic gain. The growing understanding that it is not technology per se that is at fault, but rather the way in which it has been applied or not applied will have widespread consequences.

The more balanced and discriminating application of technology, which characterizes the posttechnological age, will require the assessment of the secondary and higher order effects and costs of technology.

This is because the complexity of technology is accelerating at a rate so rapid that it causes instability in institutional relationships. This concept relates to the management principle operative in a cybernetic system, by which a system grows, exhibits stability, adjusts, adapts, and evolves. When

139

the laws of self-regulation and self-organization are no longer operative the behavior governed by the dynamic structure of the system is no longer viable and the system self-destructs.

Solution of this situation will in part require introducing into the decision-making process an analysis of the possibly negative social costs of technology. It will also cause more research and development funds to be channeled into areas having high social value in the long run but may cause unfavorable economic costs in the short run.

National toward International—Clearer than almost any other change in the environment of the corporation is the extent to which societal interactions have become international and global. Communications, transportation, production, and distribution systems are bringing nations closer and closer together. Obsolescence of traditional political, economic, and ideological boundaries is occurring because of population growth, decreasing costs of transportation and communication, and emergence of new patterns of economic interaction.

The world has thus become increasingly dependent on the resources of the entire planet. As a result of this increasing interdependence, there is a growing interlocking of economies, technological development, and social progress. Some of the most important problems resulting from this emerging international environment are the increasing gap between developed and less-developed countries; the decreasing ability of the United States to compete in low-technology industries such as textiles, leather goods, and clothing; and the increasing dependence of the United States on foreign raw materials and fuels. Perhaps the most visible example of this trend is the growing importance of the multinational corporation.

Meaning for the Corporation

Resolution of the central problem, a definition of the social responsibilities of business, can be accomplished through the integration of the conflicting demands on the corporation created by the emergence of the four environmental changes. This can be achieved when the demands of the constituencies of business (shareholders, employees, consumers, the public, and government) are integrated into a new and internally consistent pattern.

The impact that the four environmental changes will have on the five constituencies of business can be illustrated in a matrix, Table 1. The entry, at the intersection of each row and column, illus-

trates in summary form some of the possible effects.

A broad outline of a possible scenario that might emerge is as follows:

The corporation will have been led to a reexamination and reformulation of its basic goals and a restructuring of its basic form. As a result of political and legislative processes, and spurred on by increasing public awareness and desire to redefine the corporate role in society, several private-public sector legislative and administrative guidelines and incentives will be formulated. Such guidelines and incentives will reflect national objectives, provide mechanisms for greater corporate involvement in the public-sector goods and services market, encourage a balanced development of new technology, reflect a more sophisticated understanding of manpower planning, and facilitate international trade.

Two other major groups will be more involved in the corporate enterprise: consumers and employees.

The postindustrial age, which is now emerging, portends a much higher standard of living, a decline in the importance of manufacturing, and the rise of service-oriented and knowledge-oriented activities.

Consumers will play a major role in influencing product planning and design; employees, in influencing basic changes in corporate structure, goals, and work environment. The next result will be a shift by the corporation toward greater involvement in public-sector goods and services. This shift may aggravate problems of raising corporate capital and problems of meeting increasing foreign competition; ultimately it may lead to restructuring, or public-sector financing, of some basic industries (e.g., transportation, steel, power, and so forth). Opportunities for foreign investment and the increasing role of multinational corporations may also accelerate these processes. In short, the corporation will exist increasingly in a "fish bowl" environment where the public, government, consumers, and employees participate with shareholders in setting corporate objectives.

Some Alternative Initial Adaptations

In attempting to paint a representative and plausible picture of impacts on the corporation, some important details have been omitted. These

TABLE 1—SOME POSSIBLE IMPACTS OF SOCIAL TRENDS ON THE CORPORATION

Corporate Constituents	Economic toward Social	Industrial toward Postindustrial	Technological toward Posttechnological	National toward International
Shareholders	Encourage corporate social involvement but retain largely economic concept of profit	Encourage gains in productivity through applications of information-related technologies	Seek mechanisms for sharing costs with government for development of new technologies	Encourage development of new technology to meet foreign competition Look to multinational investment opportunities
Employees	Seek meaningful work Seek a less-structured work environment	Seek voice in corporate affairs Seek shorter workweek and increased fringe benefits	Seek means for hedging against delays, uncertainties and additional costs of new technologies	Seek mechanisms for easing dislocations to employees from foreign competition
Consumers	Press for useful, safe, reliable products that serve genuine consumer needs	Demand publication and dissemination of production data Seek voice in corporate affairs	Insist on thorough assessments of new technologies affecting consumer	Encourage trade measures for reducing costs of consumer products
Government	Reexamine and reformulate national goals to reflect public-sector priorities Provide legislative guidelines and financial incentives to stimulate private initiative in public-sector areas	Revamp manpower planning programs for retraining, for mid-career changes, and so forth Encourage productivity gains	Encourage balanced development of new technology	Facilitate international trade
Public	Seek redefinitions of corporate objectives to reflect increasing role in social goals	Seek mechanisms for greater public involvement in corporate boards	Demand that corporations understand environmental effects of new technologies	Support measures for balanced development of international trade

details concern the differences in responses or adaptations that may be made by individual corporations and industries. For some, the changes may be minor, and the present market mechanism for allocating resources may continue to be used. For example, this is likely for such activities as retailing and personal services, where the impacts from postindustrial, posttechnological, and international developments may be minimal. For others, the changes may be extreme, and basically new corporate public-private forms may emerge in housing, education, and health services. Diversity will be the end product, while incremental trial-and-error rather than grand strategic planning or comprehensive conceptual theories will show the way.

Many difficulties concerning underlying corporate purpose may arise in seeking adaptations to environmental changes. Many of these have been eloquently described by a number of authors, but perhaps Milton Friedman [6] captures the essence most effectively. His central theme is that the proper business of business is economic profit. Unresolvable dilemmas arise if we veer away from this basic principle, for we are then asking the agents (managers) of corporate owners (shareholders) to make social choices by allocating private capital for public purposes. Such agents are neither qualified nor authorized to do this. The result will be an obfuscation of roles and, ultimately, perhaps the demise of the most efficient mechanism known to man for allocating scarce resources—namely, the corporate enterprise.

Such difficulties must be squarely faced. One way is to explore how expected environmental changes may suggest redefinitions of corporate purposes and roles. For example, it is unlikely that the solution to the steady degradation of the quality of our public-goods and services sector will come from dependence on voluntary assistance from the private sector operating under present ground rules. So far, such efforts can be considered miniscule by any measure. It is unjust and unwise,

141

as Friedman says, to expect individual corporations to hasten their possible demise through such efforts. In the short run (e.g., less than five years), government, reflecting societal desires, must specify through legislation and administrative guidelines the requirements for meeting societal responsibilities, be those in the fields of pollution, minority employment, or consumer goods. This will provide a common frame of reference for each corporation. In addition, incentives—financial and otherwise—must be provided to make some socially important markets economically attractive. There is no reason why essential corporate purposes, including economic profit as a central objective, may not be retained as some corporate resources are redirected toward the public sector. In these adaptations, government will play a key role.

In the longer run (e.g., 5 to 10 years), however, some basic changes may take place as a result of impacts on the other claimants of the corporate organism. For example, already some signs have appeared that particular institutional and individual shareholders will invest only in those corporations that pass some minimum social audit.[7] Also, consumers directly influence the corporations through their "votes" for consumer products; as dissemination of product information and consumer coherence increase, the effect will become even more pronounced. But perhaps the most important influence will be registered by employees, particularly those destined to assume management positions. The signs are already fairly clear that the new breed of future managerial talent is oriented differently from his present-day counterparts. This may be the single most important and most sustaining factor influencing corporate adaptation.[8] Finally, the general public exercises its influence through its general awareness of corporate activities. A recent case study brings this forcefully into focus. The study suggests that corporations in a particular industry that rank high in social concern (i.e., concern for pollution) also are the most profitable.[9] The conjecture is that the correlation is due not only to reduced operating costs from health insurances, maintenance, and taxes, but also to reduced costs in raising capital and marketing its products (i.e., projection of a "clean company" image).

In any case, however impacts are ultimately felt, and, however each individual corporation adapts, a number of public- and private-sector mechanisms can be considered for making some initial adaptations. Six are described as follows:

Responses to New Social Demands

Human-Resource Planning

Changes in career requirements are becoming so rapid at every level that virtually no one is immune from job obsolescence. This problem will intensify as the shift to a postindustrial, posttechnological, international-oriented society continues. One urgent need is for government to revamp completely its manpower forecasting and planning policies. A supplementary approach is the development of a scheme for voluntary career insurance, supported by the employee, the employer, and perhaps government.[10] Under this scheme, as an individual approaches job obsolescence, he would be provided with career counseling, retraining and, perhaps, income maintenance during the period of transition. If the posttraining position were at a lesser income rate than the original one, the income maintenance might be on a sliding scale to account for the difference in income levels. In fact, such plans may become agenda items in union-management negotiations in the near future.[11]

Technology Assessment

Technology assessment is the evaluation of the second and higher order consequences of new technology before it is developed and applied, so that a more effective balance can be made of total benefits and costs.[12] This function must be performed far more effectively than in the past. A search for improved mechanisms for technology assessment is under way, largely in the public sector. The basic problems center on performing this function objectively and without raising further the risks of new technology development so that it becomes, as has been admonished, "technology arrestment."

To date, industry has not taken full cognizance of the responsibilities it has in future assessments of technology. It is likely that industry may need to develop its own assessment capability to minimize its own risk in new-product development. If this is not done, the prospects of increasing government intervention in product innovation, increased costs of product development, and loss of public confidence may be materially increased.

Voluntary Associations

Buried in the backwaters of corporate relationships are a number of dormant mechanisms that may be revitalized to serve future socially related purposes. One of these is the industry trade association.[13] The attractiveness of using such a mechanism is that it already exists, involves the possibility for joint industry action, and is based on private initiative.

The list of areas in which such associations can be effective social agents is almost endless. They can set safety and performance standards; they can act in concert on pollution abatement, hard-core hiring, public-private partnership forms; and so forth. Antitrust laws may have to be redefined, but this should not be a major obstacle.[14]

Social Auditing

There appear to be few, if any, standards to determine how well a corporation is responding and adapting to socially related demands being placed on it. In view of the variety of more or less suitable responses that can be made, such assessments are extremely difficult to make. Various attempts to devise relative rating systems have been suggested,[15] but, at best, these efforts can be considered only exploratory.

Ultimately, the social-audit function may be performed by independent nonprofit corporations operating under a set of independently determined and continuously refined criteria. Other approaches related to social auditing are possible. One is the creation of a Staff Corporate Ombudsman,[11] perhaps chosen by the staff and reporting to the president. The position might be filled by a fairly young staff member for a period of, say, two to four years.

New Public-Goods Divisions

It has been suggested that business skills and resources will not be turned to the public goods and service sector unless business begins to view it as a normal risk-taking, profit-making enterprise.[14] At least two broad approaches can be taken. In the first, a detailed analysis may be made of the opportunities present, the roles possible, the risks involved, and the incentives required. Preliminary work in this area indicates that a number of unexplored opportunities exist in housing, education, health, and possibly transportation. Using another approach, a search can be made for social and technological inventions that might meet high-priority needs. Among the areas suggested for research and development are: nonharmful and inexpensive substitutes for food additives now thought to be harmful; inexpensive power sources; freshwater production and distribution systems for irrigation; and fertilizer production methods for use in developing countries. To promote such areas, patent laws might be amended to allow patent life to exceed the normal 17 years, and special cost allowances may be given to support research and development by corporations.

New Public-Private Partnerships

At some point, the interaction of corporate and government initiatives can lead to entirely new public-private partnerships. Although much has been written about such possibilities and some attempts are being made (e.g., Postal Service, National Corporation for Housing, COMSAT), little is known about the ways in which they should be structured or the conditions under which they operate best. In the future, the possibilities for new public-private intersect organizations will increase. This increase will reflect greater corporate involvement in unprofitable but socially useful public-sector activities.

The basic notion in such a partnership is that government assumes a major role in financing, policy-making, and planning; the private sector, on the other hand, provides the technological, managerial, and marketing expertise.[16] In principle, it seems workable; in practice, some hard thinking still remains to be done.

One of the key problems is the definition of the circumstances under which private corporations are both competent for, and willing to enter into, such partnerships.[17] Included among the principal requirements are: a clearly defined and specified task; available technology and supporting systems; unambiguous methods of performance measurement; and adequate financial incentives.

The absence of any one of these conditions can lead to failure. For example, the "improvement of community health services" is too broadly defined to be useful; "reducing incidence of drug use" is too difficult to tackle given our state of knowledge; "improving the appreciation of music" is hard to measure; and "building of low-income housing" may not offer sufficient return in view of the attendant risks. Nevertheless, a number of experiments is under way—particularly in teaching reading and arithmetic skills to public-school children—that are being closely watched. Although the results are not all in and some difficult problems remain to be solved, such "performance controls" may well be harbingers of similar partnerships in other fields.

Selection and Integration

Some of the adaptive measures described may blossom into useful forms for helping to shape the social responsibilities of business; at best, however, they cannot be expected to be more than small pieces of a larger mosaic that can only be dimly perceived at this time. In the long run (10 to 30 years and beyond) the accuracy with which we can project the nature of the social responsibilities of business becomes negligible.

Perhaps one way in which we can begin to focus this image is to examine our unique societal strengths from the longer perspective. Three such strengths stand out as potentially central to shaping future policies influencing the role of the corporate enterprise. These are: uses of technology; societal diversity; and a new image of man.

Uses of Technology—It may at first be surprising—in this day of deepening public disappointment in, and distrust of, technology—to identify the uses of technology as a key force in the future development of our society. And yet, a large

---

When the growth rate of productivity falters, as it appears to have done recently, the growth in standard of living falters, and all our social goals are in jeopardy, both domestically and internationally.

---

measure of our success will depend critically on how well we learn to use it. Technology provides the economic base for meeting social needs, the resources for contributing uniquely to international trade,[18] and the leading edge for realizing the benefits of a postindustrial and posttechnological society. Without its continuous development, all our social goals become infinitely more difficult to achieve.

Our ability to apply technology in the past has made an enormous difference in our economic and social progress.[19] In recent years, we have fallen badly behind when measured in terms of percapita patents and the fraction of civilian manpower employed in research and development. A real danger facing us in the next several decades is that the present disenchantment with technology will lead us to shun it, rather than to use it to serve us more effectively.

This hazard is particularly worrisome since it is becoming clearer that we are now, and have been,

underinvesting in the kinds of technology that are most directly coupled to industrial output. This situation has been aggravated by the rates of expenditures in defense and space. Notwithstanding the differences in absolute levels of expenditures, most European countries and Japan allocate more than 20 percent of their government research and development for civilian outputs, whereas the corresponding figure for the United States is less than 6 percent.[20]

The impact of this misallocation is felt ultimately as reduced productivity. When the growth rate of productivity falters, as it appears to have done recently, the growth in standard of living falters, and all our social goals are in jeopardy, both domestically and internationally. Thus, instead of using technology less, we must learn to use it more, gearing it to meeting our social needs. Such considerations have important implications to long-range business planning in terms of investments in research and development, in new-product planning, and in capital equipment.

Societal Diversity—The second factor is societal diversity. In recent years, it has become increasingly recognized that our society is an amalgam of separate cultures rather than a melting pot. This fact of existence is two-edged, for it can be a great source of strength as well as a source for division and conflict.

One of the hazards we face is strife, divisiveness, squandering of our material and intellectual resources, and eventual decline. Few countries span the diversity of groups, subcultures, and factions that exist in the United States today. What does this all mean? Among other things, it means we will have to live in a society of unprecedented social diversity. To do so requires steering a course between anarchy on the one hand and repression on the other.

The need to encourage diversity, pluralism, differentiation, and experimentation is overriding. Simple cultures are characteristics of simple societies; societies as complex as ours is and will be must include diversity as a hallmark. From this

---

It is unlikely that the solution to the steady degradation of the quality of our public-goods and services sector will come from dependence on voluntary assistance from the private sector operating under present ground rules.

---

diversity usually emerge the most useful social adaptations—hammered out through the open competition of ideas. This is the social analogue of the economic marketplace.

Thus, what could become a disabling malady can become, instead, a source of great strength. This is because the drives for diversity are not governed, in most instances, by blind allegiance to some political, economic, or religious ideology. Rather, the drives stem from the desire to discover and realize new sets of social values and goals, as summarized by the transitions described in an earlier section. The implications of all this to business are fairly clear. Among other things, business will have to learn to become an even better listener to the variety of voices, a better integrator of conflicting demands bearing on it, and a better responder to the range of publics it will need to serve. More importantly to both business and society, out of this diversity can emerge a new image of man.

New Image of Man—As a society, we are beginning to understand more clearly how to balance the social with the economic, the technological with the environmental, and man with nature. Out of this heightened understanding can develop a more satisfying relationship of man to the society that he creates and in which he lives.

The corporate form represents the most efficient producer and allocator of goods and services that we know. The new challenge facing this system is the question of its adaptability in meeting the emerging economic and social needs of an increasingly interdependent globe. At present, no one quite knows how this is best done. Nevertheless, if business assumes a major role in searching for new social forms and new social responses, then a great step forward might be made toward the person-centered society" of Mumford, the "learning society" of Hutchins, and the "self-actualizing society" of Maslow—where man increasingly learns to realize his noblest aspirations by using the productive capacity at his disposal to serve his most basic human needs. If it cannot, we may face a period of considerable uncertainty and, eventually, decline.

The vitality of the American business system will be a measure of our flexibility in marshalling these three fundamental strengths and will largely determine the eventual structure of our private enterprise system. For these unique qualities hold the answers to the ultimate questions and challenges that will be thrust on business in discharging its social responsibilities in the future. ■

REFERENCES

1—Theodore J. Gordon and Robert H. Ament, *Forecasts of Some Technological and Scientific Developments and Their Societal Consequences,* Report R-6, Institute for the Future, Sept. 1969.

2—Raul de Brigard and Olaf Helmer, *Some Potential Societal Developments—1970-2000,* Report R-7, Institute for the Future, April 1970.

3—Earl B. Dunckel, William K. Reed, and Ian H. Wilson, *The Business Environment of the Seventies: A Trend Analysis for Business Planning,* McGraw-Hill, New York, 1970.

4—Fabian Linden, "The Decade of the Seventies," *Consumer Economics,* June 1969.

5—Committee for Economic Development, *Can We Afford Tomorrow?* Jan. 23, 1971.

6—Milton Friedman, "A Friedman Doctrine—The Social Responsibility of Business Is to Increase Its Profits," *New York Times Magazine,* Sept. 13, 1970.

7—Marge Speidel, "Investor Firm Adopts Social Concern Outlet," *Palo Alto Times,* Palo Alto, California, Aug. 9, 1971.

8—Samuel A. Culbert and James M. Elden, "An Anatomy of Activism for Executives," *Harvard Business Review,* Nov.-Dec. 1970.

9—John Cunniff, "Study Indicates Pollution Control and Higher Profits Linked," *Palo Alto Times,* Palo Alto, California, Aug. 6, 1971.

10—Theodore J. Gordon,, et al, *A Forecast of the Interaction between Business and Society in the Next Five Years,* Report R-21, Institute for the Future, April 1971.

11—Joseph A. Beirne, *New Horizons for American Labor,* Public Affairs Press, Washington, D.C., 1962.

12—David M. Kiefer, "Technology Assessment," *Chemical and Engineering News,* Oct. 5, 1970.

13—Clarence C. Walton, *Business and Social Progress,* Praeger, New York, 1970.

14—William J. Baumol, et al, *A New Rationale for Corporate Social Policy,* Supplementary Paper No. 31, Committee for Economic Development, 1970.

15—Clair W. Sater, "A Supplement to the Bottom Line: Rating Corporations on Social Responsibility," *Bulletin,* Summer 1971.

16—Committee for Economic Development, *Social Responsibilities of Business Corporations,* A Statement by the Research and Policy Committee, June 1971.

17—James Q. Wilson, "The Corporate Role in the Community," *Boston Globe,* Boston, Massachusetts, Oct. 3, 1971.

18—"The U.S. Searches for a Realistic Trade Policy," *Business Week,* July 3, 1971.

19—Myron Tribus, "Technology for Tomorrow versus Profit for Today," Winter Annual Meeting, American Society of Mechanical Engineers, 1970.

20—J. Herbert Hollomon and Alan E. Harger, "America's Technological Dilemma," *Technology Review,* July/August 1971.

The Social Responsibility of Business

Arjay Miller

B USINESS should not pretend to be something it is not. More bluntly, a business is a business, not a philanthropy. Its actions should be justified essentially on business grounds, on enlightened self-interest; not on abstract moral or ethical grounds. To try to do otherwise will only increase the credibility gap from which business already suffers. Business leaders should therefore avoid the temptation of promising too much, because some in our society already have an exaggerated notion of what business alone can do. Dr. Kenneth Clark has said, "Business and industry are our last hope. They are the most realistic elements in our society. Other areas in society—government, education, churches, labor— have defaulted in dealing with the Negro problem. It is now up to business." A black militant in Detroit put it even more bluntly when he told a group of business leaders, "If you cats can't do it, it's never going to get done."

Business, of course, can do much more than it is now doing. However, it is no more reasonable to expect business to do everything than it is to expect government to do everything. If the general public becomes too unrealistic in its expectations, and business, in turn, loses sight of the limitations of what it can accomplish working alone, we could experience a backlash of opinion that would be hurtful to the limited but important role that business can legitimately be expected to play.

Address by Arjay Miller, Dean, Graduate School of Business, Stanford University.

Proper Role of Business

What, then, is the proper role of business? At one extreme, Adam Smith maintained that the businessman pursuing his own self-interest would be guided "as by an unseen hand" to do more good for society than if he consciously set out to do so.

That was a simple concept, but for nearly 200 years it worked remarkably well. In fact, until the 1960s, most businessmen continued to believe that their exclusive function was to make the biggest profit they could, with only minimal attention to the world outside the business arena. Furthermore, society by and large accepted—even applauded—this concept.

This view still has its champions among some respected economists. Milton Friedman is one. In a recent article entitled "The Social Responsibility of Business Is to Increase Its Profits," Friedman contends that businessmen who believe they are defending the free enterprise system by saying that business is not "merely" concerned with profits but also with promoting desirable social ends are "preaching pure and unadulterated socialism."

At the other extreme is a large number of vocal critics who blame business for virtually all of the ills of society, and demand a much more restricted role for business. In their view, this society will survive only if business control is taken from private hands and placed for the most part in government—or in their own willing hands, if that be needed. They argue that because of the con-

A LOOK AT BUSINESS IN 1990: A Summary of the White House Conference on the Industrial World Ahead, Washington, D.C., February 7-9, 1972 (U.S. Government Printing Office: 1972 0—467-348) pp. 85-89.

stant focus of business on profits, it cannot be trusted to do what is right and just.

Critics holding this view fail to understand that profits are a necessary cost of production, as even Iron Curtain countries are being forced to recognize. President Nixon addressed himself to this question some months ago when he said, "It is only through profits that industry can buy the new plants, the new equipment that will make our workers more productive and therefore more competitive in the world . . . I am for more profits because I believe that more profits mean more jobs."

Without adequate profits business has no way to undertake and sustain new efforts to meet pressing social needs. We must *earn* social progress, in a literal sense.

Our approach during the decades ahead must be somewhere in between these two extremes. Neither promises to do too much, nor fails to do what can be reasonably expected of us, either alone or in cooperation with government and other segments of society.

Business Now in a New Ball Game

The central fact of business today is that we are in a new ball game. We cannot return to the old, familiar ground rules. It is really too bad, in a way, that Adam Smith and Milton Friedman are not right. Life would be so much simpler if our only task and our only responsibility was the narrow pursuit of profits.

As it happens, however, tremendous new demands are being made on this society, and these in turn are causing tremendous new demands on business. We need mention only the insistent pressures for a cleaner environment, for better housing, for improved education at all levels, for greater traffic safety, and so on through a long list. The key question is, what share of the responsibility should business undertake?

For several years the federal government has encouraged business to perform an increasing variety of social tasks that were formerly regarded as almost exclusively governmental responsibilities—training disadvantaged persons, rebuilding the ghettos, helping blacks and other minority-group members establish their own enterprises, and many more. Because these involve special added costs for most of the companies involved, the government has offered special inducements to encourage business participation.

Is this the way of the future? The final returns

are not yet in, because efforts to date are largely experimental, leaving many questions still to be resolved. But some ideas are taking root that should serve us well in the years ahead.

One of these tenets is that society will be best served if each of its major institutions concentrates on what it does best, and does not waste time and resources on tasks it is poorly equipped to handle. Business, for example, can increase the hiring and training of minority-group persons, introduce new technology and increase the level of job skills, improve the quality and serviceability of essential products, and eliminate as quickly as possible harmful air or water pollutants resulting from its operations. On the other hand, some jobs it can tackle only in cooperation with government; still others it should not attempt.

In sorting out the proper assignments, we should recognize that many of our most serious and urgent current demands are in the area of public, rather than private, goods. People want cleaner air and water, safer streets, less traffic congestion, better education systems, and so forth. These demands cannot be satisfied in the traditional private marketplace. You cannot buy clean air or a lane of your own on the highway between home and office.

Need to Establish National Goals and Priorities

Since the output of public goods cannot be determined automatically by the expenditure pattern of individuals, therefore, how should we approach the problem? What is needed first, in my opinion, is a much clearer statement of our national goals and the priority we assign to each. We as people cannot continue to "muddle through" as we have been doing—starting and stopping, making piecemeal efforts wherever the pressure is greatest and, in general, having no real idea of what the ultimate cost of any particular program will be. We must improve our decision-making process if we are to make the kind of solid, sustained progress we desire.

Decisions as to what we as a people propose to

147

accomplish are and must remain, of course, a part of our normal political process. In a democracy, only elected representatives of the people will be entrusted with the establishment of national goals and priorities.

At present, however, neither the Congress nor the Administration can make sound decisions about far-reaching social goals because they lack adequate financial and other facts that are critical in determining how far and how fast we should go. Too often Congress does not know the ultimate costs of legislation. How much, for example, will the Clean Air Act and its amendments cost? $10 billion? $100 billion? No one really knows.

It seems to me essential that we know the costs of present and pending legislation because of the increasingly severe crunch on our resources, which is not generally recognized. In testimony before the Joint Economic Committee of Congress last February, I reported that the National Planning Association had estimated that the gap between accepted national goals and our ability to pay would reach $150 billion annually by 1975. In my opinion, recognition of new social needs, plus inflation, would now make that figure much larger, and the gap will certainly continue to increase in the years ahead.

Probably the most significant figure in such a report would be the gap between the total cost of

---

Proposal for a National Goals Institute

I proposed to the Congressional Committee that, as an aid in working out realistic and enduring social programs, a National Goals Institute be established by law. It would have four major tasks:

- Estimate the general magnitude of future increases in national output—in other words, how much new money will be available for spending.
- Project the cost of presently established programs—education, health care, roads and so on—over a 10-year period.
- Project the cost of attaining additional generally recognized goals over a similar 10-year period.
- Publish annually a listing of all our national goals, together with estimated costs and the resources available to meet them.

---

our national goals and our ability to pay. General recognition of this gap would in itself be valuable, because it would open the eyes of those who believe that our problem today is overproduction or failure to divide properly what they call an "economy of abundance." It also would throw into perspective such recurrent questions as the shorter workweek and technological unemployment. As long as so many recognized needs remain unsatisfied, we are facing—along with the remainder of the world—what can only be called an "economy of scarcity" requiring more work, not less.

Focusing attention on the gap between what we want and what we can afford also underscores the importance of increasing output per man-hour because increased output is the basic source of all economic progress. And unless we make the unrealistic assumption that individuals will work harder, higher output per man-hour can be achieved only through technological advance. In measuring technological progress, however, we must make certain that *all* costs are recognized, not merely the short-term direct effects.

The annual reports prepared by the proposed National Goals Institute would have no binding or direct authority. They would simply point out directions and possibilities, and provide a factual basis for enlightened public discussion and decision making. Our concern would be to make available the kind of information that we as a people must have if we are to be able to see clearly the various alternatives open to us and to choose rationally from among them.

In all of this kind of planning—defining goals, allocating resources and shaping specific programs—a clear need exists for business participation. Business must get into the planning process early and bring its experience to bear *before* programs are baked into law. If business does not cooperate in such planning, we can be sure that others will move ahead without us, leaving it to business to pick up the check, which will be larger than it might otherwise be.

It is unrealistic today to contend that business must be free to pursue its own goals without reference to the broader needs and aims of the total society. All of us in business must recognize and accept the necessity for an expanded government role in our economic life. We must make the most of the situation by cooperating fully in setting the new ground rules.

This could mean, for example, that we must be prepared to disclose certain kinds of information that have, up to now, been considered confidential. This need not be a harmful development if it is done in such a way as to protect the confidentiality of the figures of any single company. As a case in point, the automobile companies have been supplying safety and pollution cost data to the Bureau of Labor Statistics for some years without prejudice to their own individual competitive situations. The Bureau has used these data to compile average industry-wide cost increases, which are then released to the public and reflected in the Cost of Living index.

Before leaving the subject of national goals, I would like to emphasize that the establishment of goals by government need not restrict the important role business can and should play in the attainment of those goals. In some cases, such as air and water, the government role can be essentially limited to the establishment of standards that everyone must meet. Each individual firm can proceed in the most efficient manner to meet the standards, safe in the assumption that in so doing it will not place itself in an untenable competitive cost position.

Government Incentives

In many cases, however, government financial support will be required to attain established goals. In the case of low-cost housing, for example, private business is unable to make a more significant contribution at present because the families with the greatest need do not have sufficient funds to enter the market. What is needed in cases like this are government-provided incentives adequate to "turn-on" the private sector.

The type of incentive to be used should depend on the particular need to be met. In housing, for example, both rent supplements to low-income families and subsidies to building contractors are appropriate. In other cases, such as the procurement of goods and services, more use can be made of direct negotiations and contracts with private firms. As an underlying principle, maximum reliance should be placed on private enterprise and the effectiveness of management techniques that have proved so successful under our free enterprise system.

Businessmen have for too long been stereotyped as men who always react negatively to any kind of social progress that interferes with traditional ways of doing business.

For special situations, however, we should be willing to create new institutions, such as COMSAT, Amtrak, and the new Postal Service. Where neither private nor public resources alone can get a job done, there should be no hesitation at joining both to whatever extent is required to achieve the desired results.

Specific Suggestions for Corporation Executives

I will offer six specific suggestions to corporation executives as to the social responsibility of business in the next twenty years.

First, *I urge that executives integrate social objectives into the basic fabric of their company,* treating them just as they would any regular corporate activities. Although there is a role for a staff "Director of Public Affairs" or some such, the task of responding to new social needs must be accepted by all layers of management in all components throughout the entire organization. The general manager of a division or a subsidi-

Focusing attention on the gap between what we want and what we can afford also underscores the importance of increasing output per man-hour because increased output is the basic source of all economic progress.

ary, for example, should feel the same responsibility for meeting established corporate social objectives as he does for meeting profit objectives.

This means that "reporting" and "scorekeeping" for both sets of objectives must be subject to the same internal accounting procedures. Also, to be consistent, the reward system must be structured so as to penalize a manager for failing to meet either kind of objective.

Does all of this sound like too much to expect of a typical business firm? On the contrary, I believe it represents a minimum kind of effort, and one that we cannot avoid if we are to gear our operations to the needs of our time.

Second, in establishing social objectives for the corporation, use a rifle, not a shotgun, approach. Here it would be best to *have the line and staff managers participate in the setting of specific, measurable objectives,* including the time period over which each goal will be met. Although the objectives and time periods would vary from industry to industry and from company to company, they might typically include:

- Hiring objectives for minority-group persons and women expressed as a percentage of new hires, and projected perhaps five years ahead.
- Equally important, objectives for the upgrading of minority-group persons to higher levels of skill and responsibility, with specific numbers targeted in each of the higher salary grades. Where qualified new employees are not available, this would require in-house training programs aimed at increased upward mobility.
- Quotas for the purchase of goods and services from minority-owned firms, again with specific year-to-year dollar targets. This might require special help and encouragement for potential suppliers, but some firms are now doing this successfully. Much more can be done. For example, a letter from the business firm promising to make a substantial deposit would be helpful in starting a minority bank. Or, perhaps you would justify a long-term contract to a struggling new minority-owned advertising or consulting group.
- Use of minority-owned firms to the extent possible in your distribution or sales network.

As a third suggestion, I recommend that corporate executives, as individuals, *participate actively in public organizations of all kinds* at local, state, and national levels. One plant manager who is active in local organizations puts it this way: "Being a member of these groups enables us to keep a finger on the community's pulse, and lets us feel how residents think about whatever might come up . . . And we get out in the shop and tell the people to get involved in whatever interests them, to lend a hand where they're needed."

Fourth, I urge businessmen to *speak out more on current issues.* You have something to say, and you will be listened to. But I offer two cautions: Do not speak up only when you are *against* something. Be positive and constructive. Be honest and candid when the chips are down. Do not add to the credibility gap that has hurt much of business in recent years.

Fifth, where a company finds that it cannot tackle a worthy program or correct some problem

Our society will be best served if each of its major institutions concentrates on what it does best, and does not waste its time and resources on tasks it is poorly equipped to handle.

on its own, I suggest that it *make greater use of its trade association or some other voluntary grouping* to achieve its purpose. Representative ones are the National Alliance of Businessmen, which has helped many companies in the minority-hiring area, the Better Business Bureau, the Urban Coalition, and other groups that are ready to help individual companies on a collective basis do what a single company might not be able to undertake on its own. Do not be afraid to cooperate with academic organizations. At the Stanford Business School, for example, I have been impressed with the sincerity and purpose of a student-organized Committee for Corporate Responsibility that cooperates with business firms in seeking positive approaches to common problems.

As a sixth and final suggestion, *accent the positive.* Businessmen have for too long been stereotyped as men who always react negatively to any kind of social progress that interferes with traditional ways of doing business. This need not be so. People have demanded a small, low-pollutant automobile and we are now fast approaching that goal. We *can* do more to clean up our environment through the recycling of cans, bottles, and waste paper. We *can* clean up our lakes and other waterways through more careful planning and through the introduction of new systems and methods. We *can* relieve congestion in our cities and make better housing available for more people. We must endeavor to find ways to get them done, either acting alone or in conjunction with government, rather than in explaining why they cannot be done.

We must not be satisfied simply to react to pressures. How much more can be done, at less cost and with less pulling and hauling, if we make up our minds to anticipate trends and problems, and then devise a strategy to meet the situation.

The industrial world ahead—or in broader terms, the very destiny of this nation—depends in large part on how this country's businessmen respond to the new environment. I am optimistic that our business leaders will both recognize the importance of their role and carry it out in a bold, constructive manner. ∎

The Paradox of Corporate Responsibility

Henry G. Manne

CORPORATE social responsibility occupies a peculiar role in business intellectual history. It is peculiar because the underlying idea persists in spite of the absence of any rigorous justification of the concept. It has never been integrated into a coherent theory of economics or human behavior, and few of its scholarly proponents have ever analyzed the real economic implications of the idea. Yet this idea provided significant intellectual fuel for the Populist movement, the Progressive era, the New Deal, and the present antibusiness movement, sometimes euphemistically termed consumerism. It is likely to be with us until at least 1990.

It might be instructive to inquire into reasons why the idea of corporate social responsibility persists before we examine the merits of the notion. Probably some private interests are being served by the perpetuation of the concept, apart from whether it has any effect on corporate behavior. This, at least, is the hypothesis I shall examine.

The Support of the Corporate Social-Responsibility Concept

Americans seem to enjoy being told that business has a personal responsibility to them outside

Remarks by Henry G. Manne, Kenan Professor of Law, University of Rochester, Rochester, New York, and Visiting Professor, Stanford University Law School.

the marketplace. Perhaps this provides a sense of power and comfort to millions of people who cannot comprehend a complex market system no matter how well it performs. Furthermore, the successes of the capitalist system provide little opportunity for the political gore mass audiences seem to favor. Little is to be gained by those seeking either large audiences or political power from trying to explain the dull concepts of economic cost and competitive markets to the citizenry.

Government officials are maximizers just as much as are investors or industrialists, and their own utility is generally served by increases in governmental power. The concept of corporate social responsibility suits them almost perfectly. Today, as in years past, much new legislation is vaunted as making business more responsible to the public and as controlling the venal instincts of the capitalists. In fact, our political system is such that these regulatory provisions are often beneficial mainly to the politicians while carrying a high price tag for the public.

It is easy for politicians to take credit for vanquishing polluters while making no disclosure to the public of how much the cleanliness will cost them. And if for these and other reasons prices rise, then obviously price controls must be needed to guarantee socially responsible behavior by the corporations. The concept of corporate social responsibility is truly ideal for government officials who wish to claim credit for all public benefits and accept no responsibility for increased costs and

A LOOK AT BUSINESS IN 1990: A Summary of the White House Conference on the Industrial World Ahead, Washington, D.C., February 7-9, 1972 (U.S. Government Printing Office: 1972 0—467-348) pp. 95-98.

long-run antisocial effects.

American intellectuals of the left have also found happy hunting in the realm of corporate social responsibility. From Veblen and Ripley to Berle, Galbraith, and Nader, we have long been treated to one strained explanation after another of why free markets are not good for us. The alleged assumptions of the free-market model are derided; the myth of growing monopoly is constantly repeated; and the free market's inability to cope with certain externalities and social problems is blown out of all proportion.

The idea of a social responsibility fits all the liberal intellectual's predilections. It makes a moral issue out of business behavior; it accentuates the

---

A stock price will decline just as quickly whether corporate funds are given to charity, expended on social-welfare projects, stolen, or simply used inefficiently in the business . . . The stock market is ruthless, objective, and without social conscience. And for that we can all be thankful.

---

monopoly issue, since without some monopoly power, nonprofit-oriented behavior is unlikely; and it fits snugly with the recently discovered ecological crisis. The idea of corporate social responsibility becomes a convenient peg on which to hang every hackneyed criticism of business conduct and even a few new ones, like the lack of democracy and due process in dealing with employees, customers, or the community. We are, I might add, still awaiting the serious intellectual defense of all this.

Still another group who enthuses about corporate social responsibility is businessmen, particularly some prominent executives of large corporations. Several explanations can be given for this phenomenon. First, businessmen as a group are at best only slightly more expert in economic theory than the general population. And, like others, they espouse popular ideologies regardless of the underlying implications even for their own behavior.

Further, the concept of corporate responsibility flatters businessmen that they are the divine elect, as Andrew Carnegie would have had it. They are not only merely responsible for producing diaper pins or corrugated sheet metal or rock crushers,

but also they are obliged to look after us lesser beings. It is thus easy for some businessmen to believe that universities would collapse, the air become unbreathable, and civilization be lost if they did not thrust out their chins, flex their muscles and do good according to the gospel of business statesmanship—without even spending their own money.

Justification for Corporate Social Responsibility

But I do not believe that business advocacy of corporate responsibility is principally a matter of ideology or psychology. I think that it is economic. Corporate responsibility is good business because it is good public relations. Certainly in the economic propaganda war that has been waged for so long now, business would be ill advised to let politicians and consumerists claim all the credit for taming the corporate beasts—at least so long as the voting public thinks that corporations are beasts that must be tamed. One has only to look at the public pronouncements of General Motors since the Nader-inspired Project on Corporate Responsibility began its Campaign GM. Parts of the annual report now read like chapters from a corporate activist's text, implying that management operates the company as a public-service institution devoted to improvements in social welfare but not to profits.

But the talk may have consequences. As public expectations are built up both by politicians and businessmen, it becomes more and more difficult to do nothing when a new problem is identified. Then business must engage in otherwise unwanted behavior so as to stave off even more onerous political or regulatory burdens. If by these actions the public can be made to believe that business is already operating in a socially responsible way, the political threat may be defused or moderated at a relatively low cost. Better yet, the situation may be turned to positive business advantage if the situation can be used to gain "self-regulation" for the industry. The phrase is widely recognized today as meaning that potential competitors may, under a variety of ruses, be excluded from the market. But businessmen who covet this status claim that it will maintain ethical standards of business for the public's protection.

And if specific regulation ensues, that too will inevitably affect one group of firms in an industry differently than it does others. Typically the larger firms are the ones preferred. They can normally accept new regulatory costs with less effect on their total average cost because their volume is higher than that of smaller firms. And again we can see the possibility of some significant anticompetitive implications of corporate-responsibility proposals.

These then are some of the reasons why arguments for corporate responsibility continue to be made, and some of the substantive arguments against the concept. Other objections exist as well. For instance, cleanliness, safety, and nondiscrimination do not come free. Yet the ultimate incidence of the costs of these goods is rarely known. Costs can be passed forward to consumers or backward to suppliers of labor, goods, or capital. But there is nowhere else they can go. No entity called the corporation can be made to suffer or bear ultimate costs. Only people bear costs. If the costs cannot be shifted, they rest ultimately on the shareholders of the company. But only the most hardened capitalist-baiter can take satisfaction from that. Most of the shareholders will have bought their shares for prices that did not discount these new costs. Thus the financial burden will fall on those who did not receive the economic benefits of the misdeed now being corrected. And even where that is not true, the effect is still that of a tax arbitrarily placed on certain individuals to provide a general social benefit.

Many of the goals specified for corporate largess cannot be accomplished satisfactorily by firms acting individually. This may be because competitive pressures will not allow the altruistic corporation to survive, as has been claimed by some steel companies; or because the do-good firms simply are not large enough to solve the social problem on their own, as may be the case with minority hiring; or because other firms will simply continue to dirty the water or the air even if one or more stops voluntarily. A solution then will require either collective decision making by all firms, which is normally illegal under our antitrust laws, or government regulation.

Thus government has a special role in most of these areas, whether it is in determining acceptable levels of pollution, training the unskilled, or making foreign policy by outlawing trade with certain nations. But to talk of corporate responsibility for such issues does no more than muddy the water by suggesting that there is some effective way to reach the desired goal without government action. Literally no evidence can be found that voluntary corporate altruism has ever made a significant dent in any but the most insignificant problems addressed.

Many of the goals specified for corporate largess cannot be accomplished satisfactorily by firms acting individually . . . A solution then will require collective decision making by all firms, which is normally illegal under our antitrust laws, or government regulation.

Latitude of the Corporate Manager

Perhaps, indeed, the most crucial question about this subject is the extent to which nonmarket-oriented discretion is actually available to corporate managers. Berle, Galbraith, and others have long claimed that managers of large corporations are autonomous, self-perpetuating oligarchs who are free to use corporate funds in almost any way they see fit, whether it be for the shareholders, society, or themselves. Until recently this idea was widely accepted. But careful investigators have begun to test this thesis empirically and have found it strangely wanting in substance. Even Galbraith has admitted fundamental error in this regard.

No one should have been surprised by this discovery. If an industry is fully competitive, significant nonprofitable behavior is, of course, impossible. A firm insisting on such behavior would be unable to survive and function at all. We know, however, that competition is rarely this stringent, and that some surplus may be available for social-welfare purposes in large corporations. Such firms should thus find it possible to engage in some limited but significant amount of nonmarket-oriented activity without depriving the shareholders, the managers, or anyone else of their market rate of return. But, in fact, this is still not the case unless such a corporation is personally or closely held, in which case the owners are simply giving away their own money through a corporate conduit.

If public shareholders exist and without significant legal barriers to takeovers, mergers, or proxy fights, managers who actually engage in nonprofitable activities will soon be displaced. This time the market forces that will discipline the managers will not be those of the product market in which the company sells, as with competitive firms, but rather of the capital market. A stock price will decline just as quickly whether corporate funds are given to charity, expended on social-welfare projects, stolen, or simply used inefficiently in the business.

Corporate Responsibiltiy
Paradox

We find several phenomena surrounding the issue of corporate social responsibility. One is the large amount of talk on the subject. Another is the support of this notion by corporate executives, including support of government programs in no sense conducive to competitive capitalism. And still another is the meager amount of truly charitable behavior we actually witness in the corporate world. Herein lies the paradox of the corporate-responsibility notion.

And when stock prices decline sufficiently, a takeover of some sort by individuals who will manage the company in a different fashion becomes inevitable. The stock market is ruthless, objective, and without social conscience. And for that we can all be thankful.

For good public-relations reasons, corporations must continue their efforts to buy political and social goodwill by asserting noncapitalistic values. Even if everyone understood the tremendous social benefits to be derived from competitive capitalism, no individual firm could profit from voluntarily advocating the traditional values and ethics of the free enterprise system. Gain comes only from promising something for nothing.

The late Joseph Schumpeter argued, in his *Capitalism, Socialism and Democracy*, that as corporations grow and become bureaucratized, business executives cease to think and act like entrepreneurs, and therefore, cease to defend capitalism. Schumpeter may have been correct for the wrong reason. Contrary to his view, businessmen still behave precisely as classical economic theory prescribed. But today's maximizing behavior includes advocating the nonmaximization of profits. So, it is true that businessmen have largely ceased to defend business, but only because that was the businesslike thing to do.

Probably businessmen will continue, along with intellectuals and politicians, to advocate a second-rate economic system and to denegate a better one. The saving grace, at least for now, is that what businessmen say and what the market constrains them to do are two completely different things. The danger is that ultimately the talk will have so much political effect that the market system will be destroyed. When that process is complete, the only cry heard in the land will be for social responsibility from an all-powerful, overwhelming government. ∎

Role of the Corporation In The Economy

W. M. BATTEN

The role of the corporation in the economy has not enlarged in recent years. As an owner of tangible wealth of the economy, the corporate sector's share has remained stable at around 28 percent during the past half century. Over the past 20 years, rewards going to the corporate sector in the form of profits (before taxes) have declined from 16 percent to 11 percent of the national income, while the rewards of employees in the form of wages and salaries have risen. In addition, government's share of the wealth has been expanding at the expense of other sectors. The profit-seeking corporation is, indeed, a vital institution, but the United States is not, nor is it becoming a "corporate" economy. By most measures, the corporate sector has maintained a stable relation with the remainder of the economy for at least a generation. ■

Remarks by W. M. Batten, Chairman of the Board, J. C. Penney Company, Inc.

Redeploying Corporate Resources toward New Priorities

Hazel Henderson

T HE NEW "postindustrial values" transcend the goals of security and survival. They are, therefore, less materialistic, often untranslatable into economic terms and, in turn, beyond the scope of the market economy. They constitute a new type of "consumer demand," not for products as much as for life styles.

New Social Values

Ironically, these new values attest to the material successes of our present business system. They represent validation of a prosaic theory of traditional economics that holds that the more plentiful goods become the less they are valued. For example, to the new postindustrial consumers, the automobile is no longer prized as enhancing social status, sexual prowess, or even individual mobility, which has been eroded by increasing traffic congestion. Such a consumer has begun to view the automobile as the instrument of a monolithic system of auto, oil, highway, and rubber interests, and client-group dependencies, which has produced an enormous array of social problems and costs. These include decaying, abandoned. inner cities, an overburdened law-enforcement system, an appalling toll of deaths

Remarks by Hazel Henderson, writer, lecturer, and consultant on current social problems.

and injuries, some 60 percent of air pollution, and the sacrifice of millions of acres of arable land to a costly highway system.

While such consumer sentiments are often discounted as those of an affluent minority, many other postindustrial values held by the affluent groups are also being expressed by the poor and less privileged. Some groups, whether welfare recipients or public employees, less-powerful labor unions, or modest homeowners and taxpayers, seem to share a demand for greater participation in the decisions affecting their lives and disaffection with large bureaucracies of both business and government. For example, we have witnessed the real suspicions of the labor movement expressed in the charges that President Nixon's New Economic Policy was tailored much more to the liking of business interests than it was to labor. Similar charges were made by consumers, environmentalists, minorities, and the poor concerning the unfairness of tax credits "trickling down" from business rather than "trickling up" from some form of consumer credits to create instant purchasing power.

Further, environmentalists who are sometimes viewed as elitists have found themselves agreeing with labor and minorities that human-service programs, which also tend to be environmentally benign, should have been expanded rather than cut. They believe that a federal minimum-income pro-

A LOOK AT BUSINESS IN 1990: A Summary of the White House Conference on the Industrial World Ahead, Washington, D.C., February 7-9, 1972 (U.S. Government Printing Office: 1972 0—467-348) pp. 99-104.

gram is more needed than ever. Such a program would create purchasing power for instant spending on unmet basic needs, such as food and clothing. It would permit the poor greater mobility to seek opportunities in uncrowded areas, thereby relieving the overburdened biosystems of our cities. Or, to recast the disenchantment with our automobile-dominated transportation system, we may note the different but equally vocal objections of the poor. Some one-fifth of all American families do not own an automobile. This decreases their mobility and narrows their job opportunities, while the decline in mass transit and increased spatial sprawl permitted by extensive use of the automobile worsen the situation, and the relentless construction of new highways continues to ravage their neighborhood.

New Challenges to Industry

The middle-upper-income, postindustrial consumers represent a new and different challenge of vital concern to corporations. Their opinion-leadership roles and trend-setting life styles will continue to influence traditional consumer tastes as they have in several important respects, such as: the new anarchism and casualness in clothing fashions; the popularity of bicycling; the trends away from ostentatious overconsumption toward more psychologically rewarding leisure and life styles; and the astounding growth of encounter groups and kindred activities. Their increasingly skillful political activism and acceptance of concern for social injustice is already producing new political coalitions. Their growing confrontations with corporations over their middle-class issues, such as the environment and peace, have led them to discover the role of profit-maximizing theories in environmental pollution, and the role of the military-industrial complex in defense expenditures and war. These insights are leading to convergence with other socio-economic group interests so much in evidence in the movement for corporate responsibility.

Many of the corporate campaigns have been concerned with peace, equal opportunity in employment, pollution, the effects of foreign operations, safety, and the broadest spectrum of social effects of corporate activities. Campaign GM was typical. It sought representation on General Motor's board of directors for minorities, women, consumers, and environmental concerns. The same convergence is evident in the newly formed Washington-based Committee to Stop Environmental

Some groups, whether welfare recipients or public employees, less powerful labor unions, or modest homeowners and taxpayers, seem to share a demand for a greater participation in the decisions affecting their lives and disaffection with large bureaucracies of both business and government.

Blackmail, composed of labor unions and a cross section of environmental groups. It is pledged to oppose the growing number of corporations that attempt to prevent implementation of pollution-control laws by raising fears of unemployment, plant shutdowns, or even relocating in more "favorable" states or other countries. Labor unions and environmentalists view such tactics as more often power plays and bluffing, or poor management, than bona-fide cases of corporate hardship.

This growing understanding of the political nature of economic distribution has naturally focused on the dominant economic institution of our time: the corporation in both its political and economic role. Nothing displays the political power of our large corporations more vividly than their own managements' concepts of the corporation as power broker, mediating the interests of virtually all other constituent groups in the entire society! Such an all-encompassing role is traditionally ascribed to popularly elected governments in a democratic system such as ours, rather than to private, special-purpose organizations. Acknowledgment, by both businessmen and their critics, of the overriding social power of the large corporations points up the fallacy of Dr. Milton Friedman's argument that corporations do not have the right to make social decisions, but only to maximize stockholders' profits. The reality is that corporations in pursuing their profit motives regularly make ipso facto social decisions of enormous consequence.

One might conclude, therefore, that if our corporations remain as powerful as they are today, we might also expect them to collide more extensively with other social forces. This will lead to unprecedented challenges to corporate activities that are based on traditional economic theories. We can expect greater numbers of confrontations with citizens who become more radicalized as they are more affected by corporate efforts to expand, apply new technology, increase production, or move into new areas such as large-scale agri-business operations with specially severe social repercussions. It is to be hoped that these confrontations, whether boycotts, picket lines, or politicizing annual meetings and proxy machinery, will eventually find civilized channels for expression, and will lead to new structures of social mediation.

Technology Assessment

Technology assessment will surely advance beyond today's rudimentary stage. As technology-assessment methods improve, become democratized, and institutionalized at every level of government by public demand, we can expect that these former areas of management prerogative will give way to a more open, consultative public-decision-making process.

Similarly, we can also expect currently stepped-up funding to produce workable sets of social indicators of human well-being, as well as better documentation of social and environmental diseconomies generated by current production. These indicators must take into account data on depletion of resources and other environmental capital, the social health and welfare costs passed on to taxpayers by corporate automation, relocation, or various standards for employee occupational health and product safety. They must be sensitive to sub-

---

Corporations in pursuing their profit motives regularly make ipso facto social decisions of enormous consequence.

---

jective data concerning states of relative satisfaction with quality of life as perceived by the citizen. These might be based on polling techniques, or monitoring citizens' complaints funneling into government agencies or city halls, and using them as inputs into social indicators of the gap between expectation and performance of government.

As macrolevel social indicators are developed and begin to reformulate and enhance the accuracy of current narrowly defined economic indicators, the information on which individual companies base their decisions will also change. As social and environmental costs are factored into the GNP, company decisions will be framed in terms of a much more slowly growing "net national product." As these externalities become more explicitly quantified and publicly disseminated, pressure will increase to internalize these formerly unacknowledged costs of production and add them to the market price of products. The definition of profit will necessarily change to apply only to those activities that create real added wealth, rather than private gain extracted by social or environmental exploitation.

At the microlevel, community groups are already asking their local chambers of commerce penetrating questions concerning their euphoric development plans. Some communities already demand that exhaustive cost/benefit analyses be prepared on a broad range of development options, including the option of *not* developing at all.

Public-Interest Economics

As a result of all this reassessment of economic concepts and qualification methods, one would expect to see the growth of "public-interest economics groups" to join those in public-interest law and science. Such groups will eventually find foundation and other institutionalized support as citizens' groups learn that they must have their own economist present testimony on such matters as the diseconomies of one-way bottles to counter the testimony of the container companies' economists at public hearings. Similar insights will lead to demand for interest-group representation on all governmental economic decision-making bodies, such as the Federal Reserve Board, the Treasury, and the President's Council of Economic Advisers, on which consumer, environmental, and minority groups have already sought to expand for this purpose.

Corporations will find similarly stepped-up demands for interest-group representation on their boards of directors. It is also likely that other corporate publics, particularly stockholders, consumers, and environmentalists will organize themselves into coherent negotiating blocs, and engage in annual bargaining with corporations just as labor unions today.

Meanwhile, efforts are under way on Wall Street to broaden traditional security analysis to cover the social and environmental performance of corporations, following the pioneering work of New York City's Council on Economic Priorities, of which I am a director. The Council's bimonthly *Economic*

158

Priorities Report counts among its subscribers a growing list of banks, brokerage houses, mutual funds, and other institution and individual investors, and citizens. It publishes comparative information about the social impact of corporations in various industry groups in five key areas: environment, employment practices, military contracting, political influence, and foreign operations. The need for this type of corporate analysis is highlighted by the fact that there are now no less than six new mutual funds whose stated purpose is to invest only in those companies with superior social and environmental performances.

A report on an in-depth study of pollution in the pulp and paper industry, by the Council on Economic Priorities, disputes the widely held contentions that a) pollution control is achieved only at the expense of profits, and b) that pollution control is a close function of profitability. On the contrary, many companies in that industry with excellent environmental performance were shown to also have superior profitability. Several possible explanations were advanced: better management; lower cost of capital, which a favorable corporate image can sometimes command through marginally higher stock prices and lower borrowing costs; and lower operating costs in labor, health insurance, maintenance, taxes, and particularly in the cost of pollution control itself, when it is an integral part of the design of manufacturing equipment, rather than added later. This suggests the U.S. capital markets are becoming more sensitive to socially related aspects of business performance. Social-performance ratings sheets on companies will be as common in the future as are those rating traditional performance today.

Changes in Corporation Operation

If this kind of future domestic environment is a likely scenario for the U.S. corporation, then it will have to change considerably so as to maintain its current broad mandate, or embark on a restless search overseas for short-run advantages in politically or economically prostrate nation states willing to provide sweated labor and resources, and a blank check to pollute. Some U.S. corporations, driven by profit-maximizing imperatives, are already eyeing such less-developed nations. Japan has already declared its intention to transfer its own labor-intensive, high-energy, polluting industries to such areas of the world.

Corporations choosing such a strategy will surely gain their short-term, narrowly defined profit objectives, but they will incur social and

Social-performance rating sheets on companies will be as common in the future as are those rating traditional performance today.

environmental debts that will eventually lead to further social conflict both in the United States and in international relations. Meanwhile U.S. labor unions, fearing the further export of jobs, are themselves going multinational. Consumer and environmental movements are gaining strength in the industrialized nations of Europe and in Japan. Therefore, let us assume that companies will refrain from such a destructive course, and, instead, attempt to modify their policies and practices so as to bring them more into harmony with emerging social goals and the diminishing resources of the ecosystem on which they and society ultimately depend.

New Definition of Profit

One of the most vital and far-reaching new corporate strategies must be that of learning to live with the new definition of profit, and with the internalizing of the full social and environmental costs of production. This will alter markets and production as it more rationally assigns such costs to the consumer, rather than the taxpayer. For example, in the face of the coming energy squeeze, current promotional rates for electricity will likely be restructured to include external costs and remove subsidies from heavy users, such as the aluminum industry. One outcome might be the wholesale replacement of aluminum in many consumer products; another might be the disappearance of the throwaway aluminum can. A more realistic definition of profit would also result in the discontinuance of many consumer items whose production is profitable only with formerly hidden social or environmental subsidies. As resources become scarcer, we would see the gradual replacement of high-energy/matter-input goods with low-energy/matter-input goods, and the continued growth of services in the public and private sectors that is already evident.

All of this may be initially inflationary while readjustments are occurring, and may cause many American products to face even stiffer competition in world markets. However, this is disputed by Professor James B. Quinn * who believes: that the new environmental costs will eventually be sold as value added in products; that the new pollution-control processes will result in raw-materials savings; and that the possible initial disruption caused by foreign competition may be offset by rising ecological awareness in other nations; added exports from a growing domestic pollution-control industry; and other factors.

The only possible avenues for future profits seem to lie in four general areas:

Better energy-conversion ratios—For example, we will no longer be able to afford the thermal inefficiencies of the current generation of light-water, nuclear-fission reactors or the internal-combustion engine. Only by developing inherently more efficient energy-conversion systems, such as fuel cells or nuclear fission, can we hope to achieve actual economy and environmental benefits.

Better resource management and rehabilitation—Production loops must be closed by recycling. However, this will probably not be in the current mode of volunteer recycling of bottles and cans, because it does not constitute a valid negative feedback loop for the container industry, and permits them to continue externalizing the severe costs of collection.

A more realistic definition of profit would also result in the discontinuance of many consumer items whose production is profitable only with formerly hidden social or environmental subsidies.

Better "market-failure research" into needs for basic consumer goods unmet because of inadequate purchasing power. Some 10 million families with incomes of less than $5000 per year, as well as those with annual incomes between $5000 and $10,000 per year, represent one of the greatest challenges to our business system. These will require conceptual breakthroughs as far reaching as the invention of consumer credit, federally underwritten home mortgages, or the G.I. Bill's massive investment in human resources. All these families, even those below the poverty line or on

*Of the Amos Tuck School of Business Administration in the Harvard Business Review, Sept.-Oct., 1971.

welfare, have explosive aspirations for better housing, education, vacations, and consumer goods so widely advertised.

One obvious strategy for corporations is to support an adequate national minimum income, not only for humanitarian reasons and to prevent further erosion of our human resources and to equalize the unfair distribution of welfare costs among our taxpayers, but also to irrigate our economy with instant and much-needed purchasing power. For those families in the annual income range between $5000 and $10,000, corporations and labor unions alike should explore the strategies of building purchasing power by broadening of corporate ownership by cutting employees in on "a piece of the action" after the style of Louis O. Kelso's Second Income Plan Trusts, which has already proved effective in many corporations and has also reduced labor strife and increased motivation. These employee stock-ownership trusts permit corporations to finance new capital equipment with tax-deductible dollars, while apportioning out newly issued shares representing the expansion to the workers, without payroll deductions.

Better "market-failure research" into those areas where individual consumer demand is inoperable unless it can be aggregated, i.e., the potentially enormous public-sector markets where the backlog of unmet group-consumer needs is greatest. Examples are such services as mass transit, health care, clean air and water, education, retraining, parks, and all kinds of public amenities. Many of these needs might well become coherently aggregated with a little corporate support of the necessary political activities of coalitions of potential consumers now working to underpin them with government appropriations.

Strategies for Public-Service Needs

If corporations can lobby to procure government contracts for military and space products, they can also learn the methodologies of the new multistage public-sector marketing. Companies interested in developing new markets in the public sector must first contact citizens' organizations pushing for new priorities in public spending and assess which new needs they are best equipped to serve. Only these grass-roots coalitions of potential consumers can create enough genuine political steam to capitalize these new economic activities. Corporations must learn to see these groups as indispensable allies instead of enemies. Companies must then determine the citizens' expectations for

160

the performance of the new public-sector goods and services. Then, together, they can begin to formulate the design criteria and functional goals, with the companies providing technical and other supporting services to develop more detailed plans.

These processes are particularly vital in such areas as the design of mass-transit routes and facilities, so as to include the greatest number of riders. The size and shape of the total market must be measured by extensive polling and interviewing. New technology for social choice is now in the experimental stage, which has proved capable of increasing citizens' motivation and participation in articulating such new demand, assessing and formulating community goals, and then used to analyze and profile the resulting feedback.* For example, using computers and television, we might model all the alternatives for a town's transportation mix and assess outcomes for such options as: do nothing and permit continued ad hoc growth of highways and auto use; make more provision for safe paths for short trips on foot or bicycle; build mass-transit lines for high-density areas, based on route desires of potential riders; start a dial-a-bus-on-demand system with computerized dispatching; or designate open lanes for express buses on major freeways so as to lure commuters out of their cars with the faster trip. All the variables can be plotted and simulated on television as "games." Audience feedback can be profiled to change the plotting of the diagrams on the screen as the "votes" are recorded. Currently corporations hoping to serve the incipient mass-transit market are circling and waiting, or developing expensive hardware designs that they will try to put across with lobbying efforts, instead of becoming involved with all the clamoring civic groups demanding such facilities, so as to learn their needs and thereby design systems that they will use.

Finally, corporate-marketing men should begin to sell these groups of potential consumers on the merits of their systems or services, and then join with them in lobbying efforts to pass legislation or bond issues necessary to create the market for these big-ticket items.

The new consumers are not Luddites; they are realists. They do not reject technology. Rather, they seek an end to the gross, wasteful, "meataxe" technology that has characterized our receding in-

dustrial age. They envision a second-generation technology, more refined, miniaturized and organically modelled along biological analogies. For instance, we might deemphasize the high-energy transportation side of the coin of human interaction and increase the communications side. This could mean decentralizing of population into smaller, more organic-sized communities, managed locally by cable-TV-based "electronic town meetings," all linked by mass media. Likewise it might mean decentralizing corporations by breaking them up into more functional units as we learn more of the growing phenomenon of "diseconomies of scale." Smaller production units, while somewhat more costly, can be offset by lower transportation, distribution, and inventory costs. It could also mean a renaissance of grass-roots capitalism, with small entrepreneurial groups providing local day-care and other community services, or cooperatives for cable-TV or apartment-building ownership and operation.

The new consumers are aware of how narrowly based economic decisions control current allocations of resources, and that large corporations and the business system in general are a predominant force in our society and much of the rest of the world. Therefore, they also understand that they must deal with this system and work within it because they are, in reality, within it and a part of it. But they also believe that with sufficient creative, vigorous, and uncomfortable public pressures, the productive forces within capitalism can be adapted to the needs of the immediate present as well as the next two decades. ∎

*See "The Computer in Social Planning: A Chance for the Little Man to be Heard," H. Henderson, The MBA, Dec. 1971.

The New Environment for Business

Paul N. Ylvisaker

T HE NEXT 18 years for business (i.e., industry)—as for all of us—will be exciting all the way. Exciting in the sense of precarious. The main preoccupation of all of us will be survival.

The principal threat will be a general retreat to social Darwinism, one form of it being a temptation to those having control over capital to build fortresses of privilege across an international landscape flooding with restive populations. The prime social responsibility of business during this period will be to confront honestly the "reciprocals" of its own self-interest, and to negotiate rather than shoulder its way through the wearying maze of these other interests.

The numbers and complexities of these other interests being what they are, and the international competition for capital being what it is, business cannot expect to avoid growing public scrutiny of its performance as the public becomes increasingly concerned with the basic ground rules by which the search for profits goes on and the industrial resources are allocated. The publics of this country and the world are not likely to be satisfied with tokenism, self-regulation, or other responses that are left to the discretion of individual firms.

Industry's self-confidence and political standing will be shaken by the growing realization that its

Remarks by Dr. Paul N. Ylvisaker, Professor, Public Affairs and Urban Planning, Princeton University. (Dr. Ylvisaker has since become Dean of the Graduate School of Education, Harvard University.)

competence does not easily extend to the concerns and problems that the general publics are restive about: viz., the redistribution of income and the acquisition of public goods and services— a better and better quality of life for more and more people.

The performance of American industry on this score has not been impressive. Discretionary giving for charitable purposes has been only one-fifth what is allowed under the tax code. It has not done well with multipurpose ventures that involve multiple consents, e.g., the building of new communities, the renovation of old communities, even housing.

The employment it offers is heavily involved with manufacturing. Because of automation, this sector of employment is not expanding, certainly it will not increase the number of jobs this country will need to absorb its vast growth in labor force between now and 1990. Jobs in the service sector are subject to strong inflationary trends, tied to the monopolistic tendencies of the guilds that provide them. Industry is used to a simpler logic of efficiency and growth than prevails in the public-service sector.

Industry has not been notably successful in providing the critical services essential to a quality of life and the creation of sufficient jobs to ensure full employment, health, education, etc.

As industry becomes more involved with international activity, it will also be caught in crossfires of conflicting social responsibilities with relatively less feeling of responsibility, or option to

A LOOK AT BUSINESS IN 1990: A Summary of the White House Conference on the Industrial World Ahead, Washington, D.C., February 7-9, 1972 (U.S. Government Printing Office: 1972 0—467-348) pp. 105-106.

be responsible, to the immediate interests of the United States with its high labor costs and standard of living. One can therefore expect most of the "action" to move toward the service sector, toward the public sector, and to the process of arbitrating competing social demands. The prime skill and the most in demand will be that of weighing diverse and even incompatible interests.

Also on the rise will be buffering and packaging organizations and the public-development corporation, responsible for building and rebuilding cities, for designing, building, and maintaining pub-

---

The realities of the coming decade will be too harsh to expect the process of mediation and balance to be entirely or even predominantly rational and humane. The intervening years will be full of conflict and confrontation—a good deal of it violent.

---

lic infrastructures, for structuring and financing critical public services, such as health and education. Ideally, these could be joint ventures. But the probability is that the rate of return on capital invested in these public services and social goods cannot ever reach the levels expected and obtainable on the free capital market. Public allocations of capital will be made at lower rates of return. Stormy debates will occur over those allocations.

Ideally, the same qualities of enterprise and social responsibility will permeate both the private and public sectors—and certainly everything should be done to achieve a growing community of shared values. But the realities of the coming

---

Business cannot expect to avoid growing public scrutiny of its performance as the public becomes increasingly concerned with the basic ground rules by which the search for profits goes on and the industrial resources are allocated.

---

decades will be too harsh to expect the process of mediation and balance to be entirely or even predominantly rational and humane. The intervening years will be full of conflict and confrontation—a good deal of it violent.

The temptation will be to rely on force to resolve these tensions. But force by itself is counterproductive. The better answers are continuous negotiation, continuous change and adjustment. We should hope that an international pluralism will grow rapidly, so that no one, or single set of polarizations can develop or last for long. We are moving from one level of complexity (the industrialized nation) to an even greater order of complexity (the multinational corporation and denationalized society). Our fear should be that the transition will not come quickly enough; and we should be ready if not willing to take some rough riding so as to accelerate our way to survival.

The most encouraging prospect for survival is the exploding awareness of the public and especially the younger generation who have developed a tolerance and capacity for rapid change. Both industry and governments can count on accelerating public acceptance of accelerating change. The challenge will be for government and industry not so much to lead as to keep pace. ∎

Consumerism, 1990—Adapting to Today's Values for Tomorrow's Imperatives

Aaron S. Yohalem

O UR TECHNOLOGY and industrial performance has all too palpably lacked clear, resolved, and balanced social perspectives. It has lacked a critical sense of itself; lacked an awareness of the social context in which it operates and the social impact it necessarily generates. In many major areas of our economy we have had a kind of mindlessness for which we are paying high costs.

Thus far, we in industry have not even questioned, let alone attempted to direct or control our technology, production, and distribution with a view toward consciously maximizing the public weal while minimizing public risk. Not that individual companies have not been mindful of this defect, for they have. But insofar as industry-wide or business-wide consciousness is concerned, our performance has been nonexistent.

Listen to the New Winds

The traditional cost/benefit factor, the short- and long-term profit orientation are seen as motivation and the foundation of our economic system. But the myths of business-as-usual, and the market-will-right-itself simply will not suffice in the

Remarks by Aaron S. Yohalem, Senior Vice President, CPC International, Inc.

face of the consumerism of today, let alone 1990. Nor will our own long-term best interests, including our profitable well being, be served.

We in industry can anticipate, of course, that as we seek to adapt to changing values, the very process of adaptation will impact on those values and alter them, bringing about the need for still further industry readjustments. But the inexorable vigor of the consumer movement permits little room for leisurely contemplation on an optimum course of action. It is clear that if business does not get moving well ahead of the consumerism train, we shall see one of the biggest wrecks in our economic history.

The potential threat, in my view, is that corporate lethargy, married with political timidity, may procreate unworkable alterations in the economic system. This would needlessly frustrate the nation's existing capacity to meet totally legitimate consumer demands, as well as other national imperatives.

The existing system of free markets and open competition is not immutable. Although it excelled in meeting yesterday's demands for economic growth, and for abundance at reasonable prices, those achievements are widely regarded today as insufficient. Today's concern is increasingly with "quality of life." There is a disquieting lack of public confidence as to the capacity of the indus-

A LOOK AT BUSINESS IN 1990: A Summary of the White House Conference on the Industrial World Ahead, Washington, D.C., February 7-9, 1972 (U.S. Government Printing Office: 1972 0—467-348) pp. 107-110.

trial system to add this new requirement.

To be sure, today's consumer shops for products and services with a flinty eye on the price tag. But that is only one consideration. Now the consumer is likely to ask questions about such matters as the safety of the product, completeness of the information provided about it, its performance, the recourse if it does not perform well, hiring practices of the manufacturer, pollution created in its manufacture or use, and its social relevance.

Surveys of consumer attitudes reflect the depth of these concerns. Over half the public approves of Ralph Nader, an eloquent symbol and summary of consumer aspirations. Two-thirds want Congressional legislation assuring consumers of better value.

Consider, also, the attitudes of today's students. Researcher Daniel Yankelovich, a specialist on the restless generation, notes that: "What is new is not the presence of a small group of radicals on the campus but the mushrooming growth of a much larger number of students who agree with the radicals' diagnosis of what is wrong with America, even though they do not endorse their tactics. This larger supportive group is estimated at a whopping two out of five college students."

Their overriding concern, and the growing concern of many of their parents, is that the country's institutions, especially its business institutions, are indifferent to social needs—and incapable of voluntary change. This concern is highly emotional, often not susceptible to intellectual argument. It has taken a totally *political* turn.

Probably the most articulate expression of industry's social responsibility—embracing employees, stockholders, communities, and suppliers—would be to respond imaginatively to consumer demands.

This development is also reflected in the society at large. In just the last eight years, more than two dozen federal consumer laws have been passed. But they fall far short of what consumer activists find desirable. Consequently, they are pressing aggressively and effectively for personal involvement and for reform through the judicial system.

So long as the business community retains any

appearance of ignoring the revolution in consumer values, the consumerism train will gain speed, trip another series of political signals, and the consequences may tangle our economic tracks to the satisfaction of no one—with the exception of a handful of committed extremists. Probably the most articulate expression of industry's social responsibility—embracing employees, stockholders, communities, and suppliers—would be to respond imaginatively to consumer demands.

Need for Consumer-Trend Analysis

This suggests to me the need for industry to study the new dimension of consumerism with the same scale of investment in time, money, research, and analysis that it devotes to a major new service or product line prior to its introduction. Individual corporations, in the interest of improving on the best of the competitive system, should:

- analyze the demographics of consumerism as they affect their specific operations
- define those areas where consumer segments are correct or misinformed
- make the adjustments necessary to meet legitimate complaints
- undertake the communication effort required to alert the public, and its elected leaders, to the adjustments made and to areas of public misunderstanding or misinformation.

This is not a simple assignment. I suggest the only choice is to grasp the nettle. The question we in the business community must ask ourselves is: Are we smart enough to see what is happening? Have we the will to work at it in a methodical, professional way? Particularly, do we have the good sense to open up our communication channels to listen to, and learn from, even the most militant of the groups who oppose everything we believe in?

Are we in business and industry prepared to question the eternal validity of the GNP? Will we sit still to consider the arguments of the ZPGers and the ZEGers—respectively, the Zero Population Growth and the Zero Economic Growth advocates? Will we be able to derive any insight from the concept of static growth as opposed to dynamic, purely one-dimensional, linear growth?

I trust the answer will be a positive one; it had best be.

It is essential to realize that consumerism has long ago ceased to have the circumscribed limits of customary marketing concerns. Consumerism has a far more comprehensive, sophisticated relevance to our society as a whole. Consumerism further encompasses such controversial issues as:

- The use of stockholder proxies to propose resolutions affecting corporate policy, including public representation on corporate boards
- How to determine, and who to charge for, the cost of "negative externalities," such as air or water pollution
- "Product performance insurance"—and its effect on freedom of choice and the living standards of the poor
- Meaningful methods for auditing the social accountability of business
- The role of advertising and other promotion forms as they affect society's best interests
- The social obligation of investors, individual and institutional
- "Nationalizing" private systems, or "commercializing" public systems or both
- And the federal chartering of publicly held corporations

I am trying to emphasize that the complexity and intensity of the consumer movement cannot be overestimated. It is only a part, if a large part, of a pervasive public concern with increasing the social responsibility of business. Consumerism will not just go away. Coming to grips with it will inevitably take the form of a new but operative aspect of management responsibility.

While this movement is not new to our nation, it has never enjoyed more favorable conditions for nurturing it to full and robust bloom. To underscore the point, consider an extreme example: Bangladesh, which is light years from any concern over slack-fill, unit pricing, or grade labeling. Its single consumer demand is at the first plateau of Maslow's tier of hierarchial values: survival. America's consumers, on the other hand, are concerning themselves with his highest plateau: self-actualization and spiritual or humanistic rather than material considerations.

The consumer movement is today riding a flood tide characterized by a fundamental shift in national attitudes toward legislation affecting private enterprise. Historically, government has sought to proscribe those things that institutions *cannot* do. Today, however, government increasingly seeks to circumscribe those things institutions *can* do.

Clearly, then, if industry wishes to affect the shape of consumer legislation, the time is now, not the '90s, to take an introspective look at business performance as against new consumer attitudes toward "quality of life." Will we have the wisdom to recognize that the dollars involved in

rearguard movements and holding actions normally exceed those required to bring about solutions?

Industry cannot, nor should it, undertake all the initiatives in seeking a rapprochement among business, government, and the consumer movement. Nor have I the naive hope that consumerists will ever be totally satisfied, which, indeed, would impede social progress. But I do believe, given the kind of industry-wide effort required, that the business community can introduce The Rule of Reason to the consumer-industry dialogue. It will not be possible for each of the diverse elements striving for a better consumer society to have its own aspirations fulfilled, *totally*. Each will have to succumb to the rule of reason and make some accommodation to the needs of others. This, after all, is the definition of society.

Possible Results to Response to Society's Objectives

- The consumer movement itself should be prepared for still higher prices and even deeper employment dislocation if it seriously expects all of its demands to be met immediately.
- Labor leadership should prepare itself for the possibility that consumerists will one day ask what unions can do to encourage improved workmanship and to retard inflation.
- Perhaps organized labor will concern itself not only with wages, hours, and working conditions but also with such issues as balance of payments, currency convertibility, quotas, production/cost ratios, and the impact of protectionism.
- Government, on its part, should be prepared to resolve the present incompatibility between consumerism and antitrust policies. It is virtually impossible for industry to develop an effective program of cooperation or self-regulation to resolve consumer or environmental problems without violating antitrust, as currently interpreted.
- State governments will be asked to share their sovereignty by supporting, when and where needed, federal preemptive legislation in the consumer field. National or regional companies cannot offer maximum savings or service to consumers when they are forced, as now, to meet varying and even conflicting state requirements.

The rule of reason demands that all of the sectors involved listen with comprehension—not merely take turns talking. It demands that we seek, in our own self-interest, to share understanding of common problems so that we do not exhaust our energies on the impossible or, un-

---

Along with our own corporate committees on the environment, minority employment, the cities and the like, we must make certain that we maintain in industry the most realistic kind of self-criticism.

---

wittingly, the undesirable. It demands, too, that we distinguish carefully between our own point of view and the genuine insight of others, and that all of us accept the democracy of man's frailities. It may behoove us to consider some of the role reversals, as set forth in the box on page 109, that, if society is to be properly served by industry, might possibly occur.

While the public utterances of industry on the matters of consumerism are encouraging, words hardly constitute actuality. I am concerned with its performance; that it matches its words. More to the point, I am concerned that our performance responds to the demands and needs confronting us. Only with performance can we begin to build a credibility that is today sorely missing, but which is a necessary foundation for the future.

Along with our own corporate committees on the environment, minority employment, the cities and the like, we must make certain that we maintain in industry the most realistic kind of self-criticism. We need, in effect, to maintain some form of corporate counter-culture or sub-stratum thereof that will make its business the task of continuously keeping us disabused so the better to keep us on our toes and performing credibly.

Business necessarily has to become more involved socially and more responsive to business in society. Business must be able to detach itself from its own myopic traditions. It must seek out, not automatically reject, reasonable critics. It must anticipate, indeed provide, progressive leadership in the march of consumerism to the 1990s.

The question remains: Not, do we have the foresight to understand the future, but, do we have the courage to change it? ∎

Society Will Determine the Corporate Form

ELISHA GRAY II

It should be perfectly clear to any thoughtful businessman that the *form* of the enterprise system in the final analysis will be what our society thinks it should be. The corporate charter is not the Holy writ.

The public has been modifying the original freewheeling character of the institution of business for three centuries or so—particularly since the Industrial Revolution began. Since the turn of this century the process of change has accelerated until now the regulations affecting business cover everything from whom they may employ to what words they may use in selling their wares.

This process of change shows no sign of tapering off and our challenge is to try to forecast what will be expected of us 20 years hence. ∎

Remarks by Elisha Gray II, Chairman, Finance Committee, Whirlpool Corporation.

SECTION V

TECHNOLOGY AND RESOURCES FOR BUSINESS

Section V presents an overview on the technology and resources for business now and for the coming two decades through the following articles.

AN OVERVIEW ON TECHNOLOGY FOR BUSINESS

AN OVERVIEW ON RESOURCES FOR BUSINESS

TECHNOLOGY AND RESOURCES FOR BUSINESS

FACTORS AFFECTING THE RATE AND DIRECTION OF TECHNOLOGY AND RESOURCES

INTERMEDIATE INSTITUTIONS

THE POSITION OF AGRICULTURE

MAN'S HABITAT IN THE ENVIRONMENT

THE OUTLOOK FOR RESEARCH AND DEVELOPMENT

TECHNOLOGICAL TRANSFER

COPING WITH ENVIRONMENTAL PROBLEMS

169

An Overview on Technology for Business

Michael Michaelis

TECHNOLOGICAL innovation is one of the principal stimulants of economic growth. In this context, innovation is that process through which scientific and technological knowledge is translated into economic benefits by providing better products and services and by creating jobs. Invention, research, and development generate the knowledge: they are necessary but not sufficient prerequisites for innovation.

The most important figure in the process of innovation is the entrepreneur—committed to the value of an idea and to the creation of a business based on it. The second key participant in the process is the venture capitalist—a wealthy individual, a dynamic company, or an imaginative bank willing to provide risk capital.

If we are to continue—let alone increase—the sustained economic growth that has characterized this nation's economy in this century, we must achieve further productivity gains through technological innovation. This is all the more urgent as business and government intensify their efforts to solve social problems as well. Only more rapid growth in the real gross national product can provide us with the resources for the large-scale improvements—e.g., abolishing poverty, eliminating pollution, urban renewal—to be achieved in the coming decades.

Productivity increases will be particularly essen-

An issues paper prepared by Dr. Michael Michaelis, Manager, Arthur D. Little, Inc., Washington, D. C.

tial in the services sector of our economy, such as housing, transportation, health care, and education. These are the big users of resources, and are the main triggers of consumer dissatisfaction. The keys to creating and delivering new technology in this sector include: resources for innovation; scale of operation; accountability; accurate diagnosis of drags on productivity; assembling the market and integrating it with providers of technology; increased business risk-taking; public cost-sharing in demonstrations and assessments justified by the need to raise the level of productivity throughout the economy.

It is evident therefore that our attention must be focused on new arrangements if technological innovation is to play the role we propose for increased economic growth and social betterment. Recognizing the need, the federal government has begun to create new institutional approaches within the public sector and to stimulate parallel action in the private sector. A principal purpose of these moves is to assemble otherwise scattered strengths and resources for "lift-off" of dormant know-how, e.g., in energy, cancer, and housing. These recent government commitments would seem to have their policy roots in performance expectations and each has predictable social pay-offs that exceed the costs.

Technical innovation makes and shapes institutions. The automobile led to the national highway network and to the creation of large numbers of supply and service industries. Electronic inven-

A LOOK AT BUSINESS IN 1990: A Summary of the White House Conference on the Industrial World Ahead, Washington, D.C., February 7-9, 1972 (U.S. Government Printing Office: 1972 0—467-348) pp. 123-131.

tions led to TV and a revolution in mores. The computer—information technology—presages a whole array of institutional changes and problems. Technology is indeed a singularly powerful agent for change. Yet, productivity of the functions served by technology often has not been fully realized and social costs have been high. This has led to suggestions in recent years that assessment of the performance effects and goals of new technologies needs to be made so that responsible guidance—and accountability—can be exercised in the process of technological innovation. In short, the interplay of institutions and technology is a two-way street.

It is my purpose to explore briefly some concepts for institutional change that may more effectively

- provide guidance for technological innovation
- couple user needs to providers of technology
- increase the rate of technological innovation, and thus the rate of economic growth and social gain

We must, of necessity, oversimplify. Some assertions will raise unanswered questions. Although we will speculate about changes in business structure and practices—to be specific, selling performance rather than products—we suggest no basic change from the profit-motivated, capitalist, market-oriented system that has served us well. Rather, our intent is to explore new links between the consumer market and business, potentially conducive to technological innovation and productivity gains. The vital roles of the entrepreneur and the venture capitalist must not only be preserved but also expanded.

In this context—considering incentives and rewards for creative entrepreneurs—one might well want to examine the desirability for a kind of profit-sharing in which an industry that dedicates its creativity to new technology would share (possibly through tax benefits) in the payoffs from enhanced productivity; in other words, recover as a reward an increment of the cost of risk-taking. Institutional change to stimulate technological innovation thus encompasses both the public and private sectors.

Technological Innovation

Space exploration, sophisticated defense systems, and nuclear energy are frequently cited as examples of major achievements made possible through rapid and deliberate use of advanced technology. These achievements illustrate two important points:

- The major technological advances made demonstrate that technology need no longer be a limiting factor (as it was even 20 years ago) in attaining specified goals. One can almost assert that whatever our needs, technological innovation to meet them can be attained (R&D being, of course, a necessary but not sufficient prerequisite).
- The success of these high-technology enterprises rests largely on a special government-industry relationship, in which the former is the sole buyer of all the R&D and all the advanced equipment needed. This aggregation of total market demand, and the relatively predictable behavior of the buyer, combine to create a risk-taking situation in which the supplier industry is induced to respond with a posture that is technologically much more innovative than most of its counterparts in the commercial, pluralist, consumer market.

To illustrate the reverse, consider housing. This is an industry that traditionally—at least until recently—has not enjoyed a government market for its R&D and hardware, and that operates in a highly decentralized demand and supply market. Its record of technological advance leaves much to be desired. This is not to discredit the housing industry. It is laboring under severe restraints of all kinds that inhibit technological advance and that themselves cannot be overcome by technology alone. The point is that, although we have technical knowledge to improve housing, the policies and practices of business, finance, government, and labor impede the use of this knowledge. This state of affairs is regrettably all too prevalent in many sectors of our economy.

One might, therefore, be tempted to conclude that government purchasing power is the dominant stimulant of technological advance. Indeed, this view is leading to extension of the special government-industry (buyer-supplier) relationship, so well proven by results in aerospace and defense, to other socially directed goals.

But, we must not forget that similar high-technology success has also been gained in at least some parts of the private sector alone. Our voice-communication system—the Bell System in essence—is an example of corporate action to create and respond to an aggregated market demand not relying on governmental purchases. Foresight and imaginative entrepreneurship created the nationwide system, second to none in the world. It is built on and supported by remarkably advanced technology.

171

Performance vs. Products

Rather than get sidetracked on issues of public vs. private enterprise, we should note that all the cited examples of successful technological progress have a common feature that seems to us of overriding importance. In all these successes, the enterprise is structured and motivated *to provide performance of complex systems that meet functional needs of society*. The key words are "performance," "systems," and "functional needs." That is to say the operation of the complete system of defense, of space exploration, and of voice communications—each a functional need of society—is specified, executed, and measured in performance terms related to perceived or anticipated needs.

We suggest that such "functional performance" orientation of an enterprise can substantially increase its innovative behavior.

The distinction here is between "functional-performance orientation" and "product orientation." We mentioned the Bell System as having the former. Other examples can be cited:

- Firms have grown up around "institutional feeding." They provide meals to specification for certain numbers of people in certain institutions—hospitals, schools, airliners. They control not only the purchasing of raw materials, the preparation of intermediates, and the final preparation, but also the design and manufacture of equipment, utensils, and maintenance. They retain, at each point, the freedom to decide on "make or buy," own or franchise, single or multiple suppliers. Such a firm stands an excellent chance of orchestrating the various innovations required to optimize the feeding system. If the economic use of infrared ovens depends, for example, on the uniform slicing of meat to certain thickness, the firm can assure that uniformity.
- RCA in Italy operates an "entertainment system" whose elements include: a managing firm that holds contracts for and manages the careers of musicians and artists; recording studios; record and tape companies; chains of retail distribution outlets for records and tapes; a television station; a firm specializing in installing stereophonic tape recorders in automobiles.
- Corn Products Corporation is engaged in a Latin American country in performing a set of functions analogous to work of the Agriculture Department in the United States: introduction of new crop varieties and methods; construction of packaged food-processing plants; training of farmers; provision of technical assistance.

In contrast with these emerging examples of functional performance, the prevailing product orientation of much of industry is exemplified by companies, for instance, whose business it is to make and sell building materials; others who construct a house out of such materials; others who supply it with utilities; others who engage in land speculation for siting the house, and so forth. All these enterprises are involved in the shelter system. Their individual aims and motivations may strive toward the whole system, but their respective business strategies and decisions are circumscribed by the specific product or service they offer. The interrelationship between them lacks orchestration to get the most out of technological performance of the system as a whole and thus

---

Representative Desirable Results of Functional-Performance Enterprises

- Aggregation of functional markets with related performance requirements.
- Development of new business practices, more capable of higher risk-taking, stemming from the ability to control all the elements that make for systems efficiency and innovation.
- Increased perception of and demand for continuous technical and institutional innovations.
- Increased rate of technological innovation.
- Guidelines for innovation aimed toward performance objectives.
- Greater potential to act in anticipation of needs rather than by reaction to crisis: disruptive impact of innovation—"future shock"—is eased.
- Increased demand for higher skills in management, engineering, and labor; employment opportunities are upgraded.
- Increased efficiency of performance-based systems serving functional needs. This permits reallocation of resources of all kinds to attain more national goals simultaneously.
- Increased exports since superior components (of total functional systems) sold abroad will likely result in tie-in sales of other components if not the whole system.
- Improved quality of life—through humane technology—inasmuch as the advent of new technology can be significantly influenced by consideration of societal good through a functional-performance business pursuit of profits. The generation coming into being, here and abroad, is exceptionally sensitive to these issues. 1990 will see them at the helm.

limits productivity. To be sure, some firms—such as Boise-Cascade, Weyerhauser, Westinghouse—have begun efforts to orchestrate this system. Such experiments should be encouraged and supported.

Functional Markets and Performance Requirements

Functions needed by an industrialized society include shelter, food, health, education, transportation, communication, energy, recreation, and physical security. Traditionally, industry responds to these functional needs by offering goods (and services), with individual corporations specializing in one or more product lines. The consumer

---

The successful innovation in product-oriented industries seldom comes from within the established industry. Most often it is an invader.

---

chooses those within his means that taken together—he judges to provide him with the maximum satisfaction of his functional needs. This classical model of the competitive marketplace serves us well—up to a point. This is where the supplier fails to recognize the total functional needs his particular products partially help to fulfill. Often, indeed, he fails to consider which of the several functional needs he serves.

What refrigerator and freezer manufacturer, for instance, operates his business consciously as part of the "food" function? Food-service plans, by which both a freezer and a continuous supply of meat are provided, are a small step in this direction, but they are still tied to a specific product—the freezer. Should not the prime concern be to make those technological innovations that may preserve food more economically than by freezing—particularly when we think of the world's multitudes that cannot afford such home appliances? Freeze-drying at the factory and shelf-storage are possibilities. There may well be others as we consider the whole food chain from farm to table.

The corporate strategy of appliance manufacturers should be heavily influenced by such considerations. Being primarily product-oriented, however, they must perforce be motivated principally to maintain or increase the share of their present product in the market. Obsoleting a product line and replacing it by a technologically, socially, economically superior one, often requiring wholly different distribution, marketing, and production practices is difficult for obvious reasons. Indeed, the successful innovation in product-oriented industries seldom comes from within the established industry. Most often it is an invader.

Yet, the functional needs cited—and their subdivisions, e.g., voice communications as part of the whole communication function—are recognizable markets and would behave as aggregated ones if the customer had the opportunity to buy as much performance of the function as he needs. This he can do now when he picks up the telephone. He buys voice-communication performance. That business system in all its ramifications—finance, manufacture, research, and innovation, equipment operation, and maintenance—is geared to sell him performance and is motivated to optimize the performance of the system as a whole, so as to serve the maximum number and kinds of customers. As Fred Kappel, former Board Chairman of American Telephone and Telegraph said, "In the Bell System our continuous purpose has been to find and *use every resource* that will contribute to the advancement of *communication.*"

Product orientation forecloses such widened horizons and their related business perspective and strategy. Functional-performance orientation can raise the aim of corporations by targeting on enduring functional-system needs as a market instead of solely on specific products that are separate components of the system.

As companies begin to experiment with these concepts, trials and errors are evident. RCA recently got out of computers, and CBS some time ago relinquished radio-TV phonograph manufacture because each lost large sums of money in these endeavors. Each now looks at "communications" from a different viewpoint—print media as well as broadcast.

The aggregated markets representing functional needs obviously bear relation to each other. Advances made in providing communication performance affect the need for transportation and vice versa. Other interrelationships come readily to mind. The point here is that function-oriented business can—and must—assess the technical, economic, and social consequences of these functional interactions to develop corporate strategies. It is unlikely that any of the basic functions—shelter, food, health, education, etc.—will ever become obsolete while man exists. Where product orientation can spell total corporate demise in face of the innovating invader, function orientation places the risks and rewards of innovation, within any single enduring functional need, on the shoulders of existing corporations. Some corporations may, indeed, straddle more than one function—much as businesses now straddle more than one product line—and thus ride the complementary crests and troughs of related functions.

Development of New Business Practices

American business firms have been, and will continue to be, primary vehicles for the development and application of new technologies. The increasing rate of application of new technologies implies faster organizational and operational response by the organization intent on innovating. The American business firm is second to none—be it government or foreign competitors—in its ability, when so motivated, to effect rapid, inventive, structural transformation of itself without flying apart at the seams.

The evolution of corporations over the last 60 years looks roughly like this representative business:

1915—In the "weaving" business (for example)
  • Technology static
  • Primary planning effort: to match supply and demand

1940—In the "textile" business
  • Multiple products, each built on different technology, production methods, channels of distribution
  • Innovative capacity broadened
  • Primary planning effort: to assess new product need .

1960—In the "textile-chemical-plastic" complex
  • Invasion by science-based industries
  • Locking clusters of product-oriented industries
  • Primary planning effort: to develop new commercial ventures

In this development, the firm has tended to evolve from a pyramid built around a single relatively static product line to a constellation of semi-autonomous divisions, each with product lines that tend to bear a family resemblance reflecting their processes of development.

It is now possible to conceive "business systems" even though they are still made up of separate companies. Consider the function of "keeping man in clean clothes." It is carried out through interacting elements of what are now separate industries including:
  • the textile complex from fiber through weaving to apparel
  • the soap and detergent manufacturers
  • the appliance industry making consumer and commercial laundering and cleaning equipment
  • the service industry operating laundry and dry-cleaning establishments
  • the consumer wearing clothes, having them cleaned, or doing it himself

This complex of entities, related to one another in the performance of a social function, is a business system. On this particular business system, the nation spends about $5 billion per year—about the same as was annually expended on space exploration at the height of the lunar-landing program.

In contrast to the NASA system, innovation in the "keeping-in-clean-clothes" system turns out frequently to be a response with a lag in one part of the system to what another part of the system has unexpectedly done. Significant system transformation can occur through a kind of system interaction—but it is managed by no one. The diffusion of product innovation, as waves of new requirements follow a single innovation in one part of the system, contributes to an overall system transformation whose consequences become clear only after the fact.

The "functional performance" concept can take us further. We can conceive of an enterprise with the total objective of "keeping customers in clean shirts." Such an enterprise has started in California, we are told. It contracts to keep their customers regularly supplied with clean shirts—an adult diaper service, so to speak—meeting specifications of size, color, style, and cleanliness. It retains the decision to supply the customer with a new shirt or a laundered one. It has the "make or buy" decision. And, most importantly, it controls enough of the elements of the business system (at least as it applies to shirts) to be able to manage system-wide innovation by anticipation rather than by hindsight: for example to introduce new cleaning methods to match new kinds of fabric. Such a firm defines itself as functional-performance oriented. Its customers buy as much performance as they wish to use or can afford. This operation is not a rental service as presently conducted, say, for tuxedos. It does not just rent the products that happen to be available at any given time in the market-place. It is an operation that has the resources and incentives to engineer the interaction of many products to keep us in clean shirts, and to innovate in doing so.

Such a firm has a new strategy for growth by integrating a mix of elements of a business system that combines to perform a major social function. To control this mix of elements, new business practices are necessary—analytical, financial, technical. One should expect a higher ability for innovative risk-taking than in a product-oriented firm. This is because of the more enduring and predictable characteristics of the functional market, and because of the firm's ability to control all the elements that can achieve efficient system performance in relation to market needs. This kind of business system differs from those now termed "vertically integrated" or "horizontally integrated." It has some features of both, and its distinguishing mark is the system orchestration achieved by a set of separate corporate elements under the guidance of a single entrepreneurial unit.

The pressures on this firm are likely to be competitive because it should not, by nature of the particular function served—clean clothes—expect to be a monopoly. In other functional areas, such as transportation, energy, and communications—by nature of the technologies serving them—some degree and kind of monopolism (possibly on a regional basis) may be tempting. But, there is no obvious reason why single ownership of all the business elements in a functional-performance enterprise is essential. Contractual relationships (not necessarily exclusive) between the business elements, each a separate corporate entity as today, could provide the orchestration needed.

Continuous Technical and Institutional Innovations

Under the combined stimuli of a function-oriented market and of performance requirements related to social needs, it is evident that the higher risk-taking ability of the enterprise will have to focus heavily on technological and institutional innovation. The institutional behavior of those who make automobiles, say, will be quite different from those who sell multi-modal performance through an integrated transportation system. The latter will, perforce, have to create an environment in which business, government, and labor have established a permanent—albeit ever-changing—working arrangement with the technical community, in which technological and institutional in-

novation—moving in step—are an integral part of everyday life.

Such an environment does not, by and large, now exist in product-oriented institutions. It is resisted by them and by the individuals who work in them. This resistance to change is born out of the natural fear of uncertainty. Conversion of this uncertainty into manageable risk must be an objective of new institutional frameworks to be established. Function orientation makes it easier to perform this task because each component activity can be more readily understood, by the men involved, for the part it plays in the whole enterprise and the reason for and benefits from changes that it must undergo.

Functional performance provides an environment where institutional survival and growth should be perceived as directly related to innovation, i.e., innovation in all those component parts and operations that combine to make up the whole integrated system serving any specific functional need. When the consumer is in a position to buy "system performance," he judges the value of his purchase on improved performance and lower costs of the whole, rather than on those of any of its component parts. Both—improved performance and lower costs—can be achieved in great part by technological innovation. Such innovation has to be managed for the system as a whole rather than be allowed to occur haphazardly by unexpected interactions of component parts. It is all the more obvious therefore that technological innovation has to go hand in hand with institutional change—even if this fact were not already apparent from presently existing institutional impediments to technological advance. All participants in a functional-performance enterprise will therefore perceive institutional and technical change as a must.

Increased Rate of Technological Innovation

Functional-performance corporations will more readily assume the responsibilities for research and development, particularly those leading to major innovations on which their competitiveness or market share depend. Fewer vexing debates and political battles will therefore ensue on whether industry or government should pay for R&D. The one who properly perceives it as an integral need of his operation will be motivated to do so.

Also, an increased rate of innovation requires a sound base of pure science research—in the social, as well as the physical, sciences. Though govern-

175

ment may well remain a source of funding for basic research, the functional-performance enterprise can be expected to devote considerably greater resources to it than product-oriented companies have done.

The engineering professions will assume increasing responsibilities as matching of total system performance to perceived social needs becomes the main objective. The scientist's role, as the guide to potential new advances, will become more socially relevant and can be seen as such in a beneficial way—contrary to the currently growing apprehension of "what will be invented next?"

Guidelines for Innovation Aimed Toward Performance Objectives

Inasmuch as both enterprise and customer will see the operations of the enterprise as performance of a functional need, they will be able to judge its total performance. It will be necessary to assess both its beneficial performance as well as its adverse impacts. It should be easier to make trade-off decisions so as to minimize the latter, because interactions of component parts are controllable. Accountability for both benefits and adverse impacts is more clear-cut and visible, and a discerning citizenry and regulatory agencies can act with greater purpose and success to resolve issues.

The steadily growing interest in the social responsibilities of business corporations will, for a functional-performance firm, be a matter of everyday concern. . . . What is today considered as enlightened self-interest—the corporation's stake in a good society—can become the primary goal to be achieved with profit.

If, for instance, public regulation were to prohibit the use of a type of detergent, the "clean shirt" company would have to respond so as to stay in business. Its motivation to innovate with a new cleaning agent would be considerable, and accountability for compliance with regulations and for success with innovation is clearly defined.

The development of measures, such as "social indicators" and related analytical tools, could provide new capability for management of functional-performance firms to match performance to social needs, and for regulators to determine both the effectiveness of performance rendered and the extent of adverse impacts. Should it not be the role of government to develop such techniques to the point of demonstrating their usefulness? Would functional-performance firms then not be particularly responsive in using such techniques in their self-interest?

The steadily growing interest in the social responsibilities of business corporations will, for a functional-performance firm, be a matter of everyday concern. It is implicit in the goals of the firm, and it should be a recognized measure of its success. The business of such corporations is the problems of our society. What is today considered as enlightened self-interest—the corporation's stake in a good society—can become the primary goal to be achieved with profit.

It follows that technological innovation would be used to maximize social benefits and minimize adverse impacts. "Technology Assessment"—a new and as yet embryonic art being developed mainly for public-policy makers to predict beneficial and adverse consequences of technology—will have to become as integral a part of the corporation's activities as its research and development work.

Reaction to Needs Instead of Crisis

One of the most widely recognized of recent technological innovations is the transistor. It was invented in the Bell Telephone Laboratories, and is now used by countless industries throughout the world. The place and manner of its birth are of interest here.

Without derogating in the slightest the brilliant scientific effort of its inventors—which earned them a Nobel prize—it is well documented that this invention was a consciously managed one, rather than a haphazardly occurring flash of genius. That is to say, the Bell "voice-communication" system (the term "telephone," in its product connotation, is misleading) had evolved a set of performance requirements for a component without which the system could not be expected to handle efficiently the anticipated volume of traffic and demand for quality some 15-20 years hence. Having set a conscious goal, a corporate decision was made to use major technical resources for the development of such a component. The best brains—multidisciplinary teams of basic research scientists—were motivated, not only out of scientific curiosity but also with a social goal—improved communications—which spelled profit

> *The unexpected invention will not necessarily be pushed into application for its own sake of technical accomplishment. Rather it should be assessed for its usefulness to improve the whole system performance, and its application will have to be programmed so as to effect a smooth transition.*

for the company. Scientific success—in the transistor—was not long in coming, followed by engineering ingenuity.

As a functional-performance company, Bell then proceeded to make the sweeping changes in its network of operations made possible by the transistor. Although the network was basically re-engineered, the changes had to be compatible during transition with the existing equipment. On the whole, transition was made smoothly, and disruptive impacts were eased. A programmed innovation had taken place—in anticipation of needs and stimulated by them.

Without intending to generalize directly from this example, it is fair to suggest that functional-performance orientation can create an environment in which deliberate efforts can be made to ease the impact of transition—of change—on those most affected, be they consumers, workers, engineers, or managers. Action by anticipation rather than by reaction is potentially more easily achieved.

This is not to suggest that the unexpected—the flash of genius—will be driven out. Quite the contrary, as implied in our earlier remarks on increased support for basic research. But the unexpected invention will not necessarily be pushed into application for its own sake of technical accomplishment. Rather it should be assessed for its usefulness to improve the whole system performance, and its application will have to be programmed so as to effect a smooth transition. A functional-performance company can least afford disruption of its performance, and continuous, smooth change is essential. Smoothness of transition is a prerequisite for productive social and technical innovation in tomorrow's world, where the only constant will be change.

Demands for Higher Skills in Management, Engineering, and Labor

In an environment where innovation is imperative—a challenge rather than a threat—the demand for high-grade skills increases. Unusual combinations of skills, creativity, and responsibility will mark the successful manager, engineer, and worker of the functional-performance firm. In particular, considerable flexibility of human, and therefore institutional, attitude is needed if we are to succeed in experimentation, a prime prerequisite for successful innovation.

Such experiments should clearly be carried out by those who have the decision-making power in those vested interests concerned with all aspects of satisfying specific functional needs. Intimate personal participation is needed, since commitment to action is the key outcome. Simply communicating the results of experiments—the pressure of information—seems all too often insufficient to stimulate action.

A successful example of such experimentation was carried out a few years ago by the California School Construction System Development project. It was charged with the task of developing better components to permit the building of less expensive schools more quickly and better adaptable for changing educational practices. The key features of the experimental process used were:

- Through a consortium of school systems, markets were aggregated, large enough to spur technical innovation.
- The object of development was recognized as the whole system—the school in all its functions as "shelter for education"—not just a part or component.
- In the course of experimentation, the system was divided into interconnected subsystems.
- Performance criteria were developed for these subsystems.
- A process was set in motion that led to the making of a variety of alternative inventions meeting these performance criteria, and cost-benefit analyses were made to select the best.
- The whole shelter process, including its social and political problems, was taken as the subject of experimentation, and an attempt was made to design that process.

Building contractors, material suppliers, labor unions, government regulators (building codes), and customers (school superintendents) participated in this experiment, catalyzed by men with particular innovative skills. It became a forum for more rational discussion than traditional animosities would have suggested. All participants

177

were members of an experimental innovating team, an experience that few had had before. From mutual enlightenment came changed institutional relationships. The component interests began to act a little more like a functional-performance entity. The transition from the drawing board to hardware was accomplished and the results are school buildings now in existence that meet the specified functional-performance objectives.

The learning process that all the participants underwent in this experiment is but a first step to the upgraded skills required in a fully operational functional-performance enterprise. Upgraded employment opportunities are therefore to be anticipated.

Increased Efficiency of Performance-Based Delivery Systems Serving Functional Needs

Many economists have warned that the nation's productive performance (GNP) will be insufficient to attain—simultaneously—the many social and economic goals implicit in the problems we face. Painful choices of priorities— health vs. education, transportation vs. shelter, for instance—will need to be made.

These predictions are based on the assumption that growth in productivity will not be greatly dissimilar to recent history. Much of this growth, as we have seen, depends on relatively haphazard and often narrowly motivated interactions of component parts of what are not yet treated as functional systems. Though production and distribution of each part may in itself have reached a high degree of efficiency (benefit/costs), the total system efficiency is often quite low.

Functional-performance orientation focuses on total system efficiency, and should thus serve to optimize allocation of resources. This means that resources now used inefficiently—be they material, financial or human—can be freed and reallocated to other purposes, responsive to market demands. It stands to reason that the simultaneous attainment of more national goals is a possibility.

Increased Exports

High-technology products have become a main staple of our export trade. As functional performance increases the rate of technical innovation, one should expect that more such products will become available and will find buyers abroad. Moreover, since each component is designed to fit optimally into providing total performance of a functional system, tie-in sales of related components should occur. Indeed, complete system export is by no means unlikely, particularly to developing countries not yet burdened with outmoded systems and related vested interests.

Improved Quality of Life

Any and all of the foregoing potential consequences of functional-performance orientation can improve the quality of life. In combination, they total to a powerful reorientation of industrial society requiring complex mutual adjustments.

Our adaptive traditional culture will need to articulate explicitly its ethical values and preferences, if direction and control of the evolving global culture of technology is to be achieved. In our acute awareness of the disruptive nature of accelerated change, we must find room to accommodate the realization that such sustained rates of change may become a new norm. Science and technology, substituting reason for obedience and inquiry for ideology, can move mankind forward in great steps—but whither? The value-free criteria of the culture of technology must find their counterbalance in the value-laden beliefs of the traditional cultures, lest we be engulfed by the depersonalizing possibilities of a technologically controlled world. This balance, too, would require revealing experimentation for an optimum to be achieved and maintained.

It is admittedly difficult to conceive how philosophical considerations of this kind can mix with market mechanisms and a technological imperative. But performance-oriented technology has to come to terms with values: not simply environmental values, but such things as tastes, the work ethic, perception of good and bad in industrial organizations, which may be so presumptuous as to attempt decisions on what is high and what is low performance. We are conscious that "performance" is still a somewhat fragile concept in this context. Much soul-searching and deliberation will be needed to refine it, to develop measures for it, and to relate it operationally to accountability.

I believe that it will be worthwhile to take up the concept and work it into our plans for the industrial world ahead. If we are successful, the advent of new technology can be expected to be significantly influenced by consideration of societal good as an integral part of the profit motive. ∎

An Overview on Resources for Business

Joseph L. Fisher

I N DEPICTING the industrial and economic future of the United States in a target year two decades ahead, it is sensible to begin with the likely population in the United States at that time.* The 205 million figure for 1970 was up about one-third from 1950. The 1990 U.S. population could fall between 235 and 265 million, although it is probably safer to allow a little tolerance at both extremes. By the year 2000, which is the more typical target year, the range would fall between 265 and 320 million.

These figures conform roughly to the two-child and the three-child family estimates. Should the national fertility rates continue to fall as they have during the past decade, the population range for the end of the century would be markedly lower. About one-fifth of the annual population increase in recent years has been made up of net immigration, which might not hold constant either because of changes in the desire of people to come to this country or because of deliberate changes in immigration policy.

The 1990 population, at the higher and lower estimates, translates into a labor force of 105 to

110 million. Imbedded in the labor-force projections are assumptions of a slowly rising proportion of women in the labor force and a continuation of recent trends in age of entrance and leaving the labor force. Average hours of work are expected to move slowly downward in line with recent trends. Much will depend here on the general condition of the economy, especially the amount of unemployment.

The number of persons employed times the average number of hours worked yields the total labor input into the economy. If this then is multiplied by a productivity factor (output per man-hour increasing in line with historical trends) and expressed in terms of dollars, the result is an estimate of gross national product. Assuming a fairly high level of economic activity, the 1990 GNP will be more than twice that of 1970. Assuming the higher level of economic activity, GNP would rise by the end of the century to more than three times its 1970 level. Disposable income per capita, an indicator of the material well-being of people, would increase by 1990 at least by half with the higher population and by as much as two-thirds with the lower population.

An issues paper prepared by Dr. Joseph L. Fisher, President, Resources for the Future, Inc., Washington, D.C.

*The statistics presented in the following paragraphs are drawn mainly from work done or in progress at Resources for the Future, including that being prepared for the National Commission on Population Growth and the American Future.

Requirements for Raw Materials

The consequences of growth of this general magnitude on raw materials will be considerable. The following estimates of 1990 requirements

A LOOK AT BUSINESS IN 1990: A Summary of the White House Conference on the Industrial World Ahead, Washington, D.C., February 7-9, 1972 (U.S. Government Printing Office: 1972 0—467-348) pp. 132-139.

compared to 1970 sketch the picture:

- Aluminum up more than two and one-half times
- Copper nearly double
- Iron nearly double
- Lead about double
- Zinc slightly more than double
- Lumber more than double
- Wood about double
- Petroleum nearly double
- Electricity up nearly two and one-half times
- Coal slightly less than double
- Natural gas slightly more than double
- Nuclear energy up maybe 100 times or more
- Food somewhat less than double
- Cropland harvest up slightly
- Commercial forest and woodland down slightly
- Recreation land up sharply
- Urban land up sharply
- Residual and wasteland down
- Water consumption up considerably

These estimates will vary depending on whether the higher or lower population in 1990 is assumed, and on the rate of increase in productivity overall and in the relevant industries between now and then. Food and water are more influenced by population than by productivity, for most of the other items productivity is relatively more significant. Indeed, for the economy as a whole during recent years the typical four-percent annual growth rate has been made up of something over one percent increase in population and labor force, and something less than three percent productivity increase.

For each item estimated here, particular technological and economic developments may have decisive effects on the amount required; policy changes similarly may have decisive effects. For example, the amount of cropland required to produce needed food and forage in 1990 will hinge to a noticeable degree on the future improvements in seeds and fertilizing techniques; it will also depend on the legal constraints placed on the use of pesticides and perhaps fertilizers. The size of farms will also have a bearing, as will price-support levels, availability of credit, and improvements in farm management.

The consumption of electricity in 1990 will result in part from cost and price trends, the availability of competitive nuclear power, the success of efforts to reduce peaks in power loads, and new rate policies designed to hold growth of electricity consumption in check. The amount of energy raw materials that will be required in the future for electric power cannot be read simply and directly

Actions Necessary for Best Use of Materials

Among the principal actions that will have to be taken are these:

- The vigorous pursuit of research and development programs leading toward technological innovations
- The maintenance, and if possible expansion, of the world trading and investing system so that the various countries can draw on plentiful supplies wherever they occur in the world, but with due regard for the necessity of industrial development in those countries less developed economically
- Underlying everything, the need for expanding and improving the education and training of all of those who participate in the economic life of the country

from the electricity-consumption estimates; conversion efficiency will make a difference as will the shifting advantage among oil, gas, coal, hydro, and nuclear, both in conventional processes and new ones.

Along with a much larger total economy two decades hence and the greater inputs of raw materials will be, in between, more houses, industrial plant and equipment, automobiles, trucks and buses, processed food products, electricity, public works of many kinds, military equipment, and so on. In addition, the wide-ranging services category, including such activities as trade, government, and the professions, no doubt will continue to expand more rapidly than the goods category. The supplying of services also involves raw materials and resources, although generally less than equivalent expenditures on goods.

Environmental Effects

Turning now to an aspect of the economy that until recently has been more or less neglected—environmental effects—one needs to remember that what is commonly called consumption of products doesn't really extinguish them. Their form is merely changed, as required by the law of the conservation of matter that states that no matter is ever destroyed. Worn out cars pile up in auto graveyards, and some portion of them may be recycled as scrap into useful products. Garbage makes its way through the kitchen disposals and sewer lines to a treatment plant, whereupon some of it is discharged into the water, some dried and deposited on the land somewhere, and perhaps a little eventually contributes as fertilizer to agricultural production. Gasoline, after delivering its energy to propel some vehicle, adds hydrocarbons, carbon monoxide, and other pollutants to the atmosphere. The chemical and other residues from pulp-and-paper plants typically are discharged into bodies of water, sometimes treated first and sometimes not. Whatever transformations take place as things are consumed, the total amount has to go somewhere—into the air, into the water, onto the land, or back into products for consumption again.

Estimates of the amounts of various pollutants that the environment may have to absorb are hard to make. In addition to uncertainties as to future population and level of economic activity are such complications as the kinds of raw materials and industrial processes that will be utilized in 1990, the mix of final products and services that will be demanded, the emphasis given to recycling and treatment, differences in pollution concentrations among regions, and the preventive and corrective policies that will be applied during the coming years. Despite these and other estimating difficulties, a rough indication of 1990 pollution loads can be offered assuming a continuation of policies in effect during the 1967-70 period (e.g., before the legislation requiring a 90-percent reduction in most air pollutants emitted from automobiles) and only such technological changes as are clearly in view now:

Air

Hydrocarbons up more than half
Sulfur oxides up about one-quarter
Nitrogen oxides up one-half or slightly more
Carbon monoxide up one and one-half to two
  times
Particulates up slightly

Water

BOD (a measure of organic pollution) up 50
  percent or slightly more
Suspended and dissolved solids also up 50 per-
  cent or slightly more
Nitrogen up about half
Phosphorous up by half or more

Solids

Solid waste nearly double

Of these pollutants solid waste is probably most sensitive to changes in population. The others respond more to industrial and economic growth generally or to some particular component. For example, in the case of carbon monoxide and hydrocarbons, the amount of automobile use is the determining factor. Because most of these pollutants are dissipated within a few hours or days, the estimates of emissions tell something about the concentrations in the air and water, but do not preclude the possibility of serious short-term situations.

With active, successful pollution-abatement policies the condition of the environment by 1990

One needs to remember that what is commonly called consumption of products does not really extinguish them. Their form is merely changed. . . .

could be vastly improved. Many of the pollutants that plague Americans now could be reduced by 80 or 90 percent; a few such as nitrogen oxides in the air, and nitrogen and especially phosphorous and dissolved solids in the water would most likely present greater difficulties. The level and effectiveness of treatment will be critical for achieving and maintaining a cleaner environment. Fortunately, the prospects for dealing with most pollutants are encouraging provided policies are adequate to assure favorable responses from industry and the public.

The exact costs of achieving higher standards of environmental quality are uncertain but undoubtedly will be high, in dollars if not as a percent of total national income. Advanced water treatment is costly; the management and reclamation of solid wastes will strain the budgets of industrial firms and local governments; the reduction of air pollution from internal-combustion engines is already challenging the ingenuity of the automobile industry, and will add to the cost of cars.

Expenditures in 1970 more or less attributable to pollution abatement apparently were around 10 billion dollars, more than half of which went for solid-waste disposal. By 1990 these expenditures may well be three to four times as much, with water and especially air-pollution abatement rising more rapidly. As a percent of GNP, antipollution expenditures can be expected to be twice or more

*The pollutants that threaten the qual-
ity of the genetic inheritance of man
and other forms of life must be watched
with greatest care and controlled at
levels of minimum risk. The same is
true of contaminants that might destroy
the viability of whole ecosystems on
which life depends.*

what they were in 1970—up from around one percent to perhaps two and one-half percent.

Obviously the extent to which industry through
research and development can find new and economical ways to recycle waste materials, utilize
nonpolluting raw materials, and reshape whole
processes and products, the less these costs will
have to be. But even with good success along
these lines the end of large outlays for environmental improvement is nowhere in sight. Quite
new and unimagined kinds of pollution will no
doubt come along as an unwanted accompaniment of industrial progress, and a larger population with higher incomes will expect even higher
standards of air, water, and landscape quality.

Other types of pollution than those already
mentioned will trouble American industry in 1990.
Pesticides and certain other chemicals have yielded
benefits to the American consumer and profits to
the American businessman. They also inflicted
damages on the environment and in some cases on
people and wildlife. Some of them spread widely
through the atmosphere and in fresh water and
the oceans. They may persist for a long time. Certain radioactive isotopes used in industry and
science or resulting from nuclear fission have half
lives of hundreds of years. A number of toxic
metals and their compounds also persist stub-
bornly. Each of these, and more yet to come into
use, will have to be coped with. Those pollutants
that threaten the quality of the genetic inheritance
of man and other forms of life must be watched
with greatest care and controlled at levels of minimum risk. The same is true of contaminants that
might destroy the viability of whole ecosystems
on which life depends.

At the other end of the scale of seriousness are
numerous nuisances, any one of which in certain
situations may become disruptive. The total dimin-
ishes the quality of life for millions of people.
Noise and unsightly features such as inappropriate billboards and ordinary dirt are in this category. Traffic congestion, poor housing in either the
city or the country, inadequate parks and other
outdoor recreation places, and ugly architecture
and city planning are sometimes included in the
catalog of environmental problems.

Labor-force requirements can be loosely
matched to the projections of production patterns
in 1990, industry by industry, and skill by skill,
once the amounts of various items and the relevant labor productivities are specified. Because
technical and professional workers, who make up
an increasing fraction of the total labor force,
cannot easily transfer from one job to another and
because the lead-time for adequate training frequently is long, the task of providing properly
trained workers is a difficult one, made more so
by the unwillingness of most persons to be sched-
uled in and out of jobs and training programs like
raw materials or machines. If productivity in agriculture and the extractive industries continues to
rise somewhat faster than in industry generally,
as it has during the past few decades, and if this
component of the economy continues to fall as
a portion of the total, then the requirements for
additional labor arising in this sector will not be
great. On the other hand these assumptions may
not hold throughout the next two decades, in
which case the demand for workers in natural-
resource industries will be more lively. In either
event, more persons will be needed in materials-
recycling work, pollution abatement, resource
management, and the development of substitute
materials.

Key Determinants

What are the key determinants of this future?
Where will the supplies of needed raw materials
come from, and at what cost? What are the
possibilities for checking the general increase of
environmental pollution and setting the course of
industrial development in the direction of a cleaner environment? What kinds of technology will
be most helpful? What will be required to support
technological innovations with research and development, and what amounts and kinds of investment will be required to put the new technology into action? Finally, what does all this
mean for the preparation of the labor force of

1990 through education and training if the hopes of the future are to be realized?

Three groups of determinants will be considered here although there would be other ways of dividing the field. First will be the cluster involving research, development, and the application of new technology generally in industry. Second will be a cluster of factors comprising the human side: population and the labor force, education and training programs, and even the alteration of life styles. Third will be the management of industrial enterprises with particular attention to planning and investment decisions that bear critically on resources and the environment.

The Role of Technology

The way in which requirements for raw materials are met will hinge largely on the state of technology, as will the success of efforts to provide a cleaner environment. I shall trace briefly the key role of technology as it applies to energy, although the story would be similar for other natural resources. At present three quarters of total energy consumption comes from oil and natural gas. Looking ahead a few decades most observers foresee nuclear reactors as the rapidly growing energy source with the relative shares from the more conventional sources declining. By 1990 it is quite conceivable that 15 percent of total energy would be nuclear, approaching the share provided then by coal. As the years go by an increasing portion of the primary energy inputs will be converted to electricity rather than used directly for heat and propulsion. By the year 2000 approximately half of the energy commodities may find their way into use as electricity. By the end of the century half or more of total electric generation could be in nuclear plants.

Major shifts in energy sources will not come about all by themselves; they will require continued research and development leading to technological innovations in industry. Cost reductions in what by now can be called conventional nuclear reactors will be necessary, and beyond that breeder reactors will be needed. None of this will happen in the absence of significant technological progress. If one looks into the 21st century, further increases in consumption of electricity probably mean successful adaptation of controlled fusion in reactors not yet designed and through processes only dimly perceived at present. As this century runs toward its close, conventional sources of liquid fuels may begin to run dry requiring that industry turn to oil shale, coal, and tar sands. These changes will not happen by themselves either but will await technological improvements and perhaps whole new approaches.

Conservation and more efficient use of energy resource will also help, but these too are most readily achieved through technology. New technology in exploration and drilling is a key to finding more oil and gas, especially in offshore locations. More complete recovery from existing oil and gas fields hinges also on better technology. Improvements in the conversion of energy materials from one form to another—from coal to oil and gas, from shale to oil, from atoms to electricity, from coal to electricity—will result from well-selected research activities leading to the employment of new technology in industry.

Technology, embedded in a framework of economic incentives and institutions that give it the desired direction and momentum, has a similar role in reducing pollution that results from the use of energy resources. Removing sulfur oxides and fly ash from the stacks of conventional electric-generating plants is a matter for technology, as is the suppression of harmful emissions from the automobile engine, and the handling of radioactive materials in nuclear power plants. No matter where one turns, one confronts the irony that technology must solve the problems technology creates.

Because technology has become so diversified it will be desirable for future workers to be educated in such a way that they can readily be retrained for new technical jobs as the unpredictable course of economic development may indicate.

Consider the case of water resources. The growing American economy will undoubtedly require more fresh water of reasonably good quality to meet the needs of human consumption, industrial use, and irrigation. New supplies can be acquired, not only through construction of additional dams and reservoirs and interbasin transfers, but also by preventing evaporation losses especially in the arid west, by control of useless water-consuming vegetation, possibly by winning fresh water from the clouds, and especially by various techniques for restoring used and polluted water to usable condition. Finally the salt may be removed from ocean and brackish water. Progress in any of these directions is largely a matter of technology, some of which is known and some is yet to be discovered.

Another approach to the problem is that of increasing the efficiency of water use for such purposes as cooling in electric-generating plants and steel plants, and for industrial process in pulp and paper and chemical plants. A glass of water to drink is without substitute, but in industry, where water use has been increasing most rapidly, used water can be recycled in many instances, salt water can be substituted, alternative processes can be employed such as air cooling instead of water cooling, and in other ways technology can come to the rescue of difficult situations.

Needs in Education and Training

A second major determinant of the industrial future is the kind of labor force that will be available to meet the economic needs of a larger American population and to cope with environmental degradation. To the extent that directions of technology and economic development can be foreseen, educational and technical training programs can be planned accordingly. Many keys can be found here as to the direction and content of training programs for the labor force of the future.

The oceans and the ocean beds offer sources of many needed products but understanding of how ocean systems operate, where the usable resources are located and how they may be obtained, the requirements for maintaining ocean water quality, and the creating of international institutions to guide ocean development—these are among the challenges that education, training, and human ingenuity will be called on to meet.

Air pollution has become a major and besetting problem for those countries more advanced economically and for cities everywhere. As in the case of the oceans, existing knowledge of atmospheric systems is inadequate and, of course, effective ways for reducing the materials, machines, and form of behavior that cause air pollution are problems still to be solved.

As particular metals and other materials become scarcer and higher in cost, it will be desirable to find cheaper, more plentiful substitutes. One thinks of substituting plastic materials for metals, ceramic materials for lumber, low-grade ores plus new technology for high-grade ores,

synthetic fibers for natural ones, reclaimed paper and other used materials for virgin ones, and so on.

In a larger context, increased attention will be given to matching desirable properties with stated functions and end uses, and a corresponding deemphasis on the employment of a particular material. Increasingly through "molecular" engineering wholly new materials will be made to order.

Because technology has become so diversified it will be desirable for future workers to be educated in such a way that they can readily be retrained for new technical jobs as the unpredictable course of economic development may indicate. Increasingly the normal working career of a member of the American labor force should be thought of as comprising several periods in which different lines of work are followed with appropriate retraining as a normal part of life. What has occurred recently in the aerospace industry— that is, widespread unemployment among technicians and workers alike—has resulted in a concentration of effort to deal with the problems constructively. Thus far these efforts have been less than adequate in nearly every direction including retraining, relocation, and short-term financial relief. But some lessons can be learned that will be helpful in similar future situations.

The preceding survey of future resource and environmental needs shows the importance of education and training of a much larger number of persons to deal with problems of environmental quality. More sanitary engineers, public-health administrators and workers, environmental monitors, conservation officers, ecologists, producers of pollution-abatement equipment, and a long list of others will be called for in the years ahead if the country is to win back a higher level of environmental quality. A similar story can be told with respect to labor and professional training to meet the country's major social problems including poverty, urban renewal, the development of new towns, the reduction of crime and delinquency, the extension of rapid mass transportation, and so on.

The Challenge to Management

Third, a key determinant of the resource and environment future will be the response of industrial management and government management to visible and emerging problems. The managers of the American economy are the ones who have to "put it all together," to use the popular phrase. The challenge of seeing into the future with some clarity and then laying the plans and establishing

184

the actions through which individual enterprises and agencies can successfully move into that future is a complicated and exceedingly important undertaking. It is an art form requiring both decisiveness and subtlety.

Managers and policy makers need the best layout of projections of the national and regional economic future obtainable. They need also the refined analysis and sense of judgment to gauge the potentialities of their own individual firms within the broader framework of what is possible. Managers especially need the techniques and the wisdom for translating potentialities of the firms into realistic plans and investment programs, market analyses, personnel policies, and production and sales activities. In a real sense the long-range investment program is the crux of the matter.

Management decisions and long-range development programs will be urgently needed to take account of the environmental damages and social costs that accompany industrial advance. Partly this will be a matter of establishing broad standards of quality and performance, and then requiring compliance through enforcement procedures. An alternative, but not inconsistent approach, is to require that the costs of reducing harmful environmental and social effects be incorporated in the decision making of individual enterprises and agencies so that the prices of their products will cover the indirect, external, social kinds of costs. Whatever mechanisms are found to accomplish the purpose, American industry in the years ahead will have to accept major responsibility for the amelioration of environmental and social problems. For the future, efficient production to meet market demand, while continuing to be important, will not be enough. Most Americans will insist on more.

Problems and Directions Ahead

Whether the industrial world of 1990 in the United States will be satisfying and productive or tense and disfigured will depend largely on what business and governmental leaders do during the next two decades. Within rather broad limits established by what the population and labor force are likely to be, how productively the economy functions, and the kinds of products and services people want, opportunities for making significant choices will be available. The American economy will almost certainly remain predominantly an industrial and service economy dependent on large inputs of raw materials and a skilled labor force,

and the private sector is also likely to continue to predominate (although with increasing regulation and coordination by government). Hence the decisions of business leaders will be decisive. What are the major resource matters on which industry will be called upon to act in the years ahead and what are the directions that seem indicated?

For raw materials the broad objective for the next few decades will be to meet reasonable requirements efficiently and at low cost. The directions will be toward cheaper, more plentiful, more reliably available raw materials, toward technology that will economize on the use of scarce items, toward efforts to find new materials and new sources of old ones, toward much more recycling of used materials and full development of by-products, and, one hopes, toward designs that facilitate recycling and re-use.

Looking at resources as natural environment rather than strictly as raw materials, the object must be to improve the quality of the basic air, water, and land and to make certain that the serious threats to whole ecosystems and to life itself are held to the lowest possible level. The direction of movement will appropriately be toward:

- less polluting and disfiguring materials, products, and processes
- increasingly high standards of environmental quality
- the application of incentives that will induce industry and consumers to improve their environmental performance
- a vigorous response to the wide public demand for a cleaner environment

Research, development, and technological innovation will be desperately needed for dealing with the sophisticated pollutants of the modern industrial economy and the complex effects they have on people and their natural habitat. Regional, national, and in some instances world quality standards will have to be established and refined for numerous air, water, and landscape pollutants, many of which result from industrial processes. The working out of these standards will require much more information than now exists about pollutants and their effects, and the enforcement of standards implies a level of interregional and especially international cooperation yet to be achieved.

Many of the issues that will be faced in moving toward a higher quality environment will be similar to those faced in providing an adequate supply of low-cost raw materials. In fact, one of the more difficult problems for industry will be to find new

No matter where one turns, one confronts the irony that technology must solve the problems technology creates.

and viable trade-offs between production of goods and protection of the environment. For example, maintaining agricultural output without using DDT and other chlorinated hydrocarbons for fertilizers will undoubtedly cost more at least for a while. The locating of electric-generating plants farther away from cities will raise the cost of electricity. The restoration of landscapes after strip mining will add to the cost of the mineral products. But these cost increases may well be justified in terms of environmental and social benefits.

The industrial enterprise system that gives the American economy its dynamic character will have to reorient itself in some fundamental ways if the indirect and unintended environmental and social damages that have accompanied industrial activities in the past are to be brought to manageable proportions and reconciled with the traditional business emphasis on production for profit. The spread of life styles that place much less emphasis on industrial products, economic growth, and material well-being will be a factor; whether such life styles will be sustained by any appreciable number of persons remains to be seen. Finally, new and imaginative efforts in education and training, within industry and elsewhere, will be required if environmental problems are to be held in check, let alone in some sense solved.

In the last few years this country has been moving through a series of crises, among them a population crisis, an environmental crisis, a social crisis generally. The several crises are interrelated and call for an appropriately integrated approach. As the cutting edge of the future, industry will be expected to adjust itself to new imperatives, reorient its modes of behavior, and try to show how the crises can be resolved. At the minimum, industry will have to accept new constraints set by government policy and public insistence regarding its treatment of the natural environment and the sources and uses of resource materials. More than that, industry should participate in the working out of constraints that can be made to operate equitably, without cramping the innovative capacity of industry, and that will in fact make possible the improvements desired. ∎

REFERENCES

Hans H. Landsberg, Leonard Fischman, and Joseph L. Fisher, *Resources in America's Future,* Johns Hopkins Press, Baltimore, Md., 1963.

Allen Kneese, Sidney Rolfe, and Joseph Harned, (editors), *Managing the Environment: International Economic Cooperation for Pollution Control.* Published for the Atlantic Council of the United States and Battelle Memorial Institute by Praeger Publishers, New York, 1971.

Roger Revelle and Hans Landsberg (editors), *America's Changing Environment,* Beacon Press, Boston, Mass., 1970.

Barry Commoner, *The Closing Circle,* Alfred A. Knopf, New York, 1971.

Scientific American, Special issue on Energy and Power, September, 1971.

Sterling Brubaker, *To Live on Earth.* Johns Hopkins Press, April 1972.

Resources and Man, National Academy of Sciences, Washington, D.C., 1969.

Environmental Quality, the second annual report of the Council on Environmental Quality, Washington, D.C., August, 1971.

Man's Impact on the Global Environment, MIT Press, Cambridge, Mass. (Report of the Study of Critical Environmental Problems sponsored by the Massachusetts Institute of Technology), 1970.

Rapid Population Growth, Consequences and Policy Implications, published for the National Academy of Sciences by Johns Hopkins Press, 1971.

Technology: Processes of Assessment and Choice, Report of the National Academy of Sciences, Committee on Science and Astronautics, U.S. House of Representatives, July, 1969.

Technology and Resources for Business

Simon Ramo

THE WORLD between now and 1990 will have an abundance of technology and resources issues—problems, opportunities, development, breakthroughs, controversies. Typical problems are: a growing gap between developed and underdeveloped nations in per capita consumption of critical materials in increasingly short supply; increasing pollution; and failure to adjust social systems in response to rapid technological change. These negatives will be accompanied by the positive potentials of vastly improved communication and transportation, plentiful energy by nuclear techniques, fresh water by de-salting the seas, weather control, new means for tapping the earth's hidden resources, superior birth-control techniques, and, even, perhaps, control of aging.

Pessimists are convinced the civilization is already doomed by our rate of consumption of the earth's limited resources and the attendant impact on the environment. Optimists are picturing a fantastically better world that future technological development can bring us. But neither's list necessarily leads us to useful anticipations. We are more interested in prediction so as to prepare for change, to anticipate and plan for the inevitable, to recognize and select alternatives early where the developments are not inevitable but are subject to our discretionary actions. We must be fully aware that nothing will happen unless permitted by the laws of the physical universe. But not everything that can happen will happen. Social, economic, and political aspects, not technological alone, will determine what actually does occur. Politically, our goals and priorities will select (even if often in a most subtle manner) how we allocate our resources. Economically, the matching of production and distribution with demand will have powerful votes also, certainly ahead of mere technical feasibility.

So if we want to arrive at useful anticipations we are forced to consider the interface problem of technology with society. Developments on the resources and technology front will cause business to be different by 1990 in many ways. There will be new products, for example. However, much more important is that business will be greatly changed as to its goals and tools because it is a part of the greater society that will itself change as a result of technological and resource considerations.

We shall look toward 1990 through a series of specific examples. At the outset, however, let us set forth part of what these examples will suggest. These are given in the insert on page 141.

Information Technology

Some examples will bring out these key social-technological issues. Consider first the new technology many see as the most important of all because it amounts to the creation of synthetic

Address by Dr. Simon Ramo, Vice Chairman and Chairman of the Executive Committee, TRW, Inc.

A LOOK AT BUSINESS IN 1990: A Summary of the White House Conference on the Industrial World Ahead, Washington, D.C., February 7-9, 1972 (U.S. Government Printing Office: 1972 0—467-348) pp. 140-148.

Some Prospects by 1990

- For real progress by 1990 toward the best use of our resources and technology a systems approach will be needed, emphasizing interactions amongst numerous technological and nontechnological, social-economic parameters.

- Great economic and social return will result from intelligent investment in advanced technology, with increased productivity alone more than compensating the cost.

- Intensive political pressure, resulting from public demand to solve "social-engineering" problems—urban development, pollution control, improved health care, better education, superior transportation—will exert a powerful, selective effect in the coming decades on the allocations of resources and the application of technology.

- Our hybrid economy, part free enterprise and part governmentally controlled, will take on a new form constituting a virtual Social-Industrial Complex by 1990. This teaming of government and business will be greatly influenced by resources and technology matters.

- In contrast with the present apparent surplus of engineers and scientists, a severe shortage will emerge with a need particularly for new interdisciplinary professionals, who can be termed "socio-technologists."

---

brainpower. Developments in electronics are making it certain that by 1990 man will have far greater ability to handle the information basic to all his pursuits—production, distribution, education, accounting, banking, medicine, law, government. Equipped with these technological aids, he will be able to sense, acquire, store, and process information, and will be able to communicate, display, categorize, deliberate, and perform other logical operations with vastly greater capacity, speed, versatility, interconnection, and geographical spread than is possible for the unaided human mind and senses.

Applied to business and industry, the coming information technology will enable human managers to operate closer to total awareness and control. Optimum scheduling and on-line measurement of deviations from plan will be possible. Incoming orders will be processed virtually instantaneously for better scheduling of labor, materials, cash flow, product distribution, and inventories. A logical step by 1990 is interconnection of information flow to industrial entities whose harmoniously interlocked schedules will act in response to market actions and production operations in real time. Payment for each other's services and materials would flow through the network, the banks dealing with money transfers on an electronic basis. The government may even take its tax cut automatically.

The development of new man-machine partnerships to make possible the superior handling of information should be eagerly anticipated. Such an advance is perhaps the greatest boon that science and technology can give society. With the enormously increased overall brainpower, the machine partner would take on the more mundane tasks, resulting in the high-capacity handling of needed information with geographical span and speeds appropriate to our busy, complex life. The human-brain partner could then be free to rise to higher plateaus of judgment, creativity, decision making, social and cultural attainments. Greater productivity would ensue. The U.S. attainments would be exported, helping improve our balance of payments.

To achieve these benefits, some corollary difficulties must be dealt with between now and 1990. For instance, the modifications of the structure of business and the pattern of all other activities needed to exploit the new information technology will involve massive start-up costs. Almost everyone involved would have at least a small console to tie him into the information network. Indeed, most of these electronic information systems become economical only with millions of terminals (even as with telephony or TV). Billions of dollars, properly reckoned as operating losses, are required, with many more billions at risk for years before turnaround into a profit period.

The pioneering capital needed exceeds what even the largest American corporations are likely to consider sensible. Despite the potential of economic and social gain inherent in the productivity increase and greater flexibility the technology would provide, the speed with which this kind of technology can come into being is greatly contingent on new organizational teaming of corporations and government. The government may need to sponsor large-scale experiments to develop the basic ideas, perhaps seeking improved information flow in government operations as the first proving ground. It may be necessary for government to allow, even encourage, the setting up of private-industry teams to share risk.

The Robot Society vs. Instant Democracy

There is more to consider on the nontechnical side of the matter before we can assess the probabilities of the realization by 1990 of the development of information technology that will revolutionize business and many other activities of man. The average citizen believes we are moving inexorably into an increasingly technological society not of his asking. The specific advance that extends the human intellect—the handling and control of information—is a leading symbol of the technological threat. Here he sees the human participant losing out as the electronic machinery moves into partnership with him. Not only is he frightened of a computer-controlled robot society, but he is also afraid of the "planned economy"—an automated socialism with no free decision making, individual initiative, or personal incentives.

The availability of advanced information technology does not inevitably lead to a state-controlled economy. Instead, we can use it to reach a higher form of free enterprise. In a "computerized" society, to oversimplify a little, all of the information needed for control—from airplane schedules to pickle distribution—is made available at the right place at the right time. Tens of

---

Developments in electronics are making it certain that by 1990 man will have far greater ability to handle the information basic to all of his pursuits— production, distribution, education, accounting, banking, medicine, law, government.

---

millions of interconnected electronic devices would be everywhere, picking up, processing, and disseminating information. In effect, each citizen would be associated with a "super telephone-TV set" telling him where to be and what to do. However, the same system—a national network of computers, communication gear, electronic memory, and information input and output consoles —that can tell millions of people exactly what to do, as though they were robots, can just as well ask them to choose a preference from a group of well-presented alternatives. The public in 1990 could tune in on the issues and take part by expressing its reactions electronically in two-way communication—"instant democracy." Information technology could be used to achieve by 1990 a more informed citizenry with an extent of participation in decision making never before imagined.

Freer Enterprise

As to the feared planned economy, remember that the foundation of true free enterprise is the free market. The closer people get to a free choice of how to spend their money and the more that all goods can be offered for sale in a free market, then the closer we come to realizing full free enterprise. Thus, if the nation attains a high flow of information reaching every nook and cranny of its economy, the ingredients are present for a free market in which everyone could quickly know what is available. A proposal to produce something by a manufacturer could be immediately considered by potential purchasers. In 1990 we could respond electronically in our homes to a "commercial" that describes contemplated future automobile models with a substantial discount for orders placed immediately. We could step to our consoles and push the right buttons to make our commitment, automatically depleting our bank accounts electronically in the process.

Applied nationally to cars, air conditioners, vacations, furniture, refrigerators, clothes, frozen foods, and educational courses, such direct communications could be used by the network's clients to schedule manufacturing and distribution in advance. The result would be highly efficient industrial activities from the ordering of basic raw materials to the setting up and manning of plants and transportation facilities. The profit-to-risk ratio would rise dramatically as the entrepreneur and the consumer would be involved together in an "on-line" market exchange.

A natural role for government would exist in such an electronicized, free-enterprise economy, and not as a rival to the private sector. The government would have to set the rules, referee, license, and insure objectivity and fair opportunity in the workings of the information service.

Advancing technology in this instance, as in every other, merely offers us choices. It does not determine the direction in which our society must go.

Environmental Technology

Despite all the controversy about pollution, if all scientific knowledge and technological developments were applied to the fullest worldwide in an optimum match with social and economic factors, the problem of pollution could be solved by 1990. Disturbance to the air, land, and waterways would not be zero in that optimum situation. However, the effect on the environment would be of a nature and amount calculated and designated as to be not only tolerable but also would provide economic and social payout on the investment.

But such an all-out, wise use of technology simultaneously by all nations in harmony with agreed-upon social criteria is an absurdly unrealistic ideal for attainment by 1990 or any decade near 1990. What we can see is our endeavoring earnestly to approach such a condition and a contest between such efforts and the parallel continuation of chaotic actions that determine our environment.

Consider, for example, as a rather typical situ-

Information technology could be used to achieve by 1990 a more informed citizenry with an extent of participation in decision making never before imagined.

---

ation, a concentration of a million or so people around a bay, the waterway already badly polluted. One alternative would be to freeze the population and industry at its present size and then go about duplicating facilities and the organization of specialized skilled personnel elsewhere to provide for necessary expansion of population and industry. At the new location, presumably we could then go on to pollute the nearby waters to arrive at the same bad density point, at which time the whole exercise could be repeated.

A more satisfactory possibility economically is to accept the penalty of the added costs of depollution, and then allow the area to grow rather than be arbitrarily limited by a pollution situation that arose without anyone's planning for it. With technology put to work fully, it is probable that for only a few percent penalty added to present costs —for manufacturing plants, public sewage facilities, transportation operations, utilities—a successful depollution program could be carried out. By "successful" we mean that the community might be able to scale-up its population from its present one million to two million with the environmental degradation held constant or perhaps even improved.

Private industry alone cannot assemble a market in which to sell pollution goods and services. Without organized citizen action—meaning government action—no meaningful customer-supplier relationship exists to depollute an ocean bay, lake, or river. To emphasize this, ponder an extremely large project. A decade ago the then President announced that we would spend some tens of billions of dollars to land a man on the moon "within the decade." Suppose the present President announces a similarly bold government program for this decade: "Before the '70s are over we shall depollute the Great Lakes."

With the cost again several tens of billions of dollars, he assigns an agency to direct the job. Contracts go out to find out how to depollute the Great Lakes, as well as to develop and analyze alternatives in the necessary modification of the practices of all who now pour waste into the lakes. New engineering advances are turned up, showing how to do the job with the least cost and how to choose the right solution to meet specific economic and social criteria.

But a great deal more than the basic science of environmental control is brought forth. Goals concerning population and industrial growth are established. Deep confrontations occur on how much we are willing to pay to preserve the purity of the environment. Limiting growth of some industry around the lakes implies industry being established elsewhere with a corresponding population shift. A whole train of events is started as the project influences not only planned growth and the pattern of society all over the United States but also other nations with which we are in competition and that have similar problems.

Mistakes will be made. Money will be spent to equip some cities on the Great Lakes with an ability to grow where the growth is not justified, and some industry potential is handicapped, unable to compete against similar enterprises elsewhere that need not add pollution controls to their costs. However, just as we succeeded in landing a man on the moon, we succeed in depolluting those lakes. Mistakes will show us how to do things more sensibly the next time.

We would have to regard a "Great Lakes Depollution Project" as a pioneering effort, an attempt to push forward the frontiers, like the moon-landing program. However, here the project is broader and much more difficult. When we speak this time of pioneering, we mean not only in technology but also in understanding what we should do about environmental control in relationship to our goals of social and economic development. But, having engaged in the project, our technology in pollution control would lead the world. Other nations would follow our lead; we could export high-technology services and equipment.

The big first steps in pollution control rest on government leadership. Private industry will join later with large investments to produce equipment and services. No combine of American companies is imaginable, without strong government sponsorship, to implement the job of depolluting the Great Lakes. Immunity from antitrust action would be necessary to set the stage for the essential free motion of data, analyses, and ideas among participating companies. Even then, the risky return on the great investment and the high start-up costs to perform the systems studies and to develop the needed methods and equipment would stand in the way.

Urban Rapid Transit

Allocation of resources and technological-development effort on projects pertaining to urban problems will deserve high priority in the '70s and '80s. Urban rapid transit is an example

An employee in a large city may live 10 miles from his work with no real choice, in view of the city's "design," to live closer. Without access to a rapid-transit system, he drives his car this 10 miles in one hour, polluting the air as he goes, and using much of his energy and patience in the miserable traffic. He leaves his transportation investment to stand all day in the parking lot. He is tired before he starts to work; his 40-hour workweek accomplishes 30 hours work, but it takes him 60 hours portal to portal. The same applies to the rest of his and his family's life, whether the transportation needs are concerned with education, medical care, shopping, or recreation.

Look at the productivity waste, or better, the productivity improvement potential. We have a 60-to-30 ratio—a two-to-one gain to shoot for —not the two or three percent usually mentioned for annual productivity increase. The potential economic payoff of soundly designed rapid transit is sinful to ignore; it is unlikely that we shall continue giving it little attention from now until 1990.

About half of us, say, 100 million people, live in cities large enough that the introduction of effective rapid transit would make a significant change. For each million people a billion dollars or so would be required to design and build a good rapid-transit system, an investment for the

nation of some $100 billion. To establish such systems by 1990 would involve a five-billion-a-year design and building program—enough to absorb considerable unemployment of engineers.

Much of what needs doing in urban rapid transit lends itself to private investment for profit, the profit coming out of the economic return that will be the consequences of effective programs. However, unlike the development of the now-established consumer business of the nation, solving

---

The big first steps in pollution control rest on government leadership. Private industry will join later with large investments to produce equipment and services.

---

urban problems requires strong government participation. Private industry alone cannot design urban rapid-transit systems, build them, and deliver them to consumers. The only system that will provide good return on investment for their users will be those whose design takes account of meticulously detailed aspects of the economic and social future life of the given community. The government, as pointed out in the inset, would probably have to fund research and development programs with industry to bring the needed apparatus into existence through prototype stages. Beyond this it could be expected that private industry would take substantial investment initiative, seeking hardware sales, and installation and maintenance contracts.

Urban Transit

The federal government needs to launch substantial programs for detailed system design of urban transit, done concurrently with broader system studies of urban community requirements and design. This must be accomplished for a dozen or so communities, the results describing thoroughly implementable rapid-transit systems, calling out the components to be developed and built, the relationship between the system and the community's anticipated life, the performance traded off against the costs.

For actually implementing the individual systems, funding would be required in each community, of course. But if the systems design were done well enough the economic return to the city would be clear, which it is not today. It then becomes possible to imagine that cities could float the necessary financing, perhaps with some federal-government guarantees, the investment funds so raised being paid back out of operating revenues.

Political pressure to meet articulated need, anticipated productivity increase and, thus, economic payoff and a recognized requirement for minimum energy utilization in a match with minimum pollution will conspire toward rapid-transit systems operating in most of America's cities by 1990.

Electric-Power Generation

On the technological horizon few possibilities for 1990 are more exciting than the availability of virtually limitless, clean electric-power generation by controlled thermonuclear fusion. A primary fusion fuel, deuterium, occurs naturally in water and can be separated from it. Therefore, it is virtually inexhaustible. Thus, successful development of fusion-powered technology would permanently solve the problem of the rate of depletion of fossil fuels. As a power source, thermonuclear fusion presents no radioactive waste products; it could never explode, only collapse.

Substantial experimental work has been carried on to learn the principles of controlled thermonuclear-fusion power generation, with promising results. However, to arrive at practical designs will require many more years of the greatest of efforts. The combination of increasing power demand, shortage of conventional materials and the pollution problem (the solutions to which in all its forms requires more rather than less energy consumption) suggests that new thermonuclear approaches gradually will be recognized as meriting more support. By 1990 such techniques may emerge successfully. Of course, as has been the case with another nuclear-energy approach, the nuclear reactor, this cannot happen without large government-sponsored programs, the ratio of return to risk, and the enormous start-up costs again being beyond practical, exclusively private investment. Perhaps by about 1990 a government-private-industry team effort will be formed to carry the fusion development to completion.

The Pervasive Importance of Wise Use of Technology

Even a half-hearted attack on our top priority, technology-related problems, will require the strongest effort of which we are capable in allocation of resources and in technological development backed by scientific research. It is hard to predict the specific resource and technology developments that will emerge by 1990. It is not difficult to anticipate that between now and then we shall be engaged in a contest, on the one hand, to use science and technology to the fullest, and, on the other, to control the nature and speed of technological development. By 1990 it may become crystal clear—the evidence is available today—that these two sides of the contest are not and should not be placed in opposition. We cannot attack problems soundly without full use of science and technology even as we can no longer tolerate their misuse.

Many other examples of the course of future technology could be cited. New educational technology has the potential of broadening the tools of the educator and making possible systems of education that will provide high returns on the investment. Or, take health care, where present procedures, simply extended, will utterly fail to provide for the increased expectancy. Clearly we need, and science and technology can provide part of the means to new approaches: a trained paramedical personnel force; improved preventive medicine; better testing and categorizing procedures; creative hospital designs based on superior information handling; instrumentation; scheduling; patient monitoring; and other key aspects. The same kind of comments can be made about crime control, housing technology, use of ocean resources, and other high-priority fields.

More examples would merely strengthen the conclusion that almost every priority need of the society between now and 1990 involves issues of resources and technology. Sometimes the problem is adjustment to technological change. It may be the difficulty of prudent use of resources and technology. Equally often, the intelligent application of our materials and technological tools is vital in arriving at solutions to the problems. Most often we are in a position to do something effective about our problems. Application of our creativity and our means at hand will yield economic returns and social benefits. However, we possess great weaknesses, including organizational inadequacies, lack of established means to set goals, to compare alternatives, and to put together the pattern of private and governmental entities necessary to get on with what we want to, and can, accomplish.

Thus it is the organizational problem that must be licked by 1990 if technological advance is to yield social advance by then.

The Coming Social-Industrial Complex

In the United States during the early part of this century we learned how to mass produce by the fullest partnership of free enterprise and technology. Free enterprise was the means for joining the financial investment, the know-how, and the customer. The government had only to provide rules, refereeing, and protection. But, just as private industry alone cannot depollute the Great Lakes or provide urban rapid-transit systems, it also cannot cut down wasteful energy consumption in operating transportation systems when that waste results from antiquated government regulation. It cannot presume to set national goals on growth of electric-power generation capacity vs. pollution. The new wave of broadened use of science and technology that is inherent in the teaming up of government and industry to go after these vital areas will give the United States a strong lead in new high-technology products for export. The remainder of the developed world has the same kinds of problems. What it does not have is our size of market over which to spread the costs or

Social-Engineering Projects

In providing for defense of the nation we went beyond consumer-free-enterprise organizational concepts. A combine of government, industry, and science and technology was formed and it met the nation's requirements for weapons systems. Similarly, a new combine will be needed to utilize our basic capabilities to meet the new public demand for social-engineering projects. The military-industrial complex involved at most less than 10 percent of our gross national product. In contrast, half of the total activities of the nation is tied in with the priority "social-engineering" matters—urban development, health care, improved education, environmental control, rapid transit, housing technology, and the mass use of synthetic brainpower through electronic information networks. The coming social-industrial complex will involve more jobs, more private investment, and more of the nation's resources. Its influence for good and for bad will thus be proportionately greater.

The new wave of broadened use of science and technology that is inherent in the teaming up of government and industry . . . will give the United States a strong lead in new high-technology products for export.

an integrated national or regional economy as is ours. Nor does it have a potential for aligning needs, resources, and technology so as to work out fully coordinated programs for solution to problems within a single political entity. In addition, it lacks as a starting point now, in the early '70s, the large body of trained engineers and scientists we possess, backed with ample and readily extendable laboratories and manufacturing facilities. Europe considered as a total entity and Japan have some of these qualifications, but by comparison with us the difference is as great by any quantitative measure as is our gross national product compared with theirs.

To create the new pattern of private-government cooperation, some of us must get over the hangup that insists government is already too involved in the planning of change and should leave the making of advances and the removing of ills wholly to the private sector. Many of the rest of us must abandon the line of thought that says private action is "selfish interest" and bad, so we must become a totally government-directed nation. Almost everyone knows we are actually operating a hybrid society, part free enterprise and part government controlled.

This awareness, however, does not prevent many from espousing one simplistic view or the other and avoiding in this way adequate discussion of innovative, cooperative organizational schemes. Consider that for most of the coming, large-scale advances involving resources and technology, effective use of private enterprise resources (even with considerable government participation) will involve private corporations in cooperative efforts that would be precluded by existing, but out-of-date, antitrust law interpretations. Our organizational concepts defining the role of business and government were based on an earlier non-technological and non-international society. They must be modified soon to meet the problems of the next 20 years.

193

The Missing Profession

The '70s have opened with an apparent surplus of scientists and engineers, many of whom are now unemployed. Moreover, there is widespread belief that we are producing too many Ph.D.'s in general. This over-supply hardly jibes with the picture we have painted of social and economic forces driving us to apply the most direct, forceful, mass effort with all of the wisdom and creativity that we command. Urban development, controlling the environment, the changeover in the way we operate business, government, and the professions in response to the availability of electronic information systems—each of these fields and others, alone, if directed properly in its development, should be able to absorb quickly all trained, intellectually qualified individuals we can conceivably produce.

Granted, the problem is one of organization— clarifying goals, arriving at decisions, setting up teams, working out the national bookkeeping so that we can apply funds where they are needed to get on with the projects that we need and can afford. But the existence of these great organizational and administrative difficulties, which must somehow be surmounted, should not confuse us into believing we have a surplus of capable, educated people. The appearance of such a surplus should be, in fact, a signal that we are poor organizers and planners. How absurd, for example, to say, as some do, that we cannot afford to tackle the problems of learning how with least cost and best results to depollute our waterways while engineers and scientists who could make progress on such efforts are drawing unemployment relief funds.

Long before 1990 it will become apparent that we have a shortage of properly trained people, particularly the interdisciplinary, the practical, the intellectual. We cannot suddenly turn a large fraction of our engineers into experts on the social side of the problems or opportunities. Because it will be the only way to get started to get the job done, we shall, for a decade or more, create "social technologists (perhaps we should say "poly-socio-econo-politico-technologists") in the school of hard knocks. These will be key performers in applying science and technology fully to the needs of our society. They will become expert at doing so by pragmatic, day-to-day synthesizing of arts and disciplines and experience and motivations and human ingenuity.

Probably by 1990 our universities will be turning out graduates who have specialized in these social-engineering problems. It may take until then before this interdisciplinary "technology-society" field is properly understood and categorized, with enough general principles tied to it that it can be taught as an intellectual discipline. For one thing, the "people" problem is vastly more difficult than the problems of physical science and technology. Large and powerful industrial organizations make products and distribute them but their products are physical. When it comes to filling our needs, we are strong on things and not so strong on man. This imbalance will handicap us, possibly forever—at least until 1990. The disciplines that make up our professions today will split, merge, expand and readjust themselves in the academic institutions and in the real-life world, where the new professions now missing will take root partly on the old and partly in response to new needs and opportunities.

Penalties and Benefits

Doing it wrong means to continue to countenance an antitechnology wave, confusing this tool of man, technology, with its misuse by man himself. It means going on without setting goals, without planning, without study of alternatives, with selection by crisis. It means using all of the materials we can lay our hands on, and feverishly building our technological systems, our energy consumption, and our production as though it were our contemplated, determined goal to do so at the highest rate. If such action and our per-capita consumption of materials and energy are emulated to the maximum extent by the remainder of the world, then we shall surely create even greater world instability. We shall inadvertently promote contests of increasing severity amongst nations for acquisition and control of resources. Under such circumstances, it is difficult to see how the world can survive to 1990 in any state except one of increasing waste and pollution, fear of each other, and decreasing moral and ethical values.

On the other hand, doing it right means we recognize that we will have shortages of materials. Accordingly, we must apply technology to the fullest to avoid waste of materials, discover new materials, use them most effectively, invent and create substitutes. It means we recognize that the whole world will suffer from pollution unless nations cooperate on goals and controls. We must

194

acknowledge that pollution will be minimized by wise technological development and ample energy supply.

Doing it right means, in short, using technology to the fullest to preserve and increase our resources whether it be more brainpower or more electric power. It means recognizing that to use technology fully, and not misuse it or fail to use it, to get the most of our resources, to influence the other nations of the world to cooperate toward these ends, we shall often have to invent new roles for government and new patterns for government-industry-science cooperation. Doing it right means to discard inhibitions about accepting government-industry-science teaming and deliberate goal-setting activities. It means serious study of social-technological-economic interfaces, much planning, and considerable control. We must abandon the idea that to articulate objectives and study alternative plans is to embark on a one-way road to a complete state control of the economy and the life pattern. Instead, it may be that to have freedom where it counts will require planning for freedom. Neither a state-controlled life nor a completely free-enterprise one will suffice or satisfy us. Instead, new and developing organizational hybrids of varying kinds, depending on the projects to be performed, need to be accepted as the pattern for 1990.

Because of the potential of social and economic payoff, and because citizen appreciation is increasing as to this potential, political pressure will predominantly grow in the direction of action and soundness. Thus, I believe that we can look to 1990 as a time when the resources and technology situation of the world might improve substantially. As we stand in 1990 looking at the year 2000 and beyond, we might have more hope then than we have today for the long-time stability of our highly technological society. ■

Factors Affecting the Rate and Direction of Technology and Resources

Howard W. Johnson

THE MOST important resource to be considered is the human resource. The first determinant will be the size of the population. In short, the rate of new births will have most to say about many of the questions before us. The rate for the United States is expected to decline further. Beyond that, the prime characteristic of the '90s will be the intense interrelationship of the human being with his physical environment and with his fellowman. Partly this will be due to the population growth, perhaps more so to the geometric increase in individual and group interrelationships. It will be a difficult world from which to withdraw. Human pressures and human communication, encouraged by technology of all kinds, will force a higher sense of interdependence than ever. Important new voices will be heard and will have to be considered. Greater involvement by women in the affairs of the marketplace, and more particularly in business decision making, will be a large factor. Minority groups will have a more equitable participation in the workings of the decision process.

The most important new fact of life in business in the decades ahead will be participation and involvement to a much greater degree and more di-

Remarks by Howard W. Johnson, Chairman of the Corporation, Massachusetts Institute of Technology.

rectly than ever. This involvement will be expressed in the marketplace, of course, and in the reward structure, but it will also be expressed within the firm itself and in terms of the structures of government requirements surrounding business. Two effects of this fact are to be considered. The first is that, in requiring business to consider many more relevant voices in its decision making, there will be large limits to action and a large frustration in functioning. The second, clearly positive, is that it may well be possible to emerge with a higher quality of conclusion and a more solid sense of support.

This higher involvement, greater participation in decision making in business, also impinges on human structures, governmental, educational, and public institutions of all kinds. This requirement for involvement has a special relevance to technology and resource maintenance. People, within the firm and without, will want assurance that technology is widely used, that natural resources and the physical environment are being protected. The definitions of "wisdom" and "protection" need much clarification. They are not to be left in the hands of a few special pleaders of special interests, either groups or individuals. If greater participation can be achieved, a sense of direction, purpose, and support will add much to the sense of life in the '90s. This leads to the question: will it be possible to

A LOOK AT BUSINESS IN 1990: A Summary of the White House Conference on the Industrial World Ahead, Washington, D.C., February 7-9, 1972 (U.S. Government Printing Office: 1972 0—467-348) pp. 149-152.

involve a whole new range of participants and still keep a sense of efficiency and direction?

Technology in the future will, I believe, be devoted to those areas of a clearer human significance than heretofore. These goals tend to be those for which the market mechanism, either from demand or from supply, have not yet proved effective. Some of these goals, for which technology will be available are:

- Large-scale improvements in the city, if the goals can be set and if the resources can be mobilized.
- Improvement of environmental quality, which will clearly be in our grasp in the '90s if the problems of improvement can be defined, if the goals can be stated in terms of a reasonable time cycle, and if the capital base can be developed.
- Delivery of large-scale services, such as health care and transportation, if the problem can be defined, goals set, and financing secured.

Need for More Attention to Research

An assurance of the availability of technology is not automatic, of course. That will require a new kind of research, and, closely related, the development of a new educational process. As to research, large problems growing out of our present practice must be resolved if technical and social solutions are to be available. Present support of basic research comes from the federal government, largely to university researchers and laboratories, but also to private and public companies. The level of support in basic areas of research is simply not adequate. Worse, because the time cycle for research is long, the tendency to provide stop-and-go financial support for research is wasteful. Efforts should be pressed to support basic research more evenly over long time periods. The full replacement of support that has come from the Department of Defense does not now exist. A vital requirement for effective development of human progress in the '90s is a regular and intensive searching of the frontiers of science.

As to applied research, the needs are more obvious if no less involved. One of the problems in applied research is to find solutions to complex systems problems. This requires an interdisciplinary approach in problem definition and goal setting as well as method. The mechanisms here are not yet clear. Technology has performed brilliantly for society; whether technology really benefits

The level of support in basic areas of research is simply not adequate. Worse, because the time cycle for research is long, the tendency to provide stop-and-go financial support for research is wasteful.

mankind is without question. It does, but only in terms of what mankind asks of it. It is the statement of what is desired of it that is lacking. If we can develop realistic goals and provide long enough lead times to achieve them, technology will be the route by which the grim predictions of the decaying state can be avoided.

Education As It Relates to Technology

A review of our requirements for research in technological development leads directly to the requirements for education in the coming two decades. Much thought—long overdue—is now being given to a revision of the form of education related to technology. We are seeing once again the cyclical decline in student interest in engineering and science, for example, as well as a decline in demand for students with such preparation. This decline, incidentally, can result in a large shortage in major engineering ability during the next two decades.

One such review is proceeding at M.I.T. It provides an example of the kind of thinking that must be given priority now if the young men and women who will direct the application of technology in the '90s will be ready. This analysis starts with the idea that engineering education must be responsive to a broader requirement by society. Solutions must take into account not only devices that achieve limited progress but also the social and economic factors that surround them. Engineers must participate with others in defining these requirements, and proceed, in systems terms, to solve those problems. Engineering requirements move from hardware devices, whether in transportation, agriculture, or manufacturing, to hardware systems such as power systems or transport systems, and finally to whole systems, with emphasis on the "software" development required to make the system more responsive and more regenerative.

Such an expansion of the concept of the engineer's role puts new emphasis on a broader range of costs to be considered. These include not only the direct and immediate costs but also the longer range costs of the social and human costs of technological development. It places emphasis on the development of a conceptual framework *to decide what to design.* This requires the effective involvement of those affected, both presently and in the future, in the development of technology. It puts emphasis on the necessity to analyze requirements, and to the realization that each subsequent addition to technology changes the situation and its future requirements in real ways.

Translating this new framework for engineering and the management of technology into educational terms has led Dean Alfred A. H. Keil of M.I.T. to designate four distinctive types of engineers required for our society. These are set forth at right. All four classifications proceed from a firm base in engineering science to learning and experience in the demands of their particular specialization. To me, the most significant part of this concept of engineering education is the necessity to bring into the teaching process other sets of understanding: the social sciences and management, as well as the pure sciences, for complete comprehension of the breadth of the problem and the process.

Construction of a new concept of engineering education is one of the most critical requirements for our society in preparing for the 1990s. Most important is that this new conceptual effort must begin now. Efforts along these lines deserve national emphasis.

Economics and the Technology and Resources Partnership

Far too little understanding exists of the process by which the capital base will be generated and allocated for financing the expansion of sound

---

Types of Engineers Needed

- *The technologist* whose main concern and interest are with the existing technology in the fabrication, operation, and maintenance of engineering products and industrial processes. This education requires background in the related sciences and the development of basic skills in his field of technology, coupled with an understanding of industrial practices in his field.

- *The practicing engineer and designer* whose main concern is the application of science and technology in the conception and development of new "hardware." His education requires development of a strong background in related engineering sciences, technology, systems analysis, and engineering economics, as well as the development of capabilities for synthesis.

- *The engineering scientist* whose main concerns are the advancement of the engineering sciences and laying the foundation for new technology. His education requires development of a strong background in related sciences as well as the development of research abilities.

- *The broad systems engineer* whose main concern is the determination of the broad design characteristics for systems to meet actual needs of society. His education requires the development of a strong foundation in engineering and systems analysis as well as the development of capabilities to relate engineering solutions to society's needs.

---

technology in the 1990s. Whether we can generate the capital required to finance the diverse needs of society, both public and private, cannot be easily assured. It is too early to predict the demands of the various markets of the '90s. It seems likely to me that if our demographic factor is favorable, and provided we can fully protect the incentives for savings and for profit, capital resources will be adequate. Private and governmental agencies alike must reexamine the functioning of the capital markets in our society so that optimum market development rather than the heated pressure of events will become the most important factor in adapting the system.

The most important new fact of life in business in the decades ahead will be greater ·participation and involvement to a much greater degree than ever.

Need for Able Managers

Beyond the tasks I have outlined, a final crucial determinant in the beneficial use of technology and resources in the '90s remains: the need for managerial talent of breadth and quality. If we can develop a sense of the priorities arrived at on a broad basis of interaction of all the relevant sources, and if, with an appropriate research base we can develop the requisite technologies, there will still be the scarce resource of people, especially in managerial roles, to make the system function. The constraints on an effective functioning system in the '90s will, I believe, be more human than technical. The natural constraints on the system will change sharply. Shortages will occur in space, air, and materials. The time-frames to be considered will be longer. But the most difficult constraints will relate to the need for managers in all sectors of the society who can make the largest strategic judgments on a more visible stage of operations. Legal requirements, governmental

---

Construction of a new concept of engineering education is one of the most critical requirements for our society in preparing for the 1990s.

---

pressures, and the decisive interest of many more of our people will combine to place an extraordinary need for management people. They will require a constant reeducation within the context of what society wants to become. This requirement for effective management will bear as heavily on federal and local government and other institutions as it does on private business. Of all the factors that relate to the wise and humane development of the future of our society, this requirement for effective managers strikes me as the most complex.

The need for management must be expressed in terms of people with the highest sense of standards and values for the advance of our human society. In understanding the basis for the gulf between many young people and the world of business as they see it, I am struck by the way in which the production of wealth—the material base

for human advance—is considered by many of them completely separate from the creation of values. Any discussion of business suffers from appearing to emphasize only the economic factor. In the increasingly interdependent world of the '90s, the relationship between material advantage and high values must be more clearly understood. It seems apparent to many businessmen that one cannot develop a high sense of values without an adequate economic base. But I would go further. If we are to enter a better age at the end of this century, the creation of value and the creation of wealth, the sense of service that best describes man's purpose must be understood and communicated to our young people. ∎

199

Intermediate Institutions

Robert A. Charpie

THE CRITICAL problem about technology and resources is man's relationship to them, both as it is now and as it changes with time. This relationship creates working organizations of men, who incorporate the necessary capabilities to effectively approach man's problems. Future institutions must combine the capabilities and efficiencies of man in private enterprise with the broad responsibility and representation of man in public agencies. Preferably, of course, with a minimum of the disadvantages of the two.

Man can achieve little by himself. His achievements are represented in the institutions he creates. They manifest the intelligence of his mind and the values of his emotions. Sometimes these institutions leave monuments, such as the pyramids, the cathedrals, or the amphitheaters. But the basic forces are the institutions, which made these works possible as a concerted expression of society. Institutions and their change mirror the ability of man to manage his society. They never have been truer than today.

I wish to stress the urgency of creating new intermediate institutions—institutions that lie between industry and government—that will better resolve present and future problems. These institutions must fulfill the idealism of the young, satisfy the needs of the poor, protect the aged, provide health care for the sick, equalize social justice,

Remarks by Dr. Robert A. Charpie, President, The Cabot Corporation.

A LOOK AT BUSINESS IN 1990: A Summary of the White House Conference on the Industrial World Ahead, Washington, D.C., February 7-9, 1972 (U.S. Government Printing Office: 1972 0—467-348) pp. 153-156.

preserve the environment, and treat all men humanely.

In the early days, when man strived to improve the amenities of his life, it was important to make things possible. To this end, he invented technology. But technology for the future has a changed role. Our predominant problem is no longer to make things possible, but to satisfy human likes and preferences. Thus, technology can begin to play its rightful role as a tool. Its application must be designed carefully in a broad new framework, which then becomes a new institution of modern man, governing technology rather than being it.

We have a spectrum of institutions ranging from private enterprise to governmental services, with a host of special institutions in between. There are nonprofit think tanks, and profit-making schools (yes, indeed, some of these still exist). There are churches and hospitals. There are authorities and foundations. Even such complex hybrids as COMSAT.

In this rich spectrum of institutions before us today, private enterprise and government are the two extremes. Private enterprise is probably the oldest institution man devised. It improved his life through effective use of his skills and trade with his fellowman.

But, benefits and profits are rarely the only motivation in man. The enjoyment of life requires security. To obtain security, man developed the institution of government. Government has since taken on a myriad of other functions, most of them concerned with society as a whole. This satisfies the individual only in an indirect way. The benefits from man's efforts and skills for government accrue to everyone, and are therefore unnoticeable to the individual himself. His rewards are nontangible, and therefore his motivation often wanes.

Neither of these institutions is, therefore, without weakness. Man needs institutions in between, preferably with many of the advantages of the two extremes and with few of their faults.

The Historic Role of Intermediate Institutions

America has traditionally been blessed with many intermediate institutions, obviating government bureaucratic programs and overcoming the limitations of profit-oriented business. Until recent times, such institutions were created to suit many different needs, and to embody many suitable structures. Yet, of late, at the very time when such intermediate institutions become most important, they have become jeopardized and are threatened with serious survival problems.

One area in which intermediate institutions of the independent sector have been and still are active and successful is medicine. Hospitals, medical schools, and research have been set up by independent organizations and many are still supported by them. Most of this activity is done with little publicity or public recognition. It includes donations of manpower as well as funding, and often satisfies human emotional or idealistic needs left unfulfilled by regular jobs in business or government.

Another traditional area of the independent sector is education. Initiated by local groups, churches, or special interests, education at all levels has until recently retained a remarkable independence. In fact, there seemed to exist a healthy mix of public and private education, which provided a friendly competition in which public schools strived toward the quality of private schools, and the latter justified their invariably higher costs through noticeably better educational effort. But now, this balance has eroded and a public educational monopoly seems inevitable.

Where America had once an effective tripartite of business—special institutions—government, we have now focused on the dichotomy between the private and the public sector, at the very time when this "establishment" is under serious question and

needs new approaches to solve those problems it cannot solve either unilaterally or bilaterally.

The Creation of Intermediate Institutions

The successful creation and redevelopment of intermediate institutions depends on active participation and involvement by business, by government, and by all special-interest groups of our society. The institutions must be designed to focus on the many problems thrust on us by the rapid change in our environment.

We need to do more than reexamine and encourage the role of nongovernmental activities in medicine, education, urban improvement, rehabilitation, poverty, and many other areas. We need, in fact, to work extensively on those problems that are just now emerging or recurring, such as alienation of the young, technological unemployment, transportation, drugs and their underlying causes. None are easy problems.

Neither of these institutions (industry and government) is without weaknesses. Man needs institutions in between, preferably with many of the advantages of the two extremes and with few of their faults.

Government has tried in one way or another to tackle all of these problems, few with convincing success. In fact, government is not an ideal framework for many of the approaches now being tried. What is needed are organizational structures, tailor-made for each specific problem and supported more effectively and lastingly than such organizations can be supported now, either privately or publicly.

Changes for Viable New Institutions

Business will surely change in the future, probably much more than it has in the corresponding past. Some of these changes will occur without our effort, others will need concerted and intelligent action by us, the business community.

Human satisfaction—Our present institutions are geared to maximum production, rather than to maximal human satisfaction. But, what is human satisfaction? We do not have answers to this question. We cannot even ask this question intelligently, because we do not have the organizational structures that can focus on it. Industry is still product oriented: a better car, rather than better mobility; a better aspirin, rather than a cure for headaches. Medical science is still reducing disease and increasing longevity, without consideration for the boredom people may find in lonely old age, or the economic strain they face in extended periods of retirement. What do people really want? What would they like to do with themselves? The fundamental question is: What is the most satisfactory life people can find in today's or tomorrow's set of opportunities? We cannot, and do not want to change the increasing concern for general happiness. But we certainly can organize to support this goal.

Profit motive—We see increasing numbers of bright young people being not only concerned about material wealth, but also actually disdaining it. Undoubtedly, this is affected by the affluent environment, in which many of these young people have been brought up. This change of values is probably fundamental and lasting in the young people, so that they are not as much dominated by the desire for material wealth as the older generation has been. This is likely to have some effect on our whole business structure.

Search for relevance—Many people avoid going into business because they dislike the profit orientation and the lack of individuality that often exists in highly structured, large business concerns. Yet, these young people will have to find work to do, not only to earn their living, but to justify their life. Many of these young people are looking for positions of social service.

Profit from business ownership—In the past, stocks and bonds were strictly papers expressing monetary wealth. But this position is weakening. For several years pressure has been to vote stock portfolios not merely on a profit basis but also for social responsibility. This is not a trend to be taken lightly, nor is it a trend to be scorned. It gives businessmen opportunities they did not have before. The trend is likely to continue as more young people inherit stocks from their elders. Thus, future business management may be dominated less by profit and more by social and environmental responsibility.

Money and other values—In our society, affluence has already diminished the absolute value of money in human life. Few incidences remain in which money is the critical difference between a good and a bad life. Other values of human life

begin to dominate, such as the coherence of the family, and the compatibility of a person with other persons around him.

Consumer protection—Consumer-protection organizations have given much strength to consumers as a group or as individuals. Add to this a general increase in social responsibility among ever increasing numbers of people, and we can

---

What is needed are organizational structures, tailor-made for each specific problem and supported more effectively and lastingly than such organizations can be supported now, either privately or publicly.

---

expect more customer-oriented business activity than ever.

Adjusting the Rules

Besides these changes, which are occurring now without our help, adjustments in business rules must be made to encourage or at least allow the development of new organizations.

Obtaining general support—Basic to all this is general, public support for such changes. Traditionally, business has sought support for changes from government. More recently, public reaction has become less acquiescent. The decision on the SST, for instance, has demonstrated the need for basic public support. A coherent program of education and publicity is needed to explain broadly what is needed and what can be done:

Removing regulatory restrictions—Business today is entangled in ever increasing laws, rules, controls, etc. Some of these make it difficult to develop innovative approaches. Government is reluctant to change any rule once established, no matter how badly out of date. Government has also indulged in the other extreme, providing incentives and support, but failing to remove them once they were outdated. Procedures need to be developed to communicate with government on these problems.

Establishing incentives—Many of the changes needed for future institutions need substantive support to get going. Government can provide some of it through tax breaks, direct grants, alleviation of restrictions, etc. These actions must, of course, be sought and justified by business, individually or collectively. This requires organizational support in itself.

Broadening the profit motive—Business still is locked into the profit motive. Thus, nonprofit, social or philanthropic efforts cannot be accommodated in the business structure. But they can be taken on in an independent institution, in which service—rather than profit—is the motivation.

Assuring continuity—One of the critical failures of the independent institutions is their dependence on the general economy and on the social image. New institutions to be successful now must give sufficient assurance of continuing performance, both financially and manpower-wise.

Responding to change—In today's pace of change on all fronts, programs have increasingly limited periods of useful life. The establishment of new institutions must, therefore, consider at the outset an effective process for adjustment and eventual discontinuance.

Conclusion

The next 20 years in business and society will be dominated by a humane renaissance, which occupies the minds of most people of this nation and, indeed, of the world. For the business world, this points to the prevailing need for new institutions that effectively integrate the advantages and capabilities of private business with the responsibilities and facilities of government for representation and service to the people.

I have tried to point out how natural changes and adjustments in values of the people, and in the rules for business, will particularly help develop the needed new institutions. The additional changes we need to make represent a challenge for business.

Private business will continue to have a critical role in the success and, indeed, the survival of the freedom of man in an ever increasingly complex society. However, this role of private business is not automatic. We must work earnestly and intelligently to effect changes for a new type of business structure, responsive to the changing needs of tomorrow's society. ∎

The Position of Agriculture

William J. Kuhfuss

THE PERCENTAGE that agriculture holds in our total business economy is about the same as it has been for many years, although fewer people are producing the agricultural output than ever. Today we have about three million farms in the United States. Of these, 1.8 million produce agricultural products commercially; by 1990 this may be reduced to 1 million or fewer. These farms will be larger and more specialized.

Consumers in the United States spend 18 cents of their disposable dollar for food. This is the lowest relative food cost ever reported for any people anywhere in the world. According to some projections, by 1990 this will drop to 14 cents.

With today's agriculture operating at 70 percent of parity, which is the lowest since the depths of the depression in the early '30s, it is difficult to project a prosperous agriculture even though it is an important segment of our total economy. We must have a continued increase in the efficiencies of farm production if we are to increase the net returns to producers, unless the comparative relationships change.

We cannot relegate American farmers to the status of poverty-stricken peasants and expect to retain a healthy and dynamic total economy. Farmers must prosper to be able to invest in resources and technology. For efficiency to increase,

Remarks by William J. Kuhfuss, President, American Farm Bureau Federation.

our methods and techniques must be further improved; machinery must be made more efficient to produce the foodstuffs to feed America and the world. We will have some increased efficiencies in agricultural production. We can expect improvement in methods, plant breeding, and in the use of fertilizers, pesticides, insecticides, and herbicides. However, it will be most difficult to maintain the rate of increasing efficiency that agriculture has achieved in the past 20 years when productivity has increased more rapidly in agriculture than in the remainder of the economy.

Farm mechanization will improve as long as economics are allowed to dictate the direction of agricultural development, and as long as economics justify it. If a greater return can be obtained by modernizing than by the use of present methods, which may require larger labor inputs, farms will continue to utilize new equipment.

Farm-labor cost must be reckoned with. For equity between groups, the monopoly that has been granted organized labor must be eliminated so as to allow more equitable position for proper negotiations between producers, labor, and business. All segments of the economy would benefit from the establishment of legal guidelines that would provide an opportunity for equitable negotiations between the different groups. A monopoly in any segment in our enterprise economy is indefensible.

If we are to be a part of a dynamic world we must compete in that world. With our great re-

A LOOK AT BUSINESS IN 1990: A Summary of the White House Conference on the Industrial World Ahead, Washington, D.C., February 7-9, 1972 (U.S. Government Printing Office: 1972 0—467-348) pp. 157-158.

Requirements for a Progressive Agriculture

American agriculture will have the technology and resources in 1990 to produce an abundant supply of food and fiber, provided that:

- Farmers are permitted to enlarge, specialize, and change as the production and marketing picture changes. We must avoid farm programs that put the farmer in a straightjacket.
- Inflation is kept under control. Over the long pull, farm costs outrun farm prices during inflationary periods. Net incomes are squeezed and farmers cannot invest in needed resources and technology.
- Market expansion continues at home and abroad. If we lose the export market, we will have weak markets and low incomes, and farmers will not be able to invest to improve efficiency.
- Farmers have the ability and the right to organize and manage the marketing of their products. Production needs to be geared to market needs.
- Consumerism trends do not harass farmers and limit their ability to perform efficiently. We must avoid programs that will fix farm prices. We must be certain that limitations on the use of pesticides, antibiotics, and feed additives are reasonable and realistic. We must have reasonable rules on disposal of animal wastes, antipollution, and zoning.
- Adequate farm credit continues to be available.

sources, modern equipment, know-how, and working in a system that motivates the individual by giving him at least a share of the fruits of his labors, we must and can compete with less efficient production areas. But to achieve that we must have equity among groups—the producers, laborers, processors, distributors, and business. Enterprise will provide the discipline; it will keep us competitive and in balance in our total market. With this we will not need wage-price freezes. In the long run, commodities will be produced where they can be produced at the lowest price. We are a part of the world market, which is directed by the buyers and users of commodities.

The changes rapidly taking place in agriculture well demonstrate that agriculture is not static. I predict that by 1990 many accepted practices of today will be considered antiquated. This applies to methods of tillage, fertilization, irrigation, weed control, harvesting, and probably to the movement of products from farm to market as well. I expect many innovations to circumvent the monopolistic merchandising patterns now common.

In my lifetime the traditional midwest grain farm has increased in size from 160 acres to 600, 800, or 1000 acres, or more with no increase in

It will be most difficult to maintain the rate of increasing efficiency that agriculture has achieved in the past 20 years when productivity has increased more rapidly in agriculture than in the remainder of the economy.

the amount of labor or the number of people involved in the operations. New technology, better methods, better equipment are the answer. Consumers have benefited from this increased efficiency.

And we have not achieved the ultimate in agricultural efficiency. Really, we have only begun. With the development of the air-transport industry we can readily imagine revolutionary changes in many areas relating to agriculture. Air freight is still in its infancy. With the proper use of air freight for repair parts, foods, and drugs, inventories can be greatly reduced. Supplies, especially perishable products, will be fresher. The development in air travel itself may be far from its final achievement.

We must preserve the competitive enterprise system and be determined to be a real part of the world market, recognizing that the best market we have is right here in America. We need to emphasize and support the profit system as the means to a greater GNP. ■

Man's Habitat in the Environment

Nathaniel A. Owings

RECENTLY I came across a handsome photograph of Half Dome in Yosemite Valley. The caption below the photograph read: "A scenic scar in the west flank of the Sierra Nevada granite—engraved and polished by the slow tools of an ice sheet." Nature had turned a geologic disaster into a scenic wonder, carved by a vast press of oversweeping ice. I thought to myself of our man-made scars, carved by a vast press of oversweeping population. I ask you, can't we, too, gradually turn these modern environmental disasters into a triumph of aesthetic beauty?

This cannot be done by our professional sociologists, city planners, architects, and engineers alone. We all loom small on a large horizon. Neither can this be done by government. In a democratic society the creative impulse must come through the *pro bono publico civitas,* with the help of science, commerce, and industry. But if our generation cannot handle it we can always pass the buck, and turn this impending threat of environmental disaster over to our sons. God bless them. I sincerely believe that they can turn it into a triumph. I wish to address myself particularly to youth—for it is the young men, the coming generation, that must meet the crisis. I firmly believe in the guts, drive, and imagination of youth. It has what it takes to pioneer our new frontiers in this, our

Remarks by Nathaniel A. Owings, Founding Partner, Skidmore, Owings & Merrill.

chaos of opposites.

Youth may know that the practice of commerce and industry is, by and large, much like war: individual prerogative, survival of the fittest, and the principle of free competition. We put high value on the profit motive. We may deny this, but it is usually profit in terms of dollars. Within this code of ethics, and within the scope of this area of operation, we have produced the most powerful industrial nation the world has ever known.

Wasteful Us

Soon we will have about 9½ percent of the world's population. At that time we—this 9½ percent—will be consuming about 83 percent of all the raw materials and resources in the world. Consider the envy the rest of the world feels, not only when they watch us *use* these resources, but also when they watch us *misuse* them. When they watch us waste them. When they watch us pile up junked cars along our highways, destroy our rivers, plunder our forests, strip mine our mountains, and pollute our air. Does it not give you pause when you consider heavy industry moving into the last sanctums of natural beauty in quest of clear water to cool the power plants; industry and housing moving into our prize agricultural belts; the Grand Canyon turned into a reservoir. The techniques of science have been harnessed to production for short-term gain, minus just one vital, scientific fact: *production that ignores the aesthetic is simply bad economics.*

A LOOK AT BUSINESS IN 1990: A Summary of the White House Conference on the Industrial World Ahead, Washington, D.C., February 7-9, 1972 (U.S. Government Printing Office: 1972 0—467-348) pp 159-163.

Conviction is growing in the land that we must restore beauty where it has been ravaged; that we can preserve it where it now exists, and that we can create it as we build anew. Is beauty something one collects but rarely creates?

In Madison Avenue jargon, what about a new image for commerce and industry? Why not develop a program designed to revitalize our too often negative psychology? Why not adopt the

---

We need to reanalyze what is meant by progress. We need to weigh progress, with its profit and loss, against waste. We need to define waste, and question its relation to untouched resources. Is wilderness waste—or a savings bank?

---

offensive, using our own techniques to prevent impairment and to create new solutions? These gifts only commerce and industry bestow on a nation that is concerned deeply at every level of government. True, most of these ideas would require drastic changes in the law, but the government is ripe for legislation favoring and recognizing beauty and conservation, constructive enabling legislation permitting radical new concepts of the use of tax-money credits, in kind, in the form of natural resources themselves.

Our fathers and grandfathers were concerned with setting up a system that would guarantee security, with the establishment of a sound, free enterprise system, a sound environment for their specialties, be they beef, trains, or pills. Today we face the same problem with a different set of circumstances for our specialties, which is no longer economic security or public health but something else far more subtle, far less easily defined. We need to reanalyze what is meant by "progress." We need to weigh progress, with its profit and loss, against waste. We need to define waste, and question its relation to untouched resources. Is wilderness waste—or a savings bank?

We are learning that our superb country has an economic value in its unexploited state. We are learning that man is the trustee—more than the owner—of our natural resources. We stand at the crossroads. Each of us with our own discipline and foresight, and with what may appear to our forebears as radical concepts, will find, I trust, a better

balance between the utilitarian and the aesthetic—and will take action to establish it.

If, as man claims, he has produced a great technological age and has proven his capacity to shape and control his environment, then he should be thoroughly ashamed of himself. The result is the present widespread degradation of a good chunk of the United States, environmentally and socially. If Detroit, as the headquarters of U.S. No. 1 product, is an example of our technological age being responsible for the production of 10 million new cars this year, isn't it somewhat embarrassing that Detroit is the nation's No. 1 culprit in the terms of blight, crime, drugs, unemployment? How does this square with the vaunted claims of our technological success?

One of the background papers prepared for the Conference has this to say: "Man has this great power to alter his primary environment as he wishes." Who is *he*? Which man? The corporate executive, the laborer, or just the consumer? Can this man speak for himself? Has this man been identified? Are his appetites, desires, and needs really understood? Are they being shaped by the desires, appetites, and needs of the insatiable maw of commerce and industry? Market-wise, are we shaping our technological advances and our use of resources to fit business, and forcing man—this undefined creature—to absorb it like ducks being stuffed for paté? Or are we willing to identify the little man's needs and shape the *technological* resources of commerce and industry to satisfy them in terms of the *environmental needs of nature,* with another partner—perhaps the landlord—certainly holding most of the stock?

Suggestions have been made as how to "develop new mining techniques for low-grade ore, the extraction of oil from low-grade shale." In those apparently simple, innocent words lies a real threat to the predacious ravaging of the environment on the scale of entire states such as New Mexico and Arizona and those adjacent thereto;

Those who talk of new cities in unspoiled open space are simply walking away from a problem they have failed to solve. What right have they to start a new one when they cannot solve the old one?

207

Cannot we gradually turn these modern environmental disasters into a triumph of aesthetic beauty? . . . This cannot be done by our professional sociologists, city planners, architects, and engineers alone . . . Neither can this be done by government. In a democratic society the creative impulse must come through the pro bono publico civitas, with the help of science, commerce, and industry.

the skimming off, gathering together, crushing and squeezing out of low-grade ore from the surface of those states. What could possibly justify such action?

The labor force of 1990 is alluded to as more a question of the quality of that labor force than the quantity. What will be the quality of the spirit and the willingness to work of this labor force? If it follows present trends, it should go below the zero point on the graph by that time. I see the necessity for a major restructuring of the basic assembly-line system so that the man and the woman who spend their lives tightening a bolt on that line can be given a greater share in the creation of the product, with a variety of interests. A new type of assembly line has already been suggested where groups assume more responsibility. This in itself is a good example of how technology must readjust to the basic principle of the human being as something more than a faceless cog in a piece of machinery.

I have a high regard for leaders of commerce and industry. I should. They and I have been building their corporate headquarters, their plants, and their various facilities for some 45 years. But in a curious way they and I have been plagued by a kind of over-success. I begin my suggestions, my prescriptions for the future, by asking that we remember the word humility. Starting with that, I suggest that commerce and industry remind themselves that they are not the end in themselves, but they merely offer the means of a better life for man through the utilization of their powerful and dangerous know-hows. Commerce and industry are tools to be used *not* to produce more products,

but to create goods that will aid in the final goal—improvement of the environment and the habitat in which man lives.

I believe the leading difficulty is also the source of commerce and industry's greatest success: their unremitting pursuit of mono-culture; their single purposeness. I believe that we all must take another look at nature. We must analyze her basic functional cross section, which can be described in one word: diversity. When nature adopts a mono-cultural approach, like a typhoon, or an earthquake, the results are disaster. Man, especially since the Industrial Revolution, has been approaching all of his problems on a mono-cultural basis. Generally the end result has been a disaster. We must begin to think about the total problem, say, of transportation for example, rather than highways and concrete. Transportation is part of the diversity of the problem of man's share in the environment and must be treated as a diversity. If this seems obvious, then it also seems obvious that we should know better and shouldn't have been making the mistakes we have consistently been making for at least the last 30 or 40 years in this area. Most of what I have to say is obvious. Each thing affects another, like the domino theory. But, like the Ten Commandments, most obvious things are ignored instead of followed, and I see no harm in bringing them up again.

I suggest that the executive leaders in commerce and in industry take a look at their own final objectives, personal and individual. They are diverse, not mono-culturist. I suggest that each of them—indeed all of us—are looking beyond the mad struggle to produce, expend and produce again, to the time when we can use and conserve and enjoy those things. And from each and every one, enjoy the benefits of diversity—the diverse benefits each offers in terms of joy, happiness, rest, and peace.

Restructuring Cities

In this regard, another item on my laundry list for business—commerce and industry—is to choose another goal, a more realistic goal. That goal would be a personal participation in an all-out drive to build our cities into a habitable habitat for man, combining our know-how and resources on a total basis toward meeting the diverse needs of the existing cities, as I have spelled out more fully on page 162. This can be done only through the genius, and the financial and construction knowhow of commerce and in-

Cities As They Should Be

- The cities of this country are already there. Their locations are fixed points at the crossing of desire lines of people and goods. Those who talk of new cities in unspoiled open space are simply walking away from a problem they have failed to solve. What right have they to start a new one when they cannot solve the old one? I firmly believe that the solution is before us, and possible within the next 20 years.

- Our central cities should be low rise, high-density habitat, where the central city is taken over and treated as one great unit. Every city has at least a third to a half of it in streets. At the lowest levels of this habitat structure I propose the heaviest things would be done: heavy traffic, heavy transportation, heavy industry. Then, rising through successive layers of wholesale, retail, light industry, cottage industry, would be open parks, terraces, green space, on which rest apartments and housing for the city dwellers—and there must be city dwellers. They could rest up on top where the sun is.

- The Secretary of the Interior made the statement recently that the land-use policy of the United States is one of the prime objectives and necessities to be established before any working order could be arranged. This land-use policy must require housing within the city, walk-to-work operations, the elimination of the automobile within those cities and the cleaning up of the open space around. All of this involves long-term commitments, heavy machinery, heavy industry, all forms of manufacture. The product, however, would be fitted into the warp and woof of the diverse needs of the city itself.

- I see the end of the single-purpose skyscraper, and of the senseless burgeoning of the little cubicles in which human beings sit at sterile, faceless desks punching little buttons, never seeing the beginning of the process or the end. It seems intolerable that we should ask young people, or anybody, to do this. Why shouldn't that be relegated to the computer? Why not use half or more of each of these great structures that we at Skidmore, Owings & Merrill are designing and building for housing of the people who work in them—or at least work in the city? Why not raise the high art of topiary, or horticulture, of service trades, to the point where the 85 or 90 percent of those who live in town can find employment? We must find ways and means of raising the dignity of human labor to the point where it will be acceptable again, or I really see no answer to the future. We must develop service industries to help fulfill the void between the rat race of manufacturing expendable products and getting back to the slower, lower key kind of living involved in the full recognition of the development of habitat.

dustry. No government can ever do this. If there is any doubt about this last statement, then look at the record of both parties since 1930. It is the road of disaster in housing, urban renewal, highways, transportation; every aspect of man's habitat is defective. Their failures rest to a large degree on the lack of understanding at all levels of government, and perhaps in commerce and industry as well, that man can only be led, guided, and aided—but *never* managed. To understand this requires some humility and some love.

I suggest that we turn to the capital structure of a sound ecology as the basis for our major investments for the next 20 years. Man has a huge slice in this investment, but not all. At best, not more than 20 percent. Let us withhold our technological genius rather than exert it until we know where, and how, it should be applied. Too often we have plunged ahead blindly and destroyed the subject area in our enthusiasm, with an unawareness of the damage we have done until it is too late to correct. Witness a great percentage of our highway programs across the country.

Let us start out on a new basis. Let us recognize that 85 percent of us live on 10 to 12 percent of the land. Let us organize each section—the 10 to 12 percent for man and the 85 to 87 percent for food, fibre, bird, animal, coastal estuaries, lakes and rivers. Let us give equal time for all, and spend our energies, brainpower, and ingenuity on how *not* to use copper and oil and tin, instead of how to use more. Let us learn the word "waste," and its meaning. Let us reanalyze the term "use," and remember that many things unused are of higher value than when expended.

Opportunities Offered by Communications

Of all the developments in technology it seems to me that communications offers us the greatest opportunity to be of help. If our cities are jammed with traffic, could not the communications breakthrough offer great help in solving business travel, for example, where whole board meetings could be held intra-city through closed-circuit television, reducing travel to that for impulse items only.

Let us learn the word "waste," and its meaning. Let us reanalyze the term "use," and remember that many things unused are of higher value than when expended.

Could not the corporate structure be modified to supply service needs on a closed-cycle basis instead of the constant striving for the spiral upwards?

I suggest, with all humility, that we quit passing the buck to government and start a war of our own on the total problem of the environment, recognizing man's place as being but a part of it; where we begin to make sacrifices with excitement: give up the third car, the electric razor, turn off the lights at night in our cities. Enough GNP potential is available to build sewers, to build high-speed railroads between high-density cities, to keep us busy for a long time. We can create a physical environment for man in which we can work with personal commitment on problems still unsolved, with the excitement of finding out whether they will or will not work. The goal of all this is to create for ourselves the kind of living we all really want and have never had.

I suggest that we quit kidding ourselves into believing that what we are doing now is the answer, admit we are wrong, and start off fresh on this great, new, exciting vision of the garden cities of the future. ∎

The Outlook for Research and Development

W. O. Baker

S CIENCE and technology are but other words for understanding and learning and discovery. But they will be used for the benefit of all mankind only when coupled with organization and productivity, which are other words for business. We shall discuss briefly the outlook for research and development in terms of how new basic science and engineering can enhance the service of industry in its social and economic goals of the coming decades.

Bold discovery is the most individualistic of human enterprises. The record shows conclusively that it occurs in an atmosphere of social freedom and entrepreneurship, aided by a pluralism of institutions, where planning is modulated by possibility. Progress under such circumstances is best helped by the system of free markets.

This credo of individualism is inherent in our discussion of the future: that American industry and its technical production is an element of international policy that says starvation, suffering, and conflict are not the inevitable lot of man in a free, personalized society. I shall consider the guidance we have for the enhanced creation of industrial science and technology, and the ways it applies to the opportunities for business in global advance.

Remarks by Dr. W. O. Baker, Vice President for Research, Bell Telephone Laboratories, Inc.

Advanced Training Graduates— Supply and Demand

The vital core of science and industry—human talent—must be cherished as we have it now. One estimate of what we are doing with it is provided by the number of awards of doctoral degrees in all subjects. The estimates of the total national output for the next decade vary from that of Cartter of about 380,000 to those of G. W. Hagstrum of about 520,000. This entails an increase from about 31,000 in 1971 to perhaps 60,000 in 1980 and, according to Hagstrum's most generous estimate, as many as 121,000 in 1990. Only a minority of these is in science and engineering, and only a minority of those may be oriented toward business. However, the needs in economics, sociology, language, and many other fields in business will grow drastically. Thus this particular pool of talent is extremely limited, even under generous assumptions. It is believed that only about a quarter of these new doctorates will be required as college and university teachers. If so, industry should find new, better ways to use people with this training and intelligence.

Among those doctoral scientists and engineers who, in 1969, did not go into academic work, 76 percent went into research and development, and 24 percent into other activities. According to some NSF projections, only about half of those in this

A LOOK AT BUSINESS IN 1990: A Summary of the White House Conference on the Industrial World Ahead, Washington, D.C., February 7-9, 1972 (U.S. Government Printing Office: 1972 0—467-348) pp. 166-171.

decade who go into nonacademic work will be employed in research and development. That suggests a bad trend. It is even guessed that in engineering, which encompasses most of the elements of modern business practice, perhaps a third of the doctorates in this decade will not even be occupied professionally.

Strong action toward a national advanced education policy is needed . . . Industry must exert leadership in the employment of the most talented and best trained of our population, such as the winners of doctoral degrees.

This cannot be taken to mean that in the 1970s and 1980s a projection of 2.3 times the number of doctorates awarded in the natural sciences, and a doubling in the social sciences and humanities, should be discouraged. These factors are already much less than the tripling of doctorates in the natural sciences in the 1960-70 decade. Such a slackening is not the way to achieve modern evolution of society or of industry. Equally ominous is Frumkin's projection that, with present trends, especially in nonacademic work, the number of doctorates "required" during the 1980s will be less than half of the number expected to be added during the 1970s.

National Advanced Education Policy Needed

We submit that strong action toward a national advanced education policy is needed. Trends suggest the beginnings of unionization and collective action in which the faculties and universities as "sellers" of Ph.D.s will oppose in self-protection the free-market movements. The answer is that industry must take a strong responsibility not only in research and development, but also in other segments of business as well. It must exert leadership in the employment of the most talented and best trained segment of our population, such as the winners of doctoral degrees.

If a nationally supported program is necessary, it should be undertaken promptly. It would yield long-term gains reaching far beyond large national projects such as those of the last two decades, which have been largely technological. One of its principal by-products might indeed be the stimulation of industry to recognize its phenomenal dependence on intellectual and personal excellence!

Bearing of Environmental Factors on Technology

For industrial progress, especially in science and engineering, human resource is the dominant, but not the only, factor. Foremost is money, which is one measure of many of the things business has to do. Presumably, too, it is a measure of value that must be taken into account for the quality of life and preservation of the environment.

Science and engineering provide the crucial bond between straight economics, which deals in terms of profit and product volume, and the maintenance of a livable world. Many examples are possible, but I shall cite but two with which I have been associated. Lead mining presents a severe environmental hazard. Nevertheless, lead has been a central element in civilization for centuries, beginning with its use for tubing and piping as symbolized in the generic term "plumbing." More recently it was the principal protective sheath for cables used for distribution of electrical power, and much of modern communications. Thus lead, with its high environmental costs, was embedded in much of modern social need. Indeed, one telecommunications firm alone, at its present demand levels, would consume a sixth of the world's lead production under traditional practices. This would amount to more than a billion pounds annually. This demand, plus that required for the growing distribution and communications systems around the world, would have made lead mining and refining an extensive burden on the ecology. Beginning some 20 years ago, a sophisticated scientific study, followed by new chemical engineering and electrical and mechanical design techniques, led to the replacement of lead sheathing and plumbing by synthetic polymers. New industries and new technologies are evolving from this.

In another arena, an exactly parallel science and engineering of macromolecules led to the development of synthetic rubber. As a consequence, the efficiency of agriculture has been enhanced by the use of rubber-tired implements. The densely populated areas of Southeast Asia and Africa, relieved from growing natural rubber, have shown dramatic improvements in the world's food supply at minimal deterioration of the earth's surface.

Equally striking from the point of conserving

agricultural and forested land has been the displacement of the world's dependence on natural fibers from cotton, cellulose pulp from trees and rayon, wool, and silk as well as linen flax, by a host of vastly improved synthetic fibers and textiles. Their sources are almost wholly petrochemical, derived with minor disruption from hydrocarbons or other subsurface resources.

Examples of these effects could be repeated in the realms of medical care, transportation, and so on, but they certify that appropriate science and engineering can contribute both dollar and human values, dwarfing all other ingredients of value scaling.

R&D Costs and Benefits

It is clear that the dimensions of present dollar costs of R&D should not be decisive in planning for the future. Current dollar costs are, in fact, however, determining the research and development planning of the next few years in business. This is a reflection of management judgment and not of national resources or dollar availability. This judgment, as implied in the commentary in *Science* for December 17, 1971 describing the drastic cuts or elimination of some of the most respected industrial research in the nation, is clearly related to the elements of management quite different than the perspective of the White House Conference on Business in 1990.

It is exciting to consider the opportunities for further resource allocation to industrial R&D, which now barely exceeds one percent of the GNP, and is well below one-half of the spending on advertising. Further, it is a much smaller fraction of GNP than that of net profits after taxes, capital spending for new plants, and various other values by which management is guided.

A wide range of opportunities is shaping up for the new business leadership of the next decades. That is the reassessment of the principles of resource allocation, and a sharper cognition of what really new science and engineering might do for the business community of America. Even now much of that community has had no experience with significant research and development, even though it is fundamental to economic growth. Four industrial companies spend 20 percent of all the R&D funds used in manufacturing industries; a hundred companies spend more than 80 percent. With respect to federal work, which is now about 29 percent of the total U.S. annual funding of industrial

R&D, four companies spend a third of this total. The remainder is relatively heavily concentrated in aircraft and missiles, electronics, and to a modest degree in the machinery industries. Among the roster of American industrial activity engaged in R&D activities, the concentration for instance in foods, which is virtually all privately financed, is the lowest, with four companies accounting for 30 percent. As might be expected, in motor vehicles, four companies account for 90 percent of such technical effort. To summarize, nearly 60 percent of American industrial R&D comes from company funding, with accordingly only 11 percent representing work done by federal support.

The "D" portion of R&D takes the lion's share of R&D expenditures. In 1971 total national spending, including all industry, for development accounted for $15,615 million, nearly double the figure of a decade ago. Applied research, as defined by the National Science Foundation, amounted to about $3500 million in 1971, and basic research at $645 million, barely higher than five years ago, with an annual growth rate of less than one percent.

Opportunities for Industrial Progress

At least two bold, new paths for industrial progress in the decades to 1990 have appeared in our discussion. One is in finding ways to employ large numbers of holders of advanced degrees who have gained some experience in the practice of learning and discovery, which is the route of initiative and innovation in economic and industrial progress everywhere.

I can hear the remarks about all those Ph.D. paint salesmen. But I also recall the survey of consumer price changes from 1965 through the first half of 1971, as compiled from Bureau of Labor statistics surveys, which showed that the cost of repainting rooms went up 68 percent, second only to the 110 percent rise of hospital-room occupancy. The cost of paint itself went up 18 percent, fourth in a figure of product and service price increases.

I believe that these rises would have been much

Appropriate science and engineering can contribute both dollar and human values, dwarfing all other ingredients of human value scaling.

less if higher skills and talents had been employed in such industrial operations. This faith is supported by the observation that in the highly technical industries, with greater expenditures of R&D funds, the price increases were vastly less, being five-percent for drugs and prescriptions, a seven-percent decrease for television sets, a five-percent increase for telephone service, and only eight percent in the technologically growing food and agriculture segment represented by pork chops.

A second pathway is through the drastic allocation of more R&D funds in that large segment of industry that makes little or no use of R&D. Difficulties exist, we realize: the balance sheet, the cash flow, the shareholders, the stock market and its emphasis on annual profit growth, etc. The federal government certainly needs to know more than it has seemed to know about this matter. This administration is deeply concerned about reviewing tax incentives, antitrust, and various aids to industry for discovery, innovation, and productivity enhancement, which can all lead to profit growth. But for this to occur, industry itself must take a stronger lead than has been seen recently.

We are only now beginning to realize the accumulated benefits of the new basic science acquired in this century, but especially in the past two decades. Nuclear energy, materials science and engineering, and the realm of digital automata have provided intellectual as well as practical access to levels of understanding, design, and innovation whose economic and social impacts are just beginning. Thus, diverse industry should shift its tactics to take advantage of ever more sophisticated human talent, so that both business methods and business products are more quantitatively specified. One major tactic already being adopted is wider use of systems engineering, which must be supported by much enhanced levels of systems research. At one extreme the global modeling proposed by Professor J. Forrester* can hardly be realized with the present paucity of valid empirical information on the behavior of technology, markets, people, politics, etc., in the real world of business. At the other extreme, we have the slow but steady accumulation of data banks and knowledge of the behavior of known physical systems ranging from power generators to artificial hearts, and other elements of organic beings.

Some of the most urgent needs lie with physical

---

*Recently summarized in his new book *World Dynamics 1971*, a fitting successor to his earlier one, *Industrial Dynamics 1961*.

systems, such as breeder reactors for the future electric power supply. Much needs to be done, not only in further analysis of the first U.S. demonstration plant of 300-500 megawatts, but also in related system elements such as a transmission, cryogenic transformer and machinery, and probable materials behavior. High among the needs is for suitable economic tests of this and other modeling. Fast neutrons in the core of a breeder reactor cause radiation damage in the stainless-steel structure leading to swelling and ultimate fracture.

No computer program will solve the multiplicity of concurrent problems. Only the most modern data handling and theoretical modeling can be expected to lead to technical and economic success in a vital national program.

Between these extremes of the upsurging dependence of industrial technology on computer processes lies a new universe of skills. High among them will be what is now called a kind of social

---

Even now much of the business community has had no experience with significant research and development, even though it is fundamental to economic growth.

---

engineering. New statistical methods, such as multidimensional scaling, implemented by computers, will enable industry to estimate behavioral and other social and economic positions with respect to new products and services, or massive financial commitments. Environmental qualities, and other elements of technological assessment, can be factored in with early experimental trials. Such analyses will also aid in explaining how, in a recent nationwide sample of attitudes toward business, the Campbell Soup Company outranked all of our high-technology, high-innovation industries in the esteem of the public.

Wider Use of Existing Technology

High priority should be given to finding ways of applying various high-technology, high-productivity components already available to existing commercial systems. The history of modern electronics and integrated circuitry is a classic case of such synthesis of new systems with the discovery of new scientific components. Many other cases remain as yet little exploited. For example, research on the physics of superconductors has, in the past decade, produced more chemical compounds having zero electrical resistivity at exceedingly low temperatures than were discovered in all the prior decades. The whole electrotechnology of cryogenics has opened up. Superconducting magnets are already serving in important studies of plasmas, thermonuclear-fusion experiments, radio-spectroscopy studies, and a host of other fields.

The point is that, with the appropriate systems parameters known, as has been true of electromagnetism for a long time, rapid and effective insertion of new technology—in this case superconductivity—can lead to major technical and commercial advance. When we can begin to talk about the biosciences in terms of enough systems parameters, such as the molecular weight and structure of polynucleotides, and the qualities of cell membranes, new domains of chemotherapy and physiotherapy will occur quickly, with great benefit to people.

It seems possible that the spread of new technology would strengthen small-and medium-sized businesses, if we but allow reasonable balance with very large enterprises that can generate and make it available as needed.

Consider the more prevalent case in which the technical systems parameters are unknown or unheeded. This is particularly true in the processing of materials, which is a dominant phase of manufacturing. Some progress has been made, particularly in chemical engineering unit processes, such as distillation, where both computer modeling and detailed theoretical analysis have tied down many of the most wasteful and, indeed, environmentally undesirable features. On the other hand, the laser, with its remarkable capabilities, has experienced slow and fumbling insertion into industrial processes. Traditionally wires have been drawn through inefficiently drilled diamond dies. Still it took some years even to use the laser, which can apply megawatts of radiation power to minute areas, to that simple process. Recently the Burroughs Company needed 20,000 holes in a steel sheet about the size of a postcard, each hole to be smaller in diameter than a hair. A laser drill is now machining these parts.

Similarly, the laser has been applied to the alignment of tubes, pipes, and tunnels with striking improvement. It is claimed that, with the laser, contractors lay chemical-plant waste lines 30 to 40 percent faster than the best prior schemes. About 15,000 lasers were provided for surveying systems for the construction industry, and for machine control in 1971. Some estimates indicate a market of $500 million worth of industrial laser units by 1980. This would be considerably expanded if some of the dramatic information-handling and communications capabilities of lasers are in commercial use by then. Thus, the semiconductor laser is just coming along for practical use.

All this activity emphasizes the need in the process industries for more systematic analyses of opportunities that may reduce the expenditure of the billions of dollars now going into metal working, fiber spinning, plastics molding, mineral extraction, etc. An interesting program of the National Bureau of Standards is taking shape in the creation of Standard Reference Data. The plan is to standardize sets of mechanical properties for a whole industry. This will be of immeasurable value for process control.

Some of the opportunities here are indicated by the recent work of Dr. Gilbert Chin in our laboratories. Bronzes have been processed into wires and other forms for millenniums. Great ingenuity has been displayed in making empirical improvements. Despite all this, Chin has found ways to double the strength and yield stresses of bronzes by fundamental control of crystal texture during processing and subsequent heat treatment. Anyone who thought we had passed the Bronze Age a thousand years ago is sobered by this finding, as well as cheered by the opportunities ahead. Incidentally, Chin's x-ray studies would have been impossible without the ability to make massive computer analysis of the vast number of possible states that cold working of metals can produce.

We will advance to ever more challenging endeavors. Other examples are the formation of artificial organs for humans, and joints made of the new carbon-fiber composites. For their manufacture to become practical, better knowledge and more precise process control will be critical. Millimeter transmission systems employ waveguides capable of carrying more than 100,000 voice channels per conduit. For their manufacture it has been necessary to evolve new methods of providing straightness and uniformity that are orders of magnitude better than the whole tubing industry had been able to achieve even with the stringent demand for precision in nuclear reactors.

The central theme is evident everywhere. The exciting new components of research and development must be accompanied by systems analysis that will enable them to fit into existing markets and economics, so as to eliminate the jerky and financially erratic modes of innovation so far prevalent.

Faster Information Handling

Finally, business must accelerate its improvement in organization by the use of still other kinds of emerging technology based on its own research and development. Business-information systems supported by computers, graphical displays, and modern communications are gradually pervading our more advanced commerce. Obviously banking and financial institutions must convert ever faster to such aids if they are to avoid paper paralysis. Again, neither the education nor experience is adequate to optimize the systems that are even now in prospect. Here, too, public policy must recognize the dimensions of the issues far more astutely than has so far occurred. For instance, the size of technical effort, including research and development necessary for the formation of new information and communication capabilities, is often in deadly conflict with old or social conceptions of size, monopoly, and cartels.

It would be quaint and comfortable to believe that small personalized enterprises could achieve such resources for a nation of more than 200 million. However, world competition, as well as the realities of science and engineering, make this a dangerous fallacy.

We have accepted for more than two decades the hypothesis that great national programs in defense, space, and others will have a commercial spin-off, or fall-out that will yield an effective transfer of technology into important national commercial advances. The record demonstrates— in time to give us warning for the future—that this has not happened.

All sorts of social, political, and economic reasons can be given for this failure. I shall accent one that is particularly prominent in the field of organization technology, but occurs elsewhere too. Modern information and communication science and technology are so complex in concept and in hardware, with such remarkable economies of scale, that to convert discoveries into practice commercially requires massive resources and risks. This, of course, imposes an enormous responsibility of conscience and social role on the large enterprises that have these resources and can take these risks. Just the same, it is a direction we must take, not toward fragmentation. The focus of whole communities of expert scientists and engineers, carrying right into field operations, is essential to create new networks of information processors and com-

High priority should be given to finding ways of applying various high-technology, high-productivity components already available to existing commercial systems.

munications support. The profit-and-loss statement is an invaluable focusing method, unique to industry, and generally effective only in one corporate unit, although the Europeans have sometimes adapted this to groups, and the Japanese have a special group-government methodology.

I am saying that the content of new science and engineering for business, especially in the whole realm of organization, econometrics, and information is becoming sufficiently difficult that really large critical masses of effort are necessary to show the financial gains that are potential. This may be particularly prominent in the power-generation field of the next decades, and can probably extend to many other environmentally sensitive businesses as well.

Indeed, sophisticated information systems will be necessary just to determine whether new knowledge is being generated, as well as being critically disseminated in the corporate system. It seems possible that the spread of new technology would strengthen small- and medium-sized businesses, if we but allow reasonable balance with very large enterprises that can generate and make it available as needed. An orderly patent and publication arrangement is essential. The patenting of computer software, as well as stimulation of widespread mechanized access to the technical and scientific literature, can be a great help in maintaining the American principle of giving everybody a chance.

I have the conviction that, heeding these principles noted, industrial research and development can indeed comprise the "endless frontier" of advance toward peace and social justice, profits for those who labor, and the preservation of a livable world. Consider what you have now that is good— what you eat, keep healthy by, wear, ride in, look at, listen to—and then recall how it came about. ∎

Technological Transfer

George Kozmetsky

HISTORY is full of records of successes and failures of private business and government's role in producing, inducing, consuming, and distributing new knowledge in the form of technology and science. Nor has the last decade produced the necessary mechanisms for effective dissemination of technology for the creation of "human society" (in the words of Bill Harman) or for a "postindustrial society" (in the words of Herman Kahn).

The next two decades will be dominated by a thrust that will be user oriented as contrasted to technologically motivated advances. The user orientation will perforce place greater emphasis on mechanisms for technology transfer to business and other institutions. In other words, the transfer process itself will become a segment of what will be known as "information technology," which means the collection, storage, processing, dissemination, and use of information.

The immediate concerns with information technology have arisen from the fact that in the past two decades it has become an increasingly larger proportion of our GNP, and that it provides an increasingly larger proportion of employment opportunities. These concerns take on added significance when they are related to our growing concern over

Remarks by Dr. George Kozmetsky, Dean, College of Business Administration, University of Texas, Austin.

national productivity and our balance-of-payment problems.

Information technology has become an indispensable part of the web that holds society together. It has been developed in a piecemeal fashion through a myriad of individual decisions. Nevertheless a major portion of our nation's resources has been invested in one way or another in information technology. The capital investment, both public and private, is large—possibly hundreds of billions of dollars. A commensurate return is obviously desired. In addition to invested capital, our society has given high priority and valuation for the education of our scientists, engineers, technicians, and managers in and for information technology. There is yet no consensus or means to measure the effectiveness of such investments of national resources in terms of costs and benefits to our nation's economy and social and political betterment.

What is discernible today is general frustration. It is not clear how one can apply information technology by itself to increase our nation's productivity, rebalance our payments, and add to the general welfare and satisfactions of our citizens and institutions. This has led both the supporters and critics of information technology to seriously question the values of current information technology and the worth of continuing to invest more of our nation's resources, private and public, in the same manner as in the past.

A LOOK AT BUSINESS IN 1990: A Summary of the White House Conference on the Industrial World Ahead, Washington, D.C., February 7-9, 1972 (U.S. Government Printing Office: 1972 0—467-348) pp. 172-176.

Concerns Regarding Technological Transfer

Of the problems related to transfer of technology to the business sector, I have selected two that I consider to be of major import:

- The amounts directly invested by the federal government are large. The desire is to get maximum pay-out from these sums.
- The human resources utilized are among the most valuable in our society, e.g., scientists and engineers. Their utilization needs to be inspired.

To understand the process of technological transfer, one must examine the process by which technology is created. As Professor A. Shapero has stated: "The technology-transfer process entails a large number and variety of institutions and organizations, and flows through a large number and variety of channels. The process is affected by a number of social, cultural, and behavioral factors, and, as one might expect from the number of variables, the process is shot through with change. Enough is known about various aspects of the process, however, to make it reasonable to state that it is possible to substantially improve the extent, volume, and quality of the country's technology transfer by means of a deliberate, data-based effort to design appropriate and feasible policies, strategies, procedures, and institutions."

Technology is unlike physical and human resources. In fact, information technology can be regarded as a major national resource. The characteristics of this resource are these:

- It is a body of knowledge.
- Its utility depends on hardware, software, and communication devices.
- It is a higher order of resource than human and physical resources in the sense that information technology is essential to organize and effectuate not only human and physical resources but also all other technologies.
- It is homogeneous and heterogeneous at the same time. It is homogeneous in the sense that it can be generated, stored, and used in a standardized form. It is heterogeneous in that individuals can take "standard" pieces and combine, store, and use them in highly individualistic and nonstandardized ways. Interestingly enough, the nonstandard can in time become standard.
- It is not an expandable resource in the usual sense; it can be used in a manner that is contrary to the laws of entropy. In other words, it permits us to organize our resources in such a manner as to enhance the sum of them all. It is not used up in the process.
- It is created by human beings and not by nature. In other words, it is not a recombination of natural resources. Since it is man-created, man alone can determine its relative abundance or scarcity.
- It is the one resource that permits man to take data about perceived complexities, process it, and organize the information that results in a manner that allows man, with his limited capabilities, to extend both his understanding and his control of his environment.

For the past two decades the federal government has been the prime motivator in the creation of science and technology as a national resource. As John J. Corson wrote in *Business in the Humane Society*: ". . . Throughout the postwar years, expenditures in support of military technology and related space technology have made up 80 percent of all government spending for research and development.

"By the mid-1950s, leaders of this nation's scientific community were vigorously voicing three elemental facts. They contended that technological advance is dependent on a substantial and prior investment in basic research; that the research required to expand fundamental knowledge should not be governed—and distorted—by the needs of the military; and that this country could no longer afford to rely on the uncoordinated activities of scientists in universities, in private research institutions, and in business enterprises pursuing their individual interests with limited resources. The new knowledge thus acquired and the balance maintained among various sciences simply would not suffice to serve the needs of an expanding population and to keep this nation competitive economically and militarily—in an ever-more-compacted world."

The process of transfer was limited by the fact that scientific and technological knowledge was placed in the hands of a limited number of institutions. Of federal funds for university research allocated in 1968, 42 percent was given to 10 major universities; 31 percent to 8 nonprofit "think tanks"; and the remainder distributed among 900 universities, 10 institutions, six federal agencies, and seven others. Developments for the military and space programs were also allocated to a limited number of firms, e.g., about 40 firms have over 70 percent of these contracts. These statistics are not surprising in view of the limited number of trained scientists and technologists and the demand for rapid solutions of national problems. One could hardly expect any other solutions under those circumstances. However, it is inappropriate to expect such allocations for development of technology to continue between 1972-1990.

Changes will and must come. They will be in the form of meeting the market demand, thereby requiring the further development of information technology in the transfer process. In this respect, we can view what is currently referred to as the information explosion as primarily a market demand. The flow of published technological materials as patents, journals, and books has been pri-

---

Other nations have not cut back on their technological training and development. They could well provide a higher order of competition for newer technologically based products, systems, and services . . . This will provide a new dimension of competition to American business in the next two decades.

---

marily to satisfy the market demands of those who generate the knowledge. It has been a closed market system specially for scientists and engineers. It has not been user oriented, i.e., business. Therefore it is not surprising that the information explosion has not been effective in the transfer process of technology to broader based business.

The potential-user market for technology is substantially greater, but we have yet to develop an adequate transfer process. In other words, we will need to develop information technologies to enhance such transfers. In the case of commercial enterprises, which number over six million, the continuing pressure is to achieve and maintain their competitive positions. These pressures lead to a normal consideration of new products, new services, and improved products and services.

To date it has been possible to bring about effective technological transfer through human interaction. This has been primarily by the transfer

of scientists and engineers between universities, government agencies, private laboratories, and companies. However, in the past two years this process has been shifted through cutbacks of funds, reordering of national priorities, and the economic conditions in the nation. The perceived results are that less students are being educated as scientists and engineers and many of the trained scientists and engineers are seeking other nontechnical careers. In brief, this could be, in the short run, a misuse of our skilled human resources. Furthermore, other nations have not cut back on their technological training and development. They could well provide a higher order of competition for newer technologically based products, systems and services, especially if they develop their technology transfer process to become more market oriented. This will provide a new dimension of competition to American business in the next two decades.

Suggested Propositions and Initiatives for Transfer of Technology

The movement of information technology from its origination to a potential user entails the various formal and informal channels through which information flows, the nature of the sources and receivers of the information, the form in which the information is sent and the nature in which the transmissions occur. The transfer and dissemination process helps to establish major criteria for effective technology transfer strategies for business, government, and education as well as to identify the defects in past transfers so that more constructive dissemination processes can be averted to meet current and future needs of users.

Three propositions can be made:

1—Top-management executives need complete and up-to-date information to enable them to identify and assess the policy options affecting the national development, use, and regulation of information technology. This information must come from a source or sources that are:

- independent and objective so as not to be dominated or unduly influenced by any single sector, institution, or group
- comprehensive in its integration, analyses, and formulations to ensure a commonly shared body of knowledge, predictions, and assessments on which decisions can be based
- a full-time service to ensure uninterrupted attention to the myriad of developments and decisions in and relating to the information

industry, and to their cost and benefits to the public interest

- nondirective in the sense that it neither "sets nor" imposes policies on decision makers; instead, it should inform and identify alternatives as a management-information input to all institutions

2—Decision makers need to perceive and understand information technology much more in terms of:

- an interdependent "industry" that is one of the major producers of goods and services and a major source of employment in the '70s and '80s
- an emergent national resource whose value as a management tool may be a decisive factor in our efforts to cope with national problems and to maintain our international competitive position
- a source of economic and political power requiring policy decisions to ensure that it is used to serve the national interests

3—Research and development efforts in information should be more systematized and better managed (without overcentralizing or overmanaging) to:

- correlate public and private research efforts to the extent necessary to provide in timely and economic ways those products, services and innovations essential to the private and public interest
- identify those areas of research that have high economic risks requiring possible incentives to make the market mechanism more responsive and profitable
- identify those areas of information technology in which the nation should have technological and economic advantages in international markets, so that our capabilities can be extended
- set standards that serve as guidelines for hardware, software, and communications systems

4—There is a need to design a comprehensive educational-program information technology to develop and maintain the professions, managerial talents, and skills essential to an information-dependent society.

As to the first proposition, the following initiatives can be taken:

Initiative 1—Create an independent center that has the capability for formulating alternative national policies in the area of information technology. This center might be created at the behest of the President, by an organizing committee of eminent citizens from the private and public sectors. It should be a nonprofit center, under the leadership of a distinguished board of trustees and with a staff of recognized credentials. It should be financed in part by business and foundations, in part by the federal government, and with provisions for assessing its value and for "writing it down and out" every five years if it is not performing to the satisfaction of all concerned.

As an "integrative" center, it would draw on the research already done in other centers of information technology, contract out research by way of filling existing gaps, synthesize that research, formulate national policy alternatives with assistance from experts in business, government, and education, and employ the most effective means for introducing these alternatives into the policy-formulation channels for consideration by those who must finally make the policy decisions. It should be available for private consultations with leaders in all sectors, and it should endeavor wherever possible and appropriate to make its findings public.

As a nondirective center, it should not set policy. It should seek to inform, not lobby; propose, not impose. Its effectiveness should be periodically and vigorously assessed.

A policy center on information technology would constitute a valuable source of policy-related information for an institute for national objectives, which is also under consideration. It is at this latter point that policies options for information technology can be correlated with policies options in such areas as human resources, economic growth, international balance of payments, and so on. In short, these constitute the genesis of a more systematized policy-formulation network for the United States.

Among the first steps that might be taken are the following:

- creation of an organizing group of eminent citizens from diverse positions but with one common interest, namely, the new center
- determination that this organizing committee will bring together the first board of trustees, propose to the board of trustees an eminently qualified president, secure from business and foundations as much as 50 percent of the first five-year funding
- determination that the President of the United States is prepared to authorize the remaining 50 percent of the first five-year funding
- disbanding of the organizing committee once the board of trustees is legally constituted and the aforementioned prerequisites are guaranteed

If the center is to be truly effective, it must be in close and continuous contact with appropriate sources in business, the executive and legislative branches of government, at all levels, education, and the scientific community, and the people-at-large, both here and abroad.

Output from the center would take the form of private and public seminars and conferences, private and public reports, educational programs, and so on.

Such a center could be brought into being within a year of the formation of an organizing committee. An assessment process could begin about the third year and be completed at the end of the fifth year. The process could be repeated thereafter.

Initiative 2—Develop a corporate-consumer interface system to evaluate the implication of new information technologies on the consumer environment, and to communicate these assessments to top management.

Initiative 3—Assess the role of industry associations for purposes of recommending broader and more relevant roles consistent with developments in information technology. This initiative should come from the major constituents of these industry associations, rather than from any single association. The cost would be minimal. Expertise is available on a consulting basis in conjunction with association representatives. Costs are extremely modest; the results can be significant.

Initiative 4—Survey existing regulations covering information technology and recommend changes so as to enhance our international competitive position with respect to this technology.

As to proposition number two, the following initiatives can be taken:

Initiative 1—Develop periodic and comprehensive reports profiling the character, scope, and composition of the information industry in terms of investment, R&D, employment, products, services, demands and priorities, costs and benefits, and competitive technological developments at home and abroad.

Information products, services, and systems permeate the very fabric of society. Reports such as those proposed above, if they are to accurately reflect the influence of the information industry, would have to take this into account.

Initiative 2—Top management within each company and institution should appoint a small staff to study the specific implications of information technology for management objectives and policies, products and services at home and abroad.

Initiative 3—Professional societies, industry associations, university centers, and special public-interest groups are becoming more involved in information validation and policy assessment. Consequently, they should take steps to evaluate their own understanding and assess their own effectiveness in this regard.

Initiative 4—Because information technology, products, services, and systems are the very links that hold society together, meetings held to assess information as an industry or a resource should include representatives of all groups developing, using, and assessing information technology.

As to the third proposition, the following initiatives can be taken:

Initiative 1—Encourage the National Science Foundation and/or the National Academy of Sciences to allocate more research funds for information technology on the premise that it is a highly interrelated and growth field essential to the national well-being.

Initiative 2—Encourage the President's Scientific Advisory Committee, in conjunction with the Office of Science and Technology, to establish the more important requirements for R&D efforts in information technology in terms of perceived national priorities and needs.

Initiative 3—Promote the development of essential talent and innovation in the area of information technology by means of scholarships, awards, and other incentives.

Initiative 4—Establish, possibly in the National Bureau of Standards, an interinstitutional task force to determine the feasibility of standardization and compatibility requirements for information technology.

Initiative 5—Determine the feasibility and desirability of establishing a government data bank for information technology that would be a recognized point from which business, education, and others could draw on government-produced and held information on this technology.

As to the fourth proposition, the following initiatives can be taken:

Initiative 1—Determine the anticipated manpower requirements of the information industry as an integral part of the country's economic projections for the next ten years.

Initiative 2—Develop the knowledge and talent essential for the education of people required to manage information as an industry and as a national resource.

Initiative 3—Design educational programs and instructional methods, including the structured means of validating these programs.

Initiative 4—Conduct periodic assessments of personnel policies and practices and make such modifications as necessary to accommodate to personnel requirements created by information technology. ∎

Coping with Environmental Problems

Athelstan Spilhaus

T WO COMPARATIVELY new aspirations of people will affect business and industry profoundly in the next generation. These deal on the one hand with an increasingly protective attitude to people and, on the other, with the concern for a clean environment outdoors. Both of these worthwhile objectives harbor the danger of being overdone to the extent of inhibiting national productivity.

In our drive toward "zero risk," we may stifle inventiveness, initiative, and the production of new things for people's health, for their increased mobility, and for their improved shelter. Innovations can be inhibited by excessive assessments of side effects and risks.

No one argues that proper assessment of the effects of new chemicals, new drugs, new materials, and new modes of transportation is necessary. However, few among the public recognize the danger to our overall national productivity if this protective assessment is overdone. Without minimizing the great efforts required to prevent further pollution of our lands, air, and water, unrealistically stringent standards imposed with impossibly short time scales can also act as inhibitors of the productiveness needed to stimulate the muscles of a waxing business and industrial effort. That effort

Remarks by Dr. Athelstan Spilhaus, Fellow, The Woodrow Wilson International Center for Scholars, The Smithsonian Institution.

is essential to provide the resources to accomplish the desired clean-up.

We need to move toward a better public understanding of what I call an "ecolibrium" position—balancing the desires in ecology and environmental quality with the necessary stimulation of economic well-being to accomplish these desires. This involves more realism in the education of the public to recognize that all activities involve an acceptable risk, which is not zero. In the use of the components of our environment—air, land, and water—there is an acceptable burden of man's wastes of the proper kind that they can carry. This is not zero.

Social Demands Will Spawn New Industries

The proper use of water and air is to dirty it, whether we use it in the organisms that are our bodies or in the organisms we call industry. This water and air, after use, must be cleaned for reuse. Water and air, therefore, become commodities that we must use, clean and reuse just as the commodity—food—is grown, used, and regrown. Perhaps as we think of agriculture today, we will have atmoculture and hydroculture in the future. The cleaning of air and water is not a one-shot proposition. It is something that we will have to do continuously and the cost of cleaning these new commodities for reuse will be part of the cost of producing the things and the energy we need.

We are already seeing what can be called the

A LOOK AT BUSINESS IN 1990: A Summary of the White House Conference on the Industrial World Ahead, Washington, D.C., February 7-9, 1972 (U.S. Government Printing Office: 1972 O—467-348) pp. 177-178.

next industrial revolution where a whole counterpart of the businesses and industries that produce things for people's use must be stimulated to grow up to take what have been considered wastes, reprocess them, recycle them, find secondary uses for them, and reuse them. This industry has as its products cleanliness, reducing waste, saving resources, using waste.

The technological steps necessary and the methods of financing, the institutional practices, and the proper training of people for this new industry will require more sophisticated inventiveness and ingenuity. This will be as interesting and more demanding as that required in the original production of things because it is easier to get people to pay for physical products than for ephemeral desires, however strongly they wish for them.

The saving of resources, if effective, will lead to a per capita decrease in the production of the mature industries such as engaged in mining and winning nonrenewable resources from the earth. It is logical that perhaps these mature industries should be the ones to look toward this new, massive, after-use development—the mining or refining of the bulk material after use.

We need, also, a revitalization of the basic bulk mature industries. These have largely been neglected in our universities and research laboratories in

---

Water and air, after use, must be cleaned for reuse . . . Perhaps as we think of agriculture today, we will have atmoculture and hydroculture in the future.

---

the enthusiasm for those exploiting frontier scientific technology. Because all of these measures consume energy, we must examine in a balanced way the least energy-consuming methods of winning the real resources, whether from nature or by after-use. We must also apply modern high technology to energy economy and resource economy in our most basic industries. Otherwise, in achieving these intermediate steps we will find ourselves faced with an inflated demand for energy, which in itself might not be able to be met within the nation's economy. Even in the popular concept of recycling, we must recognize when it is energetically economical to recycle, when it is necessary to re-

A U.S. Planning Board Recommended

Long-range planning in business and industry, assisted by long-range planning in our laboratories and other institutions is needed as we prepare for the coming decades. Also, there must be a focus in government of a long-range planning group with tenure of appointment commensurate with the time scale that has to be planned for. For this reason, I have proposed that there be set up, reporting to both Congress and the Executive Branch of Government, a United States Planning Board with terms of appointment somewhere between the 14 years of the Federal Reserve Board and the life tenure of the Supreme Court. Without such a focus for long-range planning in the federal government, even the best future planning of business and industry has no focus in the total society.

---

cycle because of seriously threatened natural resources by depletion, and also when it is not energetically sensible or economic to recycle.

If, in addition to controls on the quality of our new commodities—clean air, clean water, and clean land—we can provide incentives to these new industries to produce them, we will be able to use our successful business and industrial institutions and enterprises to achieve the necessary balance between ecology and economy, which represents the ecolibrium of the future.

We will move inevitably toward a higher and higher technology society and at the same time desire full employment for people. We must recognize that employment in the businesses and industries will differ from the employment that we have regarded as productive. ∎

SECTION VI

THE HUMAN SIDE OF ENTERPRISE

Section VI presents an overview on the human side of American industry now and for the coming two decades through the following articles.

The Human Side of Enterprise

Max Ways

WHENEVER I write an article touching on the years ahead, I receive letters and telephone calls from readers of *Fortune* who say, in effect, "Thank God for a writer who views the American future optimistically and cheerfully." These well-intended messages both embarrass and infuriate me. I am not angry at the readers, but at myself. Apparently I have not expressed clearly what I think and feel. True, I am ardently hopeful about the future of the United States. True, the main underlying trends of this society, especially in the last twenty years, seem to me profoundly right. Nevertheless, the American prospect does not fill me with complacency.

My anxiety derives less from objective conditions actually present in American society than from the way so many of my fellow Americans interpret recent trends. Many who call themselves conservatives, many who call themselves liberals, many who call themselves radicals see the present condition of the nation differently from the way I see it. If they are right, but few grounds exist for optimism or even hope. But, even if they are wrong, their views may continue to dominate public discussion and to shape the public mind. Should that be the case, the future of American society will in fact be as dark as these gloomy observers believe the recent past has been.

For, in human affairs, trends are not like geo-logical movements of land masses or the inexorable tides of the oceans. The American future, especially, depends on how the American people, their leaders, and their thinkers handle the opportunities and the dangers confronting us. And the quality of our decisions about the future will depend largely on how well we understand the present and the recent past.

We are considering formation of policy, public and private, in the years between 1972 and 1990. Policy, as I define it, is a pattern of action designed to get from where one is to where one wants to be. The conventional wisdom says that the first step in policy formation is to establish goals. This proposition was valid in the past when we all knew—or thought we knew—where we were. Today the setting of goals is the *second* step in policy formation. The first step is to find out where we are and to correct false impressions about the direction in which we have been traveling.

Nowhere is the misunderstanding more serious than in the subject "The Human Side of Enterprise." This embraces many issues that are more actively debated today than they were a generation ago. The old argument about whether the American enterprise system was the most efficient way of producing goods has quieted down. Not even a dedicated Marxist is eager to argue, in terms of efficiency, with a trillion-dollar economy.

Address by Max Ways, Member, Board of Editors, Fortune magazine.

A LOOK AT BUSINESS IN 1990: A Summary of the White House Conference on the Industrial World Ahead, Washington, D.C., February 7-9, 1972 (U.S. Government Printing Office: 1972 0–467-348) pp. 196-204.

An Attack on the Enterprise System

So the discussion has shifted to a ground that we must recognize as more fundamental. As we gain confidence in the ability to rise far above the level of material subsistence, we become more interested in the human side of enterprise. We become more intent on judging the economic system in psychological, esthetic, and moral terms.

Those who now denounce the enterprise system say that, while it gorges American society with goods, it debases people. They say that workers are dehumanized into mere cogs in the corporate machine, that consumers are diddled into buying worthless things that they do not want, that business managers are corrupted by an excess of arbitrary power, that the corruption of their concentrated power spreads to the political life of the nation.

I urge you not to underestimate this attack. That many people in other countries hold this view of the United States not only damages our country's moral and political credit, but it also confuses the other nations in their own internal decision making. Equally alarming is the fact that millions upon millions of Americans, including many of the best educated and most influential, share—more or less—this negative view of the human side of the enterprise system. The prevalence of this belief is a deeply demoralizing factor in our national life. It could weaken or paralyze our efforts to deal with the much more difficult challenges of tomorrow.

The attack on the human side of enterprise is not as easy to refute as was the attack on its productive efficiency. On the purely economic side, we now have a number of firm, objective measurements that almost everyone accepts. Before those yardsticks were developed, all economic trends could be interpreted subjectively. For instance, writers who, 150 years ago, opposed the industrialization of England persuaded many of their countrymen that the population of the island was declining and the realm was becoming poorer, when, in fact, rapid upward movements in both population and prosperity were occurring. While those particular fallacies could not be successfully spread around today, it is still possible for critics of the United States to argue that power in this society is becoming more concentrated, although strong indications exist that the opposite is true. We still lack—perhaps we shall always lack—objective, quantitative measurements of such matters as the distribution of power and the incidence of freedom.

Millions upon millions of Americans, including many of the best educated and most influential, share—more or less—this negative view of the human side of the enterprise system. The prevalence of this belief is a deeply demoralizing factor in our national life. It could weaken or paralyze our efforts to deal with the much more difficult challenges of tomorrow.

Setting the Past Straight

But the absence of an accepted G.N.L.—an index of gross national liberty—should not force us to remain silent in the face of false observations about the social trends that have been running in this society. We will not illuminate planning for the next 20 years unless we clear up some of the public confusion about what has been happening in the past 20.

Is it, for example, true that machines have taken over so much work that there is less and less for humans to do? If we interpret presently available evidence in a way that projects a relatively effortless future, then we can make right now some dreadful mistakes of policy. A young relative of mine, who wants to be an elementary school teacher, enrolled last year in a teacher-training course at a university. A professor told the class that the first and most important thing to understand was that three out of five children now entering school will never have a job in their lives. If enough teachers believed this prophecy, it could conceivably guarantee its own fulfillment. Possibly, society 20 years from now might be in desperate need of workers only to discover that three out of five young adults have been expensively trained for non-work. That three out of five of today's American children will never work on farms or on assembly lines is almost certainly true. But, if the last 20 years provides any clue to the next 20, then it is more likely that five out of five will have jobs—and many will have two jobs at the same time.

All my life I have been hearing the promise—or threat—of a leisured society. Every great technological advance—the computer was the most recent—brings on a new spate of predictions of widespread unemployment or lotus-eating leisure.

227

I have not seen much leisure coming my way—and the statistics indicate that I am not unique. Since 1940 the workweek in the United States has shrunk slowly, while millions of women were entering the work force. With more than 80 million people—40 percent of the whole population—holding jobs, with another 30 percent in schools and colleges, it would appear that the United States is becoming busier.

Yet I have heard a university president say that most undergraduates were in college because society, which had nothing else for them to do, had parked them on the campus. I interpret the 20-year increase in college enrollments differently. I think that most Americans sense, with a kind of deep social instinct, that in the years ahead enormous tasks face this society. They sense, especially, a shortage of highly educated men and women. And I believe this national instinct correctly judges the future.

The basis for my belief is, as usual, the flow of the last 20 years. Public discussion has distorted the picture of which kinds of occupations have the most rapidly rising incomes. An

---

It would be much less expensive in the long run to attack the problem [of unemployment] at its roots by educational and social programs that will give the chronically unemployed the skills and personal attitudes that will enable them to hold jobs.

---

unconscious conspiracy attributes all sharp pay increases to labor-union action. Many labor leaders propagate this view, for obvious organizational and self-serving reasons. Many employers also propagate it, in an effort to mobilize public sentiment against the power of unions. The press and television propagate it, because labor-management confrontation contains the dramatic quality of conflict that is precious to all journalists.

But when one looks back at what has happened to annual incomes by occupations over 20 years, it is hard to escape the conclusion that the doctors and lawyers and corporate managers and scientists and professors and public officials and economists—without benefit of unionization—

have done at least as well proportionately as unionized workers. Almost all professional occupations have been in a sellers' market for the last 20 years. I believe we can reasonably assume—happily—that this surging demand will continue during the next 20 years.

While the incomes of those employed in the jobs requiring higher education have been rising, their numbers have also increased rapidly. The only possible explanation for all this is a standard market explanation: demand for labor, especially highly educated labor, has been exceeding supply.

Notions about Unemployment—and Employment

This talk of labor shortage seems to be contradicted by the grim presence of unemployment, which now extends to some highly trained groups. By 1990 the United States ought to make real headway in reducing unemployment—which is really three separate problems. Cyclical unemployment has diminished during the last generation primarily because the swings of the business cycle have become less severe. Visible today, however, is a large group who are unemployable or who have jobs only when production is at peak levels. The punishment we have taken from inflation indicates that it is not wise to try to handle this kind of unemployment by a chronic overheating of the economy. It would be much less expensive in the long run to attack this problem at its roots by educational and social programs that will give the chronically unemployed the skills and the personal attitudes that will enable them to hold jobs.

The truth is that the skill levels of the economy have moved up beyond the present reach of this group. Because this upward movement of skills is almost certain to continue, we will have more of the chronic unemployed unless we improve their ability to be assimilated into productive work.

The third unemployment problem is exemplified by the present situation in the aerospace industry. This is probably not a one-shot phenomenon. As change continues to accelerate, many highly trained people will find that their skills are temporarily unwanted or permanently obsolete. There are obvious policy decisions here for adult education, which might retrain those displaced, and for corporations that will need to do a more thoughtful job in shifting such people to other lines of work.

As a society, we have had a kind of emotional obsession, dating back to the '30's, with cyclical unemployment that has prevented us from paying adequate attention to the other two kinds of unemployment. And this same obsession has distracted our attention from the increasing demand for white-collar labor, which now accounts for more than half of all jobs. This rising demand has major implications for the human side of enterprise, for the quality of work and life in the United States.

All of us are familiar with the story of how rising productivity, powered by technological advance, by education, and by improved organization, released from the farm and the factory floor millions who would otherwise be required to produce the present volume of goods. Less vividly, we understand that those so released (or their more numerous children) have been absorbed into a rather vague category called "services" and into white-collar jobs generally. But there is little discussion—and no clear picture in the public mind—of why this sudden multiplication of white-collar jobs came about.

Four words, four characteristics of today's society, explain the rising demand for white-collar work. These are: change, knowledge, individuality, interdependence.

Decision Making Comes of Age

To provide a contrast against which to examine our own time, consider a typical European society of the pre-industrial centuries. The lives of ordinary people changed little. One of the most important resources was muscle. Knowledge in those times accumulated slowly and could be transmitted from generation to generation without any special or conscious effort. The idea of individuality had been deepened by Christianity, but this idea did not get much secular reinforcement in day-to-day life, where one man's work, one man's way of life, was very like another man's. Cooperation, when needed, was governed by tradition or commanded by hierarchical authority, political or ecclesiastical.

That kind of society required but little decision making, little attention to planning, little communication between one segment and another, little need for persuasion or for the adjustment of differences. A tiny fraction of the whole population—mainly nobles, assisted by some of the better-educated clergy—took care of such social decision making and such organized communication as was necessary. For the remainder, the sheep increased—or the sheep unaccountably

sickened and died. The turnips grew—or they didn't. What was there to communicate from day to day? What was there to be discovered or changed? What was there to be decided?

With us, however, a huge demand for manpower has arisen out of the need to handle masses of information. Within any enterprise, between one enterprise and another, within the society as a whole, we achieve cooperation and make decisions through the flow of information. Technology helps us to do this, but essentially the coordination of society must always remain a human responsibility. That is what the rise of white-collar work is all about.

The present pace of change is so great that routines must be constantly scrutinized and frequently altered. Knowledge, now vastly overshadowing muscle, has become the central human resource. We are the first society where teachers outnumber farmers, where people who work with words, ideas, and other symbols outnumber the factory operatives who produce material things.

These millions of symbol handlers, these white-collar workers, are not parasites, not extras. They are dealing with the primary product of today's society, which is nothing less than the quality of the society itself. As the organism becomes more complex its nervous system becomes more elaborate. In banks, in universities, in the world of art and entertainment, in government bureaus, in social-service organizations, in the communications industry, in every kind of management are those who are now needed to build and maintain the relationships between man and man.

For knowledge, our central resource, is now highly specialized, both in exploration and in its practical application. This fact sharply differentiates one man's work from another's, a diversity that powerfully reinforces and accelerates the long, slow trend toward individuality in western culture.

Interdependence Is Today's Rule

Yet the specialization that permeates our society has another result, one that apparently—but only apparently—runs counter to the trend toward individuality. That other characteristic is interdependence. Never was there a society where so few men could say, "I stand alone." Without one another we cannot work, we cannot live. Whether or not we feel brotherly, brotherhood is, in fact, our present condition.

The immense cooperation that our society requires can no longer be mandated by arbitrary authority from above. No one can achieve effective cooperation within his own enterprise by personal whim or fiat. The President of the United States cannot operate the executive branch of the government that way. President Nixon has said that he "struggles with the bureaucracy." Those whose minds are still stuck in the past may wonder why the President does not simply tell the bureaucrats what he wants. The truth is that he, along with every corporate chief executive, every university president, confronts almost daily some nominal subordinate who is, in truth, his superior in knowledge of some critical aspect of decision making.

Back in the 13th century, a lawyer, Henry of Bracton, noted some limitations on the power of the Plantagenet kings. The king needed a court to carry out his will. The earls who surrounded the king were called his companions, "and," said Bracton, "who has a companion has a master." Today, far more than was the case in the 13th or any other century, virtually every man's work depends for its quality and its effectiveness, somewhat on the work or the judgment of others. These others may be his helpers or his superiors, or his peers, or his competitors, or his customers, or his suppliers, or the constituency of stockholders, or citizens that he represents. Today, we all have companions and, therefore, in Bracton's sense, masters.

But this does not imply that we are all helpless or enslaved. On the contrary, in our lifetimes a vast distribution or democratization of power has quietly occurred, not primarily because those formerly at the top of society wished to be generous, and not primarily because those below reached up and grabbed power. The true reasons for this shift were more fundamental and more enduring; these reasons, too, emerge from the four characteristics mentioned above.

The human side of enterprise, both in its external and internal aspects, has been profoundly altered by the wider distribution of power. Between now and 1990 we will see many issues, requiring difficult decisions, arising out of this trend.

The individual consumer, for example, has much more power of choice than in previous generations when nine-tenths of all purchases were made under the pressure of immediate necessity. Mass prosperity, along with the variety and complexity of goods and services now offered, opens an immense new range of individual consumer freedom. All sellers of goods and services are now competing with one another for the consumer's favor across the old, narrow product-market lines, which have become, in some contexts, almost meaningless.

Anxiety Accompanies Change

But new freedom has brought, as always, new difficulties. The vulnerability of all products and all markets to innovation and to unpredictable consumer tastes has increased anxiety throughout the world of business. No doubt, this anxiety is most conspicuous at upper managerial levels, but I think that it also affects, in one way or another, all the people who work in the enterprise system. Under present and future conditions, any specific job or skill can become obsolete. Every now and then some young man tells me that he has modest career goals; all he wants is a secure, comfortable job. I tell him that not many of these jobs are left. And they will get fewer every year. Even the civil service now feels the premonitory breezes, if not yet the winds, of change.

And the newly empowered consumers, who threaten all the producers, are themselves victims of anxiety and frustration. Many of the products and services spread out on the counter of the national market are hard to appraise, hard to compare. To the extent that the consumer lacks knowledge of what he buys, his power is undermined. He resents that—and he should resent it. In the years ahead business and other organs of this society, including government, education, and the press, must greatly improve the consumer's ability to obtain and to handle product information.

Advertising is one way consumer information enters the market. As an indication of the true character of today's enterprise system, nothing is more revealing than the rise of advertising. Great national corporations now spend billions begging people to buy their wares, people whose grandparents formerly bought, under the goad of dire necessity, in narrow local markets where they had little choice.

But the consumer will not sit back and feel flattered and grateful because advertising has demonstrated the huge increase in his own economic power. He will, I think, continue to step up his demands for a more explicit and more candid informational content in advertising. He will in the next 20 years increasingly assert, as a right, his need for more accurate knowledge concerning the goods he is asked to buy. He will demand better information not merely for the sake of greater economic efficiency as a consumer. He will demand it also in terms of human dignity, of his right to increase his own control over his activities. He will resent advertisers who seem to envision him as a moron or a child.

A Shift from Material to Social Demands

In the realm of material things, every great advance for a hundred and fifty years has stimulated popular desire for still further advances. Signs now appear among the more prosperous half of the U.S. population that this spiraling appetite for goods is slowing down. But it is being overtaken by another spiral of desire that seeks such nonmaterial objectives as dignity, freedom, and personal responsibility. Life inside the American corporation is one area where this newer spiral of desire can be observed.

A high proportion of people employed in enterprise, including many of those at middle- and top-management levels, feel frustrated and unhappy. They say their responsibilities are too constricted. They say they want more scope. Somebody—whether the government, or their bosses, or their colleagues, or the labor unions, or the stock-market analysts—is always getting in their way.

In one sense, this widespread desire for more responsibility is profoundly wholesome. It fits a fundamental trend of our time, the trend that gives everybody more power than his ancestors had. It fits the future when, if I am right, our children and grandchildren will deploy more power than we deploy.

But it makes all the difference whether we see this desire for more responsibility as a revolt against a repressive system or whether we see it as a wish to accelerate a trend that is already running. Recently my TV screen brought me an interview with a disgruntled professional football player. He complained that his particular club had what he called an "antiquated management" that promulgated a lot of "Mickey Mouse" rules for its players. Up to that point, I was with him. But then he went on to say that people now coming out of college would not stand for such tight control, that they would rebel against the repressive measures of the establishment. He would have made a far better case if he had said that the game of football, as now played, requires participants who are capable of initiative and self-discipline.

The managements of most football clubs, knowing this, have indeed relaxed in their efforts to control their players. The managements of military organizations are evolving in the same way because modern military technology cannot be properly handled by robots trained on Frederick the Great's model. The game of business enterprise many years ago began putting a higher and higher value on such individual qualities as personal initiative, personal knowledge, personal judgment. In 1960 when Professor Douglas McGregor published his book, *The Human Side of Enterprise,* the actual trend toward what he called Theory Y management was already running strongly.

The facts of American business life still run

Without one another we cannot work, we cannot live. Whether or not we feel brotherly, brotherhood is, in fact, our present condition.

far ahead of the formulation of theory. I have heard it said that there are only three or four companies in the United States that practice what can truly be called participative management. By some ideal standard of perfection that may be true. But it is more significant that there can be few successful managements in the United States today that do not give their employees more scope, more responsibility than they did 20 years ago.

I am glad, in a way, that recent college graduates, after their own peculiar fashion, are finally catching on to the tendency of the world outside the classroom to thrust personal responsibility on individuals. As an editor, I was getting a little weary of young journalists who wanted to be told what to do and how to do it. In today's world of enterprise young newcomers will find few processes as regimented and depersonalized as the multiple-choice examination. They will find few power structures as hierarchial as the classroom.

Frustrations and Rewards of Change

The real frustrations of today's business life come not from the imposition of concentrated power from above. Many of them come from the increase of freedom—other people's freedom, the need to consult and persuade others before we can get anything done. More serious are the frustrations that come to every one of us from our inability to meet our own internal standards of performance. Somehow, in the midst of floods of information we seldom seem to know what we need to know to make, with certainty, the right decision. We all grope insecurely in a maze of contingencies and possibilities, dependent on the interplay of a multitude of individual judgments and wills.

That large segment of American life idiotically called the Establishment suffers especially, and will continue to suffer, from the anxieties and insecurities of the new freedoms. Significantly, most other Americans would like to enter, or would like to see their children enter, this uncomfortable life of leadership. Not all will succeed. For many years a large, though diminishing, proportion of Americans will work on assembly lines and in other kinds of jobs that do not depend on highly personalized qualities. Between now and 1990 the tension between the less educated and

Every now and then some young man tells me that he has modest career goals; all he wants is a secure, comfortable job. I tell him that not many of those jobs are left. And they will get fewer every year.

the more educated will probably intensify.

One way to mitigate this conflict is to recognize how dependent each group is on the other. If you fail to see your dependence, come to New York some time when we are having a strike of sanitation men. And if workers in such jobs fail to see their dependence on the highly educated millions, let them sit through a series of public meetings on urban renewal where lawyers, architects, engineers, sociologists, psychologists, environmentalists, businessmen, and politicians are locked in dubious and painful battle over how best to compromise the conflicting housing objectives of people who cannot afford to move—or do not want to move—to the suburbs.

Those who hold routine, impersonal jobs in this society shrewdly suspect that the rest of us, despite all our frustrations, are getting huge psychic incomes from our work, incomes that are at least as important to us as our salaries. A society that is—and will be—hungry for many levels of labor, will have to pay through the nose for workers whose jobs produce little in the way of personal satisfaction. As the cost of unskilled and semi-skilled labor rises, the economic incentive to mechanize such jobs will increase. And the labor-hungry society will have new recruits to the massive ranks of the symbol handlers.

I have been describing a society that would not be comfortable or tranquil even if we all understood what was going on. But our relation to our work and, indeed, our whole national life is made much more difficult—perhaps it is even endangered—by the highly inaccurate picture of the condition that is presented to the public. A society that is so dependent on communication ought to be especially careful with the most important symbols, those it uses to describe itself and express its own values. I am sorry to say that the intellectuals and professional communicators have been doing a sloppy job.

The image of U.S. enterprise presented in drama and novels and songs and folklore is about 40 years out of date. This would not be a serious discrepancy in those centuries when conditions changed slowly. But it is serious today. Talented young men and women, needed by the enterprise system, reject business careers because they have been given a picture that simply is not true. More distressing and more harmful in the long run is the demoralization of those who enter the business world in the cynical belief that they are accepting for the sake of money, a morally depraved system that will try to thwart their own growth as human beings.

I have encountered this belief in all age groups and at all levels of business life. The power of beliefs, including wrong beliefs, is such that not even opportunity to observe the truth will always correct the preconception. Businessmen themselves talk about their careers as a "rat race," when, in fact, most of the pressure comes from efforts to meet their own rising standards of excellence. This is, morally speaking, a situation quite different from a rat racing other rats toward a piece of cheese. Many businessmen proclaim that their only goal is personal success, when, in fact, they spend their lives in organized cooperation with other men in joint tasks that have great social value. They say they are slaves to the system when, in fact, they are gradually changing the system from day to day in ways that give more responsibility and more freedom to more people. Is it any wonder that so many young people reject—or accept with reluctance—careers that have been presented with a kind of reverse hypocrisy, a pretense that the moral situation of business is worse than it is?

Confusion over Our Image

There are still broader and more important symbols that confuse our picture of American society. Let me refer to two famous literary symbols. One is Robinson Crusoe, a civilized man reduced to a state of nature, extracted from the complexities of having to deal with other men—except, of course, for Man Friday, who does the dirty work at Robinson's command. We all met Robinson Crusoe in our childhoods and he reappears whenever we need a symbol of freedom. Well, he was free. But his was not the only or the best kind of freedom. Unless we suppress Robinson Crusoe we will never be able to understand our own kind of freedom, the kind that flourishes amidst complexity and interdependence with other men.

There will not be much Robinson Crusoe in the American future—and even less Man Friday. All the old subservient types—blacks, women, even children—will demand and receive a much larger share of control over their own lives and over the terms on which they will cooperate. These trends, too, have been running strongly in recent decades. It has been about 40 years since I heard an American boast that he had an obedient wife—and he was lying. We want our wives to love us—a much more ambitious and difficult objective. We still try to instill—temporarily—some measure of obedience in our children. But obedience is no longer the paramount objective in child training, no longer the central way of preparing the young for life. At early ages we start encouraging them to think for themselves, to develop wants and wills of their own; to learn the hard social lessons of compromise and persuasion on which cooperation depends. Even our religious and moral formation swings from obedience and toward more emphasis on love and on seeking the good for its own sake.

So there is more trouble in the churches, trouble over ethical standards, trouble in the home, trouble between husbands and wives, trouble between parents and children. And, for parallel reasons, there is more trouble in politics and within business enterprises. In every sphere we are simultaneously increasing both our individual freedom and our dependence on one another. And that's hard.

The other great literary symbol that confuses our image of ourselves appeared more recently than Robinson Crusoe. It is George Orwell's *Nineteen Eighty-Four*. It was perhaps intended to satirize the totalitarian political dictatorships, but it was interpreted by a wide public as a valid caricature of all modern industrial society. The book was published in 1949 when we had just finished a great war with one dictatorship and were engaged in a cold war with another. The question whether we ourselves were ripe for regimentation and tyranny then seemed pertinent.

Now, the year 1984 is only twelve years away. How real is Orwell's spectre? Not very. We braced ourselves—indeed, we are still braced—to repel Big Brother whether he approached in the shape of the U.S. government or in the shape of a corporate manager. And while we were so

Talented young men and women, needed by the enterprise system, reject business careers because they have been given a picture that is simply not true.

braced, trouble hit us from exactly the opposite direction. Orwell warned us against regimentation. Our problem turns on diversity. He warned us against authority. Our problem is how to achieve voluntary cooperation. He warned us against thought control. Our problem is the achievement of consensus. He warned us against a too rigid social order. What we have is crime in the streets. Big Brother's only chance will come if we fail dismally in the next 20 years to evolve along the lines we have been following, while solving the problems that come with that line of development. Meanwhile, let's put Big Brother on that island with Robinson Crusoe and forget them both.

233

Have I made it clear this time that I am not optimistic or cheerful? Have I spoken emphatically enough of present and future conflict? Have I adequately stressed that the tasks and risks that loom between now and 1990 will be even more formidable than those of the last 20 years?

Assuming that I have, I shall turn for a moment to grounds for hope. Our new kinds of trouble originate mainly in advances, not merely material advances but in the intellectual and moral framework of society. Americans never really supposed that the piling up of goods was the be-all and end-all of existence. We always believed that "the good society" had something to do with personal freedom, personal development, and voluntary cooperation. And that is the direction in which we have moved. We are not on the wrong road. What has really been happening in the human side—the essential heart—of American enterprise is an important part of the unfolding of man's spiritual destiny, his responsibility to seek in freedom for higher forms of order.   ■

Labor-Management Relations

Charles M. Brooks

THE FACTORS in labor-management relations that seem most likely to shape the future of the "human side of enterprise" appear to be the pressures for an abundance of the material goods; what is commonly called "full employment"; personal fulfillment of all people; and no hardships or inconveniences due to strikes.

The major challenge in labor relations that I think we might expect to emerge from those pressures is this: Can we somehow or other eliminate our inflationary expectations and meet our social-progress goals, while retaining our free-labor, free-market system?

Stating the challenge differently: if the demands of the work force are not lowered to realistic levels, if the rate of industrial productivity is not raised significantly, if the public's growing intolerance for strikes is not stemmed; then we can expect free collective bargaining to be nothing but a memory by 1990.

Many indicators show that the path we are now treading will lead to the death of free collective bargaining by 1990. Instead of a free market and free collective bargaining we would have a permanent and enforced system of government controls of wages and prices. Some prophesied that a system of wage and price restraints is inevitable in our industrial system.

Remarks by Charles M. Brooks, Manager, Labor Relations, Texaco, Inc.

Conflicting Pressures

Consider the pressures that are likely to lead to this prediction. I see the desire for an abundance of the material goods of the world as a strong and continuing pressure. With all the talk about the "quality of life," the concern about ecology, communal ownership of property, personal permissiveness, and the like, the demand for the material things of life is just as strong as ever. As a rule, when the final speeches are made in our election campaigns around the country, our politicians will still talk loud and long about unemployment, poor housing, hunger, and poverty. Those are economic matters; they are bread and butter issues!

Dr. W. Allen Wallis, Chancellor of the University of Rochester, has said it this way: "For the overwhelming majority of the population, restrictions on what they can buy or sell, and on what terms, have far greater impact on their personal lives than restrictions on expression."

The demand for material goods—even luxury items—is still growing faster than the population. Since 1965, family income has risen about 50 percent; cost of living rose 30 percent; wages and salaries rose 63 percent; and corporate profits after taxes were *down* 3 percent. The indicators point to a continuation of this pressure for higher compensation, even in the face of sliding profits.

We live in an industrial-relations climate, where higher and higher compensation is de-

A LOOK AT BUSINESS IN 1990: A Summary of the White House Conference on the Industrial World Ahead, Washington, D.C., February 7-9, 1972 (U.S. Government Printing Office: 1972 0—467-348) pp. 210-212.

manded for fewer and fewer hours of work for more and more people. We all favor this desirable goal. But we cannot enjoy forever these material blessings with an inadequate growth in productivity.

Personal fulfillment is fine, but if we are to enjoy the fruits of our private enterprise system, investors must have a fair return on their capital. It is capital investment that makes jobs available. The unassailable truth is that the whole structure of our private enterprise system will crumble unless the profit motive is satisfied.

These are some of the conflicting pressures that I see in our future labor relations. Labor-union leaders also are generally mindful of these and similar conflicts created by the inflationary expectations of their members. But the labor-union leadership feels even more keenly the lash from their members when the leader fails to get their demands.

The challenges then are:

- How can we "have our cake and eat it too?"
- How can we keep our freedoms when we so often are demanding that the government make our decisions for us?
- How can we expect 200 million inconvenienced people to be tolerant when a few hundred or a few thousand strikers indulge in a power play to achieve more of the worldly goods?

The challenge for both business leaders and labor leaders is to decide and act regarding the choice between a free market and free collective bargaining on one hand, and a controlled economy and government-dictated decisions on matters now negotiated in collective bargaining on the other.

Free collective bargaining, insofar as I can tell,

Many indicators show that the path we are now treading will lead to the death of free collective bargaining by 1990.

---

is cherished by those on both sides of the bargaining table. However, the uses—or perhaps abuses—of this freedom has brought us to a fork in the road.

John Kenneth Galbraith expressed disturbing views on this question this way: ". . . . the Ad-

ministration must not suppose that quarterway measures—jaw-boning, voluntary guidelines, inflation alerts, levitation, incantation or massive public prayer—will work. It must break the structure of inflationary expectations with a freeze and then work out a permanent and enforced system of wage and price controls wherever strong unions set wages and strong corporations set prices."

Can we expect "a permanent and enforced system of wage and price controls"? Have we already made our choice between free collective bargaining and government controls? Must we lose the freedom of workers to strike? Must we abandon the right of business to cease operations? What can we do to preserve the privilege of the two parties to a labor dispute to settle it by collective bargaining?

While domestic inflation must be reduced, these controls should be phased out as soon as possible to prevent serious distortions and inefficiencies that could stifle the U.S. economy. Vigorous, noninflationary economic growth over the long run can be achieved only if the government pursues sound budgetary and monetary policies, and if wage increases are kept in line with productivity gains.

We should be able to avoid "the continuation of the collective trend" and "the well-known disadvantages of centralized control and bureaucratic giantism," referred to by Willis W. Harman.

Three Propositions for Study

I suggest three propositions for dedicated study by labor, management, educational, and governmental representatives.

Out-of-date labor laws—We are trying to cope with 1972 problems in our labor relations by using laws, methods, and procedures designed for problems of 30 to 50 years ago. Why should we not go modern? Most of our labor laws and procedures were adopted in the 1930s with the prime objective being to neutralize the capabilities of one side in the labor-management arena. Congress did this because of what it deemed to be an imbalance of power, due to the weakness of unions and the economic strength of the employer side at that time.

Assume, that the several labor-relations statutes of the 1930s were needed at that time. As one who helped administer some of those laws during that period, I would agree that there were some good reasons for the laws. But this need of 35 to 40 years ago has long since passed.

The pendulum has swung to the other side. Since that time union membership has multiplied by six; unions have become politically potent and economically strong. The balance has now shifted so much in labor-management relations that the employer cannot now win and a union need not lose in an economic struggle.

This kind of imbalance, with excessive union power, inevitably must lead to a decay of our system. It is worthwhile to remember Lord Acton's famous warning: "Power tends to corrupt; absolute power corrupts absolutely." This will happen before 1990 if the present trend continues.

This condition then presents the challenge for us to revise our legal structure. No one seems willing to take the same kind of legislative initiatives that were taken in the 1930s. The result of each effort so far has been to put some patches on the old 1930-type laws.

I believe we should have a studious and objective review of our labor-management laws. I suggest that our labor laws be amended to grant government protection and assistance to the parties only to the extent that assistance and protection are needed.

Preserve the profit motive—A business enterprise grows, in the long term, only if it has a product or service that consumers need or desire. Mr. Anton Jay, a noted British management adviser, was quoted in the January 1st press as saying: "As in a tribe, those who provide the group's needs survive a period of famine; and those who don't drop off. And the survivors, of course, emerge stronger than before."

Labor, management, and the public will all

We live in an industrial-relations climate where higher and higher compensation is demanded for fewer and fewer hours of work for more and more people. We all favor this desirable goal. But we cannot enjoy these material blessings with an inadequate growth in productivity.

The right to bargain collectively, the privilege to negotiate for higher wages, and the continued operation of a free market for prices, as well as other rights and freedoms are at stake.

gain in the long run, if the relations between management and labor are conducted as business dealings, and if the need for reasonable profit is recognized by all sides.

Voluntary procedures for settling disputes— The two sides in labor-management relations must devise a voluntary procedure for settling disputes when an impasse develops while negotiating a contract, just as the parties now use voluntary arbitration to settle disputes after the contract has been executed. If they do not, we must be prepared for an eventual system of compulsory settlement.

The first efforts to agree on the details of such a system might fail. However, if everyone tries hard enough, the final efforts might succeed. The chances of success are good if the job is approached with a view to correcting earlier mistakes.

Finding a formula, setting guidelines and agreeing on procedures, I would be quick to concede, would not be an easy assignment. But nothing worthwhile is easy. Also, the other options open to the parties are not so inviting. The right to bargain collectively, the privilege to negotiate for higher wages, and the continued operation of a free market for prices, as well as other rights and freedoms are at stake.

I have faith that if both sides struggle as hard to find a solution to these problems that plague our whole labor-management relations system as they have always done to preserve their self-interest, we can find an answer long before 1990. ∎

Minority Groups and the Work Force

Solomon Harge

LESS THAN a generation ago it was widely accepted among economists that nothing was so drastically wrong with the American economy that 60 million jobs couldn't cure. Today, with employment exceeding 80 million for the first time, a consensus forecast of economists and other "experts" is for a jobless rate nationally of 5.4 percent, down slightly from 1971's average of 5.9 percent. Obviously, the trouble is that while the U.S. economy, even in a slump, can produce more than a million jobs a year, new jobs are fewer than new workers.

If we are to maintain our cherished system of private enterprise, those responsible for the shaping of future corporate policy, in their own self-interest, must come to grips with the critical need for drastic change. America is a nation dedicated to progress. But progress entails change, and in our concern for the future, we must give more consideration to sociological aspects.

Some industrial concerns, including a measurable but still miniscule involvement of nonwhites in middle management, have dealt with these special problem groups in a commendable manner. However, I sense a tendency among too many businessmen to make only token efforts in this area, and a willingness to consign the complex problem of minority utilization to the federal government. The danger inherent in assigning such planning to

government is eventual control by bureaucrats, however wise or benevolent.

The Human Side of Productivity

To provide the necessities for the increasing world population—about 150,000 people per day—we must have increased productivity of people who are old enough, healthy enough, and skilled enough to turn the world's raw materials into things that humans need. At any given time in our society, this is a relatively small number of people.

Increased productivity, in turn, depends on the creation and development of more efficient tools and techniques, both of which must be provided from profits, since in our system that is the only source.

What of the "human" state of productivity? Today's worker is a different individual from yesterday's, and he will be greatly different in 1990. The tendency of today's workers to demand more wages for less productivity is likely to become ingrained in future workers as our technological genius is given full application in the next generation.

Our gross national product, the yardstick of our industrial growth, will show tremendous gains if our plans make producers of all our citizens. This will happen only if somewhere along the line private industry develops programs and techniques designed to use, rather than placate, our newly en-

Remarks by Solomon Harge, Executive Director, Consumer Protective Association, Cleveland, Ohio.

A LOOK AT BUSINESS IN 1990: A Summary of the White House Conference on the Industrial World Ahead, Washington, D.C., February 7-9, 1972 (U.S. Government Printing Office: 1972 0—467-348) pp. 213-215.

franchised young people, and especially our young black people, and older workers who still have values accumulated in work experience, and the liberation-conscious women of tomorrow.

People are beginning to clamor for the right to participate in decision making. Industrial planners resist for two basic reasons: industry is essentially undemocratic, also the planners themselves are generally too remote from and too ignorant of local conditions.

No less a problem is the plight of American blacks, at the bottom of our industrial totem pole. What are we to do about them, this traditionally last-hired and first-fired group? The challenge faced by planners is to find meaningful and profitable programs to transform them into productivity and self-reliance.

We must stop fooling ourselves that economic problems are our only concern. A whole range of issues are only secondarily economic face us in the future. Racism, the generation gap, crime, and cultural autonomy all have economic dimensions.

American business must realize that *employment* is the number one concern for blacks; not education, not housing, not voting rights, not even social integration. No man can think of these things while he is hungry.

As complaints mount, business and industry will face increasing pressure to end job discrimination. This has already resulted in greater enforcement powers for the federal government through the Equal Employment Opportunity Commission, and

---

American business must realize that employment is the number one concern for blacks; not education, not housing, not voting rights, not even social integration. No man can think of these things when he is hungry.

---

the threat of ever more power to come. Sooner or later, action will have to come as a result of public opinion developing from the continuing lack of black participation in the labor force.

The day is past when we can depend on persuasion and conciliation to bridge these troubled waters. Management of business and industry needs to have all the facts on matters involving the

nonwhite worker and those outside the labor force, and how the opinion and action of these individuals can affect business and industry. Consider the riots in my home city of Cleveland, Ohio. It was basically a war between the haves and the have-nots. When a man has nothing, what can he lose? He may pass by a factory or business that will not hire him. He wants to hurt the business that has hurt him. The gasoline and the match can bring a business to its knees. And it happened.

The Black Man and Employment

But it is not so important that a riot occurred in Cleveland as why it occurred.

What is happening or has happened in the black community can never be revealed completely in statistics. For example, is the withdrawal of black adults from the labor force an involuntary retirement, an alternative to unemployment, or sporadic employment at low wages? Many black workers have either lost faith in themselves, have given up trying to ride the new wave in equal opportunity, or refused to believe they are included. For some, nothing can restore their faith in themselves or in "the American dream." For many, the American dream is a nightmare.

The nightmare is made up of many things. One is the realization for many that they cannot move into areas where they can be trained and qualified for higher employment because of educational deficiency. Men with little schooling, low earnings, and poor work histories tend to withdraw from the labor force, probably explaining why the proportion of nonparticipants in the 55-64 age group is higher for nonwhites (19 percent) than for whites (15 percent). .

Black men are not in the labor force for numerous reasons, including their concentration in seasonal and other temporary employment, lack of education and skills, and continuing patterns of racial discrimination, which often deny them employment or relegate them to the least desirable jobs, along with other nonwhites. For many of these men, the only doors open are those to the basement. The other doors are still locked and may have future repercussions for business far greater than the long hot summer of 1967. Drastic action is needed if we do not want to live through more riots.

Of course, we may be able to contain future violence. I am told that some plans are on federal drawing boards to meet whatever emergency arises, some of them raising serious questions about their constitutionality. But even if they are contained, disruptions are bound to result in unstable business operations and increased taxes.

I believe that many opportunities are open to the private sector to develop relations with black leadership, and through them, to communicate the positive plans and steps that are being taken to provide real equal employment opportunity. Sometimes simple, honest efforts are all that are needed. Many programs instituted by top management are not implemented down the line. Blacks quickly sense this, but frequently top management does not.

Better Communication Needed

I also suggest that management develop a line of communication with individuals in the black community who can shape public opinion. Such a relationship should be developed when things are running smoothly—before the crisis. Management should keep testing the winds of social change in the communities in which it operates. Too often, the storm can break without warning or apparent cause.

Successful experiences should be shared by businessmen. General Motors, Ford, and other big corporations have mounted some relevant programs, and they should be willing to share their successes as well as their failures with others.

Business and industry must find answers to many questions. Do we expect to make way for more nonwhite workers in our future plans, and, if so, in what areas? Can they be trained for the production techniques of tomorrow, especially since today's young blacks are better educated than ever before? Are we willing to exert our influence in the black fight for open housing, an important factor if we intend to build plants outside the central cities. If black workers can locate near suburban plant sites, the supply of labor is enhanced and costs kept within profitable limits.

What shall be the future role of private industry in the development of black entrepreneurship? Of black caretakers for plants in the central cities too valuable to abandon?

In the interim, it would seem that thousands of nonwhite workers can be attracted to and trained for the many new services to be demanded by a more affluent future society characterized by more leisure time, higher wages, shorter workweeks, a surge in tourism and in the entertainment industry.

The former bootstrap occupations once relegated entirely to nonwhites, such as sleeping-car porters, bellmen and waiters, messengers, maids, and the like, will offer opportunity for those who simply cannot catch up with advanced techniques required by production quotas.

Can these people be sold on both the dignity and profitability of this sort of employment? Can such work be given meaning enough to attract and develop a hard-core base working force?

We need to implement and sell these ideas:

- That the American dream is a dream for us all
- That equal opportunity is a reality and not a myth
- That people are important, no matter who they may be
- That economics is related to the social aspect
- That a nation that prints on its currency "In God We Trust" must do exactly that

Finally that we learn to deal with "What Is Right" as opposed to "Who Is Right." ∎

240

Labor and Environmental Factors

Joseph P. Tonelli

T HE STEPS taken today are indelible footprints that may lead to either disastrous or beneficial results for our children and grandchildren. The fact is, much of the future has already been made from both our and our predecessors' doing. After eons of time—from the time God made this world—through the glacial age and evolution, down to what we call civilization—it has taken us only about 200 years to desecrate and waste our North American continent.

Every industry, public or private, has made a dubious contribution to the mass hysteria gripping the civilized world today. Ecology was only a scientific term in the dictionary a few years ago. Today it is an institution with its own ecosystem.

In the industry whose employees are represented by my Union, wood and clean water are essential. Without them, we are out of business. The industrial use of these natural resources has undeniably polluted our air, water, and soil.

Some believe the way to abate environmental pollution is to eliminate the polluters. Fortunately, not everyone preaches a dogmatic, doctrinaire philosophy prescribing the instant death penalty for all industrial offenders. If carried through to its calculated conclusion, we would undoubtedly return to the cave-man age with pure air and water, but relatively few would be left to enjoy it.

Find an Answer to Pollution without Industrial Genocide

At present, the total fixed assets of all the paper companies and subsidiaries in the United States are approximately $9 billion. It has been estimated by the scientists and ecologists that to convert the present existing plants into pollution-free plants would cost $9 billion. We do not need economists to tell us that when the cure is 100 percent of the existing value we are faced with a destructive dilemma. No industry can absorb such costs and survive. It would be the classic case where the operation was a success but the patient died.

No one is more interested in pure water and air than my people. Industry must have clean water to produce quality-controlled paper, but we cannot approve industrial capital punishment as a reasonable means to end pollution. A solution short of genocide to meet the needs of our time and the future must exist. The solution will have to be found like most other solutions—in compromise.

Unless such an answer is found, we will continue on a downward trend of destruction of our environment or, the more likely alternative, will eliminate a large segment of American industry and the jobs that it provides.

Remarks by Joseph P. Tonelli, President and Secretary, International Brotherhood of Pulp, Sulfite and Paper Mill Workers of the United States and Canada, AFL-CIO.

A LOOK AT BUSINESS IN 1990: A Summary of the White House Conference on the Industrial World Ahead, Washington, D.C., February 7-9, 1972 (U.S. Government Printing Office: 1972 0–467-348) pp. 216-217.

241

The abolishment of much of industry would also end the economic and defense strength of America and lower its living standards.

Since 1965, a growing number of pulp and paper mills have closed, primarily because, we are told, of their inability to meet pollution-abatement criteria. In fact, 92 plants have closed, terminating thousands of workers and eliminating 1,964,500 tons of production annually.

The incidence of closings increases each year, and I need not tell you what this means in human frustration, economic readjustments, and community casualties. Our industry is not alone. Others have had similar experiences.

Without question measures must be taken toward the goal of nonpollution. Those steps must be real and effective, but they cannot be so effective as

---

Some believe the way to abate environmental pollution is to eliminate the polluters . . . If carried through to its calculated conclusion, we would undoubtedly return to the cave-man age with pure air and water, but relatively few would be left to enjoy it.

---

to destroy the paper industry in the United States and the hundreds and thousands of jobs the industry provides.

You cannot have your cake and eat it too. You cannot have jet travel without noisy air lanes and airports; abundant power and light without electric or atomic generators; or the comforts and conveniences of modern living without some destruction and pollution of our natural resources. It becomes a question as to what you are prepared to give up. Better yet, it is a question of how to reduce and ultimately eliminate the unpleasant aspects of our industrialization without giving up the advantages of 20th century living.

The fine line that we search for must encompass the help of every segment of the country's society—business, finance, labor, government, professionals, conservation organizations, and the like, so that we may proceed in a constructive and orderly fashion with a program that will eventually cure our environmental ills and still not destroy the employment and economy of this country.

Government should work in partnership with business and labor to save a threatened industry.

I, as a labor leader, plead for moderation. I fear we have gone overboard on ecological awareness to a point of self-destruction. Let us apply the brakes and slow down for the good of all of us. ■

Labor Relations and Education with Respect to 1990

Robert D. Helsby

T HE CONNECTION between labor relations and education may seem remote.
However, I believe it is possible to demonstrate that the relationship is inseparable.

Labor Relations

Several basics of our labor relations, I think, will
change radically. In many respects, these changes
will be interrelated. The most dramatic labor-relations development of the past decade has been the
demand by public employees for rights akin to
those of private-sector employees—representation
and bargaining. However, remember that in the
more than 35 years since the enactment of the National Labor Relations Act, about half of the manufacturing work force has been organized while
less than 20 percent of the nonmanufacturing work
force has been. This varies greatly by state and
region.

By way of contrast, the percentage of organizational penetration among public employees in
many states and among federal employees is much
higher. In New York State about 60 percent of all
state and local public employees belong to unions
and about 90 percent are represented by a bargain-

ing agent, although these employees do not belong
to the organizations. Hidden in these numbers are
several developments that may have a profound impact on labor relations as a whole.

*Unionization of public-sector white-collar work-
ers*—Public-sector unions are apparently able to
organize workers who have resisted organization
efforts by private-sector unions—professionals,
clericals, technicians, et al. Proportionately, the
mix in public and private employment differs. The
public sector has relatively greater numbers of professional and clerical employees and fewer people
in blue-collar occupations. Public-sector unions
could not have achieved the successes of the past
decade without the ability to organize professional
and clerical employees. I suggest that the potential
for spillover into the private sector is substantial.

A major difference exists between the collective
negotiations of professional employees and those of
nonprofessional. Professional employees are not
content to negotiate only the so-called "bread and
butter issues"—wages, pensions, vacations, health
insurance, and similar benefits. Teachers want to
negotiate curriculum, disciplinary systems, griev-
ance procedures, faculty-student ratios, class size,
etc. Other professionals believe that their professional training and experience should be utilized in
a system of participatory management to develop
the policy decisions that affect them. These em-

*Remarks by Dr. Robert D. Helsby, Chairman, New
York State Public Employment Relations Board.*

A LOOK AT BUSINESS IN 1990: A Summary of the White House Conference on the Industrial World Ahead, Washington,
D.C., February 7-9, 1972 (U.S. Government Printing Office: 1972 0—467-348) pp. 218-222.

243

ployees have been in the vanguard of the new "relevance and involvement"—in short, to be actively involved with the decision-making process that governs their work life. This is an increasingly important element in job satisfaction; it is bound to spread to other types of employees in both the public and private sectors.

Role of public-sector middle management— How middle-management employees in the public sector should be treated is much debated. Should organizational and bargaining rights be extended to them? That is one of the fundamental issues. In the private sector this problem was resolved by Taft-Hartley. However, in the public sector the Taft-Hartley provisions take on a different meaning even when literally transferred. I believe that public-sector middle management will emerge with some type of bargaining rights. Here too, the potential for impact on the private sector is substantial.

Separation of public- and private-sector organizations becomes indistinct—The line between the public and the private sectors is constantly changing. For example, in New York State private bus companies providing local transit service are rapidly disappearing and, in many instances, are being taken over by public authorities established to continue the service. This is a national trend. As things stand now, employees of a bus company taken over by a public authority move from one labor-relations system to another. The potential for some type of marriage between the private-sector labor-relations systems and the emerging public-sector will undoubtedly occur, perhaps to their mutual benefit.

The most crucial present difference between the two is the right to strike. Private-sector unions consider the strike a ritual necessity. Public-sector unions increasingly contend that they are deprived of a basic right because of the nearly universal ban on the strike. If the objective of a bargaining relationship is to give employees a voice in the determination of their terms and conditions of employment, then I would observe that about 90 percent of the public employees in New York State have such a voice as against 30 percent in the private sector. Essential to union penetration in the private sector is the ability to strike. Public-sector experimentation with procedures as a complete or partial substitute for the strike may or may not provide an answer.

Whatever the ultimate workout, I believe that labor relations in both the public and private sectors will, in another generation, have matured to the point where most employees in both the public and private sectors will have an effective voice in the determination of their terms and conditions of employment. Although a free enterprise system will always have some strikes, I believe that the strike will become increasingly obsolete. As collective bargaining relationships mature, better ways of conflict resolution will be found. The costs, waste of resources, and emotional trauma of strikes will be important factors leading to those new ways. The variety of experimentation in public-sector conflict resolution will hopefully help in this search.

As management and policy making become a shared process, employees will become more and more an integral part of the enterprise with many incentives for the financial success of that enterprise. Instead of avowed adversaries and in many cases, outright "enemies," labor and management will act increasingly as partners—albeit with differing points of view. Representatives of management, labor, and government will find that they have much more to gain by a stress on constructive relationships of mutual respect and understanding. Strikes that do occur will tend to be short, and often of predetermined duration to accomplish a mutually understood goal—more of the demonstration variety rather than the type of present-day strikes.

Although there will always be some strikes in a free enterprise system, I believe that the strike will become increasingly obsolete. As collective-bargaining relationships mature, better ways of conflict resolution will be found.

As unions become more secure in their representation of employees and thus do not have to prove and reprove their "manhood" to be reselected by employees, this security will result in a stability that will permit maturing relationships with management without the fear of displacement. Success in this regard will, to a large extent, be determined by the achievement of increased worker satisfaction. In this connection I believe that A. Harvey Belitsky of the Upjohn Institute for Employment Research states it well:

". . . The *will* to work will follow only when

workers derive satisfaction from their jobs.

"Many personally disintegrating kinds of work have admittedly been eliminated, but the deadening effects of numerous boring jobs, spilling over into leisure hours, remain a challenge to job developers; and qualitative changes in jobs must not become a trade-off for improving the economic status of persons with subaverage incomes.

"Interest in such qualitative aspects of work as variety, autonomy, and responsibility has been evident for some time, but an intense concern has been demonstrated only recently.

". . . The large-scale quest for worker satisfaction, through job enrichment, could prove to be the nation's most critical economic challenge. Although additional research, experimentation, and development are required, this important goal can be achieved, because the means have been tried and proven . . ."

The union's role in 1990 will have changed dramatically. This new partnership will enable the unions to concentrate their energies and resources

---

Some of the [campus unrest of recent years] results from the obsolescence of the educational system, not only at the college and university level, but at all levels . . . In one respect, the only thing new in education is the amount of money spent, and even this is meeting increasing taxpayer resistance.

---

on an everwidening spectrum of social and economic programs for the benefit of their members.

The growing trend in our society appears to be to find more effective ways of giving the individual a better means of controlling his own destiny. While the institutional arrangements that have evolved in labor relations go farther down this route in some respects than we have gone in other areas of society, the ultimate has not been achieved. The "law of the jungle" is not appropriate in a complex, urbanized society. Even when the conflict is as ritualized as in most private-sector strikes, it is still inappropriate. While none of the techniques that have so far emerged provides a complete answer, I am optimistic that solutions will evolve from our present confusion.

Finally, we seem to be in the process of adapting our social institutions to give the individual a greater sense of relevance and identity. This process involves the formulation of both ad hoc and more permanent groups whose demands sometimes make those of unions look simplistic by comparison. Skills for conflict resolution have been more highly developed in labor relations than in other social processes. These same skills, or an adaptation of them, may well become the essence of management not only in business and industry but also in almost every social enterprise.

Education

The restless nature of the age in which we live has had a substantial and well-advertised impact on the educational system, particularly on higher education. Much of the campus unrest of the past few years is directly attributable to the Vietnam war. Some of it, however, results from the obsolescence of the educational system, not only at the college and university level, but at all levels. To those who are, in one way or another, consumers of the products of the educational system, this obsolescence is readily apparent. At least it is obvious that the system is not working well. In one respect the only thing new in education is the amount of money spent, and even this is meeting increased taxpayer resistance. Certain factors are hidden in the present debate and controversy about the educational system that may control future developments. Several of these are as follows.

Lag between educational research and application—The lag between research and development and application is greater in education than in almost any other field. As yet, we simply do not understand how individuals learn. A substantial breakthrough in learning theory and its application could radically alter the educational system as we know it. Short of this, a reduction in the time span between research and its application could basically alter the nature of the system.

Introduce a bargaining system—The introduction of a bargaining relationship into the public-school system has the potential of expediting the process of change by forcing school management to manage in the sense of establishing approaches and goals, and evaluating results rather than acting in the traditional ministerial capacity.

Broadening bargaining participation—The bargaining relationship may well be extended to include parents and pupils. It is quite apparent, for example, that city school systems are not adequately meeting the needs of the clientele they increasingly serve. It also is apparent that teaching methods and curricula that are suitable for the needs of middle-class suburbia, however adequate, are simply not working in the inner city. The melting-pot theory, among others, appears to be no longer valid, if, indeed, it ever was. The solution to these problems may be found in the extension of the bargaining process so that teachers, students, parents, and administrators can work out educational goals and methods to meet particular needs. We may even determine how to make a federalized-type system work—central financing and local control.

The educational period—We may resolve the inherent conflict between the educational and the custodial functions of the educational system. On the one hand we say that our young people are more mature and act accordingly—the lower voting age for example. On the other hand, the educational process keeps getting longer, even though it is obvious that 12 years of elementary and secondary education plus four years of college could

---

I suspect that the [secondary] schools will increasingly limit themselves to the so-called basic and tool subjects, and leave much of the remainder to the employer . . . The employers will increasingly be in the training and retraining business, probably with increased government assistance.

---

be condensed without serious loss. The State University of New York, for example, is about to initiate an experimental three-year Bachelor's Degree program. At the college level the concept of *in loco parentis* is pretty well dead, but most of the custodial function of the educational process remains intact. In the next 20 years, I think we will have to face up to the contradiction, but a guess as to what the result will be is uncertain. I submit that we cannot afford to continue the education system in a holding pattern to keep young people out of the job market for whatever reason. A more realistic correlation between the system and the ability-maturity level of students must be achieved.

A more flexible educational system—Many factors—public needs, pressures, and demands; the rapidly changing needs of business and industry; the needs of the individual for a lifetime of learning to meet his changing work requirements—will combine to force the education establishment to abandon much of the rigidity and inflexible pigeon-holing of individuals into society. When a flood of veterans returned from World War II with GI Bill qualifications, only to find the existing stereotyped college system jammed and unadaptable, the two-year college system with its Associate Degree responded with unparalleled swiftness and flexibility. Similarly, medical education must be radically revamped to provide the needed services, as demonstrated by increasing medical knowledge to prolong and enrich life, as the latest war on cancer; increasing affluence to meet the costs of medical care; mammoth government subsidies, i.e., medicare and medicaid. The realities of the situation will simply not tolerate nine to seventeen years of higher education to prepare an M.D. Many types of paramedical professions will emerge with a wide variety of training possibilities. In short, the entire medical profession, and particularly medical training, will be drastically revamped.

Occupational training in secondary schools—As part of the reevaluation of what the schools are supposed to do, I anticipate a complete rethinking of the role of secondary education in occupational training. I suspect that more of this burden will be transferred to employers as the schools are increasingly unable to keep up with the rate of technological change. I suspect, moreover, that the schools will increasingly limit themselves to the so-called basic and tool subjects, and leave much of the remainder to the employer. The corollary is, of course, that employers will increasingly be in the training and retraining business, probably with increased government assistance.

The only viable and better alternative is for a much closer interrelationship between industry and education. Under this option, systems would need to emerge that would ensure that facilities and equipment were kept current as well as the relevant instructional processes. A constant and viable personnel interchange between education and industry would become a way of life. Which of these alternatives will be selected will largely depend on the ability of the education enterprise to adapt itself to the exploding changes of industry. The job will get done; it simply is a question of who will do it and with what resources.

Education to meet social changes—I anticipate that at some point the present lock-step system of

246

education will finally be broken to the extent that it will come much closer to meeting lifetime needs rather than assuming that education is a terminal process. One of the assumptions built into the present system is that 12 years of elementary and secondary education plus four years of college plus graduate work, if any, take care of an individual's educational needs for life. This simply is not true and never really has been. I strongly suspect that education, particularly higher education, received by two-thirds of most business and labor leaders, has little real bearing on what they now do. Even more illustrative of the point are present occupational surpluses, such as engineers and technicians, resulting from cutbacks in the aerospace industry.

The fundamental problem is how well the educational system can accommodate to the increasing rate of social change. The evidence is clear that for at least a generation we have not been making it on this front. And the rate of social change is more likely to accelerate than to slow down.

Conclusion

The world of business in 1990 will call for undreamed of adaptation by the human side of enterprise. Particular modifications will be called for in the fields of labor relations and education.

In labor relations, a whole new relationship between business, labor, and government will emerge. Indeed, it will become an interrelationship. In education, individual, public, governmental and industrial pressures will force a complete restructuring, particularly in higher education. The archaic niceties and rigidities of the past will not meet the complex and rapidly changing needs of society.

If these hypotheses are correct, the quality of life in 1990 will be inherently richer, more satisfying, and secure. If these hypotheses are accepted, the sooner we get to work on their implementation, the better for all of us. ■

247

The Human Factor in Planning for 1990

Berkeley G. Burrell

A REVIEW of the past 20 years shows so many unexpected events—particularly in the social sphere—and for which our society, particularly industry, has proved to be so ill prepared.

How then do we plan for 1990 when we cannot predict one year hence? Long-term forecasts can ignore the cyclical swings in business; they can concentrate on trends and their long-term effects.

As predictions have it, we will experience a huge GNP surge through 1990. Productivity will increase, wages and profits will rise. Everyone will have food, shelter, necessities, some luxuries, and more leisure time. People will work every other day, or nine out of fifteen days, or mornings only, or some such configuration. The work force will expand by 28 percent but unemployment will be only 4½ percent. Of course, we had full employment under slavery. Industry will give sabbatical leave to employees wishing to involve themselves in humanitarian projects. Cable TV will change the nature and programming of the television industry. Families will no longer need two or three automobiles. Cash will be a thing of the past. Society will be people and individual oriented. The association man replaces the organization man. Sounds like utopia. Will we fall prey to our own Madison Avenue rhetoric?

Toffler in *Future Shock* states that technocratic

Remarks by Berkeley G. Burrell, President, National Business League, Washington, D.C.

planning is econocentric and essentially undemocratic. I might also add that it is even antihuman. We have "economic indicators" to gauge the overall health of the economy. We have, however, no recognized social indicators to indicate the health of society. We have not learned to measure the quality of life. The human side of enterprise cannot yet be reflected on the bottom line of our financial statements.

Assume utopia in 1990, in spite of the Cassandras. And I may be one. Problems are inherent in arriving at Plato's Republic. Even Plato required a highly ordered, socially stratified community with rigid psychological and physical controls, including population controls and limits on creative endeavors. The state came first.

The increased concern for the individual in the United States will unavoidably conflict with the nation's need to increase the effective and efficient use of its technology and its greatest resource, people. Automation can lead to boring jobs, and, after achievement of physical needs and pleasures, motivation is difficult to instill. When you have everything, why produce more? In a disposable society, quality and durability are bound to lose their importance. If citizens shoplift and steal in 1972 out of boredom rather than necessity, imagine what happens when those persons have three- and four-day weekends. Weekend TV football remains as one of the few legitimate outlets for our aggressive natures. Right now, the majority of murders are homicides com-

A LOOK AT BUSINESS IN 1990: A Summary of the White House Conference on the Industrial World Ahead, Washington, D.C., February 7-9, 1972 (U.S. Government Printing Office: 1972 0—467-348) pp. 223-224.

mitted by friends and relatives, not criminals. Leisure and affluence, which we are not prepared for, are bound to lead to a high degree of anomie and boredom. This was Rome in the 5th century. Permissiveness and restrictiveness are both self-immolating.

Problems of Small Business

Nineteen ninety! Small business will still need skilled management and personnel. It will be concentrated in the service sector. Its fixed costs will be high. White-collar workers will be unionized, making labor costs even higher. New towns will attract the middle class who will want to work where they live. The hardship of relocating is less on big industry than on small business. Communities do not offer incentives to the small business to relocate. Big business can retrain professionals to meet its labor needs, but the small businessman is hampered by the time he can allocate to training programs and by the salary, plus fringe benefits, he can offer. Shorter work weeks, however the configuration, mean even more employees are needed, and good personnel will be hard to find.

The challenge is how to remain a strong and technically proficient society when the idea of work itself is becoming rapidly obsolete.

Money having lost its marginal value, small business will have to offer fringe benefits such as paid vacations to Bermuda, free family medical care, scholarships for employees and their children, free housing, etc. It may become advantageous for a small businessman to send a key employee to work in big business for a year to learn new methods and bring back this knowledge for use in his own enterprise.

The impermanence of the future society will call for a more highly sophisticated small-business operation. The key to the success of small business in the future is its greatest asset: it is people oriented. Whether it is employees or customers, the small business is concerned with the human element. It is accustomed to be concerned for the individual. The history and size of big business will make it difficult for it to make the transition without proper planning and a strong commitment.

In fact, none of us can effect the changes neces-

sary for success unless we first commit ourselves to be people oriented. We should consult with youth and with the unions, but we should not need them to tell us to care. People are this nation's greatest resource.

The challenge is how to remain a strong and technically proficient society when the idea of work itself is becoming rapidly obsolete. An affluent and technically proficient democracy, according to the *Wall Street Journal,* no longer worships productive endeavor as a national virtue. The puritan work ethic is now passe with whites. Blacks were already negated because they had no meaningful work.

If there is in fact a grand design for a 1990 utopia, I have not been privileged to see it. If there is no such design, then let us get urgently about the task of developing a community that allows for individual growth within a system that responds rather than reacts.

We need a plan for which the goal is not merely full employment, but full employment of our human resources and its potential. If we are to lead, let us lead by example. Let us lead by learning to live lives of quality, rather than of quiet desperation. We must be the catalyst for developing man to his fullest potential. It cannot be developed ad hoc. It must be planned. ∎